Representative Americans

POPULISTS AND PROGRESSIVES

REPRESENTATIVE AMERICANS

The Colonists
The Revolutionary Generation
The Romantics
The Civil War Generation
Populists and Progressives

Representative Americans

Populists and Progressives

Norman K. Risjord

ROWMAN & LITTLEFIELD PUBLISHERS, INC.
Lanham • Boulder • New York • Oxford

ROWMAN & LITTLEFIELD PUBLISHERS, INC.

Published in the United States of America
by Rowman & Littlefield Publishers, Inc.
A wholly owned subsidiary of The Rowman & Littlefield Publishing Group, Inc.
4501 Forbes Boulevard, Suite 200, Lanham, Maryland 20706
www.rowmanlittlefield.com

PO Box 317
Oxford
OX2 9RU, UK

British Library Cataloguing in Publication Information Available

Library of Congress Cataloging-in-Publication Data

Risjord, Norman K.
Populists and progressives / Norman K. Risjord.
p. cm. — (Representative Americans)
Includes bibliographical references and index.
ISBN 0-7425-2170-2 (hardcover : alk. paper) — ISBN 0-7425-2171-0 (pbk. : alk. paper)
1. United States—History—1865-1921—Biography. 2. United States—Politics and government—1865-1933. 3. Populism—United States. 4. Progressivism (United States politics) 5. United States—Social conditions—1865-1918. I. Title. II. Series: Risjord, Norman K. Representative Americans.
E663.R56 2005
973.91'092'2—dc22

2004017331

Printed in the United States of America

∞™ The paper used in this publication meets the minimum requirements of American National Standard for Information Sciences—Permanence of Paper for Printed Library Materials, ANSI/NISO Z39.48-1992.

For My Son, Mark
Who Casts a Lengthening Shadow of His Own

Contents

Preface

The purpose of this volume, like others in the series of *Representative Americans*, is to make history human, to put some tissue on the skeletal framework of names and dates. By using a biographical approach, I hope to make the past more concrete and vivid, to recover a heritage that today's reader can feel and experience.

Like the others in the series, this book focuses on a particular time period, utilizing the life stories of individuals to explore the political, social, and cultural dimensions of that era. This volume treats people whose principal contributions fell in the period roughly from 1880 to 1920. The dates are necessarily inexact; three of the individuals studied, Carrie Catt, W. E. B. DuBois, and Margaret Sanger, lived and worked until mid-century.

As with the earlier volumes in this series, my selections are not "representative" in the sense of average or common. Instead, they are chosen to illuminate and personify historical developments. John D. Rockefeller and Mother Jones provide us with the story of the rise of big business and the early struggle between capital and labor. William Peffer represents the Great Plains' form of Populism, while Louis Brandeis represents the Wilsonian variety of Progressivism. The final group of four—Carrie Catt, John Muir, W. E. B. DuBois, and Margaret Sanger—are individuals who, in my view, were ahead of their own time. They marked the transition from Progressivism to the liberal thought of the last half of the twentieth century. That thought will be explored in greater depth in a subsequent volume.

Norman K. Risjord
Madison, Wisconsin
May 2004

PART I

Progress, Poverty, and Populists

So long as all the increased wealth which modern progress brings goes but to build up great fortunes, to increase luxury and make sharper the contrast between the House of Have and the House of Want, progress is not real and cannot be permanent.

—Henry George, *Progress and Poverty* (1879)

1

John D. Rockefeller: Robber Baron or Industrial Pioneer?

One of the remarkable features of the nineteenth century was the pace of America's industrial growth. The nation emerged from a traditional, slow-growth, rural society in the first quarter of the century, "took off" into self-sustained economic growth in the 1840s, and by 1860 ranked fourth in the world in the volume of manufactured goods. By 1890 it stood number one, and a scant ten years later it outranked the second and third heavyweights, Britain and Germany, combined. Facilitating this development of a modern economy was the legal evolution of the business corporation, from the joint stock company with a handful of shareholders into a mammoth enterprise capable of pooling almost limitless amounts of capital by selling its shares on a public market.

The principal restriction on corporate growth was antiquated laws that prevented a business entity chartered in one state from owning corporations in another state. In the last quarter of the century ingenious corporate lawyers evaded these restrictions by devising the trust, which not only allowed a business to operate on a national scale but it enabled a single corporate management team to control all the elements of production, from forest, mine, or oil well to the consumer marketplace (vertical integration). Unfortunately, the trust device also permitted aggressive capitalists to buy out competitors and create something approaching a monopoly (horizontal integration), and it was this latter practice that gave the trust an evil reputation.

State and federal governments and their law courts abetted this institutional development by creating a legal framework that made it possible. But the effect was to place unprecedented power over the shaping of American society in private hands—in the hands of railroad builders, industrialists, and investment bankers. And, having done so, the government then stood aside! There was no federal attempt at regulation of business until the Interstate Commerce Act of 1887, and no significant effort to enforce that statute until the early twentieth century. The result of this release of entrepreneurial energy was a pace of economic change that outran both the political philosophy of the time and the administrative competence of government. Businessmen of leathery conscience set their own moral standards, and the cutthroat, often wasteful competition that resulted gave rise to the image of "robber barons," a reference to the barons of the Middle Ages who sat astride trade routes and charged tolls of merchants who passed their castles—mere leeches who extracted profits from commerce without contributing anything to economic development.

At the center of this economic miracle and the moral dilemmas that it posed was John D. Rockefeller, who made himself one of the richest men in the world—and one of the most hated. Rockefeller was a pioneer in business organization, developing the concept of the trust, applying it to a new and rapidly growing industry, oil refining, and then driving out competition by methods that were often ruthless. When reformers at the turn of the century—Populists and Progressives—became concerned that competition was destroying itself, that a few cold-blooded corporate masters were monopolizing the economy, their attention turned naturally to John D. Rockefeller. Exposé journalists, whom President Theodore Roosevelt labeled "muckrakers,"[1] wrote books and articles about Rockefeller and his Standard Oil "trust," deriving most of their information from interviews with men whom he had driven out of business, fairly or unfairly. By the time he retired from the world of commerce in 1897 (at the age of fifty-eight) Rockefeller may have been the most feared and hated man in America, and another forty years of magnificent philanthropy did not entirely erase this image.

Ironically, Rockefeller regarded himself as an intensely moral man who lived by the rules of the Bible and never reneged on a contract. He even expressed the notion that the good Lord had given him his gold, not, of course, as a direct benefaction, but as the virtually inevitable reward for hard work, abstinence, and dependability. Competitors, he thought, fell by the wayside not because of any untoward behavior on his part but because they were weaker, less imaginative, less resolute than he. His critics thought that his philanthropy—which far exceeded that of any man of his time, including Andrew Carnegie, who made a philosophy of the "gospel of wealth"—was a payback for a guilty conscience. Rockefeller never saw it that way. Indeed, he deliberately concealed most of his giving, lest it be misinterpreted. He gave away money because he had more than he could possibly spend and because he realized that it had come to him through the circumstances of a free economy in a nation blessed with natural resources. If that combination was God's doing, Rockefeller was not alone in so believing. Robber baron or industrial pioneer? John D. Rockefeller remains an enigma.

1. Roosevelt's reference was to a character in John Bunyan's *Pilgrim's Progress* (1678) who, instead of lifting his eyes toward heaven, looked downward and stirred up filth.

John Davison Rockefeller. (Photograph from the Collections of the Library of Congress.)

The Making of a Businessman

There was little in the paternal stock to suggest future greatness, or even much success. The first Rockefeller had come to America from Germany in the early eighteenth century, settled in New Jersey, and acquired a sizable landed estate. The family fortunes had gone downhill from there.

John D.'s grandfather, Godfrey, was a jovial man with grand schemes that never seemed to pan out. His abortive business ventures subjected his family to an insecure existence as they roamed from village to village in southern New York. He was also much given to strong drink, a habit that aroused a great aversion to liquor in his wife Lucy, a repugnance that she almost certainly imparted to her grandson. Indeed, John D. Rockefeller all his life would tend to equate merrymaking with weakness of character, and he would associate only with individuals who were self-controlled and resolute.

In the mid-1830s Godfrey and Lucy Rockefeller settled in Richford, New York, in the wooded hill country just south of the Finger Lakes. Within a year their twenty-five-year-old son William appeared in town, coming from God knows where, with a slate tied to a buttonhole containing the words "I am deaf and dumb." Encountering a townsman, he scribbled the query "Where is the house of Godfrey Rockefeller?" William was of that breed of men that seemed to abound in nineteenth-century America—sometime peddler and full-time confidence man. The deaf-and-dumb tactic enabled him to learn a town's secrets and uncover potential customers for his various nostrums and cure-alls.

Settling in Richford where he worked the countryside with a wagon full of trinkets, William charmed and wed Eliza Davison, a pious woman who had led the sheltered life of a farm girl. Eliza's father was moderately wealthy, which, no doubt, added to her charms. Although John Davison was strongly opposed to the marriage, he gave Eliza a dowry of $500 and on that the couple started housekeeping. Eliza's first child was a girl, named Lucy; her second, born on July 8, 1839, was a boy whom they named after her father. John Davison Rockefeller was thus born during the presidency of Martin Van Buren; he would survive into the second term of Franklin D. Roosevelt.

William Avery Rockefeller almost immediately resumed his wandering existence, leaving home for months at a time, often returning with a new horse and wagon and a pocketful of dollar bills. In addition to peddling rings and trinkets at huge markup prices, William styled himself an "herbal doctor" and sold an elixir made from herbs that his mother Lucy had gathered in the woods and cooked up. When John D. was four, the family, now enlarged by the birth of a second son, William, moved thirty miles north to Moravia, New York, where father Bill had paid $1,000 for a ninety-two-acre farm on the shores of Owasco Lake, one of the prettiest of the Finger Lakes. There in Moravia, a pretty village that instilled fond memories, John D. Rockefeller grew into adolescence, while his father prospered in a logging business and continued his mysterious wanderings. Eliza, who often had to endure pregnancy while her husband was on the road, gave birth to two more children, Mary Ann and Frank.

For thirty weeks of the year, between fall harvest and spring planting, the Rockefeller children attended a one-room schoolhouse where discipline was harsh and books were few. John D., who would later describe himself as a "reliable" but not "brilliant" student, excelled in only one subject, arithmetic. He seemed from his earliest youth to be made for the counting house, and from the beginning he associated numbers with money. It was not that the family was poor. The problem was that it lived for months at a time on village credit while Big Bill satisfied his wanderlust. The children would be hungry and Eliza at her wit's end when Bill would suddenly materialize with an angelic grin and pockets full of crisp dollar bills sufficient to discharge the family's debts. Little wonder that John D. Rockefeller all his life associated money with manna from heaven.

Bill moved his family a couple more times and finally, when John D. was fifteen, they settled in Cleveland and John entered the Cleveland high school. Bill's wandering by this time included some philandering, and in June 1855 he married a woman from Ontario and adopted the traveling name of Dr. William Levingston. He thereafter lived the dual existence of a bigamist until Eliza died more than thirty years later. Big Bill lived until 1906 and made infrequent cameo appearances in his son's life, though, interestingly, he never sought to take advantage or share in his son's wealth. In middle age, John D. became increasingly hostile toward his father, but as a teenager he remained meekly under the paternal spell. It was several years before he became aware of his father's bigamy.

Bill's second marriage must have caused a lessening of financial support for Eliza and the children, for John D. suddenly dropped out of high school in May 1855, two months short of graduation, and went looking for a job. After many disappointments, due to his youth and inexperience, he finally landed a job as an assistant bookkeeper in a mercantile house. Rockefeller, whose only scholarly success had been in math, revealed a knack for accounting, and before long his employer increased his pay from fifty cents a day to $25 a month. Even in his first year of working he gave what he could to charities; his giving soon averaged about 10 percent of his pay. Eliza had brought him up in the Baptist faith, and that church was the main beneficiary of his philanthropy, though in 1859 he contributed funds to a black man so he could buy his wife out of slavery.

By 1858 he had managed to save $800 and was ready to go into business for himself. He formed a partnership with a twenty-eight-year-old

Englishman, Maurice B. Clark. Each partner contributed $2,000 in capital; John got the remainder of his share on a loan from his father—at the exorbitant interest rate of 10 percent. Cleveland was a major transfer point for meat and grain shipped by farmers from the western Great Lakes and sent by rail to New York and Philadelphia. The fledgling partnership bought and sold produce by the carload, and in their first year their profits equaled their $4,000 capitalization.

Although an ardent antislavery Republican, Rockefeller did not volunteer for service when the Civil War broke out in April 1861. His father had by then entirely abandoned the family, and John, at the age of twenty-one, was the sole support for his mother and five siblings. So he paid $300 to hire a volunteer soldier in his stead (as allowed by federal law), stayed home, and made money. The war increased Cleveland's importance as a rail head and lake port. Western foodstuffs that had sometimes been shipped down the Mississippi River now all came eastward across the lakes, and military supplies from the factories of New England flowed westward to the armies fighting in Kentucky and Tennessee. Rockefeller took on additional partners, and by 1862 the annual profits of his firm had soared to $17,000. Rockefeller was by then looking for a new outlet for his entrepreneurial energies, for he realized that war profiteering was a short-term gamble. He found it in oil refining.

Bringing Order to Oil

Oil Creek, in far western Pennsylvania, was a minor tributary of the Allegheny River. Its name dated back to the eighteenth century when the first pioneers noticed that its waters were covered with an iridescent film and tasted foul. Seneca Indians in the area skimmed off the oil for use as a skin liniment, and in the nineteenth century an occasional peddler had bottled and sold it as an all-purpose elixir. But no one had thought to burn it for warmth or lighting. Although various vegetable oils were available for lighting homes, the most popular illuminant by far was whale oil. In addition to yielding oil from their blubber, some whales also provided from their head cavities a waxy spermaceti that made the hardest and most long-lasting candles. However, by 1850 whales had become scarce due to overhunting, and rising wealth and population caused the price of whale oil to soar.

In the mid-1850s one of the more alert residents of Titusville, a village on the banks of Oil Creek, sent a specimen of the stream's water to chemistry professors at Yale. The report came back that, properly refined, "rock oil" could provide the smoke- and odor-free illumination of whale oil. The recipient of the report formed a company and sent Colonel Edwin Drake, a former railroad conductor with no training in engineering, to Titusville. Since it was evident that oil was in the vicinity, Drake's problem was to determine if it could be tapped and made to flow in commercial quantities. After digging several pits that merely caved in, Drake started to drill in a manner used for salt wells. The drilling mechanism stood well above ground and was supported in place by a wooden structure known as a derrick. On August 28, 1859, an epoch dawned when oil bubbled up from the casing of a hole that Drake had drilled the previous day.

An oil rush ensued as hundreds of fortune-seekers threw up derricks and began drilling holes all up and down the narrow valley. Since the crude oil had to be distilled, primitive refineries also sprang up, and within a year the once-lush valley was a soil-poisoned wasteland. The hubbub in Oil Valley soon attracted attention in Cleveland, only a day's coach ride away. In that city was a small group of chemists who had learned the European method of extracting kerosene from crude oil using sulfuric acid—the basic process of oil "refining." Among these was an English friend of Maurice Clark, Samuel Andrews, who was also a fellow parishioner of Rockefeller's at the Erie Street Baptist Church. In 1863 Rockefeller and Clark put up $4,000 for a half interest in a new refining venture, Andrews, Clark and Company, and thus was born the distant ancestor of the Standard Oil Company.

Rockefeller plunged into the oil business with single-minded enthusiasm. Although Andrews and Clark were older than he, they respected his business acumen. Every morning they came to his house in the predawn dark to discuss possible bargains and contracts. As John's sister Mary Ann observed, the older men usually deferred to her brother. "They did not seem to want to go without him," she wrote. "They would . . . walk in and visit in the dining room while John was at breakfast." They talked interminably of oil to the exclusion even of the progress of the war. "I got sick of it and wished morning after morning that they would talk of something else."

Rockefeller brought a bookkeeper's sense of order and regularity to the fledgling industry. On his first visit to the oil fields he was struck by the chaos and inefficiency. The threshold problem was that no one knew how much oil lay below the surface. The only other commercial oilfield in the world at that time was in Russia's Caucasus. No one even knew whether there was oil elsewhere in North America. In the California gold rush a decade earlier the forty-niners had stripped off the surface gold in a couple years and then most went broke. The oilmen and the refiners both assumed that their bonanza was similarly short term, and prices soared around $20 a barrel. Then a lucky driller struck a pressure pool, and a mighty gusher roared hundreds of feet into the air. With that single well yielding 3,000 barrels a day, the price plummeted to ten cents a barrel, far below the cost of transportation.

Transporting the oil was another problem, for the nearest rail head was about twenty miles away. The flow from the wells had to be directed into wooden barrels,[2] which were then loaded into wagons. Dirty, ragged, cursing teamsters drove the wagons over rutted roads to the train station, often tipping or losing barrels along the way, and charging three or four dollars a barrel for the service.

After visiting the oilfields Rockefeller made two key decisions. First, that refining was the place in which to invest because it was subject to ordinary business accounting methods and, as the neck between the geysers in the fields and the demand in the cities, it was the point from which the industry could be controlled. Drilling, on the other hand, was a lottery that would produce more paupers than millionaires. His second decision was to build his refinery in Cleveland, rather than amidst the oil wells of Titusville. From Cleveland he could ship his kerosene by boat or train to New York and Philadelphia. As soon as technology permitted he would connect his Cleveland refinery to the oilfields by pipeline so as to bypass the price-gouging teamsters and their wasteful methods.

Wartime demand kept prices high—they reached twelve dollars a barrel by 1864—and Rockefeller poured most of his profits into enlarging his refinery. By early 1865 the partnership owned the largest refinery in Cleveland, capable of treating five hundred barrels of crude oil a day. By then, however, his cautious partners had become worried about his zeal for continuous expansion. The war was winding down that winter, and peacetime demand was uncertain. They also fretted about the continued supply of crude, even though another bonanza had burst forth that winter at an obscure Pennsylvania valley called Pithole Creek. Clark and his brother (who had been brought into the business) were also annoyed at Rockefeller's overbearing self-confidence. In keeping the firm's accounts he minded every penny, but he would then turn to the banks and borrow tens of thousands of dollars for business expansion without consulting his partners. In February 1865 the partnership broke up by mutual agreement. Rockefeller and Clark bid against one another at a closed auction for possession of the refinery, and Rockefeller won with a bid of $72,000, a price that he himself conceded was almost twice what the physical plant was worth. But at the age of twenty-five he owned the largest refinery in Cleveland and one of the largest in the world. "It was the day that determined my career," he told a biographer years later. "I felt the bigness of it, but I was as calm as I am talking to you now." Andrews had stuck with Rockefeller through the breakup, and they formed a new partnership. Andrews slid into the role of technical adviser; Rockefeller made all the key business decisions.

Expansion and innovation were his trademarks. In December 1865 he opened a second refinery in Cleveland and installed his brother William as plant manager. He then turned to ways of reducing costs and

2. The Pennsylvania barrel, containing forty-two gallons, remains the industry standard today.

streamlining the business. Transportation was still the highest single cost. He had been paying neighborhood coopers $2.50 for barrels made of white oak. Because his demand for barrels was large and steady, he found that he could save money by making his own. He could also make better ones by having the oak staves kiln-dried in the woods, rather than using green timber as the coopers did. His firm was soon making thousands of barrels a day for less than a dollar a barrel, and the lighter, tighter barrels made of dried wood cut his transportation costs in half. He also encouraged the railroads to develop a tank car for carrying oil (they had previously tried to ship barrels on open flatcars). Within a few years Rockefeller had his own fleet of tank cars, and he paid the railroads only to haul them around. His one momentary setback was an effort to build a pipeline connecting the oil fields with the rail heads. The angry teamsters kept tearing it up.

In contrast to the audacity that speared his meteoric rise to wealth and power, Rockefeller brought a bookkeeper's caution and deliberation to the idea of marriage. He also had exacting standards, requiring a woman who would be deeply religious, like his mother, yet a partner in his drive for wealth and power. While in high school he found a likely mate in Laura Celestia Spelman (known as "Cettie") who, in addition to being physically presentable and bright, was taking courses in bookkeeping and business principles. However, the Spelmans were Cleveland gentry; Cettie's father was a member of the state legislature. John had to wait until his own fortune was improved; they were married nine years later in 1864. After a month-long honeymoon, in which they made the already conventional visit to Niagara Falls, they settled into a rather plain two-story brick house on Cheshire Street, two doors from his mother's residence. They lived frugally and without servants for the first few years, a life of Spartan simplicity that Rockefeller would later recall with wistful affection.

Rockefeller and Flagler

There were probably two key elements to John D. Rockefeller's success in the world of business. One was his opportunism—his ability to spot a promising field of endeavor and pour resources into it, tempered only by an accountant's eye for the bottom line. The other, undoubtedly, was his eye for talent—his ability to assemble a team of capable, congenial executives who would transform the Cleveland refinery into the world's strongest manufacturing company. The first of these recruits was Henry Flagler. Indeed, the alliance of Rockefeller and Flagler may have been the most successful business partnership in history.

As puritanical as Rockefeller at this time (he would later become noted for finery of dress and elaborate houses), Flagler came from a similar background and was endowed with an equally nimble faculty for numbers and balance sheets. In his memoirs Rockefeller noted that Flagler "was always on the active side of every question, and to his wonderful energy is due much of the rapid progress of the company in the early days."

Flagler also grew up in the Finger Lakes district of New York, the son of a Presbyterian minister. He dropped out of school at fourteen, moved to Sandusky, Ohio, and became a commission merchant in wheat, sending carloads, among other places, to the firm of Clark and Rockefeller in Cleveland. He went bust on a bad investment during the Civil War but was rescued by his father-in-law, Stephen V. Harkness, who made a fortune during the war on inside tips from politicians (he stockpiled barrels of wine and whiskey just before the government imposed a tax on spirits).

In 1867 Rockefeller, who like his cash-happy father mistrusted banks, approached Harkness for a $100,000 loan. Harkness agreed on condition that Rockefeller make Flagler treasurer of his company and Harkness's own personal "watchdog." A few days later the *Cleveland Leader* announced the formation of a new partnership, Rockefeller, Andrews, and Flagler with offices in a prestigious building on Public Square. "This firm," the newspaper added, "is one of the oldest in the refining business and their trade is already a mammoth one. . . . Their establishment is one of the largest in the United States." Rockefeller was twenty-eight, Flagler thirty-seven.

Flagler's first great coup was to negotiate preferential freight rates with the railroads that served Cleveland. "Rebates," as such preferential tariffs were called, were later singled out by the turn-of-the-century muckrakers as the basis of the Rockefeller fortune, a secretive device by which he cheated his competitors and drove them out of business. In fact, neither Rockefeller nor Flagler invented rebates; the railroads themselves did. Nor was it preferential treatment that enabled Rockefeller to rise to the top. He was already there when Flagler negotiated the first "sweetheart" deal with a railroad. On the other hand, the muckrakers were right in that Rockefeller's commanding position gave him extraordinary power in compelling railroad-freight concessions.

Rockefeller had the further advantage of having located himself in Cleveland. The other major refining center in the West, Pittsburgh, had only a single artery connecting it with eastern markets, the Pennsylvania Railroad. Cleveland, in contrast, was blessed with two railroads: the Erie, which ran through southern New York to the Jersey side of the New York harbor, and the Lake Shore line, which ran to Buffalo where it connected with Commodore Vanderbilt's New York Central (it would later be absorbed into the New York Central System). In addition, during the summer months when Lake Erie was open, Cleveland refiners could send their product east by boat through the Erie Canal. With three competing transportation systems, Cleveland refiners were in a good position to negotiate favorable freight rates.

Railroads, almost from their inception, had favored certain customers because of their own high fixed costs. They had borrowed enormous amounts of money simply to build their lines, and they then had to maintain both track and rolling stock. As a result they favored customers who had large, heavy loads to send (coal, oil, iron ore) and who could guarantee regular shipments. For a railroad, then, Rockefeller was an ideal customer, for a train composed only of oil-tank cars could make a round trip to New York City in only a third of the time it would take a freight train consisting of a motley assortment of box cars carrying different products to a variety of places.

In the spring of 1868 Henry Flagler went to Jay Gould, who had recently wrested control of the Erie Railroad from Commodore Vanderbilt in a famous stock market war, and negotiated a secret deal by which Rockefeller and Flagler would receive a 75 percent rebate on oil shipped through the Erie system. Rockefeller and Flagler could then have gone to the Lake Shore Railroad and demanded a similar concession, but they were much too shrewd to use that sort of heavy-handed tactic. Instead they approached other Cleveland refiners with a suggestion that they coordinate shipments in order to save money. They apparently got some cooperation, for Flagler then went to an executive of the Lake Shore line with a promise to ship sixty carloads of refined oil daily (far more than they themselves produced) if the railroad could give him a special price. They worked out a verbal arrangement (none of these contracts was ever put into writing) whereby the Lake Shore would ship oil to New York for only $1.65 a barrel, while the officially listed rate was $2.40.

The Lake Shore bargain revolutionized the oil industry and gave the railroads a vested interest in the creation of a giant oil monopoly. The rail lines soon applied the rebate system to other businesses that could promise steady shipments, and that further encouraged the consolidation of American business into giant national companies. Rockefeller was well aware that the Lake Shore bargain was revolutionary. "It was a large, regular volume of business," he later wrote, "such as had not hitherto been given to the roads in question." Neither man had any pangs of conscience over the deal. "I remember when the Standard received its first rebate," wrote Flagler. "I went home in great delight. I had won a great victory, I thought."

As rumors of the bargain flashed through Cleveland, journalists began to take an interest in the laconic young man who had become the boy wonder of American business. "He occupies a position in our business circles second to but few," wrote one. "Close application to one kind of business, an avoidance of all positions of honorary character that cost time, keeping everything pertaining to his business in so methodical a manner that he knows every night how he stands with the world." As if to confirm his arrival at social respectability, in August 1868 Rockefeller moved Cettie and their daughter Elizabeth into a multi-storied brick house on Euclid Avenue, a street that was already adorned with mansions built on fortunes in lumber, flour milling, real estate, and banking, and known locally as "millionaires' row."

In an upstairs bedroom of the new house Cettie bore a succession of children. A second child, Alice, was born in 1869 but died a year later. Then came Alta (1871), Edith (1872), and John D. Jr. (1874). Unlike his father, Rockefeller was firmly rooted in his home. He mirrored the popular image of a Victorian father—hard in his business affairs, mellow and loving in the company of his children. He even had a telegraph line installed connecting the office with his home so he could spend two or three afternoons a week at home, combining decision making with gardening and planting trees. The system also allowed him to pace himself, so that he never appeared tired or stressed. His long life alone is testimony to his concern for health and exercise. But the home was also a castle, and it might as well have been surrounded by a moat. Rockefeller hired governesses to educate the children at home, and the family's only outside social engagements were church-related. Playmates, invariably drawn from the Baptist congregation, might visit for a week or more at a time, but the Rockefeller children were never allowed to visit other homes. Nor did Rockefeller lavish money on the children. The four shared a single bicycle and, except on Sunday, the girls wore simple gingham dresses and hand-me-downs. John D. Jr., the youngest and the only boy, once confessed that he had worn handed-down dresses until he rebelled at the age of eight.

Genesis of the Standard Oil Trust

Within a year after their railroad rebate coup Rockefeller and Flagler faced the specter of ruin. High profits in the refining industry and low start-up costs had brought into the field "the tinkers and the tailors and the boys who followed the plow." By 1870 refining capacity was triple the amount of oil being pumped, and the price of kerosene collapsed. Rockefeller estimated that 90 percent of all refineries were operating in the red. Later in life he identified the years 1869 and 1870 as the moment when he decided that cooperation would be more beneficial than competition. This could best be done by creating a giant cartel that would bring discipline to the industry, reduce overcapacity, and stabilize prices.

The first step was incorporation. In January 1870 the partnership was dissolved, and the Standard Oil Company was formed under Ohio's incorporation laws. Rockefeller was president, his brother William became vice president, and Flagler was secretary-treasurer. With $1 million in capital (larger than any other manufacturing company) the new corporation owned the two Cleveland refineries, which produced about 10 percent of the nation's kerosene, a barrel-making plant, warehouses, and shipping terminals. The three officers had pooled their personal resources and owned nearly all the stock. Other investors declined to step forward because of the glut in the industry. Rockefeller decreed that the three officers would not take salaries; they would be reimbursed instead by stock dividends. In the corporation's first year of operations it paid 105 percent in dividends.

The first target in Rockefeller's imperial plan was his Cleveland competitors, the twenty-six other refiners in the city. His ally in the scheme that historians would call the "Cleveland Massacre" was an old enemy, the Pennsylvania Railroad, which had previously been the mainstay of the Pittsburgh refineries. The man in control of the Pennsylvania Railroad was Tom Scott, the most domineering, autocratic, amoral railroad man in the country. Accustomed to buying whatever he wanted from the venal Pennsylvania legislature, Scott had obtained a charter for a corporation with the innocuous name of the South Improvement Company. Under Scott's scheme the three railroads that served the western refineries—the Pennsylvania, the New York Central, and the Erie—would join with the Standard Oil Company as the principal shareholders of the South Improvement Company (SIC), with other refiners invited to join if they wished. Then refiners who were members of the South Improvement Company would receive rebates of up to 50 percent on their oil shipments. Although all refiners were theoretically invited to join, Rockefeller effectively excluded them by buying up almost 50 percent of the SIC stock (the railroads owned the rest).

While this deal was forming, the Standard Oil executive committee, on January 1, 1872, boosted the company's capitalization from $1 million to $3.5 million in order to purchase "certain refining properties in Cleveland and elsewhere." Among the new shareholders were some of the leading Cleveland bankers. In February the railroads announced a doubling of freight rates on oil for all shippers who were not members of the South Improvement Company. Protest meetings erupted from Oil Creek to Cleveland, and for the first time Rockefeller was publicly identified as a villain engaged in unfair competition. One newspaper crowned him the "Mephistopheles of Cleveland." Reacting to the uproar, the Pennsylvania legislature cancelled the charter of the South Improvement Company in early April, and a committee of Congress began an investigation of "the most gigantic and daring conspiracy" ever to threaten a free nation. When his railroad allies rescinded the rate increase, Rockefeller himself caved in.

He had by then obtained his primary goal anyway. During February and March, wielding the invisible club of the South Improvement Company and utilizing his newly acquired capital, he bought out twenty-two of his twenty-six competitors in Cleveland. He started with the largest of them and then used that acquisition to panic the smaller ones. Rockefeller later claimed that he had done his fellow refiners a favor because most of them were losing money anyway. His victims felt otherwise, and they retained vivid memories of the crude pressure tactics of the Standard Oil negotiators when they were interviewed thirty years later by the muckraking journalist Ida Tarbel (whose father was one of Rockefeller's victims). The South Improvement scheme—even though not a single railroad rebate actually came of it—and the Cleveland Massacre seared Rockefeller's reputation with lasting infamy.

He personally, however, felt that he had behaved honorably, and he resumed his quest for order. In May 1872 he induced the Pittsburgh and Titusville refiners to join him in a gigantic cartel, which would limit oil production to the nation's demand and negotiate favorable freight rates with the railroads. The cartel crumbled within a year because the refiners could not maintain discipline within their own ranks. There was wholesale cheating within the association, and small producers on the outside took advantage of the pact to gain a share of the market. By mid-1873 Rockefeller had concluded that a refiner's association was a "rope of sand" and the only way to bring order to the industry was to put it under the heel of the Standard Oil Company. "The idea was mine," he said later. "The idea was persisted in, too, in spite of the opposition of some who became fainthearted at the magnitude of the undertaking, as it constantly assumed larger proportions."

During the next two years Rockefeller moved energetically into Pittsburgh, Philadelphia, and New York, buying out his competitors. In each case he offered the owner of a refinery the choice of cash or Standard Oil stock. If they took stock, Rockefeller preserved his own supply of cash and avoided going to bankers for a loan. Unfortunately, most sellers preferred cash because they had little confidence in the schemes of this thirty-five-year-old visionary. But those who accepted stock did very well indeed. One biographer has estimated that a goodly portion of American high society in the twentieth century is descended from men who accepted Standard Oil stock in the 1870s. By the end of 1874 Rockefeller controlled virtually all the oil that traveled over the New York Central, Erie, and Pennsylvania railroads.

It was at that point that he discovered the potential in pipelines. Since the late 1860s, oil had been piped from the wells in the field to the nearest rail head. There were at the time no long-distance pipelines. But in the summer of 1873 Rockefeller's some-time ally and long-time nemesis Tom Scott set up a pipeline subsidiary of the Pennsylvania Railroad. Scott resented Rockefeller's control of the flow of oil through his ownership of railroad tank cars and hoped to create a monopoly of his own, an interstate pipeline. Rockefeller perceived the threat and immediately began buying up local pipelines in Ohio and western Pennsylvania and tying them to the Erie and New York Central roadbeds. Within a year his pipelines were handling a third of the oil coming out of Pennsylvania, and he had more monopoly power than ever. By simply turning off the spigot he could ruin any refiner that stood in his way. It is splendidly ironic that by the time the Standard's railroad "rebates" became a political issue in the 1880s they were utterly irrelevant. By then, Rockefeller was moving nearly all his oil through pipelines that he controlled.

Throughout this period of rapid expansion in the 1870s Rockefeller and Flagler had been skirting the edge of the law. The Standard Oil Company, as an Ohio corporation, was confined by the terms of its corporate charter to the state of Ohio. It had no legal right to own companies domiciled in other states. Rockefeller and Flagler evaded this restriction by a simple expedient. Although they purchased a competitor with Standard Oil's cash and stock, the stock of the other company—and hence its ownership—was transferred not to the Standard but to Henry Flagler, treasurer of the Standard, as trustee. The concept of trusteeship had arisen in the common law out of the need to protect the rights of minors when a parent died prematurely. The estate was managed by a trusted friend or relative in the interest of the minor children until they came of age. Business partnerships also used the device to transfer certain joint property to a bank as trustee. Such trusteeships became legally binding when approved by a court.

By 1879 Flagler was the trustee for dozens of corporations that had been purchased with Standard Oil cash and stock. All the trust agreements had been done secretly; none had the approval of a court. But it was messy, and it made unified control of the Standard's many operations difficult. In the course of that year Flagler and his lawyers prepared a general trust agreement and obtained court approval. Under the agreement three officials in the Cleveland office were made trustees for all the stock held by the Standard's thirty-seven stockholders (four men, the two Rockefellers, Flagler, and his father-in-law Harkness held half of the 35,000 shares), as well as Flagler's numerous trusteeships. The trio of trustees (who were mere dummies for the real owners) was to manage the stocks and other assets for the benefit of Standard Oil stockholders.

The new organization was still unwieldy. The trustees had no real power, and the trust was subject to double taxation, as Ohio sought to tax all the Standard's assets no matter where they were located. Consequently in January 1882 a new trust agreement was signed. This set up a board of nine trustees, who would take direct control of the stock of the Standard and all its subsidiaries. The former stockholders of the Standard, now forty-two in number, were given trust certificates representing their investment in the company. All profits from the Standard and its subsidiaries would be turned over to the trustees, who would then issue dividends to the certificate holders. Most significantly, the nine trustees were now the decision makers—the two Rockefellers, Flagler, and six one-time competitors who had been absorbed into the Rockefeller circle of associates. The trust was capitalized at $70 million (i.e., that was the value of the trust certificates issued), and the trustees followed Rockefeller's habit of pouring most of the profits back into the business by purchasing additional pipelines, refineries, and export facilities. By 1890 the Standard Oil Trust was worth nearly $116 million, earning about $20 million a year and paying $11 million in dividends. By that date, too, the Standard had become a model for other businesses—trusts had arisen in meat packing, sugar refining, even the self-igniting match industry. And the word "trust" had become a public ogre, a symbol of monopoly and unbridled power, and consequently a target for politicians.

Titan of Industry

When the Standard Oil Trust was formed in 1882 its head office was situated in New York. The city was the nation's financial center—on the rare occasion when Rockefeller had to resort to bank credit, his needs far outstripped the resources of Cleveland—and New York's port was the nation's busiest. By then about 70 percent of American oil was being sold abroad; it was America's fourth-largest export. In addition, New York had become a major refining center. By the 1880s crude oil was being sent directly to the coast by interstate pipeline, and Cleveland's status as a refining center was in decline. The Standard built huge new refineries in Brooklyn; Bayonne, New Jersey; Philadelphia; and Baltimore.

Rockefeller moved his family to New York the following year. Characteristically, he purchased a modest four-story brownstone house on West Fifty-fourth Street. Garlanded in ivy, the house was flanked by sizable lawns that would later serve as the sculpture garden of the Museum of Modern Art. Around the corner, on Fifth Avenue, amidst the flamboyant edifices of Commodore Vanderbilt's sons, were the stately mansions of the Standard Oil men: Flagler, William Rockefeller, and other officers. True to the family's mistrust of moneylenders, William financed his house by selling John $50,000 of Standard Oil stock, an imprudent decision that would ultimately account for the vast disparity in wealth between the two brothers.

Rockefeller brought his midwestern version of Puritanism to the cosmopolitan city. He and Cettie avoided the round of dinner parties, costume balls, and opera nights where Astors and Vanderbilts set the tone. One magazine took note of their simple lifestyle: "He never entertains notables, his home is never given to entertainment, and he follows the policy of self-effacement at all times and in all places." He continued to hedge his children from the sinful world, and they were now old enough to see the difference. John Jr. lamented the relative freedom of his cousins around the corner. "They had a gay kind of social life, with many parties which we used to wish we could have."

John D. Sr. adhered to a simple daily routine. After a breakfast of bread and milk, he spent a nickel to take the Sixth Avenue elevated train downtown to the Standard's headquarters, a massive nine-story building at the foot of Broadway (at one time the location of Alexander Hamilton's home). His mind on business from the moment he boarded the train, he made penciled notes to himself on his shirt cuff. He then slipped noiselessly into his office at the stroke of nine. "I never knew anyone to enter an office as quietly as Mr. Rockefeller," noted his private secretary of many years. "He seemed almost to have a coat of invisibility."

Through the 1880s Rockefeller continued his efforts to streamline the industry and make it more efficient. The main bottleneck was the industry's antiquated marketing system. Retail stores that sold kerosene were supplied by self-employed wagoners, with carts full of rattling barrels. This obsolete distribution system could not handle the flood of kerosene that was now coming out of Rockefeller's refineries, and it could not keep up with demand for lighting in the new factories, hotels, and office buildings that were being built in the mushrooming cities. So Rockefeller built his own fleet of tank wagons manned by Standard employees. The Standard's pipelines delivered refined oil to large storage tanks in each city where the tank wagons filled up. The wagons then delivered the oil to groceries and hardware stores where they refilled special canisters that the Standard had provided. To widen the market further the Standard sold, almost at cost, heaters, stoves, and lanterns, thus creating demand for oil while supplying it.

The new system was highly efficient and extremely profitable, but it also made enemies of many ordinary citizens. Rockefeller's direct marketing practice bypassed wholesale dealers altogether; grocers and hardware dealers often resented the requirement that they sell only Standard's kerosene as a condition of doing any illuminating-oil business. The Standard's subsidiaries, moreover, were hard to control, and local managers had few scruples about gouging customers. The Standard's marketing operations thus touched thousands of small businessmen in every congressional district, and their complaints were soon being heard in the halls of Congress.

The complaints also caught the attention of exposé journalists, most prominent of whom was wealthy, Columbia-educated Henry Demarest Lloyd. Lloyd had married into the family that owned the *Chicago Tribune*, and in the late 1870s he began writing editorials sharply critical of the Standard Oil Company. In 1881 the *Atlantic Monthly*, the nation's leading mass circulation magazine, published an essay by Lloyd entitled "Story of a Great Monopoly." Although much of his information came from Rockefeller's business victims, Lloyd shrewdly pitched his story at consumers, opening with the line: "Very few of the forty millions of people who burn kerosene know that its production, manufacture, and export, its price at home and abroad, have been controlled for years by a single corporation—the Standard Oil Company." A superb phrasemaker, Lloyd claimed that the "octopus" (a nickname that would soon become synonymous with Standard Oil) was a threat to American democracy because it regularly bought and sold congressmen and it had "done everything with the Pennsylvania legislature except refine it." Lloyd continued to pepper the Standard Oil Company through the 1880s, climaxing in a book-length exposé of its misdeeds in 1894, "Wealth vs. Commonwealth."

Such public scrutiny finally caught the attention of politicians who initially focused on the railroads and their alleged ties to the trusts through the rebate system. Beginning in the 1870s, state legislatures, responding to the complaints of farmers and other small shippers, passed laws regulating railroad rates. When the Supreme Court declared such laws unconstitutional in 1886, on grounds that only the federal government could regulate interstate commerce, an assortment of railroad users descended on Congress. The result was the Interstate Commerce Act of 1887, the first hesitant step toward federal regulation of a privately owned business. The law specifically prohibited railroad pools and rebates, and it set up the first federal regulatory agency, the Interstate Commerce Commission. Although Congress apparently envisioned that the ICC would regulate the fares that railroads charged for carrying freight, the Supreme Court gutted the statute of any such power. Rockefeller viewed the path-breaking statute with studied indifference. He was sending most of his product through his own pipelines, and in places where he was forced to use railroad facilities he negotiated oral agreements on rates that were virtually undetectable.

The Sherman Antitrust Act three years later was a more direct attack on the Standard Oil Company. What Rockefeller had taught the thinking minority of the American public was that free competition tends to destroy itself. In an uncontrolled marketplace the hardest working, most ruthless business leaders will rise to the top, buy out their competitors, and end up with a dominant market share (though rarely with a true monopoly). The purpose of business, after all, is profit, and the highest profits are to be made in noncompetitive conditions. In a perfectly free market, no one made any money, as Rockefeller discovered in the early stages of the refining industry. The corollary was that a semblance of competition could be preserved, paradoxically, only by government interference—that is, a law breaking up monopolies, or trusts, as business combinations were then commonly known.

The problem with the Sherman Act was that it could have been drafted by the businessmen themselves. The shortest statute in American history, it consisted of only two sentences. It prohibited business combinations that restrained interstate commerce, and it awarded the victims treble damages. No federal agency was created to enforce the law. In practice, it was up to the president of the United States and his attorney general to spot combinations and bring suit, although private businesses who suffered injury could also sue monopolists. Worse, only four years after the law was adopted, the Supreme Court, composed of lawyers who had not grasped the lessons taught by Rockefeller, ruled that the term "interstate commerce" referred only to the physical flow of goods across state lines and did not apply to manufacturing (such as sugar refining in the case at hand and oil refining by implication) because factories are necessarily sedentary. The statute, in short, was so riddled with loopholes that it became popularly known as the Swiss Cheese Act.

Rockefeller, who made a habit of never commenting publicly on the accusations of his critics or the antics of politicians, simply ignored the statute. As far as he was concerned, practical businessmen, such as the Standard Oil combine, had already solved the problems of free competition, and only soft-headed politicians and magazine scribblers thought there was any need for governmental tampering. Ironically, the evolution of corporate law driven by businessmen and their lawyers was already rendering the trust device obsolete. In the previous year, 1889, New Jersey passed a law enabling corporations chartered under the laws of the state to own corporations created by another state. Copied by other states eager to attract business, such as Delaware, the statute gave rise to the holding company, a corporation whose sole function is to hold a controlling interest of stock in other corporations, so mammoth in its capitalization that it could be formed only with the help of an investment banker.

The invention of the holding company, combined with pro-business administrations in Washington, gave rise to a new wave of business consolidation in the 1890s and the emergence of giants that rivaled in size the Standard Oil Company. (Such twentieth–century megaliths as General Electric, International Harvester, and International Telephone and Telegraph were created during the decade.) The wave of consolidation climaxed with the formation of the United States Steel Company in 1902, America's first billion-dollar company. Although the heart of this holding company was the Carnegie Steel Company, the genius behind it was not a steel man at all but an investment banker, J. P. Morgan. And the president of U.S. Steel was a Morgan protégé, Judge Elbert Gary. Indeed, it was said of Gary that he "never saw a blast furnace till he died."

University of Chicago

By the 1890s, Thomas A. Edison's light bulb and dynamo, together with his organizational genius in being able to illuminate entire cities, were seriously encroaching on the Standard's kerosene business. Rockefeller responded initially by diversifying his personal investments. In 1893, having learned of the discovery of a rich lode of iron ore in northern Minnesota, Rockefeller purchased nearly the entire Mesabi Range. In 1902 he sold the iron range to J. P. Morgan, and in return became one of the largest shareholders of U.S. Steel.

By the mid-1890s the stress of business was beginning to show; he suffered headaches and a series of stomach maladies. In addition, it seems likely that he felt that his job was done. He had created a gleaming juggernaut that stood astride the entire American economy. A friend noted some years later, that the business "had ceased to amuse him, it lacked freshness and variety and had become merely irksome and he withdrew." He appeared less and less frequently in the Standard Oil tower on lower Broadway, and in 1897, at the age of 58, he retired altogether.

Ironically, Rockefeller's retirement virtually coincided with two momentous events affecting his company—the discovery of oil in California with reserves that exceeded anything that had been drilled out of Pennsylvania and the growing popularity of the automobile. As Standard Oil exploited the new supply and met the rising demand by converting from kerosene to gasoline, the value of its stock rose dramatically, and Rockefeller grew richer in retirement than he had while working. His fortune stood at about $200 million in 1897; by 1913, when Henry Ford instituted the moving assembly line in the auto industry, Rockefeller was worth $1 billion.

Surplus wealth was another inducement to retirement. He received $3 million yearly in Standard Oil dividends and nearly as much from his outside investments in railroads, banks, iron mines, and two orange groves. Even if he had been given to buying enormous yachts—as J. P. Morgan was famed for doing—Rockefeller could not personally consume that much income. He had to give it away.

He had, from youth, been a philanthropist, with the Baptist church his biggest beneficiary. By the 1880s he was giving liberally to Baptist schools. One of his most important projects was a seminary for newly freed black females, founded shortly after the Civil War in Atlanta. Rockefeller rescued it from debt and financed the construction of several classroom buildings and dormitories. But he did not—and this would become a hallmark of his future philanthropy—give it a permanent endowment that would preclude the need for future fund-raising. He wanted the school to support itself. When the female heads of the school offered to name it Rockefeller College (which would have placed it alongside other schools endowed by "robber barons" of the Gilded Age: Cornell, Vanderbilt, and Stanford), Rockefeller humbly declined. Instead, he suggested the name his wife's family, and thus was born Spelman Seminary, renamed Spelman College in 1924. It remains today one of the most respected schools for women, counting among its alumni both the mother and the grandmother of Reverend Martin Luther King.

By the late 1880s Rockefeller was deluged with petitions for philanthropic grants, and he realized that he had to bring order to his giving in the same way he had systematized the oil industry. He found an agent in

Frederick T. Gates, a thirty-eight-year-old Baptist minister who had given up the capricious job of preparing souls for the hereafter and taken up the more pressing task of upgrading the herein. He did so, however, without losing faith that the Baptist Church could be a useful agent in such social improvement. In 1888, when he first encountered Gates, Rockefeller was being severely pressed by Baptist clergymen on the need for a new Baptist university that included graduate programs. Their model was Johns Hopkins University, founded in the 1870s as a graduate school devoted exclusively to professional training. It had quickly attracted some of the most distinguished researchers in the country, as well as a host of able students. (Richard T. Ely, Thorstein Veblen, and Woodrow Wilson were in one famous history seminar.) Able Baptist undergraduates, the argument went, were forced to attend Harvard, Yale, and Princeton for advanced work, and in those secular places lost their religious idealism. The clergymen pressuring Rockefeller differed only on the location of their proposed school. One wanted it situated in Manhattan (on Morningside Heights, which would have made it a neighbor of Columbia); the other preferred the booming city of Chicago, where building costs were lower and post-graduate training nonexistent.

Rockefeller was easily put off by aggressive solicitation, and he kept the two clergymen at bay for several years. Gates, a midwesterner, strongly favored the Chicago site, and he caught Rockefeller's attention with an exhaustively researched report on the advantages of the Windy City. Most persuasive to Rockefeller was the lack of similar institutions in the Midwest, and Chicago was sufficiently distant from the Manhattan headquarters of Standard Oil to allay suspicions that he would turn the school into a mouthpiece for Wall Street. In 1889 he pledged $600,000 toward the founding of the university on the understanding that the board of the American Baptist Education Society would raise another $400,000. The board approved a charter for the University of Chicago in May 1890.

Rockefeller, whose enthusiasm for the project had grown exponentially under Gates's tutelage, took it upon himself to find a president for the school. His choice was William Rainey Harper, who, at the age of thirty-five, was the foremost Baptist biblical scholar in the country. Harper, a professor at Yale, was reluctant to leave his biblical studies and drove a hard bargain. He wrung from Rockefeller a promise that he could continue his scholarly interests and serve as both professor and president. Perhaps even more important, he informed Rockefeller—and Rockefeller did nothing to disabuse him—that he would need additional funding to make the University of Chicago "from the very beginning an institution of the very highest character," on a level with Harvard, Yale, Johns Hopkins, and the University of Michigan. With Rockefeller's tacit approval of these extravagant dreams, Harper accepted the presidency in February 1891.

Within a year Harper had gone through Rockefeller's endowment, negotiating more than 120 faculty appointments, ransacking the Ivy League for its most luminous names. Among his acquisitions was John Dewey for the philosophy department and Thorstein Veblen in economics. When the school opened in October 1892, its faculty was so studded with renowned scholars that it was at birth in the front rank of higher education. Rockefeller and Gates were both "utterly appalled" at Harper's profligate spending, but Rockefeller had been drawn in so deeply that he could not turn back. He pledged another $500,000 the following year, and when the depression of the mid-nineties dried up the school's other sources of funding, he pledged an astounding $3 million, the largest sum ($50 million in today's dollars) ever given by a single individual to an educational institution. Harper permitted the football coach, Amos Alonzo Stagg (who had set up the first physical education department at an American university), to announce the gift to the student body during half time of a game with the University of Wisconsin. Chicago had been trailing at the half; following the announcement, it trounced the Badgers.

By 1910, when Rockefeller finally severed his connection with the university (he was a liability by then because the muckrakers had so thoroughly sullied his reputation), Rockefeller's gifts to the school totaled $35 million. The Baptist connection had been severed three years earlier, and the university was a self-funded public entity. (The city of Chicago's contribution to the school during its first twenty years had been less than $1 million.) The University of Chicago remains Rockefeller's best-known philanthropy, and the model he established—giving birth to an institution that would thereafter enjoy an independent existence—was a landmark in American philanthropy.

The Kindly Eccentric

Rockefeller mellowed noticeably in retirement. His life remained very private. He and Cettie settled on an estate near Tarrytown on the edge of the Catskills that eventually amounted to three thousand acres. He took up golf, and, as with everything else he did, made it a consuming passion. An account book begun in 1906 indicated personal expenses of about $500,000 a year, with an astounding amount, $27,537.80, devoted to golf. He played golf on a daily basis almost to the end of his long life.

The irony is that while Rockefeller relaxed and withdrew from the world of commerce (he was titular president of Standard Oil but had no role in decision making), the ruthlessness of his rise to power in the 1870s came back to haunt him. In the ideological forefront of the post-1900 Progressive movement were the journalistic muckrakers. Their principal outlet was a magazine founded by Samuel S. McClure in 1893. Ida Tarbell, managing editor for *McClure's*, began a series on Rockefeller in November 1902. Her father had been one of Rockefeller's early victims and, having grown up in the Pennsylvania oil fields, Tarbell had easy access to many people who hated Rockefeller. In a nineteen-part series that appeared in monthly issues over the next two years she laid out his misdeeds in grisly detail. By the time she was through one of the world's most private men had become one of the world's best known and most hated.

The silence of both Rockefeller and the Standard Oil Company in the face of this assault might seem perplexing in the context of today's world where corporations employ battalions of public relations spin masters. But both Rockefeller and the Standard had a tradition of silence and secrecy. Perhaps wisely, they realized that any refutation would drag them into the gutter with the muckrakers. In addition, Rockefeller could not dispute the truth of some of Tarbell's anecdotal evidence without admitting the truth of many others. Years later he could still express bitterness over her slanted writing and outright falsehoods (while denying that he ever read her articles), but he never made a public reply.

Railroad regulation and the breakup of business monopolies were the hallmarks of Theodore Roosevelt's Progressivism, and Ida Tarbell's series directed the government's attention once again to the Standard Oil. In 1906 the government brought suit in federal court under the Sherman Antitrust Law against the Standard Oil of New Jersey and the sixty-five companies under its control. (Although its headquarters were in Manhattan, the Standard had reincorporated under New Jersey's lenient holding company law.) The Standard and its officers, including the Rockefellers and Flagler, were accused of monopolizing the oil industry and engaging in illegal practices, including railroad rebates, abuse of the pipeline monopoly, and predatory pricing. The government wanted the Standard to be broken up into its state-chartered components, including Standard Oil of New Jersey, Standard Oil of Ohio, and Standard Oil of Indiana. A government report of the following year alleged that the Standard manufactured and marketed 87 percent of the nation's kerosene and was more than twenty times the size of its most serious competitor, Pure Oil (the company once managed by Ida Tarbell's father).

The lower courts agreed with the government, ordering the Standard broken up, and the suit wound its way to the United States Supreme Court. On May 15, 1911, Chief Justice Edward White read the opinion of the Supreme Court affirming the decisions of the lower courts. However, in ordering the breakup of the Standard, White invoked a new legal principle, the "rule of reason." White argued that the Standard must be dissolved, not because it was a near-monopoly, but because it had unreasonably abused its size in negotiating railroad rebates, predatory pricing, and other abuses. White's "rule of reason" coincided with ex-President Roosevelt's new view of big business that would be the basis for his presidential campaign in 1912. The mere size of a company, Roosevelt had concluded, was not a danger to society, for there are many economic benefits to be gained from bigness. It is only when a large corporation misuses its size and power that it must come under government purview. The "rule of reason" would remain the basis of the government's antitrust policy for the next quarter-century. In 1920 the Supreme Court would carry the rule to its logical conclusion by declining to break up the United States Steel Company on grounds that it had not unreasonably misused its power.

Rockefeller reacted to the decision with his usual nonchalance. On the golf course when the news reached him, he turned to his partner and said that if he had any money to invest in stocks, "Buy Standard Oil." It was good advice, for the public was eager to buy the stock of the newly independent companies, which would evolve into today's giants: Exxon, Mobil, Amoco, and Chevron. The stock of each instantly shot up by 50 to 100 percent. Rockefeller, holder of 40 percent of the stock of the trust, claimed 40 percent of each new independent, and his fortune pushed upward toward $1 billion.

Rockefeller had by this time further institutionalized his philanthropy. While the antitrust suit against him was pending, he asked Congress to issue a charter for a permanent philanthropic trust, the Rockefeller Foundation. The press, as usual, misinterpreted the move as conscience money, and amidst the public uproar Rockefeller gave up on Congress and obtained a charter from the state of New York. Established in 1913 the foundation had an initial endowment of $100 million, and Rockefeller gave it another $88 million by 1919, when he left it to survive on its own investments (most of which were in Standard Oil stock). Mindful of the public criticism, the directors of the foundation shunned the humanities, social sciences, and fine arts as potentially controversial and favored instead giving grants in the fields of science and medicine. The foundation financed worldwide efforts to eliminate yellow fever, malaria, tuberculosis, and other scourges of mankind. With multimillion-dollar grants to the medical schools of Johns Hopkins and Harvard, the foundation was a major factor in the rise of American medicine to world leadership.

Rockefeller developed a new persona in the 1920s, the kindly eccentric. He had a fleet of touring cars on his Hudson River estate, and he took to driving the country roads, picnicking by the roadside, and conversing casually with farmers. Abandoning his lifetime habit of secrecy, he readily gave magazine interviews, and the fledgling motion picture industry loved to photograph him and (with the advent of "talkies") record his witticisms. He began spending winters in Florida, where he entertained the heroes of the 1920s, Henry Ford and Will Rogers. After Rockefeller beat Rogers in golf, Rogers quipped, "I'm glad you beat me, John. The last time you were beaten, I noticed the price of gasoline went up two cents a gallon." Rockefeller threw his head back and roared with laughter. Shedding at last the reputation of crusty curmudgeon, Rockefeller was making himself into a storybook character, an American myth.

He lived on another decade, long enough to see his son, John D. Jr., spread the Rockefeller philanthropy in new directions, buying up huge amounts of acreage in Wyoming, Virginia, and North Carolina that would become the basis for the Grand Teton, Shenandoah, and Smoky Mountain National Parks. Among John Jr.'s other endowments were Colonial Williamsburg and the Museum of Modern Art in New York.

When John D. Rockefeller died of heart failure in May 1937, he and his son (and later grandsons, John D. 3rd, Lawrence, and Nelson) left America with a rich cultural legacy. He himself remains an enigma, an amalgam of godliness and greed, puritanical thrift and enterprise tempered by fiendish cunning. A champion and beneficiary of the system of free enterprise, he unwittingly demonstrated the need for governmental policing.

Suggested Reading

The most recent, and by far the best, biography is Ron Chernow's *Titan* (1998). Allan Nevins's *Study in Power: John D. Rockefeller, Industrialist and Philanthropist* (1953), two volumes, is a friendly portrait, aimed at correcting the half-truths and exaggerations of the muckrakers, but it remains useful today. Nevins is especially good at explaining the legal evolution of the Standard Oil Trust. An able study of Rockefeller's partner is Edward N. Akin's *Flagler: Rockefeller Partner & Florida Baron* (1988). The concept of the "robber barons" is best explored in Matthew Josephson's delightfully written *The Robber Barons* (1934). The female members of the Rockefeller family are given their due by Clarice Stasz in *The Rockefeller Women: Dynasty of Piety, Privacy, and Service* (1995). The most thoughtful overview of the era is by Robert H. Wiebe, *The Search for Order: 1877–1920* (1967).

2

Mother Jones: "We Have Nothing to Lose But Our Chains"

The energy that drove America's rise to world industrial power came from an ugly chunk of carbon that had to be dug out of the ground with pick and shovel. Coal powered the industrial revolution. Steel production was the leading indicator of industrial might—coal fired the industry's blast furnaces. The railroads revolutionized the movement of heavy goods; their locomotives were run on coal. When Edison's light bulb replaced John D. Rockefeller's kerosene to illuminate America's offices and homes, the generators that lit up entire cities were set in motion by coal. Britain, Germany, and the United States were the preeminent industrial powers in the nineteenth century. Each was blessed, to be sure, with an enterprising, comparatively well-educated people. But they were also the world's leading producers of coal.

The output from America's coal mines surpassed even the rate of industrial growth. The 2 million tons gouged out of the mines in 1840 leaped to 37 million by 1870 and 350 million tons in 1900. Until late in the century most of the miners were émigrés from the British Isles. After 1870 the insatiable demand for coal and the advent of machines that simplified the cutting and scooping processes changed the ethnic makeup of workers in the mines, as owners hired recent arrivals from southern and eastern Europe with no mining experience but who were willing to work for lower pay. Mining had always been a dangerous occupation, and the employment of inexperienced laborers increased the chances of injury. Between 1870 and 1914 about fifty thousand coal miners died in industrial accidents. Collapsed roofs and cave-ins were the most common killers, but negligence and inexperience also took their toll, as men were crushed by coal cars, maimed in blasting mishaps, and asphyxiated by methane. The number of miners who died annually in the United States was triple that of Britain or Germany.

Women almost never worked in the mines, not because of any concern about their frailty but because male miners resisted their competition. Children, especially boys, were commonly employed on the surface or at tunnel entrances. Trap boys opened and closed the doors for mules pulling the coal cars in and out of the mine; breaker boys sorted the coal from the slate and stone. Textile mills often moved into mining communities because the miners' wives and daughters were a ready source of cheap labor. The miners were paid by the piece (each miner's cart was weighed as it emerged from the tunnel), and pay was so low (about fifty cents a ton) that entire families had to obtain gainful employment in order to survive.

Prevailing economic theory posited that both capital and labor were fluid and perfectly mobile, capable of moving about in search of the highest profit or best wage. That theory had no relevance to the coal miners, who lacked the means to move about and, in any case, could see nothing on the horizon that beckoned. Moving also meant finding new jobs for wives and children. The mining community itself was a social and economic straitjacket. Most coal mines were located in isolated mountain valleys. To attract workers the owners provided housing and built stores. The owners soon discovered that the income from house rentals and the proceeds from company stores were a major source of profit. To ensure their monopoly position they forbade rival stores in the company town and ejected itinerant peddlers from company property. Many mines paid their workers only in scrip, scraps of paper that could be exchanged for goods only at the company store.

With no prospect for improving their lot, coal miners were ready prospects for labor union organizers. Labor unions had existed since the beginning of the century, but the only durable ones were trade unions, made up of skilled workers with some bargaining power. In 1887 various national trade unions formed an umbrella organization, the American Federation of Labor (AF of L). The first president of the AF of L, Samuel Gompers, a cigar maker by trade, stamped his personality and philosophy on the organization. A conservative man by nature, Gompers had no beef with the capitalist system; he merely wanted to ensure that workingmen got their share of the pie through union organization and collective bargaining.

The problem the AF of L faced in organizing the coal mines was that the miners had few skills and were easily replaced if they went on strike. In addition, any attempt to organize them by skill or specialty merely divided the workers in each mine and weakened them further. The only effective way to organize the mine workers was on an industrial basis—a single union for each mine, regardless of the specialties of individual workers, and a single national organization for the entire mining industry. In 1890 the United Mine Workers of America (UMW) was formed on precisely this formula. It became loosely affiliated with the AF of L (it was the only industrial union in the trades federation), and by concentrating on improving working conditions in the mines, striking only when necessary, during the next ten years it became the largest and most powerful union in the country. The UMW grew by sending organizers into every mining community, from Pennsylvania to Indiana and Illinois, who persuaded the miners to form their own local organizations and seek recognition from the mine owners. The most famous of these union organizers—a legend by 1900—was a woman who, by that date, performed her alchemy under the name and persona of Mother Jones.

Mary Harris/Mary Jones

In her autobiography, published in 1925, the last year of her life, Mother Jones described her childhood in five sentences: "I was born in the city of Cork, Ireland, in 1830. My people were poor. For generations they had fought for Ireland's freedom. Many of my folks have died in that struggle. My father, Richard Harris, came to America in 1835, and as soon as he had become an American citizen, he sent for his family." The next forty years of her life take up only 6 pages in a 250-page book. The autobiography, in short, is not a sentimental life story; it is a revolutionary tract, designed to inspire future generations to continue her efforts at labor organizing and radical change. As a result, the autobiography is as much fiction as fact. In addition to implying that her father fled to America as a revolutionary, she placed herself in the midst of historical events—the great railroad strike of 1877, the Haymarket Riot in Chicago in 1886—when there is good evidence that she was elsewhere at the time. She even conjured up a birth date for herself—May 1, which in the 1880s had become internationally recognized as a workingman's holiday. A recent biographer, Elliott J. Gorn, has managed to penetrate this crust of mythology and bring to light the few documents that record the existence of Mary Harris before, at the age of sixty, she assumed the legendary persona of Mother Jones.

The second child of Richard Harris and Ellen Cotter, Mary was born in Cork some time during the summer of 1837. Mary had at the time an older brother, and Ellen was to give birth to three more children, not one of whom is mentioned in Mother Jones's autobiography. When Mary was about ten her father and older brother sailed for America, joining thousands of other Irishmen fleeing the great potato famine of the mid-1840s. Ellen, Mary, and the younger children crossed the ocean some four or five years later and settled in Toronto, where Richard was employed as a railroad construction worker. Mary attended the city's common schools, and at the age of twenty she was admitted to the Toronto Normal School. Although she never graduated, she underwent enough training to secure a teaching job at a convent school in Monroe, Michigan.

When the school term ended, Mary collected her pay and moved on to Chicago to learn the trade of dressmaking. However, the wanderlust that had borne her out of Toronto and away from her family soon returned, and by late 1860 she was in the Mississippi River cotton port of Memphis. A few months after her arrival she married George Jones, who worked in a machine shop that specialized in building and repairing steam engines and steam-powered mills. Jones was a member of the International Iron

"Mother" Mary Jones in 1902. (Photograph from the Collections of the Library of Congress.)

Molders Union, a fairly strong trade union headed by William Sylvis. Sylvis was a pioneer labor leader who was the first to attempt the creation of an umbrella organization for labor, the National Labor Union (1866). Jones's activities with the union were Mary's first introduction to labor organization, and Sylvis's emphasis on the dignity of the workingman made a lasting impression.

Between 1862 and 1867 Mary gave birth to four children, and because her husband brought home a healthy wage, she was able to confine her labors to housekeeping. Curiously, there is no mention in her autobiography of the events of the Civil War or the impact of the war on Memphis. She does not even mention the vicious race riot of the spring of 1866 that helped persuade Congress to impose military Reconstruction on the postwar South. In 1867 yellow fever struck the city with disastrous consequences for the Jones family. In recounting this tragedy, the lines of her dry autobiography for the first time explode with emotion:

> In 1867, a yellow fever epidemic swept Memphis. . . . Across the street from me, ten persons lay dead from the plague. The dead surrounded us. They were buried at night quickly and without ceremony. All about my house I could hear weeping and the cries of delirium. One by one, my four little children sickened and died. I washed their little bodies and got them ready for burial. My husband caught the fever and died. No one came to me. No one could. Other homes were as stricken as mine. All day long, all night long, I heard the grating of the wheels of the death cart.

Mary returned to Chicago and took up dressmaking with a shop on Washington Street near the lake. She apparently did skilled custom work, for she described her clients as quite wealthy. Chicago in the 1870s and 1880s was the nation's preeminent boomtown. Its population had been doubling every decade since 1830. The city was a dynamo of energy, with railroads, canals, rivers, and lakes providing access to an immense hinterland. Its sawmills honed the lumber taken from the forests of Michigan and Wisconsin. Its flour mills refined the wheat of Minnesota and the Dakotas. Its stockyards treated the cattle and hogs fattened on the farms of Indiana, Illinois, and Iowa. But it was also a city deeply divided socially. The wealthiest fifth of the population, mostly native-born Protestants from New York and New England, held 90 percent of the property in the city and they flaunted their wealth with elegant mansions along the lakeshore. Immigrants, a majority of the population by 1870, crowded into tenements once inhabited by native-born émigrés from the farm. Some, like Mary Jones, were Irish, but increasingly the ethnic makeup bore the accents of southern and eastern Europe. By 1900 Chicago would have more Poles than any city in Poland except Warsaw, more Czechs than any city in Bohemia except Prague. Already attuned to revolutionary rhetoric in their homelands, the immigrant population would lend a ready ear to domestic radicals.

Sitting in the window of her dressmaker's shop Mary Jones bore witness to this social chasm and aligned herself with the needy, those whom she would eventually come to consider as her people, her "family":

> We worked for the aristocrats of Chicago, and I had ample opportunity to observe the luxury and extravagance of their lives. Often while sewing for the lords and barons who lived in magnificent houses on the Lake Shore Drive, I would look out of the plate glass windows and see the poor, shivering wretches, jobless and hungry, walking along the frozen lake front. The contrast of their condition with that of the tropical comfort of the people for whom I sewed was painful to me. My employers seemed neither to notice nor to care.

Labor strife, which invariably affected Chicago even when centered elsewhere, provided a focus for her compassion. The great railroad strike of 1877, centered in Pittsburgh, was the most violent strike in American history to that time, and it virtually severed the railroad traffic between the Midwest and the East Coast. President Rutherford B. Hayes ultimately intervened and employed the U.S. Army to break the strike and get the trains running. In her autobiography, Mother Jones places herself in Pittsburgh during the strike, though there is no evidence that she was ever in the city; it was one of the many fictions in her story, her way of validating her claim to be the "mother" of the American labor movement. Nevertheless, the strike had ramifications in Chicago that doubtless had a deep effect on her. Railroad workers roamed the Chicago streets calling on other workers to join them, while impromptu bands played the French revolutionary "Marseillaise." Sympathetic laborers took control of factories and fought the police and militia. After three days of disorder the federal troops fired into the crowds, killing thirty and wounding more than 200. Upon Mary Jones dawned the realization that labor union organization was part of a larger class warfare and that social stability could be achieved only when economic democracy paralleled the nation's vaunted political democracy. Unfortunately, President Hayes's intervention in the railroad strike demonstrated to her that even the nation's democratically elected officials were hand-in-glove with the wealthy and their corporations. Perhaps more drastic social change was needed than the limited objective, voiced by William Sylvis and Samuel Gompers, of simply gaining for labor its share of the national pie.

In 1879 Terence V. Powderly became president of the Knights of Labor, another attempt at a nationwide organization of all workingmen. Like Samuel Gompers, Powderly stamped his own personality and philosophy on the Knights. Unlike Gompers, Powderly believed in a universal brotherhood of labor, skilled and unskilled, and he sought to advance the interests of workingmen through negotiation and political pressure, rather than by strikes and violence. But due to its broad appeal, the Knights attracted men more radical than Powderly, and in the early 1880s locals on the Great Plains won a pair of strikes against highly unpopular railroads. By the middle of the decade membership in the Knights leaped to more than a million, and it was the largest labor organization in the country. Mary Jones began attending meetings of the Knights' Chicago local in the late 1870s, and she became quite active after the organization admitted women as voting members in 1880.

These meetings were another step in her education, for the Chicago local of the Knights was increasingly coming under the spell of anarchists. American thought had always had a strain of hostility toward government, but it was refocused by new philosophies of radicalism from France, Russia, and Germany. The theory (some would say it was nothing more than a pretense for violence) was that both governmental authority and capitalist power had to be overthrown because they were inseparably linked. The anarchists' aim was to restore freedom to individuals, not only in an economic sense, but as a way of life, giving the populace a broad participation in its own affairs. This line of thinking was predicated on revolutionary violence, and much of their rhetoric was drawn from European Marxists and the model of the Paris Commune of 1870–1871. Typical of the anarchists' rhetoric was the 1885 address of an official of the Central Labor Union, Chicago's largest worker organization:

> We are revolutionists. We fight for the destruction of the system of wage slavery. . . . The claim of capital to profit, interest, or rent is a robber claim, enforced by piratical methods. Let robbers and pirates meet the fate they deserve! . . . Proletarians of the world unite! We have nothing to lose but our chains, we have a world to win!

Both anarchism and the Knights of Labor went into decline after the Haymarket Affair of May 4, 1886, when an anarchist threw a bomb amidst a tense confrontation between Chicago police and striking workers (eight anarchists were brought to trial after the bloody incident, and four were hanged), but echoes of their rhetoric could be found in Mary Jones's public addresses when she began her own organizational efforts in the 1890s.

The Making of "Mother Jones"

Although in her autobiography Mother Jones claimed to have played a central role in the labor strife of the 1870s and 1880s, there was no public notice of her in either the newspapers or the police reports. This very obscurity proved to be of advantage, however, for it made her sudden appearance on the public stage in the 1890s more dramatic and furthered the legend of "Mother Jones." The name of Mary Jones first appeared in print in connection with her involvement with Coxey's "army" in 1894. The worst depression of the century had blanketed the country in 1893, and Jacob S. Coxey, a Massillon, Ohio, businessman of radical bent, conceived the idea of leading an army of the unemployed to Washington to pressure Congress into approving a "good roads bill" that would put men to work on public highways. Although Coxey recruited his own following in Ohio, thousands of men elsewhere took up the idea and began their own march on Washington.

Mary Jones's departure from Chicago goes unexplained, but we find her in Denver in the spring of 1894 (newspapers friendly to mine owners would later claim that she ran a brothel in that frontier village). She crossed Kansas to join a group of two hundred marchers who were proceeding toward Kansas City as a first step on a journey to Washington to join Coxey. She aided the men by helping to raise money for food and giving speeches to bolster morale. Most city newspapers regarded Coxey's marchers as either cranks or dangerous radicals. The *Kansas City Star*, in the first journalistic notice of her, called Mary the "mother of the commonwealers." In Kansas City the leader of the group absconded with the funds that Mary had helped raise—a total of $108—but a core of men continued on to St. Louis, with Mary traveling a day ahead to raise money for food. It is unlikely that they went beyond St. Louis, for on the first of May Coxey arrived in the nation's capital and paraded his army of six hundred through the streets. When he mounted the Capitol steps to make a speech, he was arrested for trespassing and sentenced to twenty days in jail. Although "General" Coxey's armies were brutally dispersed by police, he had unwittingly launched Mary Jones's career. She was now on the road, and she would remain there for the next thirty years, camping in the guest rooms of friends, spending overnights in hotels and Pullman cars, working tirelessly for the disorganized laboring poor.

She nevertheless remains, for the next few years, a shadowy figure, bouncing in and out of the printed record. She had apparently become an agent of the United Mine Workers by 1894, for in the summer of that year she was in Birmingham attempting to organize Alabama coal miners when the Pullman strike broke out in Chicago. Workers at the Pullman Palace Car Company went on strike against wage cuts and conditions in the company town of Pullman, Illinois. Eugene V. Debs, founder of the American Railway Union (ARU), an industrial union that sought to organize all railroad workers (as opposed to the Railroad Brotherhoods, which were trade unions), tried to help the Pullman strikers by organizing a nationwide boycott of Pullman cars. Employers countered by obtaining a court injunction prohibiting the strike on grounds that it was interfering with the delivery of mail and the movement of interstate commerce. Debs ignored the court order, and President Cleveland's attorney general sent federal troops into Chicago. After several days of violence the strike was broken, and Debs was jailed. In the landmark case of *In Re Debs* (1896) the Supreme Court of the United States upheld the right of a court to issue an injunction[1] ordering striking workers to return to their jobs.

Mary Jones was still in Birmingham in 1896 when Debs was released from prison. In prison Debs had been converted to the gospel of socialism, or at least the form that had been developed by the Fabians of Britain, who eschewed the revolutionary doctrines of Karl Marx and preached instead the gradual governmental takeover of basic industries, such as railroads, steel mills, and coal mines. When Debs arrived in Birmingham to broadcast his new message, Mary Jones brought out thousands of city workers in a show of support. She described the scene in her autobiography:

> The train pulled in and Debs got off. . . . Those miners did not wait for the gates to open but jumped over the railing. They put him on their shoulders and marched out of the station . . . through the street, past the railway office, the mayor's office, the office of the chief of police. 'Debs is here! Debs is here!' they shouted. That night the crowd heard a real sermon by a preacher whose message is one of human brotherhood.

Debs thereafter labeled Jones a "modern Joan of Arc," and they remained lifetime friends and political allies.

A year later, on June 15, 1897, several hundred members of the American Railway Union held a convention in Chicago. Debs's aim now was to fold the ARU into a larger organization known as Social Democracy for America, and he wanted to set up a pilot socialist community. The governor of Washington had invited them to build the colony in his state, and Debs gave a rousing speech in support of the idea. "When he finished," the *Chicago Evening Journal* reported, "white-haired 'Mother' Jones, who occupied a prominent position, proposed three cheers for the governor of Washington for inviting the organization to make its experiment in that state." Ten years earlier railroad workers had found a heroine in a transplanted Englishwoman, Mrs. Henry Jones, who had championed their cause in the columns of the *Brakeman's Journal*. She

1. An injunction, issued under the principles of equity, rather than the common law, is a court order designed to prevent foreseeable harm, which, should it occur, would then give rise to a suit at law. Over the next thirty-five years courts would repeatedly enjoin labor strikes on grounds that they might lead to violence against persons and destruction of property. In the case of Debs, the court's injunction was based on the federal government's obligation to preserve the free flow of interstate commerce and the delivery of the mail.

had signed her columns "Mother Jones," and by 1897 the railroad men had transferred that appellation to Mary. (Many may have assumed they were the same person.) The notice in the *Chicago Evening Journal* was its first printed usage.

By 1900 Mary Jones, in her early sixties, had finally metamorphosed into the persona of Mother Jones. People addressed her as that in letters and on the podium. She invariably signed her own name "Mother Jones" or simply "Mother." Everyone from coal miners to presidents of the United States called her Mother. The persona had tremendous advantages for her new mission in life: Jones had been brought up a Roman Catholic, had taught in a convent, and naturally viewed female leaders as "mother." To the miners, many of whom were also Catholics, the name connoted Christian martyrdom and the suffering of Mother Mary. Jones, in turn, could think of the miners as her "boys" and the needy of the world as her "family." The mother persona also protected her in the public arena, where women appeared only at the risk of scorn and insult. She deliberately exaggerated her age by ten years, wore old-fashioned black dresses and flouncy hats, and charmed her audiences with a smile as prim and sweet as any gentle grandmother. No one would dare upbraid, much less physically interfere, with such a figure, even though, once she began to speak, out of her mouth streamed a revolutionary call to arms, liberally punctuated with profanity.

The character that Mary Jones created was immensely effective; the United Mine Workers readily conceded that Mother Jones was by far its most effective organizer. A young miner from Pennsylvania who later became a UMW official described her technique in the late 1890s: "She came into the mine one day and talked to us in our workplace in the vernacular of the mines. How she got in I don't know; probably just walked in and defied anyone to stop her." He then explained how she won the miners to her side:

> She would take a drink with the boys and spoke their idiom, including some pretty rough language when she was talking about the bosses. This might have been considered a little fast in ordinary women, but the miners knew and respected her. They might think her a little queer, perhaps—it was an odd kind of work for a woman in those days—but they knew she was a good soul and a friend of those who lacked friends.

For several decades thereafter, Mother Jones, walking dusty back roads from one union rally to the next, was one of the enduring collective memories of the mine country. Why she attached herself to the cause of coal miners we can only guess. Perhaps it was the harsh conditions under which the miners worked and lived. Such conditions evoked her compassion and rendered miners susceptible to her message. She also no doubt felt comfortable working with UMW officials, many of whom were Irish. At the turn of the century she was the spearhead of two spectacular organizational drives by the UMW. Although the strikes were a mixed success, they triggered the first presidential intervention in history on the side of labor. And when they ended in 1902, the UMW, with 300,000 members, was the largest and most respected (and feared) labor union in America.

The Great Coal Strikes

By 1897 the UMW had about nine thousand members, with adherents in nearly every mine in Pennsylvania and a majority in a few. But it had no contracts with mine owners and had not achieved the status of a recognized bargaining agent. In the summer of that year the coal operators of the bituminous coal belt, which extended from western Pennsylvania across Ohio to Indiana and Illinois, asked their workers to take a 20 percent cut in pay, a reflection of the depression that had begun in 1893. No large corporation dominated this field; the mining companies were small and competed with one another. To prevent cutthroat competition they had formed among themselves an organization called the Central Competitive Field, which functioned as a sort of cartel. When the cartel announced the pay cut, tens of thousands of miners who worked ten to twelve hours a day for about fifty cents a ton walked off the job.

Mother Jones helping with children in a West Virginia mining camp. (Photograph from the Newberry Library.)

The UMW took command of the strike and sent Mother Jones into the coalfields of western Pennsylvania. She burst into the Monongahela Valley with customary energy, organizing rallies and giving spirited speeches. Capitalizing on the populist mood of the times (since 1892 the Peoples' Party had sought to unite farmers and workingmen in a lower-class political movement), she persuaded local farmers to donate food and she sent their wagons to "Camp Determination," the regional strike headquarters on Turtle Creek. In her orations, which were invariably salted with anecdotes of personal courage (her own as well as others), her fundamental appeal was to the miners' manhood, urging them to stand up for their rights against the bosses. She made a similar appeal to the miners' wives, sketching for them a new image of womanhood—the militant, working-class mother fighting for her family. The *National Labor Tribune* enthused, "She has done more missionary work for miners of the Pittsburgh district than any two of the [UMW] officials and done it better. . . . To her, more than anyone else, the miners owe much of their success in this unpleasantness."

When the strike ended in January 1898, the UMW had a contract with the Central Competitive Field that recognized it as the collective bargaining agent for the entire bituminous region. The owners backed off from their pay cut and even granted the miners a small raise and an eight-hour day. With the agreement membership in the UMW leaped to 100,000. The mine owners also benefited because the UMW was strong enough to prevent wildcat strikes (i.e., by local leaders in individual mines). The UMW contract helped to stabilize the whole bituminous industry. It did not, however, apply to the new bituminous mines that were being opened in West Virginia, nor did it apply to the anthracite ("hard coal") mines of eastern Pennsylvania. The anthracite country was the UMW's next objective.

Anthracite was a much more highly valued form of coal. Almost pure carbon, it burned at the high temperatures necessary for the blast furnaces of Pittsburgh and Chicago, and it provided virtually soot-free heating for homes. The corporate owners in the anthracite country were larger and wealthier than in the bituminous fields and more resistant to unionization. Indeed, by 1900 financier J. P. Morgan had whole or partial control of nearly all the mines of eastern Pennsylvania. As a result, only a tiny fraction of the miners had joined the UMW, and the miners were internally divided by skill levels, local loyalties, and ethnic rivalries (about half were immigrants or the children of immigrants).

Despite the UMW's victory in the bituminous field, its leadership remained rather tentative. Its young president, John Mitchell, was cut in the Samuel Gompers mold, temperamentally and ideologically inclined toward negotiation, rather than strikes and open warfare. Although he disagreed politically with Mother Jones, he recognized her value to the movement and gave her the title of "international organizer" with pay of

$500 a year. But he was not eager to confront J. P. Morgan and the other anthracite owners.

What became known as the Great Anthracite Strike was initiated by the miners themselves, not by the union. A series of wildcat strikes in the anthracite fields between 1897 and 1900 finally forced the UMW to act. When 120,000 miners laid down their picks and shovels in September 1900, the UMW officially announced a strike and sent Mother Jones with other organizers into the field. Her new pitch was to embolden the miners by making the union itself a religion, an object of faith. She scoffed at "sky pilots" (priests and ministers) and often made them the butt of the anecdotes that had become a signature feature of her speaking style. Her stories usually involved herself and some unlucky straight man:

> Not far from Shamokin, in a little mountain town, the priest was holding a meeting when I went in. He was speaking in the church. I spoke in an open field. The priest told the men to go back and obey their masters and their reward would be in Heaven. He denounced the strikers as children of darkness. The miners left the church in a body and marched over to my meeting.
>
> "Boys," I said, "this strike is called in order that you and your wives and your little ones may get a bit of Heaven before you die."
>
> We organized the entire camp.

Six weeks into the strike the UMW was gaining steadily in membership, and the miners were holding fast. As winter approached, a shortage of coal for heating homes loomed, and that spelled trouble for President William McKinley, who in early November was seeking reelection against Democratic candidate William Jennings Bryan. Knowing that Morgan and other coal operators feared Bryan more than their own miners, Republican Party boss Mark Hanna (a coal and iron merchant from Ohio) asked the coal companies to settle the strike. They agreed and offered their workers a 10 percent raise, but they refused to recognize the union. The UMW went along, and the settlement lasted for a year and a half.

In May 1902, with that contract about to expire, UMW leaders in the anthracite region called a new strike, and they asked John Mitchell to call a nationwide strike, including the Central Competitive Field, even though the bituminous contract was still in force. Mitchell, who feared that breaching a contract with owners would damage the union's carefully cultivated legitimacy, refused. Mother Jones went along with this decision for the sake of unity, but she made it clear she would have preferred a nationwide walkout. "These fights," she grumbled, "against the oppressor and the capitalist, the ruling classes, must be won if it takes us all to do it."

Although confined to the anthracite fields, the strike received the support of 100,000 workers, and it shut down the anthracite mines entirely.

Progressive reform was in the air by 1902, and public opinion leaned in favor of the miners. President Theodore Roosevelt (who had succeeded to the office upon McKinley's assassination in 1901), always tuned to public opinion, proposed an independent commission to work out a settlement. He was thus the first American president to regard a labor union not as a sinister conspiracy but as a corporate body able to negotiate and live up to a contract. Roosevelt did not like labor unions, but he could not tolerate defiance of his authority. When the coal companies dragged their feet, Roosevelt pressed harder. The presidential commission eventually worked out a compromise, with gains for the workers on the items of wages and hours, but it yielded to Morgan's insistence that there be no legal contract recognizing the union.

The UMW agreed, and the miners returned to work in what has often been regarded as a great victory for organized labor. But Mother Jones was furious. With winter approaching and a coal shortage at hand, she felt that Mitchell had missed a fine opportunity to gain a union contract for the entire anthracite industry. Although this dispute helped delineate their philosophical differences, the two papered over the tension and for a time continued to work together. Defeat in West Virginia and Colorado would precipitate an open break.

"Medieval West Virginia"

"Ah, my brothers," Mother Jones told a UMW convention in Indianapolis in January 1901, "I shall consider it an honor if, when you write my epitaph upon my tombstone you say 'Died fighting their battles in West Virginia.'" Part of her frustration with the leadership of John Mitchell was that he seemed to ignore West Virginia. In order to pour UMW resources into the coal fields of Pennsylvania in the years from 1897 to 1902, Mitchell was forced to pull organizers out of West Virginia. Rich veins of well-exposed bituminous coal had recently been discovered in that state, and its miners were the lowest paid in the country. West Virginia thus competed directly with the Central Competitive Field, and its cheap coal lessened the market for the output mined under the union contract. In the view of Mother Jones, the UMW's position everywhere was menaced by its failure to organize West Virginia.

During those years, 1897–1902, whenever she could be spared from the Pennsylvania coal towns, Jones was touring West Virginia spreading her gospel of the union as family, the union as religion. It seemed a hopeless task. The miners were racially divided—those in the southern part of the state were mostly black; those in the northern part were recent immigrants. The owners, most of them, were absentees, having derived patents to land from the Virginia legislature dating from before the Civil War. Worst of all, state and local governments were, in Jones's phrase, "medieval." Ninety-five percent of the miners lived in company towns that were not incorporated and had no elective officials. In village and county governments mine supervisors controlled the mayor, city council, and the judges. A prime qualification for state governor was experience as a coal company officer, and the state's chief mine inspector was president of several coal companies. The state, in fact, had few safety regulations and did not enforce the ones it had. The death rate among miners in West Virginia exceeded that of all other mining states.

Whenever Mother Jones or other organizers attempted to hold rallies, they were broken up by armed guards wielding court injunctions. By the summer of 1902, however, the UMW organizers had made enough progress in the northern mines of the state that Mitchell felt obliged to send in additional resources. He asked Jones to lead a group of 140 union organizers, even though such a concerted effort was almost certain to lead to violence. "I dislike to ask you always to take the dangerous fields," he wrote the woman that he always addressed as Mother, "but I know that you are willing." Despite the apologetic tone, this was an important concession to Jones's pleas on behalf of West Virginia because Mitchell must have been aware of the impending confrontation in Pennsylvania's anthracite fields.

On June 7, apparently without consulting Mitchell, the West Virginia chapter of the UMW called a strike in the state's northern fields. Within days county sheriffs, armed with injunctions from county courts, began arresting UMW organizers. One coal company went to a federal court and obtained a sweeping injunction that prohibited strikes everywhere in the state on grounds that a strike constituted a conspiracy to injure financially the mine owners. Acting on this court order, a federal marshal attempted to arrest Mother Jones as she was addressing a crowd in Clarksburg. She insisted on finishing her speech in which she added a coda condemning the courts for arresting union organizers but doing nothing about the thugs hired by operators to beat up striking miners.

Released on bond, she traveled to a UMW convention in Indianapolis where she gave a passionate description of the dreadful conditions in West Virginia. She then returned to the federal court in Parkersburg to face trial on charges of conspiracy. During his arguments before the court, the United States attorney pointed at Mother Jones and called her "the most dangerous woman in America" because she could single-handedly prevail upon thousands of otherwise contented men to quit working. She and other union organizers were found guilty, but the judge refused to send her to jail lest he make her a martyr. Instead he lectured her on being "a good woman" and following paths "intended her sex should pursue." She gave the judge a cherubic smile, noted that they were both quite old, and invited him to become friends in heaven. Outside the court, she called the judge a scab and denounced him as a hireling of the robbers who owned the mines. She then dashed off to make her presence felt in the developing anthracite strike in Pennsylvania.

During the autumn the black miners in the southern coalfields of West Virginia joined the strike, but that only added to the violence and terrorism. Backed by court orders, the coal companies hired armies of private detectives who shot up coal towns whenever the miners offered resistance. The strike was crushed in the course of 1903, and for the next ten years the UMW was barely felt in West Virginia. Putting the best face she could on the disaster, Jones proposed that the next UMW convention be held in Parkersburg "under the eyes" of the federal judge.

The echoes of the defeat in West Virginia were still reverberating in the mountains when Mother Jones sped off to Colorado where, as in Pennsylvania, miners had forced the hand of the UMW by organizing a strike on their own initiative. Large veins of bituminous coal had recently been discovered in the southeastern corner of the state, and the coalfields had been bought up by large corporations controlled by eastern investors. The biggest of these, the Colorado Fuel and Iron Company, came under the control of John D. Rockefeller in 1903. Conditions were similar to West Virginia. The companies controlled local governments and paid the mine inspectors; company towns and company stores kept the miners in virtual servitude. The Colorado Bureau of Labor Statistics found that miners' pay averaged $370 a year, compared with bricklayers, who made $969.

Although ethnically divided—including "busted" Kansas farmers, Italians, Mexicans, Chinese, and blacks—the Colorado miners had a powerful tradition of self-help radicalism, a legacy, perhaps, from the vigilantes of the gold mining era. The Western Federation of Miners, loaded with socialists boasting a radical agenda, went on strike occasionally during the 1890s and competed with the UMW for members. Although the UMW had only a few hundred members in November 1903, local leaders demanded that the coal companies recognize the union. When Colorado Fuel and Iron and other companies declared their workers happy and refused to talk, the UMW leaders called a strike. Nearly every miner in the region, union and nonunion alike, walked off the job. Miners in northern Colorado and Wyoming (the "northern field") soon joined in. Mitchell and the national office endorsed the strike, fearing that, if they did not, the striking miners would join the rival Western Federation of Miners.

The arrival of Mother Jones was much anticipated. Three months before the strike started *The Denver Republican* published a feature story on her:

> You are surprised, astonished, incredulous to be informed that this eminently respectable and strictly conventional-appearing old lady . . . should know aught of anything save the economy of a well ordered household. Political doctrines, socialist propaganda, the

> labor movement, the teachings of Karl Marx, strikes, lockouts, blacklists, riots. . . . What knowledge of these belongs to this little old woman with the snowy hair and the soft pink cheeks?

When she arrived in the town of Trinidad in the southern field, *The Trinidad Courier* reported that "many nearly broke the rubber in their neck in an effort to get a good look." After she signed the hotel register, a crowd gathered to gaze upon the scribbled "M. Jones, Chicago."

The rift between Jones and the UMW national office surfaced almost immediately. The strike was only a week old when a company in the northern field, where the owners had been willing to negotiate with the miners from the outset, offered its workers a generous contract. Mitchell and his supporters in the national office were inclined to accept so the union could concentrate its resources in the southern field where the Rockefeller-led owners refused even to talk. Mother Jones and other UMW militants, however, feared that if the northern field went back into production, there would be ample supplies to heat the homes of Denver, Kansas City, and Omaha in the coming winter months and the UMW would have no leverage against the owners in the southern field. When the northern miners met to consider the owners' offer, Jones made a stirring appeal for working class solidarity, without regard to race, religion, or nationality, in a united front against the common enemy, the capitalists. The miners were swayed and voted to reject the contract. A headline in the *Denver Post* trumpeted: "MOTHER JONES BARS SETTLEMENT PLANS: MITCHELL IS DEFIED."

Jones headed to the southern field in triumph, but she was unable to savor her victory. Mitchell's allies went to work among the northern miners, and in December 1903 they decided to end their strike. There would be no national coal shortage that winter; the strike in the southern field was doomed. The UMW called it off in June 1904. Mother Jones and the Trinidad local refused to comply, to the fury of national officers, but they too gave up in October. Mother Jones blamed the UMW executive board—a "ring of fools" she called them—rather than Mitchell for the debacle. Disenchanted with the union, she was also, at age sixty-seven, physically exhausted. She resigned her position in the spring of 1905. The Socialist Party, which Debs and others had formed in 1902, offered her a position as a traveling lecturer at $3 per day. She tentatively accepted but delayed returning to the circuit. Instead, after a bit of rest, another societal malady caught her eye—child labor.

Child Labor Laws

It has often been remarked that the nineteenth century in America, Britain, and western Europe was the century of the child. Prior to 1800 there was little concept of childhood as a stage of life. Children were treated—and dressed—as miniature adults; when they failed to act like adults, they were physically punished—usually by the father, who was in charge of upbringing. In the nineteenth century child nurturing fell to the mother; books and artworks began to portray children as children, romping and playing.[2] Tax-supported public education, beginning in the North in the 1830s, was designed in part to keep children in school and out of the workplace until they matured.

Two countertrends in the nineteenth century nevertheless delayed the enactment of child labor laws. One was that, despite industrialization, America remained a predominantly rural society, and children were expected to perform "chores" as part of their contribution to family livelihood. For the majority who remained on the farm the evolution from "chores" to "farm labor" was imperceptible. A second factor was the arrival, in the second half of the century, of immigrants from southern and eastern Europe where children were expected to be gainfully employed at an early age. As a result, according to the census of 1900, one out of every six American children was employed in a factory, mill, or mine. Twenty-eight states had codes protecting child workers, but there was no enforcement machinery.

Progressives, many of whom came from the urban middle class, made child labor legislation one of their central concerns. City-dwelling parents—working class as well as professionals—thought children ought to be in school, rather than in the factory, and school attendance rose sharply from the 1890s onward. Reformers dismissed the ancient argument that children were needed to help support the family; they argued instead that parents who relied on the income of their children were merely exploiting them, in the same way that monopolies like Standard Oil exploited everyone. Florence Kelley and the New York-based National Consumers League—one of the many female-dominated voices of Progressivism—took the lead in obtaining state and federal laws abolishing child labor. Mother Jones was on the periphery of this movement, but, typically, her voice was one of the first and, in the end, one of the most radical.

In the first piece she ever wrote for publication, "Civilization in Southern Mills," which appeared in the *International Socialist Review* of March 1901, Jones expressed her outrage at child labor. Having taken a mill job to see for herself conditions in the cotton mills, she witnessed six- and seven-year-olds beginning work at 5:30 a.m. and continuing un-

2. Parson Weems's mythical story of George Washington and the cherry tree was a literary bridge from the old to the new. The hero of that story is not George, as is commonly supposed, but his father, who declines to whip the boy even though he has told a lie. Weems goes on to remind parents that a threatened beating is more likely to produce a lie than the truth.

til 7:00 in the evening, with only a short break for a scanty lunch. "I have seen mothers," she wrote, "take their babes and slap cold water in their face to wake the poor little things. I have watched them all day long tending the dangerous machinery. I have seen their helpless limbs torn off, and then when they were disabled and of no more use to the master, thrown out to die." Creating an image that was to become a standard feature of her speeches on child labor, she contrasted the sorry lot of the mill children with the pampered poodles of the mill owners. "I shudder for the future of a nation," she concluded, "that is building up a moneyed aristocracy out of the life-blood of the children of the proletariat." To Mother Jones child labor was not simply a moral issue, as most Progressives believed; it was, rather, part of the larger problem of capital exploiting labor. Capitalists, she believed, deliberately underpaid their adult workers so that parents had to send their children into factories to supplement their income. Children thus became, for the capitalist, an additional source of cheap labor. "They have built on the bleeding, quivering hearts of yourselves and your children their palaces."

On May 29, 1903, textile workers in Philadelphia went on strike, and the uprising spread throughout eastern Pennsylvania until eventually 100,000 workers walked out. Of these some 16,000 were children under the age of sixteen. Although the cause of the strike was low pay, poor working conditions, and the resistance of mill owners to labor unions, Jones convinced strike leaders that their best chance to win public support was to publicize the plight of the child laborers. Taking a page from her experience with Coxey's army, she organized a children's parade of one hundred boys and girls carrying placards asking for "justice" and "time to go to school." Accompanied by striking workers, the children marched from Philadelphia to New York, with music and speeches to arouse public support in towns along the way.

Jones kept the press focused on the parade with daily pronouncements. "The employment of children," she told a Philadelphia paper on the eve of the march, "is doing more to fill prisons, insane asylums, almshouses, reformatories, slums, and gin shops than all the efforts of reformers are doing to improve society. . . . I am going to picture capitalism and caricature the money-mad. I am going to show Wall Street the flesh and blood from which it squeezes its wealth." This initial idea of a parading down Wall Street shifted midway through the march to a plan to descend on President Roosevelt's home at Oyster Bay on Long Island. The marchers entered Manhattan on July 23 and paraded the streets for three days under the watchful eyes of hundreds of policemen. Roosevelt never responded to Jones's request for an interview. When, on July 28, Jones and three children took the train to Oyster Bay, they were greeted by the president's secretary, who suggested that Jones write him a letter. She did, but there is no evidence he ever read it. The Philadelphia strike by then had collapsed. The children returned home by train and went back to work.

Although an apparent failure, the children's march accomplished much of Jones's original intent—publicizing the problem of child labor and piquing the consciences of middle-class voters. Although the U.S. Supreme Court in 1905 prohibited the states from regulating the conditions of labor, on the legal fiction that such laws violated a worker's freedom of contract with his employer, the states continued to tweak at the edges of the problem of child labor. They raised the legal age for employment and required parents to present written evidence of a birth date when a child applied for a job. Upon assuming the presidency in 1913 Woodrow Wilson lent his support to national legislation, and Congress responded three years later with a Child Labor Act. However, this statute was declared unconstitutional by the Supreme Court on the reasoning of the sugar trust case of the 1890s—that factory production was not interstate commerce and thus beyond the power of Congress to regulate. Although child labor continued to decline, it was not until 1938 that it was finally outlawed under a federal statute found acceptable by the Supreme Court. Mother Jones might well be pardoned for suspecting the existence of a vast capitalist conspiracy of businessmen, lawyers, politicians, and judges.

Flirting with Socialism

In 1905 Mother Jones accepted the offer of the Socialist Party to become a paid lecturer, and for the next seven years she toured the country. Labor upheavals were the main occasion for her addresses, enabling her to take up the cause of Milwaukee brewery workers, Arizona copper miners, Chicago telegraphers, Alabama textile workers, New York City garment workers, Mexican revolutionaries, and imprisoned labor leaders. The divisions within the Socialist Party also stimulated a sharpening of her own political thought.

Although socialism originated in the class warfare theories of Karl Marx, as modified by the British Fabians, Eugene Debs gave it an American flavor. Like the British Labor Party (born about the same time as the American Socialist Party), Debs favored government ownership of the basic means of production—factories, mines, and railroads. He did so on the rather hazy dream of recovering the American past, the past of small-town America, of communal efforts like quilting bees and barn-raisings, a time before giant corporations placed all human relations on a monetary basis. Debs's misty philosophy attracted a number of well-educated idealists—consumer advocate Florence Kelley, the blind pioneer Helen Keller, and novelists Jack London, Theodore Dreiser, and Upton Sinclair. Debs ran for president on a Socialist ticket in 1904, 1908, and 1912, gaining a growing percentage of the vote each time, but the vast majority of American workers ignored him. They voted by custom for one of the two major parties, or voted not at all.

Although she corresponded regularly with Jack London, signing her letters "Faithfully yours for the revolution," Mother Jones was not comfortable with the educated elite that gave the party substance. Her own experience was with the plight of the laboring poor; she could not help but question the sincerity and commitment of wealthy reformers. She was also ill at ease with the doctrinal schisms within the socialist movement, as anarchists and syndicalists scorned Debs for being too moderate and demanded overt action in the takeover of mines and factories. She was present at the founding of the most important of the syndicalist organizations, the Industrial Workers of the World, but she almost immediately distanced herself from the "Wobblies" and their revolutionary rhetoric. Jones's own speeches were full of allusions to class warfare, but she entered a fight to win, even if the victory was only local and partial. She felt that the Wobblies were more interested in posturing than in labor contracts, and their tactics were sometimes puerile (tying themselves to lampposts on city streets so they could not be arrested while making a speech).

In 1911 Jones got into a nasty fight with Socialist Party officials whom she accused of being more interested in soft jobs and fat paychecks than in fighting injustice. She was particularly annoyed when several officials attended an international Socialist conference in Copenhagen and incurred substantial travel expenses. She left the party in 1911. Without pausing for breath, she was back in the coal fields, a paid organizer for the United Mine Workers. The UMW had obtained a new president in 1908, Thomas Lewis, and although Lewis was as cautious as Mitchell, the change in leadership enabled Jones to make a self-respected return to the labor movement.

The Legend Blooms and Fades

"Medieval West Virginia," Jones wrote in her autobiography. "With its tent colonies on the bleak hills. With its grim men and women! When I get to the other side, I shall tell God almighty about West Virginia." By 1912 the state was the nation's leading coal producer, and conditions in the mines and mining communities were as forlorn as ever. Although the mine owners and their hired policemen had effectively kept UMW organizers out of the state, the attitude of the miners had changed since 1903. Racial and ethnic rivalries had yielded to a sense of solidarity. A new labor uprising was all but inevitable. It began on a tiny tributary of the Kanawha River named Paint Creek. The miners along the stream had been organized by Mother Jones in 1904. When in March 1912 the UMW asked for a small pay increase, the owners refused to negotiate and withdrew recognition of the union. The miners went on strike, and they were soon joined by nonunion miners on neighboring Cabin Creek.

The owners chased the miners' families out of their homes in the company towns, built concrete bunkers mounted with machine guns at the entrances to the mines, and advertised in eastern newspapers for replacement workers. Not permitted on company property, the miners and their families built tent colonies on the edge of highways and railroad tracks. The strike named for two obscure West Virginia streamlets, which originated with the miners themselves, became one of the longest and bloodiest labor conflicts in American history.

Mother Jones arrived in West Virginia in June 1912 and began a frenzied series of rallies in the northern half of the state. When she held a rally in Charleston, she invited the Republican Governor William E. Glasscock to attend. When the governor refused, she pilloried him publicly, saying (according to a miner who was in the audience), "You can expect no help from such a goddamned dirty coward. . . whom, for modesty's sake, we shall call 'Crystal Peter.' But I warn this little governor that unless he rids Paint Creek and Cabin Creek of those goddamned Baldwin-Felts mine-guard thugs, there is going to be one hell of a lot of bloodletting in these hills." She then told the crowd: "Arm yourselves, return home and kill every goddamned mine guard on the creeks, and drive the damned scabs out of the valleys." The miners did not really need such incitement. They lived in a land of violence, where family feuds were common, and every household had its arsenal. Even before Mother Jones arrived on the scene, the miners had organized military-style companies and were engaging the mine guards in pitched battles. On July 26 a fight at Mucklow left sixteen dead on the field.

On September 2, Governor Glasscock declared martial law and sent 1,200 members of the state National Guard into the Cabin Creek area. The army disarmed both guards and miners and arrested sixty-six persons, nearly all of them union officials and socialist stump-speakers. Army officers subjected their civilian prisoners to military courts-martial, without allowing them defense counsel or a trial by jury. On February 13, 1913, Mother Jones was arrested in Charleston, while trying to petition the governor, and transported to the town of Pratt, in the Cabin Creek area, for trial. Not wanting too much adverse publicity, the army did not put her in jail while she awaited trial and instead rented a boardinghouse and posted two sentries to guard her. (She persuaded one of them to walk with her to a nearby tavern for a beer.)

Although no record was kept of the trial, she was evidently found guilty, for she stayed under house arrest. She remained incarcerated for three months, much of it spent in ill health. The purpose, clearly, was to prevent her and other UMW agents from lending moral support to the miners. To a certain extent, it worked. In the spring of 1913, with the governor mediating, the owners offered a nine-hour day and minor pay concessions but without union recognition or an end to the guard system, which were the workers' major demands. The UMW accepted the offer without consulting the miners, who probably would have rejected it.

Throughout the spring letters protesting the violent tactics of the mine owners and the trial of civilians by the military in West Virginia had reached the Congress, and the Senate considered undertaking a formal investigation. When the senators from West Virginia contended that no investigation was necessary, Senator John Werth Kern of Indiana pulled out a telegram sent to him by Jones and read it on the Senate floor: "From out of the military prison walls, where I have been forced to pass my eighty-first milestone of life [she was actually seventy-six], I plead with you for the honor of this Nation. I send you the groans and tears of men, women, and children as I have heard them in this State, and beg you to force that investigation. Children yet unborn will rise and bless you."

As reporters streamed to their telephones, the Senate authorized the investigation, and a few days later an embarrassed governor released Jones from her incarceration. She fled to the relative security of Pittsburgh, denounced the UMW settlement, and advised the miners to hold onto their guns. She then watched happily as wildcat strikes broke out across the northern West Virginia coal fields. With the Senate investigating the abuses of the previous year, the state could not help the owners and they quickly capitulated. Without formally doing so, they indirectly recognized the union by allowing a checkoff from pay envelopes for union dues and agreeing to arbitration of miners' complaints.

It was a major victory and a landmark in the history of the American labor movement. The labor press credited it almost exclusively to the hell-raising efforts of Mother Jones, and even the *New York Times* granted her a lengthy interview. She was at the height of her national fame, and tales of her legendary exploits sprang up everywhere. Common sense might have suggested retirement on her laurels. Instead, she hurried off to organize Colorado.

The Colorado coal strike, which began in September 1913, mirrored in violence that of West Virginia. The miners were ousted from their homes in the company towns, and they set up roadside camps, using tents sent by the UMW from West Virginia. The hills around Trinidad echoed with guerilla warfare between miners and the hired guards. Unfortunately, most of the casualties were women and children, hurt when the guards attacked the tent camps. Mother Jones, who arrived in Colorado just a few days before the strike began, was banned from Trinidad and arrested when she entered the city. Released from jail without a trial, she went east to raise money for the striking miners. The governor then banned her from the entire state. Claiming that, as an American citizen, she had a right to cross state lines, she returned and was arrested when she got off the train in Denver. Said the governor: "I confidently believe that most of the murders and other acts of violent crime committed in the strike region have been inspired by this woman's incendiary utterances." When she applied for a writ of habeas corpus before the state supreme court, the governor set her free.

As in West Virginia, the incarceration of Jones and other UMW officials triggered a congressional investigation, and President Wilson sought to mediate the strike by begging the owners to offer concessions. Smelling victory, John D. Rockefeller Jr., and other others in the southern field refused. By the fall of 1814 the strike was fourteen months old, sixty-six people had died, the UMW treasury was empty, and the miners were starving. President Wilson offered to appoint a special commission to investigate and make recommendations, and the UMW accepted this face-saving device. The miners went back to work having gained nothing.

Mother Jones was at the height of her fame in the wake of the strike. She was granted audiences with President Wilson and John D. Rockefeller (both senior and junior). But such appearances only laid bare the limits of her power. She could plead the case for the workingmen but little more. An appeal to public opinion was her principal weapon, but business executives were moving to deprive her even of that. William Lyon McKenzie King (who became, in the 1920s, a much-loved prime minister of Canada) had become an important adviser to the Rockefellers, and he preached the value of public relations. Soon the Colorado Fuel and Iron Company had an entire department devoted to rehabilitating the

Mother Jones leading a street demonstration in Trinidad, Colorado, in 1913. (Photograph from the Newberry Library.)

image of both the Rockefeller family and the company. King even managed to have Rockefeller Jr., visit the Colorado mines, where he talked to the men, danced with their wives, and hugged their children.

More threatening to both Jones and the UMW, Rockefeller and King established a company union for Colorado Fuel and Iron, which negotiated wage contracts, heard miners' grievances, and provided the semblance of organization—without ever threatening a strike. The company union kept the UMW out of Colorado for many years.

The company union, which spread quickly to other industries, was not the only change in the labor movement after 1914. The Clayton Antitrust Act, passed in that year, specifically exempted labor unions from the purview of the antitrust laws and thus conferred on them the governmental imprimatur of legitimacy. The establishment the previous year of a cabinet-level Department of Labor also gave unions a new respectability. The labor movement itself was changing as trade unions affiliated with the AF of L became the dominant voice. There were fewer orations on class solidarity and more talk of participating in the success of free enterprise capitalism. Mother Jones's homilies on the family of labor seemed increasingly out of place.

In 1920 John L. Lewis became president of the United Mine Workers, and that was the end of Mother Jones's career. She regarded him scornfully as a "pie counter hunter," lining up to get his fill, in the mold of John Mitchell and Samuel Gompers.[3] Lewis, in turn, felt that Jones was a liability. In the wake of the steel strike of 1919 and the Red Scare of 1920, anyone who talked of class warfare was certain to be labeled a Communist—a term given new meaning by the Russian Revolution of 1917. He terminated Jones's services in 1921.

In her eighties, Jones suffered severely from arthritis and other ailments. She was unable, however, to give up the peripatetic life and build a home for herself. Instead, she camped with friends, as she always had. Her favorites—and obviously the most tolerant—were the Powderlys. Terence V. Powderly, the long-forgotten head of the Knights of Labor, lived until 1924. In 1923 Jones began work on her autobiography, intending it as a beacon for the struggles of future generations. Since she had no permanent home, she had no diaries, letters, or other memorabilia on which to rely. She did it from memory, dictating her stories to a friendly journalist, Mary Field Parton. Parton cleaned up the language but otherwise recorded the anecdotes as she heard them, often with a mixed up chronology. Without consulting Jones, Parton beefed up the story with long passages from the *New York Times*. The book appeared in 1925, and it was a commercial failure. The publisher printed up 4,500 copies but sold no more than 2,000.

3. The irony is that, in the 1930s and 1940s, John L. Lewis was widely perceived as the most radical, most aggressive labor leader of the day.

The tragedy of Mother Jones was that she outlived her time. The mid-1920s was a time of unparalleled prosperity. People—even most blue-collared workers—were enjoying the good life, and they were content with the social and political status quo. It was not that Mother Jones was ignored; worse, she was simply forgotten.

Knowing she was near the end and wishing for the spotlight a final time, she planned a "hundredth" birthday party for May 1, 1930. The press cooperated. Ten days before May Day the *New York Times* carried a report on the event, and the *Baltimore Sun* devoted the lead story of its Sunday magazine to the old lady, declaring that "she is willing to call it a day, the battle over, the victory won." Although declawed by the press and crippled with arthritis, she retained some of the old vinegar. When, on the day of the party, a friend tried to pin a corsage on her, she snapped, "Hell, I never have worn those and I don't want to now." When she was served water during the reception, she cursed "those old fools" who had imposed Prohibition on the country. Hundreds of well-wishers, mostly labor union officials and politicians, made an appearance, and among the thousands of telegrams was one from Rockefeller Jr. She thought he was a "damned good sport" for sending her best wishes, since she had "licked him many times." Six months later, November 30, she was dead. Her physician explained, "She just wore out."

Suggested Reading

The best biography is Elliott J. Gorn's *Mother Jones, The Most Dangerous Woman in America* (2001). A fine accont of American labor during this period is David Montgomery's *The Fall of the House of Labor: The Workplace, the State, and American Labor Activism, 1865-1925* (1987). The story of the coal strikes is well told by Priscilla Long in *Where the Sun Never Shines: A History of America's Bloody Coal Industry* (1989). Edward M. Steel Jr., editor, *The Court Martial of Mother Jones* (1995), has published the records of her trial by the army in West Virginia in 1913, with an excellent introduction on the coal mine war of 1913–1914. A good biography of Jones's closest friend is Craig Phelan's *Grand Master Workman: Terence Powderly and the Knights of Labor* (2000).

3

William Graham Sumner vs. Lester Frank Ward: The Intellectual Battleground

The evolution of life on the earth was the subject of fierce debate in western Europe for two decades before Charles Darwin published his *Origin of Species* in 1859. In the seventeenth century philosophers had theorized that the earth had evolved from a fiery, molten mass, and the fossil record developed in the following century indicated a gradual cooling and slow emergence of living things. Synthesizing this previous work in his *Principles of Geology* (1833), the Englishman Sir Charles Lyell pointed out that the earth, like mankind, has a history, a story that can be gleaned from rock strata and the fossils of primitive forms of life. The ensuing debate turned on the question of how the earth was transformed, whether by uniform forces that did not vary greatly in intensity (erosion, floods, earthquakes) or by catastrophic events (including, perhaps, divine intervention). Lyell, who subscribed to the uniformitarian theory (and thus rejected the biblical account of creation and any notion of divine meddling), did posit a "universal struggle for existence" among species of plants and animals, but he saw no creative role in this struggle that would produce more complex (and thus "higher") forms of life.

Darwin's impact on this debate was twofold. He saw that the struggle for existence was both within each species and among competing species, with the "winners" being those whose offspring were best adapted to a changing environment and thus most likely to survive. Strength, adaptability, and the growing complexity of body parts were thus the keys to the evolution of life upon the earth. His second theoretical contribution was to provide a mechanism for change—natural selection. Because each organism differs slightly from any other, even within a species, Darwin argued, some are better adapted to changes in the environment than others and thus more likely to survive. Unlike modern breeders of domestic animals, nature works her "improvements" purely by chance. Species evolve by surviving the accidents of history—changes in climate, earthquakes, mountain-building, and the rise and fall of seas.

Darwin then devoted the greater part of *The Origin of Species* to presenting evidence in support of his thesis, descriptions of reptiles, birds, and mammals gathered on his round-the-world voyage on the *Beagle*. While roughing out his theory of evolution in the 1830s Darwin saw the implications for humankind, that humans were simply an "advanced" form of animal. However, he studiously avoided such an explosive issue in *The Origin of Species*. He did not mention human beings at all until the next to the last page when he threw out the vague suggestion that "much light" could be shed on "the origin of man." Although Darwin did eventually attempt to trace human origins in the *Descent of Man* (1871), the application of the theory of evolution to human society was drawn, not by Darwin, but by another Englishman, Herbert Spencer.

Social Darwinism

Among nineteenth-century best-sellers in America, Herbert Spencer's *Social Statics* (1851) trailed only the Bible and Harriet Beecher Stowe's *Uncle Tom's Cabin*. The date of publication, almost a decade prior to *The Origin of Species*, suggests that Spencer's thinking was shaped by the pre-Darwinian debate over the earth's development. Although Spencer's thought is commonly known as Social Darwinism (a term coined by a French critic in the 1880s and that did not enter the American vocabulary until the 1890s), there is little connection between Darwin and Spencer. The term "evolution," which Darwin rarely employed, materialized out of Spencer's writings, not Darwin's, and Spencer himself was not a "Darwinian," in the sense that he did not believe that humans evolved from other "higher" animals.

Borrowing ideas from Thomas Malthus and the classical economists, rather than from Lyell and other geologists of his time, Spencer argued that the struggle of humans for survival in a free, competitive environment was the engine that drove the progress of civilization. The natural competition among people produced winners and losers, and the winners were those with more intelligence, industry, or ingenuity. By virtue of this "survival of the fittest" (a phrase he coined in the 1860s) civilization advances. The fit assume the lead and pull the entire society to a higher order of knowledge, technology, and culture. The losers, the "unfit," are left to languish or die, and in doing so raise the societal average. Rejecting the notion that progress stemmed from human's innate moral sense, which underlay the enlightened rationalism of Thomas Jefferson, the utilitarianism of Jeremy Bentham, and the transcendentalism of Ralph Waldo Emerson, Spencer posited that humans were imperfect, weak, and selfish. And it was out of their selfish competitiveness that society progressed. Social development was thus a law of nature and, as such, it was inevitable. Because it was predetermined, any attempt to manipulate it was self-defeating. Governmental humanitarianism (feeding the unemployed, for instance) merely retarded human progress because it enabled the "unfit" to survive. In this way Herbert Spencer managed to wed classical economics, which had its own natural laws, such as the law of supply and demand, with the immutable laws of biology. Government had no more role in human progress than God had in the evolution of nature. It is scarcely surprising that Spencer's philosophy was popular among Americans of the Gilded Age, for it provided a rationale for what they were doing anyway—struggling to get ahead in a free, competitive society in which government was all but irrelevant.

Herbert Spencer, a genteel Englishman with ample wealth and classical education, never experienced a personal struggle for survival, nor was he able to confront the harsh implications of his philosophy. In *Social Statics*, and more clearly in later writings, he tempered his creed by suggesting that private charity (benevolence being one of the attributes of the "fit") would help relieve the plight of the unfit. By the 1890s he had backed away altogether from the slogan "survival of the fittest" and conceded that the tendency of the poor to breed and leave progeny was an insoluble problem. He spent his last years alternating between a drugged stupor and black despair. In the meantime, however, the American edition of his writings, beginning in the 1860s, inspired a small but highly creative group of disciples, who enlarged upon his thinking and gave it an American cast. Prime among these was a Yale theologian-turned-sociologist, William Graham Sumner.

William Graham Sumner

Postwar periods are typically times of reaction, and the years following the Civil War were no exception. Americans of the Gilded Age reacted against the foggy idealism of the prewar social reformers and instead exalted material success. The Republican Party lost the farmer–labor constituency it had cultivated before the war and became unabashedly the party of big business and the status quo. The newly freed blacks of the South were left to fend for themselves, without land, education, or skills. The Puritan gospel of industry and thrift still had its hold on the American mind, but it was reconstituted to fit the mood of a property-conscious, acquisitive age. The leading evangelist for this refurbished Puritanism was a Baptist clergyman from Philadelphia (and founder of Temple University), Russell H. Conwell, whose lecture "Acres of Diamonds," a digest of his philosophy, was said to have been delivered to appreciative audiences more than six thousand times.

In harmony with the mood of the post-Appomatox years, Conwell told his listeners that the pursuit of wealth was an honorable ambition. "Money is power," he would say again and again. "Every good man and woman ought to strive for power, to do good with it when obtained. Tens and thousands of men and women get rich honestly. But they are often accused by an envious, lazy crowd of unsuccessful persons of being dishonest and oppressive. I say, get rich, get rich! But get money honestly, or it will be a withering curse." Conwell's was not only a gospel of success; it was a reminder that the successful were obliged to use their money for the benefit of society. The "stewardship of wealth" underlay Andrew Carnegie's endowment of libraries and John D. Rockefeller's founding of the University of Chicago. Fusing this brand of Puritanism with the evolutionary philosophy of Herbert Spencer was the achievement of William Graham Sumner, and in doing so he created a powerful new ethos—powerful because the reward for being good, for being industrious, temperate, and frugal—was not, as in most religions, in the hereafter, but in the here and now, in this life, in the form of success and wealth.

Sumner's father Thomas, whom William greatly admired, embodied those qualities of the Protestant ethic that would become the basis of Sumner's philosophy. He was frugal, abstemious, hardworking, and tough-minded. Unfortunately, he was also not very successful. An uneducated artisan from Lancashire, he came to America in 1836 and settled in Hartford, Connecticut, where he obtained employment in a repair shop of the New Haven Railroad. William, one of three children, was born on October 30, 1840.

Sumner's childhood was emotionally barren, and it left marks on him that affected his whole outlook on life. His mother died when he was eight, and he detested the stepmother who succeeded her. William was an oddly sober boy, self-righteous and hypercritical. He early revealed the traits of a man who would make enemies easily. Neither his brother nor his sister liked him much. To the end of his days he would scoff at the concept of human brotherhood, and he had no appreciation for beauty, whether in art or nature.

Sumner's stepmother, however chilly in her treatment of the children, did manage to salt away $1,000 toward his collegiate education. He entered Yale in 1859, intent upon becoming a Congregational minister. An early biographer described him as a young man "with few friends, reserved and repellant in manner, mature beyond his years, with strong moral and religious convictions, and with no ambition but to get knowledge." Yale at mid-century was neither a fountain of knowledge nor a source of inspiration. A citadel of religious orthodoxy, it had a narrow, set curriculum with heavy emphasis on classical languages. Sumner seemed not to object, and he graduated in 1863 with honors. Although his stepmother had died in the year he entered college, his frugal father had set aside some additional funds by the time he graduated and Sumner embarked on a year of study in Europe, spending most of his time at Gottingen, the centerpiece of German scholarship. The biblical scholars at Gottingen were his first eye-opening intellectual experience, for they viewed the Bible as a piece of history and subjected its passages to empirical tests. Their rigid devotion to scientific method and insistence on demonstrable truth left a permanent imprint on Sumner.

By the time he returned to America in 1866 he had abandoned the doctrinaire Calvinism taught at Yale and embraced the "broader" tenets of the Episcopal Church. He edited a "broad church" (i.e., evangelical) magazine, attended a theological seminary, and was ordained an Episcopal priest in 1869. For the next three years he served as rector in a succession of churches in New York and New Jersey. He married in 1871, and, while the couple would have two sons, his wife Jeannie suffered from recurrent illnesses (possibly tuberculosis) that required frequent stays in sanitariums and strained the family finances.

As his evangelical fervor faded in the routine of pastoral duties, the world of science and of laws deduced from empirical data increasingly summoned him. As a youth he had read popularized versions of the works of the classical economists Adam Smith, Thomas Malthus, and David Ricardo, and he was impressed with the laws that seemed to make economics a true science. His church sermons revealed a constant struggle to reconcile scientific evidence with religious faith. When Yale offered him a newly established chair of political economy in 1872, he lunged for it. As he later explained, "I never consciously gave up a religious belief. It was as if I had put my beliefs into a drawer, and when I opened it there was nothing there at all." Although he would give no more thought to the role of God, the authority of the scriptures, or the portent of salvation, he retained subconsciously the Puritan ideal with which he had been raised, and he would make those virtues the prerequisite of survival and success.

As a cleric Sumner claimed to have read Darwin and Spencer, and he expressed admiration for their empirical methods, while shying away from their portrayal of the violent struggle for survival. As a professor of political economy, however, he began searching for a science of society, a set of natural laws that governed human development. That revelation struck him within a year when he came upon Herbert Spencer's new work, *The Study of Sociology* (1873). Spencer's doctrine of "survival of the fittest" blended perfectly with the laissez-faire economics that Sumner was dogmatically teaching in his classroom. He expressed his developing thought in a series of essays and speeches that were eventually drawn together into a widely read book, *What Social Classes Owe to Each Other* (1883). Although laden with economic theory, the book was popular because of Sumner's gift for epigrams. "The law of survival of the fittest was not made by man," he told the Free Trade Club in 1879, it was part of the natural law of evolution. "We can only, by interfering with it, produce the survival of the unfittest."

He was, however, forced to confront the lack of ethics in Spencer's description of the struggle for survival. Spencer insisted that the "fit," by virtue of surviving, were naturally benevolent and charitable, but there was nothing in his thesis to indicate that was necessarily so. Nor did he have a mechanism by which fitness bred charity or honesty. Indeed, his weak and selfish person, struggling in a godless universe, was little different from the humankind described by the seventeenth-century philosopher, Thomas Hobbes—a people whose passions could only be kept under control by a Leviathan of government. Sumner dodged this Spencerian dilemma by proposing that the ideal human—the "fittest"—was a neo-Puritan: hardworking, temperate, moral, and frugal. When this sort of man seeks to promote his own well-being—comes by his riches honestly, as Russell Conwell would have put it—society benefits, and civilization takes another step forward.

To Sumner, then, the accumulation of capital was the primary index of social improvement. Sumner conceded that unregulated entrepreneurial endeavor would produce millionaires and monopolists, but this was not to be regretted. Capital must be in the hands of the few because only a few are capable of organizing great enterprises and handling large amounts of money in a socially useful way. If the nation were to limit the amount of wealth accumulated by its most valuable producers, it would be like killing off its generals in a time of war. Conversely, if the government were to redistribute wealth, through some sort of welfare program, the undeserving beneficiaries would waste it on beer, dice, and other frivolities, with no benefit to society.

Opposed to such artificial legal doctoring, Sumner insisted that nature alone would cure social ills. "Nature's remedies against vice are terrible," he wrote in one essay that resounded with Puritanical fervor. "She removes the victims without pity. A drunkard in the gutter is just where he ought to be, according to the fitness and tendency of things. Nature has set up in him the process of decline and dissolution by which she removes things which have survived their usefulness."

At the same time, Sumner recognized that certain men, such as Jay Gould and Jim Fisk who would be decried by historians as "robber barons," came by their wealth through political connections or iniquitous behavior. He denounced such "plutocrats," but he had no solution to the problem they posed other than to insist upon a strict separation of commercial competition and political power. Unlike other conservatives of his day, he opposed not only government relief for the poor but any sort of government aid to business. Even the protective tariff, he felt, permitted certain inept businessmen to survive by cutting foreign competition.

Sumner nevertheless recognized that consigning the great multitude of humankind to the ranks of the "unfit" was a harsh result, and one that could not be expected to be very popular. So he drafted a final chapter for *Social Classes* entitled "Wherefore We Should Love One Another," appended to the book like a hasty visit to church after a week of tumult in the marketplace. Like Spencer, Sumner relied on private humanitarianism to ameliorate the lot of the losers in the struggle for survival. Five years later, in an article entitled simply "Wealth" (1889), fellow Social Darwinist Andrew Carnegie would postulate that the opportunity to perform philanthropy was the principal objective of the accumulation of wealth, thus providing a corollary to the Sumnerian ethic, the "gospel of wealth."

In 1894, amidst the cacophony of Populist oratory and calls for government ownership of railroads and utilities, Sumner issued his final plea for free enterprise and limited government in a pamphlet entitled "The Absurd Effort to Make the World Over." It would prove to be his best-known work and left him permanently identified with Social Darwinism. Among Sumner's targets in this work was Edward Bellamy, whose widely read book *Looking Backward, 2000–1887* (1888) had introduced Americans to the Fabian Socialist philosophy of having government own and operate basic production and transportation industries. Sumner saw nothing to be gained in taking a ruthless master of industry and making him a "government functionary." Nor was he comfortable with politicians superintending the nation's economy. "Can anyone imagine," he wrote in another essay, "that politicians would no longer be corruptly fond of money, intriguing, and crafty when they were charged, not only with patronage and government contracts, but also with factories, stores, ships, and railroads?"

He had turned from the study of economics to sociology in the 1890s and begun the research for his most important contribution to that new-found discipline, *Folkways* (1906). His examination of cultural habits and attitudes among different races and over time shaped the initial premise of "Absurd Effort"—that society is a vast and enormously complex mechanism of interrelated parts and that action at any given point will produce unanticipated and poorly understood consequences elsewhere. As a result, the "social tinkerer" is as likely to do harm as good. "The student of sociology as a science," he wrote in a companion essay, "will necessarily feel a great timidity about all generalization. There are so many more things that he does not know than there are which he does know."

This was a standard—and quite valid—scholarly disclaimer, and he might have rested his argument against "social meddling" right there. But Sumner could not resist driving his antistate point a little further with an argument that the American political system was particularly ill-adapted to "make the world over." Sumner's mistrust of American democracy stemmed from his service on an electoral commission during the Hayes–Tilden presidential election of 1876. Sumner watched the Republicans literally steal the presidency by stuffing ballot boxes in three southern states that they still controlled in the last days of Reconstruction. Because a democratic government is literally "all-of-us," he argued, it is necessarily fallible and liable to error. Worse, the American government, in practice, is run by a small group of wealthy and powerful plutocrats, a self-perpetuating oligarchy that caters to special interests. To entrust the delicate mechanism of society to such soiled hands would be to compound error.

That argument brought him right back to the field of economics and laissez-faire. Society, he argued, needs to be rid of meddlers, to be let alone. The sole function of the state was to maintain law and order so that upright citizens might pursue in peace the path to success. Restrictions in the U.S. Constitution ensured that the government would be limited to this function, and it was up to the courts to enforce such limitations. The Supreme Court, as it was constituted in the 1880s and 1890s, certainly did precisely that.

The "Absurd Effort to Make the World Over" was Sumner's last dalliance with Social Darwinism. The 1890s were a major turning point in his thought. His study of cultural "folkways" led him increasingly to emphasize the importance of cooperation in human relationships, as opposed to individualistic competition. He was also disturbed by the rise of imperialist feeling, which culminated in the Spanish–American War. During the decade, which also witnessed Britain's Boer War in South Africa and the beginning of an arms race in Europe, Social Darwinists in America and Europe extended the slogan "survival of the fittest" to the competition among nations for world leadership. In the United States Theodore Roosevelt helped make popular the notion that nations, like individuals, must make themselves militarily strong and competitive, or they would wither and die. Sumner thought this a perversion of the whole concept of Social Darwinism, and he predicted (correctly, as it turned out) that such thinking would make the twentieth century as much a century of warfare as the eighteenth.

In January 1899 he addressed the Yale Phi Beta Kappa Society under the quixotic title "The Conquest of the United States by Spain." In this mistaken war, he argued, the United States had adopted the militarism, imperialism, and absolutism of the corrupt monarchies of Europe, and belligerent patriotism had silenced dissent and undermined the democratic process. It was an argument that would continue to resonate a century later.

Troubled after 1900 by the rise of giant business combinations and the emergence of powerful labor unions, who engaged one another in a Darwinian struggle for supremacy, troubled also by the intermittent warfare among nations that seemed to threaten Western civilization, Sumner concluded that the only hope for humankind was the development of social science to match humankind's industrial and military advances. He advanced these thoughts in an unpublished essay, but even if he had spoken out he would have found no one listening.

Sumner was a man of another generation. He had provided a philosophy for an age of enterprise, an age of blast furnaces, oil gushers, and transcontinental railroads. He was already outdated in the 1890s when his Social Darwinist theories yielded to the assault of his critics, who were using the concepts of Darwinian evolution to promote the cause of reform. The earliest of these critics of Social Darwinism, and in the end the most influential, was Lester Frank Ward.

Lester Frank Ward

The Wards of Connecticut and Rhode Island could trace their ancestry back to a soldier who landed in England with William the Conqueror, but a distinguished pedigree was of little help to Connecticut-born Justus Ward (1788–1857), an itinerant mechanic and jack-of-all-trades. His wife Silence was the daughter of a minister and a hardy woman who bore ten children in six different states over twenty-five years and outlived her husband by twenty-two years. Lester Frank, her last child, was born June 18, 1841, in Joliet, Illinois. The family had recently moved there from New York when Justus was employed to work on the locks of the canal connecting Lake Michigan and the Mississippi River. The Wards moved several more times during Lester Frank's boyhood, and his schooling was, at best, intermittent.

When he was fourteen they rumbled west to Iowa in a small covered wagon, living on game shot by Frank (as the family preferred to call him) and an older brother. There Justus took up farming on land deeded to him for his service in the War of 1812. Justus died two years later, and Frank went to work for a neighboring farmer to help support the family. Although he greedily absorbed every book he could get his hands on, the landscape was his schoolhouse. "Roaming wildly over the boundless prairies of northern Iowa in the fifties," he wrote many years later, "interested in every animal, bird, insect, and flower I saw, but not knowing what science was, scarcely having ever heard of zoology, ornithology, or botany, without a single book on any of those subjects, and not knowing a person in the world who could give me the slightest information with regard to them, what chance was there of becoming a naturalist?"

When Frank was seventeen he and a brother hiked east to Pennsylvania where another brother had offered them jobs in a factory. For the next two years he toiled long hours in the factory and studied Greek and Latin (the principal prerequisites for entry into college) by candlelight. When the factory failed, he taught school in the summer and worked in a sawmill in the winter. Unlike Herbert Spencer, or even William Graham Sumner, Lester Ward knew firsthand what the struggle for survival was all about. He also learned that hard work, while it might ensure physical survival, was not a sure road to success. The road to success, he concluded, was paved with education—it was a maxim he adhered to all his life.

Ward did manage to save enough money to attend the Susquehanna Institute of Towanda, Pennsylvania, but he could afford no more than a short term. He did learn, however, that he knew far more Greek and Latin than his peers, and he was eyeing Lafayette College when Lincoln's April 1861 "call to arms" summoned him. Five days before he left for the front in Virginia he married a childhood sweetheart, Elizabeth Vought. While serving in the Army of the Potomac for the next two years he sent her letters almost daily, written in French for practice in that language. His military career ended at Chancellorsville, where he took three bullets in his legs.

His war wounds opened the door to government service and, through that, to college. Upon recovery, he was first employed as a teacher in the Fairfax, Virginia, hospital that had treated him, and in 1865 he was given a job as a clerk in the Treasury Department. Two years later he applied for admission to Columbian (now George Washington) University, and his entrance examination qualified him for admission as a sophomore. Two years later he was given the degree of bachelor of arts, and after further study in botany, chemistry, and anatomy he earned a master of arts degree in 1872. All this time he had been attending evening classes in law and medicine. In 1871 he received the degree of bachelor of laws and a year later was admitted to the Washington, D.C., bar. In that year also he received his diploma in medicine. Never has the American collegiate system been so taken by storm! Having established his credentials, Ward did not bother to practice either law or medicine. He simply did not feel adequately prepared, and accordingly, "conscience would not allow it."

His wife "Lizzie" shared his scholarly interests and earned a degree of her own from the Union Seminary in Washington. She gave birth to a child, who failed to survive its first year, and then she herself died in 1871, just as Ward was finishing his collegiate schooling. Ward remarried within a year, choosing a widow, Rose A. Pierce. Their union was apparently a contented one, for we hear nothing more of her in the record of Ward's life.

After leaving college Ward held a succession of jobs in the government service, but, stultifying as it was, the civil service failed to curb his pursuit of knowledge. His researches in botany and geology led him from the country roads of Alabama to the Black Hills of the Dakota Territory, and the resulting papers earned him great respect in the Smithsonian Institution and the title of honorary curator of botany in the National Museum. In 1881 he was appointed chief geologist for the newly created United States Geological Survey.

Despite these excursions into natural science, he never lost his dream of discovering a science of society. The term "social science" had become popular during the 1860s, but the theories of Herbert Spencer and William Graham Sumner consigned it to virtual irrelevance. If any positive action by government—"meddling" Sumner called it—actually retarded social progress, as the Social Darwinists claimed, there was no point in developing a science that might guide that action. Thus history, social studies, even economics (other than the "laws" of laissez-faire) had no function. Rejecting this sort of nihilism, Ward contended that the advance of civilization instead depended on the discovery of the scientific principles governing human society. He borrowed the term "sociology" from the French philosopher Auguste Comte to describe this new discipline. Because it was informed by the discoveries in natural science and human psychology, as well as the history of mankind and its achievements, sociology was, in Ward's mind, the science of sciences.

He began work on this project in 1869, while still in school, and it took him fourteen years to complete. His research in botany and geology was a necessary foundation, and he poured through the works of the European social philosophers, from Comte to Spencer. When completed, he titled his work *Dynamic Sociology* (1883), thereby tossing a gauntlet at Spencer and his *Social Statics*. Although practically unknown to the American public (Ward's readership never came close to that of Sumner), *Dynamic Sociology* was the most important book of its time, for it cut the ground from under the Social Darwinists, established the modern discipline of sociology, and laid the intellectual foundation for twentieth-century Progressivism.

Ward began by calling into question the fundamental premise of Social Darwinism—that there was an analogy between evolution in nature and the advance of human civilization. The two are simply not comparable, he argued. Nature is blind, and natural evolution is therefore accidental and wasteful. Drawing on paleontology, he reminded readers of the number of false starts that occurred in the Cenozoic Age before mammals evolved. As a biologist he noted the number of seeds that had to be sprinkled on the forest floor to bring about a single tree. Most animals, from grasshoppers to fawns, he might have added, have camouflage coloration because those unfortunates who chance to be born with the wrong coloration (red, white, and blue frogs is the example of one scholar/comic) get eaten by predators. The losses can be in the millions before a species gets it right, and those who never get it right die out. By such hit-or-miss methods natural evolution had managed to produce the mind of humans, with reason and foresight, and in so doing had established a wholly new game plan for the earth.

Ward conceded that early humans lived in a Darwinian world governed by the blind forces of nature. Improvements in mental capacity and a realization of the value of cooperation had produced government, and social organization had encouraged cultural and technological developments. But it was not until the dawn of modern science, in the age of Galileo and Newton, and particularly the prospect of a true social science in the last half of the nineteenth century that there was real potential for human progress. Human evolution, therefore, is not blind but can be affected by the human mind. Humankind can knowingly, artfully react to its social environment, and by informed action—slum clearance, food inspection, water quality control—improve its lot and advance civilization.

While such progress might be led by social scientists, they needed broad public support, and that could come only through education. Ward, with his own experience at hand, had great faith in the intellectual capacities of the common man, and universal education would not only augment the ranks of the scientific elite, it would make the average citizen more sympathetic to new ideas and more willing to support experimental legislation. Education, Ward's cure for the ills of humankind, was necessarily a governmental function. It required public tax support to ensure quality and oversight by public officials to maintain standards. Moreover, most of the advances promised by the application of a dynamic sociology required legislation, that is, positive action by a beneficent state. Having demolished the evolution analogy, Ward turned his guns on the other pillar of Social Darwinism, laissez-faire.

In his second book, *The Psychic Factors of Civilization* (1893), Ward wrote, "We are told to let things alone, and allow nature to take its course. But has intelligent man ever done this? Is not civilization, with all it has accomplished, the result of man's not letting things alone, and of his not letting nature take its course." Laissez-faire is, in fact, inconsistent with progress, for it denies humankind the use of history and the opportunity to profit by its mistakes. The doctrine was also hypocritical, for it applied only to government and not to monopolists. Businessmen themselves did not believe in free competition, for in a system of genuine competition no one got ahead. While Sumner prattled endlessly about the virtues of free enterprise, John D. Rockefeller and J. P. Morgan were working hard to establish monopolies.

Ward regarded the slogan "survival of the fittest" as either meaningless or harmful. "Fit" itself is ambiguous. Fit for what? There is nothing about fitness for survival that promises an advance of civilization. In fact, the opposite is true. "The more advanced a society becomes the more it eliminates the struggle for existence." Indeed, the history of civilization is the story of human cooperation, the evolution of collective endeavor, whether in building a cathedral, spanning a river, or overcoming "barbarians." Even if we were to concede that a survival of the fit somehow enhanced civilization, such advances, by the estimates of Spencer and Sumner themselves, occurred in minute increments over thousands of years. Dynamic sociologists, on the other hand, in league with intelligently run government, could produce noticeable improvements within a matter of months.

Reform Darwinism

By the 1890s a group of thinkers, most of them influenced by Ward's writings, had gathered under the banner of "reform Darwinism." Where

Spencer and Sumner had hitched Darwinian evolution to the wagon of do-nothing conservatism, idealists of the 1890s suggested that it could equally well advance an ideology of reform. Accepting the Darwinian notion that humans are heavily influenced by their environment, reformers suggested improving humankind by altering the environment. Reduce the number of criminals, for instance, by cleaning up the slums and providing relief to the poor. Edward A. Ross, a sociologist at the University of Wisconsin and Ward's nephew and protégé, would later suggest that a new commandment be added to the biblical ten to encompass sins for which no individual felt responsible in the bureaucratic world of corporate business—the packaging and sale of spoiled meat by a giant packing company, for instance (*Sin and Society*, 1907). Although Lester Ward never publicly used the term "reform Darwinism," his later writings reflected that brand of thinking and furthered its cause.

Ward's two final books, *Pure Sociology* (1903) and *Applied Sociology* (1906), were a compendium of his earlier writings, and although ignored by the press and the public, they were considered by scholars—then and now—as the foundation for modern sociology. The first book focused on the social mechanism and how it worked. The second was a roadmap for the future, a collection of specific suggestions of ways in which sociologists can guide the advance of human civilization. Of particular interest to the student of Progressivism, however, is Ward's advanced view, expressed in these books, on gender, race, and class.

As with so much of his reasoning, Ward premised his discussion of these issues on biology and paleontology. Taking up the problem of gender and the suppression of women in modern society, he pointed out that nature, in its most primitive forms, did not rely on sex for reproduction. Living cells (necessarily female because of their ability to replicate) multiplied by fusion, cell division, spore formation, and other forms of virgin reproduction. The male evolved as a fertilizing agent to provide variety and complexity, but, in primitive life, he was a tiny appendix to the female, a sac filled with seed to fertilize an egg. In most families of insects and spiders the female is queen; the male is smaller and, except for one-shot fertilizing capabilities, unimportant. Among vertebrates, as Darwin himself observed, the female selects the mate, and female selectivity was an important feature of the principle of natural selection. Even when the male animals attained greater brain power, size, and strength, those qualities were used, not to control the female, but to combat other males for the female's favor.

In humankind, Ward noted, many primitive societies are matriarchal because the line of kinship is more easily identified with the sedentary female, who is nurturing a family while the male is roaming the woods, hunting and gathering. About the beginning of historical time, males used their physical strength to dominate females and then developed a cultural mythology to keep them submissive. One of the principal ways in which this was done, Ward thought, was through religion. Every major religion of the world was founded by a man and dominated by a male priesthood. Every major religion contains a mythology, like the expulsion of Adam and Eve from the Garden of Eden, that renders the female tainted with evil, a second-class saint even if she is admitted to Heaven. In Hebrew theology females were excluded from Heaven altogether; the Koran preaches that a woman has no soul, that she is like a snake, charming and venomous. The vilification, and consequent subjection, of women continued to modern times. The German philosopher Frederick Nietzsche, a contemporary of Ward's, warned his fellows: "Thou goest to woman? Remember thy whip. Women are always cats and birds, or in the best case, cows."

Ward thus concluded that woman's lowly status in modern life was due to centuries of physical and cultural subjection and not to any inherent inferiority. He noted, however, that she had improved somewhat in status in recent times, and he viewed that as a measure of civilization. In the world's most civilized countries, such as the United States, Britain, and France (he placed Germany at the bottom of the scale in this regard), women had gained important legal and property rights, and they had gained access to occupations, such as teaching, nursing, and medicine, from which they had been previously excluded. All these gains could be preserved and improved upon, Ward thought, by including females in his system of universal education. He anticipated a new stage of human experience in which "both man and woman shall be free to rule themselves."

Ward was thus the first American male thinker to advocate women's right to equal opportunities with men, and his writings provided the scientific and philosophical foundation for the feminist movement that flourished after 1900. Significantly, the radical feminist Charlotte Perkins Gilman, who believed that achieving economic equality for women was far more important than suffrage, dedicated her book, *The Man-Made World* (1911), to Lester Ward.

Ward applied a similar line of reasoning to the problems of race and class. Nothing in the past history or present condition of humankind indicated that there were any differences among the races beyond the superficial bodily variations. Racial "blood" is merely a passive factor, referring merely to the hereditary material out of which the forces of the environment—such as quality of food, sanitation, and education—mold human beings of great diversity. There is no better or nobler blood; there are no inferior races or peoples, only undeveloped ones. The difference between a primitive farmer in Africa and a college professor in England is a matter of training and equipment, not in the latent power of their brains. What separates them is education, something that cannot be inherited but which all may acquire.

By the same reasoning, the social classes that divide humankind are wholly artificial. "The chances for the discovery of native genius are the same in all classes, whether we look among the high-born and rich, the middle classes, or the poor and lowly." The solution to the problem of classes and the violence that class conflict occasions is intelligent social action that will improve the environment of the poor and provide them with education. He wrote in *Applied Sociology*:

> The denizens of the slums are the same kind of people as the inhabitants of the most respectable quarters. They are not fools by any means, but men and women with normal minds, susceptible, if surrounded by the same influences, of becoming as capable and intelligent as any. As to the criminals, they are the geniuses of the slums. Society has forced them into this field and they are making the best use they can of their native abilities. Punishment does not reform and make good citizens of them. They go back with more bitter hatred of society than before, and they finally justify their attacks upon it, realizing it is responsible for their condition.

Ward and Eugenics

Reform Darwinism had its darker side—the notion that humankind can be improved by selective breeding or selective sterilization. Darwin himself addressed this possibility in *The Descent of Man*. Of all the animals, only human beings, he noted, have the capacity to influence natural selection. "We build asylums for the imbecile, the maimed, and the sick," he fretted, "we institute poor laws; and our medical men exert their utmost skill to save the life of everyone to the last moment. Thus weak members of civilized societies propagate their kind. No one who has attended to the breeding of domestic animals will doubt that this must be highly injurious to the race of man." Darwin doubted, however, that human beings could be induced to breed selectively. "Both sexes ought to refrain from marriage," he wrote, "if they are in any marked degree inferior in body or mind, but such hopes are Utopian and will never be even partially realized until the laws of inheritance are thoroughly known."

Darwin thus addressed the problem of scientific breeding but declined to pursue it. That challenge was taken up by another Englishman, Francis Galton, a statistician by training and dabbler in heredity by avocation. He was also Darwin's cousin. Galton coined the word "eugenics" in 1883 from the Greek words for "well born," and in a series of books and essays from that time until his death in 1911 he fathered a movement for scientific breeding.

In the United States Galton's ideas appealed initially to biologists who thought that principles of animal breeding might be applied to humans. In 1906 the American Breeders' Association set up a committee "to investigate and report on heredity in the human race." The association expected the committee to bring to light "the value of superior blood and the menace to society of inferior blood." Reform Darwinists liked the idea because it promised quicker improvement in the human race than mere changes in the environment. Moreover, changes in the social condition did not guarantee social betterment. "We should remember," wrote a sociologist in 1906, echoing Darwin's worries, "that an improved environment tends ultimately to degrade the race by causing an increased survival of the unfit."

The problem was that government—the ultimate agency for social betterment among the Reform Darwinists—could do little to affect human breeding. It could, however, hinder the replication of bad traits through sterilization laws (on the unproven assumption that antisocial behavior was heritable), and that became the focus of the eugenics movement and some Reform Darwinists in America. In 1907 Indiana passed a law providing that "confirmed criminals, idiots, and rapists" could be involuntarily sterilized if, in the judgment of a committee of experts, they were likely, by procreation, to replicate their kind. By 1915 thirteen states allowed government to render sterile certain criminals and mentally defective persons in public institutions. By 1930 thirty states had such laws on the books, and by that date some 30,000 sterilizations had been performed.

In 1927 the United States Supreme Court ruled in the case of *Buck v. Bell* that a Virginia law providing for the sterilization of the feebleminded was constitutional. The Court's opinion, drafted by the progressive Justice Oliver Wendell Holmes Jr., legally endorsed the principle "that heredity plays an important part in the transmission of insanity, imbecility, etc." It is better for the world, Holmes pronounced, "if instead of waiting to execute degenerate offspring for crime, or let them starve for their imbecility, society can prevent those who are manifestly unfit from continuing their kind. The principle that sustains compulsory vaccination is broad enough to cover cutting the fallopian tubes." Then followed one of Holmes's best-known maxims: "Three generations of imbeciles are enough."

Although Edward A. Ross, Ward's most prominent student, testified before the Wisconsin legislature in favor of a law permitting sterilization, Ward himself had serious misgivings about eugenics. He recognized from the outset that it was an elitist doctrine, designed to filter out human "thoroughbreds" by encouraging certain persons to procreate and prohibiting others from doing so. Although he conceded the usefulness of sterilization in extreme cases, such as the criminally insane, he thought selective breeding in general held no promise of human improvement. Certain people were poor, he argued, not because of defective genes, but because they lacked education and other opportunities for economic advancement. Moreover, even if it were possible to selectively breed gifted people, an adverse social environment would sap their vitality and lower morale. Without changes in the environment, he implied, we would only be begetting smarter criminals. Eugenics, in short, was a gospel, not a science. It was an impractical and illusive shortcut to progress. First we must produce a social milieu in which the human seed can thrive and reach its potential—only then would it be timely to seek the origin and cure of human imperfections in the reproductive cells.

Legacy

After forty years of public service—a career that no doubt conditioned his view that government could be a useful tool for social betterment—Ward at last achieved his life-long ambition—to be an educator. In 1906 he was invited to occupy a newly created chair of sociology at Brown University. He held that professorship until his death in 1913, living in a university dormitory because his wife was confined to a hospital bed in Washington. One student remembered him fondly:

> He seemed to know everything from the beginning until the final destruction of the world. Logic flowed in his words like the gentle current of a country brook in midsummer. There was no turbulence, no strain, never a hiatus; thought fitted into thought, building always upward and onward. Every lecture was a recapitulation of evolution; not of that tremendous striving of nature with the waste and failures, the trials and errors of barbarous natural selection, but the superior artificial selection which charms the reasoning minds of men. . . . He was old when he first came to Brown—old but not decadent, aged but still active; his mental vision clear as in his prime. Only the body had yielded to time; his mind was still fresh and an inspiration to his students.

At the time of Lester Ward's death the idea that humankind could control its own destiny had largely replaced the numbing doctrine that society was governed by fixed and immutable laws. Spencer's social statics had yielded to Lester Ward's social dynamics. Thanks to Lester Ward, Americans of 1913 knew more about their society than ever before, and they had full confidence that they could reshape and improve it through collective action. In that sense, Lester Ward was the intellectual forbearer of both the Progressive Movement and Franklin Roosevelt's New Deal.

Suggested Reading

A competent, and relatively brief, biography of Sumner is Bruce Curtis's *William Graham Sumner* (1981). A modern biography of Lester F. Ward is much needed. The standard work by Samuel Chugerman, *Lester F. Ward, The American Aristotle* (1939), devotes only twenty-two pages to his life story; the rest of the book is a soporific history of sociology with Ward's contributions woven in. The most recent study of Social Darwinism is Donald C. Bellomy, "Social Darwinism Revisited," in *Perspectives in American History, New Series*, I, 1–129. Still useful, in my opinion, is Richard Hofstadter's *Social Darwinism in American Thought* (rev. ed., 1955), though the reader should be advised that some of Hofstadter's interpretations have been challenged by Robert C. Bannister in *Social Darwinism: Science and Myth in Anglo-American Social Thought* (1979). Two splendid overviews of this period are Henry Steele Commager's *The American Mind, An Interpretation of American Thought and Character Since the 1880s* (1950) and Carl N. Degler's *In Search of Human Nature: The Decline and Revival of Darwinism in American Social Thought* (1991).

4

William A. Peffer: Prairie Populist

We meet in the midst of a nation brought to the verge of moral, political, and material ruin. Corruption dominates the ballot box, the legislatures, the Congress, and touches even the ermine of the bench. . . . The newspapers are subsidized or muzzled; public opinion silenced; business prostrated, our homes covered with mortgages, labor impoverished, and the land concentrated in the hands of capitalists. . . . The fruits of the toil of millions are boldly stolen to build up colossal fortunes, unprecedented in the history of the world, while their possessors despise the republic and endanger liberty.

Ignatius Donnelly's preamble to the platform of the People's Party, 1892

Jesus was only possible in a barefoot world, and he was crucified by the few who wore shoes.

Ignatius Donnelly

In the mid-1880s the Great Plains suffered a prolonged drought that turned its prairies to dust, a grasshopper plague that devoured every bit of greenery that remained, and a plunge in the price of corn and wheat that left its farmers deeply in debt and without hope for their families. Many gave up and returned east—"In God We Trusted. In Kansas We Busted." Kansas had lost almost 50 percent of its population by the end of the decade. And those who remained were the core of a political rebellion that would rock the nation.

The Kansas–Nebraska insurgents, joined by wretchedly poor and heavily indebted farmers of the South, eventually formed a third-party organization that they called the People's Party. The concept for such a party evolved from a series of meetings in the early 1890s—at Ocala, Cincinnati, St. Louis, Topeka, and finally at Omaha, where they nominated a candidate for the presidential election of 1892. Returning home by train from the Cincinnati convention in May 1891, the Kansas delegates discussed the need for a shorthand label for their movement. Taking the Latin term for "people," *populus*, they invented the name "Populist." And thus was born the political crusade that historians have termed the Populist Revolt.

Modern scholars have been able to draw a portrait of the average Populist voter in Kansas. He lived in the recently settled central part of the state (west of Topeka); he owned only a small plot of land and was likely to be growing corn to feed his family and his livestock. Wealthier farmers in the eastern third of the state grew wheat for the export market, and, along with the urban dwellers (Leavenworth, Kansas City), were more likely to adhere to the traditional Democratic and Republican parties. The Populist voter had mortgaged his farm to buy land and tools, and he faced foreclosure by a bank when his income dwindled in the 1880s. He was minimally educated and, although not fervently religious, biblical images and maxims came readily to his tongue.

William A. Peffer did not fit this portrait at all. He had been well-educated in the East before coming to Kansas; he was trained in the law, edited the state's leading agricultural journal, the *Topeka Kansas Farmer*, and he was a staunch Republican until he experienced a sudden conversion to Populism in 1890. He quickly became a leader of the movement—perhaps because of his gift for literary expression and a deep-rooted sense of social justice. He was not a large man, nor a handsome one. Physically, the only remarkable feature about him was an extraordinary beard that masked his face from ear to ear and cascaded down his chest to his ample waist. Nevertheless, when Populist insurgents won control of the state legislature in 1890, they promptly sent him to the United States Senate. Peffer's political career over the next decade was thus a microcosm of the Populist Revolt.

A Kansas Republican

Evidently of German ancestry (Peffer is "pepper" in Deutsch), Peffer was born in a rural community of Pennsylvania in 1831. He apparently received a good elementary education in Pennsylvania schools (enough to enable him to become a highly literate newspaper editor in later life). As a young adult Peffer farmed in the summer and taught school in the wintertime. After marrying in the early 1850s (his wife, as an individual, never enters the historical record), he moved to Indiana and took up farming. An ardent opponent of slavery, he helped organize the Republican Party in that state. After four years in Indiana he moved west again to Missouri, but finding himself in conflict with his proslavery neighbors, he moved his family back east to Illinois. When the Civil War broke out, he enlisted in an Illinois regiment, which was assigned to Grant's army in Tennessee. He apparently had a clerical position, for there is no record of any battle action, and he found time to study the law. After the fighting ended he opened a law office in Clarksville, Tennessee.

In 1870 he resumed his westward drift, settling in the farming community of Fredonia in southeastern Kansas. There he became interested in journalism and purchased the *Fredonia Journal*. Combining law, journalism, and politics, he was elected to the state senate as a Republican in 1874. Ever since Kansas had become a Republican cause celebre in the 1850s, the party had dominated Kansas politics. It controlled the legislature and the governor's office for two decades after the war. Democrats, bound in a Jacksonian straitjacket of states-rights conservatism, raised their heads only in the towns along the Missouri River and in Texas-influenced Wichita. Even when the national Republican Party began to represent the interests of eastern manufacturers and New York bankers, it never occurred to Kansas farmers through the 1870s and 1880s to vote in any other way.

Peffer deplored his party's coddling of the Vanderbilts and Rockefellers and sought to keep alive the "free labor, free soil" reform tradition of the 1850s. He felt it essential that the people, through their government, harness the revolutionary changes in commerce and industry to ensure the future of American democracy, and he considered the Republican Party the only practical vehicle for such reforms. Given the intellectual fecklessness of the Democrats in Kansas, his hopes were not unreasonable. In 1881 Peffer moved to Topeka to edit the *Kansas Farmer*, the state's leading agricultural journal. He thus became an important spokesman within Republican ranks for the distressed farmers.

Kansas experienced a brief boom time in the early 1880s with good weather and high farm prices. Farmers borrowed money to increase their acreage and equipment, and by the middle of the decade the total private indebtedness was more than double the assessed value of all the property in the state. Then, beginning in 1887, disaster struck. The market price of corn and wheat collapsed, the rains ceased, and land prices plummeted. In many counties farms were mortgaged for more than their market value.

American farmers had long recognized that they were their own worst enemies, in the sense that their competitiveness contributed to their ruin. While eastern capitalists were forming cartels and trusts to reduce competition and manage the markets, farmers competed with one another for ever larger crops, thereby producing more food than the nation could eat and depressing farm prices. In the 1870s midwestern farmers had sought to cooperate with one another through such organizations as the Patrons of Husbandry (the "Grange") and the Northern Alliance.

Although these were primarily morale-building community organizations whose activities often resembled church socials, they did manage to persuade some state legislatures to adopt laws regulating freight and storage rates charged by railroads and grain elevators (popularly known as "Granger laws"). These tentative inroads on laissez-faire were gutted by the Supreme Court in 1886 when the Court prohibited the states from regulating interstate railroads,[1] and farmers were back where they started.

In the hard times of 1888 Kansas farmers turned to a new and more militant farm organization, the Texas-born Southern Alliance, which had gained a voice in Southern legislatures by demanding campaign commitments from politicians on such vital matters as mortgages and credit. In Dallas the Alliance had organized a farmers' co-op cotton exchange, which sought to eliminate the middleman in cotton marketing. Peffer was delighted when the Alliance moved into Kansas and added an "Alliance Department" to the *Kansas Farmer*. He toured the state in company with Southern Alliance officials to win new members. The relationship was far from cozy, however. Alliance leaders had formed a Union Labor Party as a people's alternative to the two-party system, and they were suspicious of Peffer's staunch adherence to the Republican cause.

The Making of an Insurgent

Peffer's faith in Republican-led reform seemed to be vindicated in that election year, 1888. Sensing the mood of rural despair and anxious to thwart the third-party movement, the Republican state convention adopted a platform pledging to reduce legal interest rates, punish usury, enact laws protecting workers, and prohibit the railroads from charging excessive freight rates. Peffer was pleased with this apparent response to the hard times, but he also had great respect for the gubernatorial candidate of the Southern Alliance-backed Union Labor Party. Declaring that "the interests of the people are far above the interests of a party," he advised readers of the *Kansas Farmer* to vote for the best candidate in each county, regardless of political affiliations.

The voters instead bought the Republicans' promises, and in 1888 Kansas became "the banner state" of Republicanism, giving its electoral vote to presidential candidate Benjamin Harrison by a large margin and electing a solidly Republican congressional delegation. Republicans also captured 39 out of 40 seats in the state senate and 121 seats in the 125-member house.

1. *Wabash, St. Louis & Pacific Railway v. Illinois* (1886). The decision prompted Congress to undertake the first federal regulation of railroads in the form of the Interstate Commerce Act of 1887.

And then came the reckoning. As the new legislature assembled in Topeka in January 1889, the Republican-owned *Hutchinson News* claimed editorially that the party platform was only a guide to candidates and was not intended as a blueprint for legislative action. The *Kansas City Gazette* agreed, announcing that the party platform was nothing more than "a little sop thrown to a half dozen who were howling so loud as to make everybody believe the woods were full of howlers." The leading Republican paper, the *Topeka Capital*, predicted that enacting the Republican platform "would put Kansas back seventy-five years." While the Republican press trumpeted the new party line, bankers and loan companies privately worked the legislative halls. The result was that every bill regulating interest rates or deferring the foreclosure on mortgages was silently buried in legislative committees.

Peffer was shocked. He pointed out editorially that the legislature in the past had permitted railroads in financial trouble to reorganize their indebtedness and reduce their interest payments. Why, he demanded, should farmers be refused similar leniency? "Is is not better," he wrote, "that the people have opportunity to save their homes after paying their debts, rather than that they should be turned out homeless? As a matter of public policy, can the State afford to pauperize its own people? Is it not the first duty of the State to protect its own citizens?" What the Republicans' betrayal of their platform proved was not that the political system was unresponsive, but that it was indeed responsive—to special interests that wielded wealth and power. The lesson drawn by Peffer and a growing number of radical farmers was that the system had been stolen from the people. While many joined the rising chorus for a third party that would represent the interests of the people, Peffer continued for the moment to favor more energetic activity by the farm organizations within the old party system. Republican intransigence in the election of 1890 would force him into third-party insurgency.

United States Senator

Abandoning any hope for relief from the Kansas legislature, Peffer turned his attention to Congress as it assembled in Washington, D.C., in December 1889. The root of the nation's distress, he had concluded, was a shortage of money and credit. The nation's money supply had failed to expand as fast as the economy, and that was because the issuance of money—a governmental function in most parts of the world—was in private hands in the United States. Ever since the government had begun redeeming its Civil War paper ("greenbacks") with gold in 1879, greenbacks had become the equivalent of gold and were nearly as scarce. Consequently, the nation's principal circulating medium was the notes issued by national banks, institutions that, though chartered by the government, were privately owned.

Since the amount of paper issued by these bodies depended on the amount of gold and bonds in their vaults, it never quite met the needs of the growing national economy. Through the 1870s and 1880s reformers had advocated various solutions, ranging from the printing of more governmental greenbacks to the unlimited coinage of silver. These proposals continued to echo through the insurgent movement, but in December 1889 Peffer developed a novel approach, which he published in his newspaper as "The Way Out."

Peffer, like other reformers, thought that the government ought to control the printing of money and issue it directly to the people. In order to avoid the use of banks he proposed that farmers be allowed to borrow money from the government on the security of crops stored in warehouses or grain elevators. The government itself would build and maintain the storage facilities, and in addition it would establish loan offices to lend money on the security of real estate. Peffer's program was thus a blend of long-term monetary reform and short-term farm relief.[2] And it was immensely popular. After publishing it serially in the *Kansas Farmer*, he issued it as a booklet in early 1890, and it went through thirteen printings in that one year.

In an attempt to make the rural depression an election issue in 1890, Peffer requested a public statement on money and credit from each of the state's congressmen. When he received only evasive replies, he focused on Senator John J. Ingalls, Kansas's leading Republican. Ingalls was up for reelection in 1891, and his political future thus depended on the composition of the legislature chosen by the voters in 1890. When Ingalls replied to Peffer's initial query that economic distress could not be relieved by legislation, Peffer reaffirmed the insurgent position that legislation was frequently used to relieve those with political power. "The Senator knows," he replied with pen dipped in acid, "that when banks and railroads and classes on the creditor side of the line want legislation, they ask for it and get it." Ingalls haughtily replied that he would respond to Peffer through some medium other than the *Kansas Farmer*.

Ingalls' reply came in the course of a mid-April interview in the *New York World*, and it completed Peffer's drift into political independence. In response to a question about the possibility of political reform, Ingalls replied irritably:

> The purification of politics is an iridescent dream. Government is force. Politics is a battle for supremacy. Parties are the armies. The decalogue and the golden rule have no place in a political campaign. The object is success. To defeat the antagonist and

2. It resonated a half century later in Franklin Roosevelt's Commodity Credit Corporation (1936).

> expel the party in power is the purpose. . . . This modern cant about the corruption of politics is fatiguing in the extreme. It proceeds from the tea-custard and syllabub dilettantism, the frivolous and desultory sentimentalism of epicenes.

Peffer was outraged, for Ingalls' cynical outburst ridiculed his very life; it mocked every reform he had embraced since antislavery. He promptly announced that the *Farmer* would oppose Ingalls in the coming legislative election and support any "competent man upon whom the opposition shall unite." The reelection of Ingalls thus became the central issue in the legislative contest that summer and fall. He personified the old Kansas and the methods and policies of the old parties. Ingalls, Peffer complained, "holds the masses at arm's length and does not enter into the joys and sorrows of the common people." By June the *Kansas Farmer* was calling for "an open rebellion on the part of the masses against existing methods of politicians and party leaders in their treatment of just demands set forth by the people."

Mass meetings became the order of the day, and Peffer's presence was so much in demand that he found himself speaking to two thousand people a day. In May leaders of the Southern Alliance called for a state convention to meet in Topeka on June 12. Delegates from the Southern Alliance made up about half of the Topeka convention; the remainder represented various farmer-benefit groups and the slowly dying Knights of Labor. The convention organized a new political party, using for the first time the name People's Party, and called for another convention in August to nominate candidates for the fall election. The August convention rejected an overture from the Democrats to back joint candidates (a foretaste of the "fusion" issue that would shadow the Populist movement throughout its history), and nominated an independent slate of candidates for the executive and state legislature. Its slate, though dominated by farmers and lawyers, included a woman, a black, a minister, and a school teacher. Peffer refused to become a candidate for governor, but it was generally agreed that he would be the party's choice for U.S. senator if it won control of the legislature.

The great majority of Kansas Populists were, like Peffer, ex-Republicans, which is scarcely surprising in view of that party's history of dominance in the state. Peffer took advantage of this during the fall campaign by appropriating Republican tradition. He likened the new party to the early GOP, the coalition of farmers and workingmen that Lincoln had attracted with his "free soil" rhetoric. Peffer evaded the temperance issue, however, on which Kansas Republicans had thrived for years, and focused intently on the questions of money, credit, and regulation of business. A fellow Populist put it more bluntly: "The issue this year is not whether a man shall be permitted to drink, but whether he shall have a home to go to, drunk or sober."

The 1890 campaign brought to the fore a number of Populist orators who would thereafter be identified with the movement. Among these was Mrs. Mary Elizabeth Lease. Born in Pennsylvania and educated, like Peffer, in eastern schools, she had married a druggist, Charles Lease, and moved to Kansas in the early 1870s. She bore four children, managed the household, and in her spare time studied the law. She was admitted to the bar in 1885 and became one of a small number of female lawyers in the state. She was a Republican until 1888 when she joined the Union Labor Party and began making political speeches. She had a natural talent for public speaking, which catapulted her into prominence as one of the most popular orators of the day. The soon-to-be-famous Republican editor of the *Emporia Gazette*, William Allen White, said he had "never heard a lovelier voice than Mrs. Lease's." He described it as "a golden voice—a deep, rich contralto, a singing voice that had hypnotic qualities." White went on to describe her powers of persuasion: "She put into her oratory something which the printed copies did not reveal. They were dull enough often, but she could recite the multiplication table and set a crowd hooting or hurrahing at her will." In the 1890 campaign Lease decried all "politicians," and especially Senator Ingalls, as hopelessly corrupt. A firebrand who preached revolution, she predicted that Kansas farmers would "win this battle with the ballot if possible, but if not that way, then with the bayonet."[3]

Another individual who emerged as a leader of the insurgents in 1890 was Jeremiah Simpson. Born in New Brunswick, Canada, he had drifted westward, first with his parents, and then on his own. For more than twenty years (except for a brief term of service in an Illinois regiment during the war) he sailed the Great Lakes as cook, sailor, mate, and captain. In the 1870s he moved with his family to southwestern Kansas and invested his savings in land and cattle. A reformer at heart, he was active in the Grange and the Greenback Party. Hard times, climaxing with a winterkill of his entire herd in 1886–1887, sent him actively into politics. He campaigned for a seat in the legislature in 1888 on the Union Labor ticket and lost in that Republican-landslide year.

He was back again in 1890, this time running for a seat in Congress. His opponent was a debonair gentleman, as well as an experienced member of the state legislature, Colonel James R. Hallowell, whom the Republican press had lovingly dubbed "Prince Hal." Hoping to expose the contrast between Hallowell and Simpson, whom the *Topeka Capital* described as "an ignorant, inexperienced lunkhead," Republican leaders proposed a joint debate. Hallowell was given the opening statement and

3. There is, unfortunately, no record that she ever actually made the statement most often attributed to her, advising Kansas farmers "to raise less corn and more hell." But it was certainly within her style, and it was the kind of advice Kansas farmers could understand.

had a grand time poking fun at Simpson's inexperience, which had been limited to service as city marshal in Medicine Lodge, Kansas. Simpson later recalled what happened next:

> When my turn came I tried to get hold of the crowd. I referred to the fact that my opponent was known as a "Prince." Princes, I said, wear silk socks. I dont [*sic*] wear any. The crowd laughed at this but it was not enough and I had to try again. Now, I said, Hal tells you that he is a law maker. That he has been to Topeka and that he has made laws. I am going to show you the kind of laws that Hal makes. Reaching over on the table and picking up a book I opened it and, tapping on the page with my finger, I said, here is one of Hals [*sic*] laws. I find that it is a law to tax dogs, but I see that Hal proposes to charge two dollars for a bitch and only one dollar for a son of a bitch. Now the party I belong to believes in equal and exact justice to all.

Simpson reported that "the crowd roared," and he knew they were with him. Having made the mistake of bringing the two candidates together in the first place, the Republican press compounded the error by chuckling over Simpson's apparent admission that he went without socks. Although Simpson probably meant that he did not wear silk stockings, not that he wore none at all, in that era of populist rhetoric, the label "Sockless Jerry" Simpson was priceless. Before long, the insurgent newspapers were referring to him as the "Sockless Socrates of the Prairie." He won the election and soon became one of the most effective of Populist leaders.

The voter turnout on election day showed the effect of this Populist oratory. The only county in the state with a turnout of less that 50 percent of the eligible voters was metropolitan Wyandotte County (Kansas City, Kansas). The counties that were predominantly rural had turnouts ranging from 75 percent to 80 percent, an extraordinary demonstration of voter interest. The election was a Populist landslide that cut Republican ranks in the legislature nearly in half. The Populists elected ninety-three members and emerged with a nearly two-to-one majority in the lower house of the assembly. They also sent five candidates to the United States House of Representatives. It was a sign of future trouble, however, that they won only one statewide election, the attorney general, and that because their candidate had the full backing of the Democrats.

Although the Populists came to Topeka on the opening of the legislative session in January 1891 with a full-blown agenda, the main order of business was the election of a U.S. senator. Despite the Populist majority, the choice of Peffer was not automatic. Republicans retained control of the senate, whose members served longer terms than the lower house, and they sought to play upon the fissures among their opponents. Democrats and some Populists mistrusted Peffer for his Republican antecedents and last-minute conversion, and old-time Southern Alliance men had candidates of their own. However, Peffer's endorsement by the Topeka convention and the popular influence of the *Kansas Farmer* proved decisive. Populist ranks closed in the face of Republican intrigues, and Peffer was elected by a nearly two-to-one majority.

Election to the United States Senate thrust Peffer onto the national stage and gave him a new forum for his plans for political and economic reform. The *Philadelphia Evening Bulletin* summarized the feelings of many: "There has been no senatorial election this winter which has attracted more attention than the one which has just been decided in Kansas. . . . Whether Peffer is a cunning demagogue or whether he is an honest dreamer remains to be seen, but his election to the senate is one of the most curious results of the political upheaval of 1890s."

Birth of the People's Party

The movement for a national third party proceeded by fits and starts. In December 1890 delegates of the Southern Alliance and some of its allies met in Ocala, Florida, to discuss the matter. They soon found themselves divided. The Kansas delegates wanted a formal third party modeled on the highly successful Kansas People's Party. Southerners preferred to reform the Southern Democratic Party from within. They would use the "Alliance yardstick," by which candidates of the Democratic Party (Republicans having all but vanished in the South) would be measured by their compliance with rural demands. The convention managed only to adopt a "platform" for a future party. A distillation of earlier Alliance "platforms," the document called for a federal "subtreasury" (low-cost government loans on security of stored crops), stronger government regulation of railroads and telegraphs, the popular election of United States senators, and a graduated income tax. In order to "educate" the public and counter the growing Republican caricature of Populism, the convention decided that paid lecturers be sent into every congressional district in the course of 1891. After the convention broke up Alliance leaders, in part to appease the third-party advocates in Kansas and Nebraska and in part to buy time for themselves, proposed an "Industrial Conference" to meet in St. Louis a year hence, on Washington's birthday, February 22, 1892.

By the end of January 1891 the Northern Alliance, the Colored Farmers' Alliance (made up of black cotton growers excluded from the Southern Alliance), and the increasingly irrelevant Knights of Labor endorsed the Ocala platform. But no one was willing to beard the Southern Alliance on its sometimes successful "yardstick" strategy. In February the frustrated Kansans issued a call for a convention to meet in May in Cincinnati to form a new farmer-labor party.

On May 18, 1891, the *Cincinnati Enquirer* carried a banner headline heralding the arrival of "THE GREAT INDUSTRIAL ARMY." As conventions went in those days it was army-sized—1,443 delegates, nearly all self-appointed and thus highly motivated. Most of the delegates represented farm organizations in the Midwest (411 from Kansas alone), and there was the usual periphery of reformers: socialists, single-taxers, prohibitionists, and women suffragists. Only about forty Southerners made an appearance, nearly all of them Texans.

Senator Peffer, elected chair of the convention, allowed both the prohibitionist leader and the suffragettes to address the meeting. The women won a minor victory when the convention passed a resolution in favor of universal suffrage, but it refused to be deflected down the temperance road. The prohibition leader, an ex-Republican governor of Kansas, left the city grumbling that the convention had simply given birth to a "third whisky party." In fact, it did not accomplish even that. It endorsed the principles of the Ocala platform, but without sufficient Southern representation it could take no further steps toward party organization. It left town after establishing a provisional executive committee and instructed it to attend the Alliance-summoned convention in St. Louis the following February.

Alliance leaders had delayed the third-party movement because they were unsure of their popular support. Peffer decided to use the time to arouse the people and force their hand. Upon returning home from Cincinnati he and Kansas activists began organizing camp meetings modeled on those that Methodists and Baptists had used in turning the Midwest into a "Bible Belt." The meetings featured songs and prayers and, above all, lectures on the aims of the Populist movement. The idea was to build a social base for the new political party. That was not difficult in Kansas where the People's Party had already demonstrated its brawn; it was the South where the camp-meeting tactic would make a difference. In midsummer Peffer, accompanied by a rotating band of third-party advocates, toured the South, from West Virginia to Texas.

These meetings promoted political radicalism—calls for government ownership of railroads and utilities—with the techniques of the camp revival. Biblical images were ever-present, for church-going farmers could easily relate to Jesus's ministry to the poor, his wrathful eviction of money-changers from the temple, and the promise of a coming kingdom of God. One Populist orator went so far as to proclaim that "Christ himself was the author and president of the first Farmers' Alliance." The success of these orchestrated camp meetings would become evident at the St. Louis convention the following winter.

In the meantime, the road to a third party remained bumpy. Returning from Texas in August 1891, Peffer took his road show to Iowa. Iowa's corn-growing farmers were as distressed as their neighbors in Kansas and Nebraska, but they showed little enthusiasm for a third party. Peffer and other Populists were mystified by this, but a modern researcher has suggested that the reason was Iowa's viable two-party system. Unlike Kansas and Nebraska where the Republican Party felt so comfortable in its dominance that it could ignore the pleas of the oppressed, Democrats and Republicans competed for farm votes in Iowa. As a result the state legislature had enacted mortgage relief legislation and "the best railroad law in the Union." Iowa farmers were thus content with a two-party system that seemed to work. James B. Weaver, the leading advocate in Iowa for a third party—and the Populist candidate for president in 1892—had little standing in his own state. In the final week of his tour, Peffer even brought out Mary E. Lease, and when she proved ineffective, the Kansans returned home.

He met similar frustration when he journeyed to Washington in December for the opening session of the Congress that had been elected in 1890. Voters in Kansas, Nebraska, and Colorado had elected eight Populist congressmen in 1890, and there were eighteen Southern Democrats pledged to the Alliance "yardstick." However, when Congress opened seventeen of the Southerners trooped off to join the Democratic Party caucus. Only one Southerner, Tom Watson of Georgia, joined the eight westerners in Senator Peffer's rooms to hold the first congressional caucus of the People's Party.

Thereafter Peffer took the lead in introducing the People's Party's reforms, most of which came right out of the Alliance platform. He introduced bills embodying the land-loan principle and resolutions (the prelude to a bill) to restrict speculation in the stock market, prohibit the formation of trusts, authorize the government to print paper money, establish a bureau of irrigation, and increase popular participation in the party nominating system. None of these measures stood a chance in the Senate, and when introduced into the House by Kansas congressmen, the Alliance-pledged Southerners showed their true colors by voting against them. The effect was to expose the fatal weakness of the Alliance "yardstick." Watson and his Southern allies were thus prepared to join the third-party movement when the long-awaited St. Louis convention met on February 22, 1892.

If size alone is the measure of a movement, the St. Louis meeting was a watershed in Populism, as 10,000 men and women converged on the city—factory workers, farmers, and reformers of every stripe, from temperance advocates to suffragists to Christian Socialists working the urban ghettoes. They overflowed the city's Exposition Hall and packed the streets and sidewalks for blocks around. Tension and purpose filled the air. As a sympathetic reporter for the *St. Louis Post-Dispatch* wrote, "Every man who sat in Exposition Hall as a delegate . . . believed in his soul that he sat there as a history-maker."

The climax came on the third day when Ignatius Donnelly, a sixty-one-year-old veteran of agrarian and monetary crusades, read a preamble to the platform that summarized Populist thinking. He reviewed the "moral and political ruin" of the nation and evoked the moral outrage of rural and working-class Americans at the condition of the country. He predicted that the popular majority would challenge the corporations and their upper-class owners and subject them to popular control through the proper use of government. To fuse the two halves of this new majority, he intoned: "The interests of rural and urban labor are the same; their enemies are identical." When Donnelly sat down, the chair of the platform committee read the short list of demands that had been evolving since the Ocala meeting: government ownership of railroads and telegraphs (an advance over the previous call for government regulation), the unlimited coinage of both gold and silver (a new emphasis on coinage), a graduated income tax, and the prohibition of monopolies. When he finished, the huge crowd exploded. A sympathetic journalist described the scene: "Hats, papers, handkerchiefs, etc., were thrown into the air; wraps, umbrellas, and parasols waved; cheer after cheer thundered and reverberated through the vast hall, reaching the outside of the building where thousands had been waiting the outcome, joined in the applause till for blocks in every direction the exultation made the din indescribable."

Its "yardstick" tactic in ruins, the Southern Alliance joined the third-party movement, and the convention set up a committee to coordinate efforts with the executive committee that had been formed at Cincinnati. The joint committee then issued a call for a national nominating convention to meet in Omaha on the Fourth of July. Unlike previous conventions where delegates were largely self-annointed, delegates to the Omaha convention would be chosen through a progression of county and state meetings. Populist leaders thus sought to create, in the months before the 1892 presidential election, a national organization modeled on that of the existing parties.

Election of 1892

In Kansas, where the Populists already had strong local organizations, the principal issue in the summer of 1892 was the question of fusion with the Democrats. A hopeless minority in the state for decades, Democrats eagerly sought joint candidates for office. Peffer just as adamantly opposed the idea. No Democrat, he pointed out, had endorsed a single Populist reform; their desire for fusion was strictly a gambit to gain political power. Moreover, he argued, fusion with Democrats in Kansas would amount to a betrayal of the Alliance supporters in the South, who had at last seen the folly of working with Democrats and were committed to an independent third party. Most Populists accepted Peffer's advice and refused to join hands with Democrats. The exception was the southwestern portion of the state where Democrats were more numerous and Congressman Simpson was more politically flexible. After being nominated for a second term by a Populist meeting in Wichita, Simpson accepted the nomination of the district's Democrats.

By setting a convention date of July 4 the Populists seemed to be giving the two major parties, each of which had scheduled a convention in June, a chance to bow to the People's Party's reforms under the pressure of the third-party threat. However, to an anti-fusionist like Peffer the sequence of conventions would have meant little, for he expected nothing from the major parties. And that, essentially, is what he got. The Republicans, convening on June 7, renominated Benjamin Harrison, even though, as president, he had proved to be too honest and independent to suit the party's bosses. The Democrats, meeting in Chicago on June 22, spurned demands to incorporate Populist principles in their platform and proceeded to nominate ex-President Grover Cleveland, who had alienated both the South and the West in the mid-1880s by a rigid adherence to the gold standard and Wall Street interests. The major parties thus left to the Populists the entire reform agenda.

The Populist road nevertheless remained rocky. On June 11 Southern Alliance president Leonidas L. Polk died of cancer, thus depriving the party of its best bridge between North and South, as well as one of its most eloquent spokesmen. Neither Peffer nor any Populist congressman attended the Omaha convention because there was important legislation pending in Congress. But they were not wanted in any case. Showing its disdain for politicians, the convention adopted a unique "Ordinance for the Purification of Politics," which made anyone holding federal, state, or municipal office ineligible "to sit or vote in any convention of this party." This was a people's party, not one for the politicians.

Although Peffer's name was mentioned as a potential candidate for president, he firmly declined to run, citing delicate health and his importance to the party as a U.S. senator. The convention eventually settled on James B. Weaver of Iowa and, as a sop to the South, chose a Virginian as his running mate. The party platform occupied the most attention, for it was the essence of the movement. It began with the apocalyptic preamble drafted by Donnelly at St. Louis. It then waded into the crucial problem of money and credit. Fine-tuning earlier Populist "platforms," it demanded that the government issue money and distribute it to the people without the use of banks, through a subtreasury or similar credit agency. It further demanded "the free and unlimited coinage of silver and gold at the present legal ratio of sixteen to one," which would further increase the supply of money. An incidental result was that it would also increase the demand, and hence the price, for precious metals in the mining states of the West, and that was expected to strengthen the hand of the Populists in the mountain states. Although Populists had not yet realized it, "free silver" would become "the cow bird in the nest" that robbed the movement of much of its reform energy. The Omaha platform also recommended a graduated income tax and federal postal savings banks.

Adopting the radical position of the St. Louis convention on corporations that served the public, the platform demanded government ownership of railroads, telegraph, and telephone systems. Appended to the platform were ten resolutions that provided a blueprint for later twentieth century reformers: the adoption of the secret ballot, protection of labor's right to form unions and go on strike, and denunciation of business corporations' use of private armies to suppress strikes.

As historian Robert C. McMath has observed, it is likely that no candidate short of George Washington could have produced a Populist victory in 1892, but Weaver was a singularly poor choice. He had first run for president in 1880 as the candidate of the Greenback Party, and he had since appeared to make himself available to every third-party panacea that came along. It was never clear whether he was driven by ideals or personal ego. His running mate was little known even in his home state of Virginia and had no discernible connection to the Populist movement. In addition, the Populists, having entered the partisan fray, had to withstand the steel-jacketed shots of professionals, who caricatured them as ignorant hayseeds led by wild-eyed firebrands. Peffer's beard, Simpson's sockless feet, and Mrs. Lease's sharp tongue came in for particular attention. In the western plains Republicans portrayed them as dupes of the Democrats and predicted that "a vote for Weaver is a vote for the solid south." In the South the Populist emphasis on class solidarity allowed the Democrats to accuse them of courting black voters. Populist leaders countered rather lamely by distinguishing between black political rights, which they had initially supported, and social equality between the races, which they adamantly opposed.

While Cleveland and Harrison adhered to tradition and declined to campaign in person, Weaver toured the West and the South, accompanied by his wife, Clara, Mary E. Lease, and other Populist orators. He was greeted by enthusiastic crowds in the West, but he made little headway in the South where Democrats heckled him for his war record as a Union general. Peffer, still in ill health, focused much of his speaking energies on Kansas. More than any other Populist orator Peffer reminded voters of the party's ideological origins. He warned against an overemphasis on silver coinage as a panacea, and he even argued—a half-century ahead of his time—that money did not require a metallic basis in order to be acceptable. Although he continued to denounce fusion, he could not prevent the Democrats from supporting the Populist candidate for governor, Lorenzo D. Lewelling, a Wichita produce dealer.

In the presidential contest Cleveland swept the South and regained the White House. The Southern Alliance had failed to convince the great mass of poor white farmers that their interests lay with the Populists, rather than the Democrats. Weaver had no charismatic appeal, and the Populists' half-hearted courtship of blacks produced more white backlash than black votes. Weaver fared better in the West where he carried Kansas, Colorado, Nevada, and Idaho, winning a total of twenty-two electoral votes—the most obtained by any third party since the Civil War. Lewelling won the governorship in Kansas, and a Populist governor was elected in Colorado. Populists also won legislative majorities in Kansas, Nebraska, and South Dakota, and in subsequent elections Peffer was joined in the Senate by William V. Allen of Nebraska and James H. Kyle of South Dakota.

The result of the elections to the U.S. House of Representatives was both mixed and portentous. Populists increased their number from eight to eleven—five from Kansas, two from Nebraska, two from Colorado, and one each from Minnesota and California. The perfidious Alliance Democrats from the South lost their seats, as did loyalist Tom Watson. The election of unalloyed Democrats in the South enabled that party to obtain firm control of the House, with a slim majority in the Senate. But the effect on Populism was devastating. Southern Populists, including Tom Watson, concluded that they had no future in their states without fusion with the Democrats. Lacking strong support in the South, western Populists began to wonder if fusion was not the only recourse for the national People's Party. Already, five of their eleven congressmen were Populist/Democrats. Before long, William A. Peffer stood nearly alone in his ideological purity.

Response to Depression

On May 1, 1893, newly inaugurated President Grover Cleveland pressed a button that turned on the ten thousand lights of Chicago's "White City" on the shore of Lake Michigan, a Columbian exposition that marked four hundred years since the discovery of America. The exposition, a blend of technological marvels and the latest urban landscape planning, was meant to celebrate the bright promise of America's future. Four days after Cleveland opened the exposition the stock market crashed, and the hard times that western farmers had been enduring for five years struck the industrial East. By the end of the year, fifteen thousand businesses had failed, and within another year unemployment approached 20 percent of the labor force. It was the worst depression of the century.

Cleveland, a classic Bourbon (after the French royal family that never forgot the past and never learned from it), had not the least idea how to respond to the depression. When the price of wheat in Kansas fell below the cost of growing it, Cleveland's secretary of agriculture lectured farmers: "The intelligent, practical, and successful farmer needs no aid from the government. The ignorant, impractical, and indolent farmer deserves none." With the government's tax receipts declining and the wealthy hoarding gold, Cleveland's only thought was for preservation of the gold standard. In the summer of 1893 he summoned a special session of Congress to repeal the Sherman Silver Purchase Act of 1890.

The Silver Purchase Act, a concession to Western mining interests, authorized the government to mint into coin the average annual output of the Western silver mines. Adhering to the gold standard, the Harrison administration made the silver coins exchangeable for gold (as the government had done with greenbacks in 1879) at a fixed ratio. Silver was a commodity like any other, and its price declined with the depression. Bankers and wealthy people thus found it quite profitable to exchange their silver coins for the government's gold. As the supply of gold in the treasury vaults dwindled, Cleveland feared for the stability of the entire monetary system. Hence his call for the repeal of the Silver Purchase Act.

Throughout the 1880s western silver interests—and the people who worked the mines—had called for "the free and unlimited coinage of silver at the ratio of sixteen to one" (a ratio of the difference in value between silver and gold that had existed since the beginning of government coinage in the 1790s). The Populists had picked up the slogan because it was one way of increasing the money supply, but "free silver" was only one plank in their platform, and a relatively minor one at that. Cleveland's call for repeal of the Silver Purchase Act divided the Democratic Party, and the ensuing debate in Congress focused national attention on the silver issue. Although Cleveland eventually secured his repeal, with the help of Republicans and "Gold Democrats," Populists and "Silver Democrats" found themselves working together. It was the first time any portion of the Democratic Party had agreed with the Populists on a major issue, and it paved the way for future collaboration.

Although Populists in Congress voted with the Democrats on the free silver issue, they were not distracted from considering more serious responses to the depression. In 1894 Kansas Congressman John Davis picked up on "General" Coxey's cure for unemployment and introduced a bill for a federal public works program. In the Senate, Peffer introduced a bill to provide $63 million to be dispensed to the states for relief to the unemployed. He proposed to fund it by using the silver dollars "lying idle in the Treasury," which New York bankers had traded in for gold. Anticipating the familiar argument that Congress lacked the constitutional power to aid segments of the population (as opposed to laws passed for the "general welfare"), he had the Senate documents clerk prepare a list of cases in which Congress had come to the aid of destitute citizens. When opponents pointed out that such "relief" measures were solely the province of the states, Peffer replied, "The time is coming . . . when for all such purposes as this state lines must be utterly abolished." Peffer and other Populists were thus the first to advance the idea—accepted by both major parties in the course of the next century—that government has a role to play in cushioning the effect of an economic collapse and in attempting to restore and maintain prosperity.

Unfortunately the high ground occupied by Peffer and the Kansas congressmen was undermined by a comic-opera "legislative war" in Kansas. While the Populists and Democrats had firm control of the state senate, the lower house was evenly divided. At the opening of the 1893 session Populists and Republicans each sought to organize the House and elect a speaker. The result was bedlam as two speakers occupied the rostrum and each side tried to out-shout the other. A temporary truce was arranged by which Republicans occupied the legislative chamber in the mornings and Populists in the afternoons. Republicans broke that arrangement by invading the House in the afternoon. Governor Lewelling retaliated by ordering the militia to oust the Republicans, but the commander, a Republican, turned his guns on the Populists instead. Bloodshed was averted through a compromise that left Republicans in control of the House. The state's predominantly Republican newspapers provided a well-slanted version of the story, and it reinforced the eastern vision of the Populists as wild men. An Ohio congressman proposed that no new western states be admitted to the Union until Kansas had been "civilized." In New York City a brash young police commissioner named Theodore Roosevelt suggested that the Populist disturbance could best be quelled by "taking ten or a dozen of their leaders out, standing them against a wall, and shooting them dead."

Free Silver, Fusion, and the Election of 1896

Utterly demoralized, Kansas Populists gave more thought to fusion with the Democrats as the off-year 1894 congressional and state elections approached. Indeed, a faction of the party—perhaps a majority—favored downplaying the Omaha platform and focusing on free silver as an enticement to the Democrats. The Kansas Democrats, overly confident with one of their own in the White House, rejected the Populist overtures, and in the summer of 1894 they nominated straight tickets for both Congress and the assembly. The Democrats fatally misjudged the popular mood nationally, which blamed Cleveland for the depression, and the congressional election that year was a Republican landslide. Even Democrats critical of Cleveland went down to defeat, in what one Democratic leader grumbled was "the greatest slaughter of innocents since Herod." The Republicans' takeover of Congress inaugurated an eighteen-year period of Republican ascendancy in national councils.

In Kansas the debacle was complete. The Republicans captured the governorship, the lower house, and the congressional delegation. Every Populist congressman but one went down to defeat. One Democratic newspaper chortled that "those Populists who told us that they could carry Kansas without the aid of the despised Democrats need not feel so sore about the results. They still have the state senate and . . . Peffer." In fact, fusion would not have helped in that Republican year, for the Republican vote exceeded that of the Populists and Democrats combined. Both of the defeated parties were severely chastened. Populist defections since 1892 had been, for the most part, ex-Republicans who returned to the GOP, and that trend accelerated. The party after 1894 was made up principally of ex-Democrats. Led by Jerry Simpson and Lorenzo Lewelling, they favored fusion, even if the only common ground was free silver. And that, of course, meant, as Peffer's biographer Peter Argersinger has written, "Populism in its original form, creative nature, and radical motivation was dead. . . . Dependent now upon those who cared little for it, Populism threatened to become only an adjunct to the Democratic Party, united on an issue of little basic importance to the party's creed in order to sustain a political life. Populism, as Kansas had known it in the days of its Pentecostal fervor to remake society, was no more."

Well aware of the drift of his party, Peffer ceased attending conferences of Populist politicians and confined his activities in Kansas to dire warnings against fusion. He directed his attention instead to the national level and labored single-handedly to help Congress see the need for political and economic reform. Noting "the mass of Pefferian bills which daily fall into the hopper" in 1894, one Washington journalist commented that "the fecundity of Senator Peffer in the matter of introducing bills has passed into a proverb." The Republican *Harper's Weekly* complained that Peffer "serves as a patient channel for the interjection into the Senate of impossible theories of legislation and barren ideas of finance." The magazine added, however, that "he is sincere and honest in his views." Another reporter observed that Peffer "seems to have won the respect and esteem of his colleagues, and to have convinced them that he represents a high standard of citizenship."

As the election of 1896 approached, the rift in Populist ranks produced a debate over the timing of the party's nominating convention. Peffer and other purists favored an early convention, prior to the meetings of Democrats and Republicans. This, Peffer felt, was more likely to produce an independent ticket, and if fusion with Democrats ultimately resulted, it would be on Populist terms. He was outvoted, however. Eleven of the thirteen Populist members of Congress favored creating an alliance with the Silver Democrats, and the Populist leadership set a date of July 22 for a convention to meet in St. Louis. "The People's Party is in more danger from professed silver friends than from any other source," Peffer wrote resignedly in the *Topeka Advocate*.

The result is a familiar story. The Republicans nominated William McKinley and campaigned on the gold standard. The Democrats turned to free silver advocate William Jennings Bryan, who had been campaigning for the party nomination for two years. As if to emphasize that free silver was their only bond with the Populists, the Democrats nominated as Bryan's running mate Arthur Sewall, a banker, shipbuilder, and railroad executive from Maine.

The nomination of Bryan put Peffer in a difficult position. In an editorial entitled "Present Duty of Populists" he noted that the Democrats had partially "espoused the people's side" by calling for an end to national bank notes and a graduated income tax in addition to free silver. He noted also that the Populists' primary responsibility was to defeat McKinley because a Republican victory would mean "class rule, oppression of the poor—debt, poverty, perpetual enslavement of the masses." Peffer nevertheless refused to support the nomination of Bryan by the People's Party, and he insisted that the party adhere to the Omaha platform.

By the time he arrived in St. Louis on July 18, four days before the convention was to open, Peffer had further modified his stance. He still demanded that the party reaffirm the Omaha platform and nominate an independent candidate for president, but he suggested that a fusion ticket could be put together after the election—and presumably before the meeting of the electoral college. The delegates that assembled in St. Louis were deeply divided, with a slight majority in favor of fusion. The convention accordingly nominated Bryan but insisted on an independent candidate for vice president, Tom Watson of Georgia. To maintain a semblance of principle it adopted the Omaha platform with an additional plank calling for a national public works program. The compromises pleased no one, and the delegates headed for home exhausted and unhappy.

The Populists' mood darkened further when Bryan refused to acknowledge the Populist nomination and ignored the Omaha platform in the campaign. Rejecting Populist pleas for genuine fusion, the Democratic national chairman bluntly stated that Sewell would remain on the ticket and the Populists "could go with the Negroes where they belong." Without funds or a national organization, the Populists were a decidedly junior partner in the free silver campaign of 1896.

Taking no notice of the Populists, McKinley and Bryan battled it out in a closely contested race that centered on the industrial states of the upper Midwest. McKinley, with a well-organized and lavishly financed campaign, won the election.

In Kansas, where Populists were relatively strong and Democrats still weak, fusion worked perhaps better than anywhere else. A Populist convention in Abilene followed the earlier suggestion of Peffer by establishing a Bryan-Watson ticket that listed the names of the same electors as those on the Bryan-Sewell ticket. The Democrats, in turn, promised to vote for Watson in the electoral college if he received more votes than Sewell in Kansas. There was similar cooperation on the nominees for state offices. The Populist nominee for governor was an ex-Democrat who had favored fusion since 1892. The Democrats, in turn, accepted Populist nominees for assembly seats. Peffer refused to endorse any candidate, but he also carefully avoided any statement that might create discord within the Populist-Democratic ranks. Most of his campaigning was done outside the state. Although Bryan got a scant 51 percent of the popular vote in Kansas, the fusionists elected a governor, obtained a majority in the legislature, and elected six congressmen. The election in Kansas thus enabled some Populists to cling to power for a few more years, but it spelled the end of the party as an organization. And with Democrats in control of the legislature Peffer, whose term expired in 1897, was doomed.

Twilight

With the legislature scheduled to meet in January 1897, the wolves began to gather. Peffer no longer had a base of support, and critics charged him with neglecting Kansas during the campaign. Lewelling and other "Popocrats" who eyed his seat set up campaign offices in Topeka in November and December. Adhering to the early-Populist rule that "the office should seek the man," Peffer departed for Washington to attend the winter session of Congress and refused to make any personal appeal for reelection. In December he sent a circular letter to legislators reminding them of his experience and promising to "keep faith with the people," but that was his only concession to playing the political game. More active electioneering would probably not have succeeded in any case. When the legislature voted on January 19, Peffer received only 24 of 102 votes. The majority then selected William A. Harris, a one-time-Democrat-turned Populist-turned-fusionist. Peffer represented the spirit and ideals of the old Populism; Harris embodied the new order.

In January 1898 Peffer published an essay, "The Passing of the People's Party," in the *North American Review*. The People's Party had passed into history, he wrote, because it had been absorbed by the Democrats. There was no better example than "Sockless Jerry" Simpson's application for membership on the Democratic National Committee. Later that year Peffer agreed to run for governor as a candidate of the Prohibition Party, though he insisted on running as a private citizen and not a member of the party. But that quixotic candidacy only underscored his isolation. If he was to remain active politically he really had nowhere to go but to return to the Republican Party. To become a Democrat was to concede the viability of fusion. In the election of 1900 he campaigned for McKinley under the auspices of the Republican National Committee. Whether he saw in the Republicans a glimmer of approaching Progressivism—the La Follette insurgency in Wisconsin, for instance—we can never know. It seems unlikely, for if he had, he surely would have said so. The switch instead reeks of desperation.

Even so, Peffer thought he had the last laugh. In 1907, after the Supreme Court had at last enforced the Sherman Antitrust Act by breaking up a railroad monopoly put together by J. P. Morgan (Northern Securities Case, 1904) and Congress had put some teeth into railroad regulation with the Hepburn Act (1906), Peffer gleefully noted that the principles he had championed as a Populist, which were "laughed to death at that time are now considered respectable." He added, "the country now hotly demands legislation it abused me for advocating." He even had praise for Theodore Roosevelt, who had vilified him in the 1890s as an "anarchistic crank," believing that the president was "applying the principles of Populism."

Although Peffer's attempt to link Populism with post-1900 Progressive reforms was quite understandable, it was not entirely accurate. Progressives had a different popular base. They were strongest in the Midwest and on the East and West coasts, weakest in the High Plains and the South. They were middle class and concerned more about the purity of food than the price of farm products. Where Peffer's brand of Populism went to the very structure of American society, Progressives were content to tinker with the system, seeking to ensure that corporate wealth not abuse its power and that competition remain relatively free. Nevertheless, Populism, by its penetrating critique of American society, laid the foundation for twentieth-century liberal reform. Peffer was right about that.

Suggested Reading

The best studies of the Populist movement are by Robert C. McMath Jr., *Populist Vanguard* (1975) and *American Populism: A Social History, 1877-1898* (1993). Although it precedes these studies, Peter H. Argersinger's fine biography, *Populism and Populists: William Alfred Peffer and the People's Party* (1974), anticipated and, in part, shaped all later scholarship. Jeffrey Ostler, *Prairie Populism: The Fate of Agrarian Radicalism in Kansas, Nebraska, and Iowa* (1993), goes a long way toward explaining why Populism was confined to the Great Plains and made little headway in the Midwest. Gene Clanton, whose earlier *Kansas Populism* (1969) was a pioneering study, provides an interesting synthesis (though still with emphasis on Kansas) in *Populism: The Humane Preference in America, 1890–1900* (1991). Clanton has recently enlarged our knowledge of the national party in *Congressional Populism and the Crisis of the 1890s* (1998). Michael Kazin, *The Populist Persuasion: An American History* (1995), adds little to our understanding of 1890s Populism, but it is a judicious analysis of twentieth-century movements that have been labeled "populist," from Huey Long to Ronald Reagan.

PART II

Architects of Empire

Take up the White Man's burden—
        Send forth the best ye breed—
Go, bind your sons to exile
        To serve your captives' need;
        . . . .
By all ye cry or whisper,
        By all ye leave or do,
The silent, sullen peoples
        Shall weigh your Gods and you.
Take up the White Man's burden—
        And reap his old reward:
The blame of those ye better,
        The hate of those ye guard.

Rudyard Kipling, *The White Man's Burden*,
a plea for American annexation of the Philippines, 1899.

5

Alfred Thayer Mahan: Apostle of Sea Power

A slow-moving revolution in naval technology reached an early, and stunning, climax in 1859 when the first ironclad warship, *La Gloire*, slid down a French quay into the sea. Designed by the celebrated French naval engineer Dupuy de Lome, the vessel was encased from bow to stern in iron sheathing four inches thick, backed by seventeen inches of teak and oak. Although equipped with an auxiliary sailing rig, *La Gloire* was principally powered by powerful and dependable steam engines. The epitome in warship design, the vessel was immune to any gunfire then known, faster than any other steamship, and had a longer cruising range. *La Gloire* created a sensation among the naval ministries of the world, and no one was more horrified than the British Admiralty in London, which for two centuries had claimed supremacy on the high seas. The Admiralty immediately placed an order for an all-iron vessel, and within two years HMS *Warrior* was put to sea for trials. Built entirely of iron, with reinforced armor covering the "vital" portions of her hull, the *Warrior* was the progenitor of all modern fighting ships.

The revolution in ship design had been in progress for more than two decades, spearheaded by commercial, rather than military, competition. The steamboat, invented by Robert Fulton in 1807, was initially used on American rivers. The first steam crossing of the Atlantic was in 1820, and regular transatlantic steam navigation began in 1839 when parliament granted Samuel Cunard an annual subsidy to carry the mails from Liverpool to Halifax and Boston. The screw propeller began to replace the paddlewheel in the 1840s, and it was one of the few innovations to be quickly adopted by the Royal Navy, which resisted change because of its huge investment in wooden sailing ships. British admirals used steam engines only as auxiliaries on their sailing ships, but they readily embraced the screw propeller because paddlewheels were easily damaged by gunfire. Iron plating was also developed by commercial carriers in the 1840s because it improved speed and lessened maintenance. The first iron screw steamship arrived on the transatlantic passenger run in 1850.

During the Crimean War (1854–1856) Britain and France (momentarily allied against Russia) experimented with ironclad rafts mounted with cannon. The iron sheet was laid flat on the deck, though some was used on the turret protecting the cannon. The rafts, called monitors, worked well enough in the sheltered waters of the Black Sea but were clearly not fit for oceanic duty. In the course of the decade the use of iron sheathing and the development of breach-loading artillery with explosive shells went hand-in-hand, cresting with the launchings of *La Gloire* and HMS *Warrior*. Thereafter the competition in ship design escalated, culminating in the 1880s with the development of the modern battleship, or Dreadnought in English parlance.

The United States Navy lagged far behind in this technological revolution, in part because of its philosophy of naval warfare. America's experience with privateers in the War of 1812 and the success of Confederate raiders in the Civil War reinforced a strategy known as *guerre de course*, a war against commerce. Naval officers and their civilian superiors thought that, in time of war, the United States must rely principally on fast, independently operated cruisers that would prey on enemy merchant vessels. The cruisers were not to contest for mastery of the seas and were to avoid an action against equal or superior forces. The corollary was a "brown water navy" (or "smooth water navy") that protected the nation's harbors and shoreline in tandem with coastal fortifications and shore guns. This strategy was further dictated by niggardly appropriations for the armed forces in the years after the Civil War. Construction of a "blue water navy" capable of meeting enemy fleets in battle on the high seas would have been horrendously expensive. No American politician even contemplated it.

There were, however, subtle differences between the two political parties on naval matters. Republicans generally favored naval appropriations, in large measure because naval officers, when they did venture onto the high seas, protected American merchant vessels and (in South America and the Pacific) helped open political doors to American traders. Democrats, rooted in the South and in rural America, saw little need for a navy and generally opposed all shipbuilding schemes. By the 1880s, however, even Democrats were beginning to share in the national embarrassment over its fleet of leaky wooden hulks, with broken-down engines and tattered sails. Among naval powers of the world, the United States ranked below Chile.

The seeds of the "New Navy" were planted in 1883, during the presidency of Republican Chester A. Arthur, when a sympathetic House Naval Affairs Committee authorized the construction of four speedy, steel-hulled cruisers. To appease congressmen who remained hostile to a navy, the new vessels were designed to operate as commerce destroyers in time of war and to promote the nation's trade and moral influence in time of peace. The chair of the House committee felt that there was "immense moral power in a 15-knot ship" and that the United States needed "all the moral power which can be crowded into iron and steel." Although built entirely of steel, the four vessels would be classed as "protected cruisers," that is only the engines and boilers were protected by armored plate. The hulls and gun housings were made of easily pierced two-inch steel. Although they contained masts for auxiliary sails (essential in the Pacific where coal was scarce), the superstructure of the new ships was lower, less cluttered, and more sleekly modern. In keeping with the theme of modernity the Navy Department abandoned its practice of conferring Indian names on its warships ("mere aggregations of harsh consonants and sickening vowels," grumbled one newspaper), and instead named the new cruisers after American cities—the *Atlanta*, *Boston*, *Chicago*, and *Dolphin*. It went without saying that the appeal to urban pride curried favor with voter-taxpayers. Conceived in the context of the old navy's *guerre de course*, the so-called ABC cruisers were the first step toward a blue-water *guerre d'escadre*, a navy capable of fighting fleet-sized battles on the high seas.

Popular enthusiasm for the ABCs fueled bipartisan political support for the "New Navy." Although Grover Cleveland's election to the presidency in 1884 brought the Democrats into power in Washington, his secretary of the Navy, New York businessman William C. Whitney, was a firm advocate of shipbuilding. In 1885 he obtained congressional authorization to build another "protected cruiser," the *Baltimore*, similar in size to the *Chicago* but much faster. The following year he took another step toward a New Navy, obtaining authorization for two fully armored cruisers, the *Texas* and the *Maine*. In conferring the names of states on these vessels the navy tacitly recognized that they were comparable to the newly developed European battleships. Indeed, when they were launched in 1893 the two were reclassified as second-class battleships, and the navy retained the tradition of conferring state names on battleships until the last ones (the *Iowa*, *Missouri*, and *Wisconsin*) were launched during World War II.

All of these vessels carried rifled, breach-loading cannon. The guns were initially mounted on the bow because all ironclad vessels were intended to double as rams, reflecting the experience of the Civil War. However, the invention of a self-propelled torpedo in the mid-1880s rendered rams obsolete, and strategy reverted to artillery fire. The cannons were placed in armored batteries near the center of the ship, fore and aft. There they could swivel in directing their fire without disturbing the ship's center of gravity. Hesitant to commit itself completely to battleships, Congress in 1888 authorized the last of the protected cruisers, the speedy *Olympia*. Propelled by either wind or steam, so as to be usable in the Pacific, the *Olympia* was Commodore George Dewey's flagship at the Battle of Manila Bay, on May 1, 1898. (The rest of Dewey's fleet was three protected cruisers and five wooden-hulled steam/sailing ships.)

By the end of the 1880s the new tack in shipbuilding, from protected cruiser to fully armored battleship, presaged a new direction for naval warfare, based on a strategy of national defense through offensive operations on the high seas. Yet the thinking in the highest echelons of the

U.S. Navy remained rooted in harbor defense and the protection of commerce. What the navy needed was a new philosophy of blue-water navalism. It got precisely that in early 1890 with the publication of a book entitled *The Influence of Sea Power upon History, 1660–1783*. Exquisitely timed—ten years earlier it would have been ignored and ten years later it would have been superfluous—*The Influence of Sea Power* would rank with *Uncle Tom's Cabin* as the two most influential American-authored books of the century. Its author was an obscure naval captain, Alfred Thayer Mahan.

A Naval Aristocrat

The Mahans were of Irish extraction. Alfred's grandfather, John Mahan, had fled Ireland during the revolutionary violence of the late 1790s and settled in Norfolk, Virginia, where he found employment as a ship's carpenter. He acquired enough land and wealth to take on the airs of a Virginia gentleman. Shedding his Irish Catholicism, he raised his family as dedicated Episcopalians and slave-tolerant Southerners. John Mahan acquired enough wealth and political influence to win the appointment of his older son, Dennis, to the United States Military Academy at West Point. A second son, Milo, took up theological studies and eventually joined the faculty of the Theological Seminary of the Episcopal Church in New York City. Seldom has an immigrant family adapted so quickly or so successfully to the American environment.

Dennis Hart Mahan graduated from West Point in 1824 and spent the next five years in France studying military engineering and fortifications. In 1830, the superintendent of the military academy, Colonel Sylvanus Thayer, named him to the faculty, and Mahan redeemed the colonel's vote of confidence by publishing a book, *Field Fortification* (1836), a study based on his experience in France. Two years later Antoine Henri Jomini, who had served in both the army of Napoleon and that of the Czar, published his classic *Precis de l'Art de la Guerre* (*Study of the Art of War*), which set forth the "natural laws" of military combat, the centerpiece of which was the principle of maneuvering a mass of men in such a way as to throw maximum power against an inferior section of the enemy's army. Through his lectures at the academy and his own textbook, *An Elementary Treatise on . . . the Rise and Progress of Tactics* (1847), Dennis Mahan trained a generation of officers in the principles of Jomini, including many of the generals who fought the Civil War.[1]

1. Among Mahan's students were Ulysses S. Grant, William T. Sherman, and Phillip Sheridan on the Union side, and Robert E. Lee, Stonewall Jackson, Pierre G. T. Beauregard, A. P. Hill, and J. E. B. Stuart for the Confederacy.

Alfred Thayer Mahan. (Photograph from Collections of the Library of Congress.)

In 1839 Professor Mahan, now promoted to dean of the faculty, married Mary Okill, the intensely pious daughter of an estimable woman, Mary Jay Okill, who operated a Christian finishing school for girls in New York City. Their first of six children, Alfred Thayer Mahan (his middle name conferred in honor of the academy superintendent), was born on September 27, 1840. The future naval officer thus grew up amidst the sounds of bugles and marching feet on a bustling military post. We otherwise know little of his childhood, for he scarcely mentioned West Point in his autobiography. He left behind no memoir of his feelings about his parents, though contemporary accounts portray Professor Mahan as an unbending disciplinarian. His mother instilled a Protestant reverence, and his grandmother, whom he adored, showered him with religious tracts. Mahan emerged with a lifelong religious faith that he channeled into the gentlemanly Episcopalianism of his paternal grandfather.

Nor did Mahan leave any record of his relationship with his brothers and sisters. His eldest sister (the Mahans' second child) suffered a childhood disease that damaged her brain and left her permanently retarded. Another sister died in infancy, and the third remained a spinster and cared for her parents in their old age. Both brothers joined Alfred in the military, one by way of West Point, the other by way of Annapolis. Mahan later recalled "those happy hours that only childhood knows" largely in terms of his reading. He loved sea stories, especially those of James Fenimore Cooper, and later claimed that he had read himself into the U.S. Navy. There is no evidence that he ever read his father's works, and he later insisted that he made his first acquaintance with Jomini while doing the research for *Sea Power*.

Following his own father's homage to the gentlemanly ideal, Dennis Mahan shipped his eldest son, at the age of eleven, to an Episcopal finishing school in Hagerstown, Maryland. Whatever the school did for young Alfred's aristocratic polish, it was decidedly inferior, in the eyes of father, in science and mathematics. After two years the lad was transferred to Columbia College in New York, where he could get better training while residing in the theologically correct household of Uncle Milo. Milo was then working on a history of the Anglican church, and Alfred emerged from his mentoring with a love of history and some sense of historical method. Nevertheless, after two years at Columbia, the sea continued to beckon him. Upon a recommendation of the president of the college, a New York congressman arranged an appointment to the U.S. Naval Academy. Mahan's father was disappointed, feeling that his scholarly son was better suited to a civilian career (a feeling that A. T. Mahan belatedly came to share), but he did not interfere.

Mahan's experience at the Naval Academy reinforced the sense of social superiority that had been cultivated by father and grandfather. Midshipmen regarded themselves as a "band of brothers" removed from the coarse atmosphere of the world of commerce and dependent upon one another for social and intellectual sustenance. Midshipman Mahan was convinced that the friendships formed at Annapolis would be "far more lasting than those made elsewhere, for here we are from every cause brothers: our association, our hopes, our profession all the same." As the nation drifted toward civil war in the late 1850s, midshipman Mahan bemoaned the fact that "the influence of gentlemen" had declined in American society and the government had fallen into the hands of "such scum as the mass of our politicians are." His attitude toward classroom work bore a similar air of casual gentility. With some application he could easily have graduated at the top of his class, but he disliked the rote learning the academy required and disdained a crass competitiveness. Without pushing himself, he graduated second in his class.

Not surprisingly, Mahan was not popular among his fellow mids and had few friends. Although he regarded the academy theoretically as a "brotherhood," he developed only one close friendship—with Samuel A'Court Ashe of North Carolina. Unfortunately, Ashe was never able to overcome the seasickness that flattened him on every summer cruise, and he resigned from the academy after only two years. As soon as Ashe reached North Carolina, Mahan initiated a correspondence in which he poured out the frustrations he endured at the academy. Ashe served in the Confederate army during the war, suffered financial ruin at its end, but ultimately became a successful lawyer, politician, and widely respected historian of his native state. The two men exchanged letters the rest of their lives, but Mahan never formed another such friendship. Never able to draw the fine distinction between social gentility and intellectual snobbery, he made enemies more easily than friends. He remained a loner throughout his naval career. Late in life his daughter referred to him as "The Cat That Walked by Himself."

The Romance and Dread of the Sea

Mahan graduated from the Naval Academy in 1859 and was assigned to a vessel on the Brazil Station. Brazil and Argentina were momentarily at peace, and there was little for the American squadron to do but cruise between Rio De Janeiro and Montevideo. Mahan loved to visit strange places, and the calm waters of the South Atlantic reinforced a romance with the sea that had begun as a midshipman. He was promoted to lieutenant upon his return in 1861 and immediately joined the fleet blockading the Carolinas and Georgia. Promotion was rapid during the war, as the Navy expanded its manpower, and Mahan emerged from the fighting a lieutenant commander.

Assigned to temporary duty in the Washington Navy Yard, he learned of a ship, the *Iroquois*, that was to embark for the Far East in February 1867, via the Cape of Good Hope with stops at such exotic places as Madagascar, the Persian Gulf, India, Singapore, and Hong Kong. When Mahan learned of the itinerary, he applied and was ordered for duty as the ship's executive officer. Mahan kept a personal journal on the two-year cruise and wrote numerous letters home. These documents reveal much about Mahan's personality, his attitude toward other peoples, and his relationship with the sea.

After arriving in the Far East the *Iroquois* was stationed in Japanese waters, and its officers participated actively in advancing American interests in the treaty ports opened in 1854 by Commodore Matthew Perry. When Japan dissolved into civil war, the American squadron landed armed parties to protect American traders and their property. Mahan admired the Japanese for their industriousness, but he thought the Chinese lazy and culturally backward. He had even less regard for the Malaysian peoples of Southeast Asia, and the inhabitants of the island archipelagoes he considered savages. While Mahan thus judged Asian peoples, the stormy waters of the western Pacific took the measure of him. His romance with the sea yielded to dread. Entries in his diary reveal a man nervous, irritable, depressed, dependent on alcohol, and living in constant fear. The following notations are typical:

> Little annoyances have made me break out. . . . Shortish with everybody. . . . Had I not better discontinue drinking altogether?. . . I have been very anxious and troubled, yet by God's grace I have been enabled to bear up against my fears and depression. . . . We have had much bad weather and I am so anxious; my mind seems half broken down by the strain. If I could only get out of the service how glad I would be to go.

In September 1869, after a bout of illness that forced him to endure a depressing Japanese hospital, he requested and was granted leave to return home. Given a six-month leave at half pay, he gratified his love for exotic travel. He left Japan for Hong Kong where he boarded a British passenger steamer to Calcutta, went overland to Bombay, thence through the newly opened Suez Canal into the Mediterranean. He spent the winter touring Italy and France and sailed home from Liverpool in May 1870. Still unsure whether he wanted to pursue a career that alternated between boredom and terror, he obtained an additional six-month leave, much of which he spent visiting his parents in New York.

At the age of thirty, Mahan decided it was time to get married. Since his days in Annapolis (a "miserable town" brimming with "lovely ladies") he had pursued women eagerly but with a shy ineffectiveness. Determining that New York City was as good a hunting ground as any, he requested and received assignment to the New York Navy Yard. Within a month his fancy had settled upon Ellen Lyle Evans, daughter of a businessman whose clan was financially comfortable and socially respectable. "Elly" was only nineteen, and her mother considered her too young to proceed rapidly into marriage. Mahan, whose ill luck with women matched Elly's inexperience, successfully concealed any haste or ardor he might have felt. In the words of his biographer, Robert Seager, Mahan "loafed along after her like an overloaded sloop tacking upwind."

The courtship was interrupted when Mahan was ordered to sea in the spring of 1871, in command of a steam merchant ship that had been chartered by the navy to carry food to France, whose people were thought to be starving as a result of the war with Prussia. On the voyage across the Atlantic Mahan experienced a round of mishaps that had come to characterize his sea duty. The engines failed shortly out of Boston, and the ship billowed eastward under sail. A boiler exploded in the mid-Atlantic, killing four seamen. The vessel then struggled through heavy gales and hurricane-force winds before reaching the English Channel, where it ingloriously ran out of coal. Upon landing in Plymouth forty men deserted the hapless ship. Mahan then learned that there was no hunger in France and that his cargo was to be auctioned off in London. He returned home and used the occasion to wheedle another few months' shore leave out of the navy. He and Elly were married in June 1872.

In November 1872, Mahan was promoted to commander, a rank he would bear for thirteen years while the navy struggled with low budgets, rotting ships, and a surplus of officers. In December he was ordered back to the South Atlantic station to take command of his first warship. The navy permitted officers' wives to join their husbands on this station, and Elly accompanied him to Montevideo where they rented a house. Their first child, a daughter named Helen, was born in August 1873. For the next two years Mahan was separated from his family for only brief intervals, when he took his vessel to "show the flag" at various South American ports. It was the best "sea duty" he ever had, in part because he was rarely at sea.

When this tour was completed, the navy had no openings available, and Mahan was forced to take a one-year leave of absence at half pay ($1,150). They went to France, where Elly's parents maintained a home, and there a second daughter, Ellen, was born on July 10, 1877. On that same day Mahan received orders to proceed to Annapolis to serve as an instructor at the Naval Academy. He had few good memories of the place, but the appointment allowed him to return to duty at full pay ($3,000)—and, equally important, it was on land.

Mahan still detested the rote-learning teaching methods of the Naval Academy, but he had learned that muddying the navy's waters brought only bureaucratic retribution. After two years of a boring, though not unpleasant, existence, he obtained another shore duty, as navigation officer in the Brooklyn Navy Yard. The family rented a house on 11th Street, off Fifth Avenue in Manhattan, and there in February 1881 was born their last child, a son, Lyle Evans Mahan.

Mahan's duties for the next three years were routine make-work, such as measuring cooking oil and establishing uniform widths for flag bunting, but Mahan did not complain. For more than a decade he had spent his spare time, both at sea and on land, studying history and naval tactics. He became a convert to the idea of a blue-water navy and was delighted when Congress authorized construction of the ABC cruisers. To his friend, Samuel Ashe, Mahan expressed hope that the United States would build a canal across the isthmus of Central America. Such a project, he felt, would facilitate a two-ocean navy and encourage further shipbuilding. Brimming with ideas but as yet without a publisher, Mahan was delighted when in 1882 Charles Scribners Sons asked him to contribute a volume to its projected series, *The Navy in the Civil War*.

With a promise of $600 and a request for speed, Mahan slapped together the work in five months, much of it at his desk in the Navy Yard when the navy's preoccupation with the size of signal flags permitted. Mahan focused on the blockade of the southern seaboard, where his own experience lay, and he corresponded with many of the participants. He was still making revisions when the book went through galley proofs. The volume, entitled *The Gulf and Inland Waters*, appeared in June 1883.

It was not a brilliant book, nor one that reflected Mahan's years of study. It was a rather straightforward account of selected naval actions along the southern coast and the lower Mississippi River. There is no hint in it of Mahan's later sea-power hypothesis. The book nevertheless had an important bearing on his career. In the course of writing he came to realize that Union naval control of the Gulf, Mobile Bay, New Orleans, and the lower Mississippi had an impact on the outcome of the war. Sea power had helped bring the Confederacy to ruin, and that was something to ruminate on. The work also brought Mahan to the attention of Commodore Stephen B. Luce, a champion of the New Navy and an advocate for the continuing professional education of naval officers. Luce had obtained authorization from the secretary of the navy to establish the Naval War College at Newport, Rhode Island, and in 1884 he invited Mahan to join the faculty. With that appointment Mahan at last found his niche in the navy—teaching naval tactics in a school alert to new ideas while receiving open encouragement to publish his research and theories.

The Influence of Sea Power

The Naval War College, as conceived by Commodore Luce, was to be the intellectual heartland of the movement for a New Navy. Luce thought of it as a postgraduate school that enabled career naval officers to keep up with the new developments and new ideas in the interrelated fields of national policy, naval tactics, and armaments technology. Luce was not interested in teachers who could give technical instructions in gunnery or fleet maneuvers. He was attracted to Mahan because Mahan had demonstrated an ability to place naval tactics in a historical context and to condense a stockpile of facts into a readable narrative. He invited Mahan to give a series of lectures at the college on the history and evolution of naval tactics.

Although Mahan's lectures were scheduled to begin in the fall term of 1885, the opening of the college was delayed a year by the opposition of conservative naval officers who thought it unnecessary and a threat to the academy in Annapolis. The postponement actually benefited Mahan, who was on sea duty off the western coast of South America when he received Luce's invitation. Bureaucratic lapses in decommissioning his ship prevented him from joining the faculty in Newport until October 1885, and the delay in opening the school gave him a year's respite to prepare his lectures. As he did so, the concept of sea power began to jell.

The role of sea power in the destiny of nations was hardly a new idea, and Mahan never said that it was. The ancient Greeks spoke often of the importance of the Athenian navy in their wars with Persia and Sparta. The Romans gloried in their land armies, but they could hardly have held their empire together without fleets of warships. The British were well aware that it was the "wooden walls" of the Royal Navy that had vanquished the Dutch in the seventeenth century and the French in the eighteenth, but no one thought philosophically to equate sea power with empire.

Mahan claimed in a letter to Luce that the "light dawned" on him while on sea duty off the coast of Peru in 1884. He was reading Theodor Mommsen's *The History of Rome* in the library of the English Club in Lima when he realized that Hannibal had been forced to make a frightful crossing of the Alps, in which he lost a quarter of his original army, because he did not have control of the sea. Had the Carthaginians controlled the Mediterranean, all of Western history might have been different. Mahan's experience with the Union navy in the Civil War and his involvement with naval missions in Japan and South America lent personal reinforcement to a thesis that sea power might have played an important role throughout history.

Despite the opposition of naval conservatives in Washington and Annapolis, Luce had managed to paste together a three-week session of the War College in September 1885. In an address, "On the Study of Naval History," to students and faculty (who together numbered no more than a dozen) Luce contended that scientific principles of naval tactics could be derived from a study of history, and he pointed to the work of the Swiss theorist Henri Jomini as the place to start one's studies. Luce thus set forth a framework for a sea-power thesis as part of the mission of the college before Mahan even arrived to take up his duties. Mahan's job would be to gather the data to support the thesis and present it in a meaningful series of lectures.

Luce permitted Mahan to live in New York while he researched his lectures, and Mahan rented an apartment for his family on East 15th Street in Manhattan. In the autumn of 1885, he was promoted at last to the rank of captain. Unfortunately, a captain's shore duty pay of $3,500 was the same as he had received as a commander on sea duty, so the promotion did nothing to improve his ever-straitened finances.

Mahan spent the winter months in the Astor Library and the New York Lyceum, studying the naval tactics of the Age of Fighting Sail. The central principle in the pioneering tactics of George Romney during the American Revolution and Horatio Nelson during the Napoleonic wars was the idea of firepower concentration, chiefly accomplished by breaking the enemy's line so as to bring a broadside of guns to bear on the enemy's smaller fore-and-aft armaments. Uncertain whether this principle could be applied to the speedy, steam-driven warships of the 1880s, Mahan turned to the works of Henri Jomini in search of a more general theory.[2]

Jomini had preached the doctrine that the destruction of the enemy army in the field, rather than the occupation of his territory or the seizure of his capital city, was the key to victory. This was accomplished by bringing to bear superior numbers of troops (and firepower) against an inferior force in combat. Pitched battles between armies or units of equal strength were to be avoided. Finally, Jomini stressed the importance of speed, as achieved by the use of cavalry, horse-drawn artillery, and swift-moving infantry (everyone remembered Stonewall Jackson's "foot cavalry" during the Civil War).

Applied by analogy to modern naval warfare, Jomini's principles suggested the use of heavily armed, fast-moving warships that could meet the enemy on the high seas under conditions where speed and firepower were decisive. Because steam and steel were so new, there were no models of such combat (the battles of Jutland in 1916 and Leyte Gulf in 1944 were in the distant future), and Mahan, to flesh out his thesis, had to rely on analogies from the Age of Fighting Sail. With the concept of sea power firmly in mind, Mahan proceeded to trace the development of naval tactics, from the line of battle employed during the Anglo-Dutch wars to the melee created by Nelson when he broke the Franco-Spanish line at Trafalgar in three places.

So well-prepared were Mahan's lectures by the summer of 1886 that he already had the rough draft for a book. At that point the naval high command in Washington threw another kink into the plans for the War College. With little regard for education in general and no concept of institutional continuity, the navy promoted Luce to rear admiral, detached him from the college, and ordered him to sea in command of the North Atlantic Station. Luce summoned Mahan from New York and asked him to take over as president of the college. Never formally assigned to the

2. Interestingly, there is no evidence that, even at this point in his life, Mahan consulted the works of his father. Indeed, there are few references of any kind to his father. Dennis Hart Mahan had suffered severe bouts of depression late in life and had committed suicide in 1871 by jumping off a Hudson River steamboat. That family humiliation, as it was regarded at the time, may explain Mahan's reticence.

post, Mahan later recalled that he "simply fell into the presidency as a first lieutenant does into command after the captain's removal." He brought Elly and the children to Newport once living quarters were set up in the college's lone building.

The facilities of the War College were not promising. It was located on the bay side of the island that gave the state its name. Its lone structure was formerly the Newport Almshouse, deliberately situated to be as far as possible from the city's seaside mansions of shipping magnates and prewar Carolina rice planters. The Mahans' living quarters were drafty and sparsely furnished. The navy provided only a single study lamp, which Mahan moved from room to room at night. Mahan provided hot water for bathing by running a rubber hose from a radiator, which probably taxed the limit of his knowledge of steam engineering.

"My own lectures," Mahan rejoiced at the end of the 1886 session, "met with a degree of success which surprised me and which still seems to me exaggerated." He immediately set to work expanding them, still with an eye on future publication. But then he ran afoul of navy politics, as he had so often before. Opponents of the War College, led by Francis M. Ramsay, superintendent of the Naval Academy, began a whispering campaign in the hallways of the nation's Capitol. They suggested that the facility at Newport was too expensive for what the navy got out of it, that it ought to be moved to Annapolis and attached to the Naval Academy, and that its facilities ought to be put under the control of the more practical Torpedo Station on Goat Island in Narragansett Bay. The whispers reached the ears of the chair of the House Naval Affairs Committee, and accordingly, the appropriations bill for fiscal 1887–1888 contained no money for the War College. Navy Secretary William C. Whitney managed to shift funds around within his budget to allow the school to limp through the 1887 session, but it was "run on a vacuum" according to Mahan.

Whitney, though an able administrator and a friend to naval shipbuilding, had the businessman/politician's mistrust of postgraduate education, and the following year he persuaded Congress, for the sake of economic and administrative efficiency, to consolidate the War College with the Torpedo Station and to place both on Goat Island. At Whitney's suggestion Congress appropriated a mere $10,000 to carry the War College through the 1888 session. Enraged by what he considered a betrayal, Mahan openly supported the election of Republican Benjamin Harrison in 1888, and he was delighted when the victorious Harrison named Benjamin F. Tracy of New York as secretary of the navy.

Committed wholeheartedly to the New Navy concept, Tracy would prove to be the greatest secretary of the navy of the nineteenth century. But before he could come to Mahan's rescue Secretary Whitney got his revenge. In January 1889 he ordered the War College moved to Goat Island to be consolidated with the Torpedo Station, and he reassigned Mahan to the most distant post in the continental United States, Puget

Sound in the Washington Territory. Mahan was instructed to determine the site of a naval base somewhere between California and Alaska. He thus ended the decade as he had begun it, counting pencils in his office to stay within budget (he subsequently billed the treasury for $1.05 that he had paid out of his own pocket) and taking soundings of salmon streams in the hushed wilderness of the Pacific Northwest.

Fortunately, it was a brief exile. After taking office in March, Secretary Tracy persuaded Congress to return the War College to the sandy spit it had occupied off Rhode Island and to appropriate $100,000 for a new building. Mahan was back in New England by April, and in September Whitney put him in charge of supervising the construction. Mahan had spent his time in exile putting the final polish on his sea power book, and upon returning to the East Coast he resumed a search for a publisher. The navy had a press of its own but no facility for marketing; Mahan wanted a commercial publisher. He had sent a draft to Scribner's before leaving for Puget Sound, but that cautious New York house considered it too specialized to sell profitably. When other publishers turned him down on similar grounds, Mahan appealed to wealthy businessmen for financial help. Millionaire financier J. P. Morgan offered $200 on condition that he share in the royalties and that Mahan raise elsewhere the remaining $2,300 in estimated printing costs.

Friends came to his rescue and introduced him to John Murray Brown, owner of Little, Brown and Company of Boston. Brown read the manuscript, recognized its importance, and agreed to publish it. With the help of Luce, Mahan obtained assurances that the army and navy would purchase at least 250 copies for placement in service libraries, and that probably convinced Brown that he could do no worse financially than break even. *The Influence of Sea Power upon History, 1660–1783* appeared in May 1890.

From Sea Power to Imperial Power

Mahan never regarded himself as a pure historian, unraveling the mysteries of the past for whatever value the present could make of it. He was a polemicist with an agenda—promotion of the New Navy, preservation of the War College, and before long, the building of an American empire that would extend the blessings of individual freedom and Protestant morality to the peoples of the dark corners of the earth.

While Little, Brown and Company sent copies of *Sea Power* to magazines for review, Mahan sent complimentary copies to prominent naval and political figures in Britain and America. In sending an inscribed copy to Luce, he thanked the admiral "for the start you gave me" and assured him that proceeds from the book would be used to extend the story through the War of 1812. He enlarged upon this theme in letters to

British naval officers, with subtle reminders of the role that sea power had played in the fall of Napoleon. In a letter accompanying a copy of the book to Secretary Tracy, Mahan emphasized the connection between the intellectual energy of the War College and his own inspiration. Sending another copy to Representative Henry Cabot Lodge of Massachusetts, a leading supporter of shipbuilding, Mahan explained that his object in writing the book was "to make the experience of the past influence the opinions and shape the policy of the future."

The reaction of Theodore Roosevelt was crucial to its success, for Roosevelt had been one of the first to arouse public interest in the navy with his 1882 book, *The Naval War of 1812*. After reading *Sea Power* Roosevelt wrote Mahan that it was "the clearest and most instructive general work of the kind with which I am acquainted. It is a very good book—admirable; and I am greatly in error if it does not become a classic." A member of the U.S. Civil Service Commission and friend of Congressman Henry Cabot Lodge, Roosevelt used his review of the book in the *Atlantic Monthly* as a platform to promote the idea of a blue-water navy. What the country needed, he told his readers, was "a large navy, composed not merely of cruisers, but containing also a full proportion of powerful battleships able to meet those of any other nation. It is not economy, it is niggardly and foolish short-sightedness, to cramp our naval expenditures while squandering money right and left on everything else, from pensions to public buildings."

With laudatory reviews raining upon him, Mahan accepted an invitation from the editor of *Atlantic Monthly* to contribute an article on naval strategy. He seized the occasion to set out the connection between sea power and imperial dominance. Published in the December 1890 issue of the popular magazine, "The United States Looking Outward" called for the abandonment of protectionism and the promotion of American trade and the penetration of overseas markets. The nation, which had become the preeminent industrial power in the world, needed such markets to overcome the problem of overproduction and market surpluses. To protect its existing commercial interests in Hawaii, the South Pacific (Samoa), and the Isthmus of Panama and to safeguard its coastline from any European threat, the United States, Mahan contended, needed a large and mobile combat navy, supported by a chain of coaling stations around the world. The time had come, Mahan told Americans, for the United States to abandon its inward-looking business arrangements and its military weakness and to assume its rightful place in the world as a major commercial, military, and diplomatic power.

While Mahan worked on public opinion, Secretary Tracy worked on Congress. In the midst of a congressional debate over an appropriation for three new battleships in the spring of 1890, Tracy bluntly embraced blue-water navalism. He belittled the cruisers and second-class battleships built in the previous decade and proclaimed that national pride required the construction of first-class vessels equal to the British Dreadnoughts. The Republican-controlled Congress obediently authorized construction of the three ships, the *Indiana*, *Massachusetts*, and *Oregon*. These would become the nucleus of the "Great White Fleet" that the United States displayed to the world a decade later during the presidency of Theodore Roosevelt.

Although their losses in the congressional election of 1890 made the Republicans shy of naval appropriations in 1891, Tracy plunged ahead with his plans for reconfiguring the service. He decommissioned six mid-century sailing ships and slipped into the congressional authorization bill one additional battleship, the *Iowa*, and an armored cruiser, the *Brooklyn*.

In the meantime, the navy, recognizing Mahan's potential as a propagandist, gave him "special duty" (i.e., freedom from any assigned duties) to work on a sequel to his book. Mahan, increasingly aware of his obligations as a professional historian, labored through primary sources for this book, notably government documents and the correspondence of naval officers. *The Influence of Sea Power upon the French Revolution and Empire, 1793–1812* appeared in November 1892, and it was history at its best—profoundly researched and vibrant in expression. Not surprisingly, it was more popular in Britain than in the United States, for it was a study in the superiority of Anglican culture as well as British sea power. While preparing to invade England in 1805, Napoleon was heard to say, "Let us be masters of the [English] Strait for six hours and we shall be masters of the world." Although he abandoned his invasion plan after the Battle of Trafalgar, Napoleon was still bent on world domination, as he crushed Austria, Prussia, and Russia in a succession of battles in 1806–1807. But, despite these victories, there remained the wooden walls of the Royal Navy, in Mahan's words, "those far distant, storm beaten ships, upon which the Grand Army never looked, stood between it and the dominion of the world."

In the meantime, in January 1892, Mahan had accepted Secretary Tracy's offer to serve as president of the Naval War College. He could not, after all, remain on special duty indefinitely, and this assignment allowed him to remain on land and continue his writing. Unfortunately, the appointment brought him head to head with his old foe, Admiral Ramsay, who was now head of the Bureau of Navigation, the second most powerful administrative post in the navy. Since the bureau had charge of all naval training schools, Ramsay was Mahan's immediate superior. Although the two strong-willed men maintained for the moment a correct cordiality, Ramsay became increasingly angered by Mahan's insistence on running the War College in his own way and by his easy access to Secretary Tracy. Mahan would have done well to have treated his superior with a bit more tact, but his own sense of superiority and propensity for vindictive hatreds precluded that.

Grover Cleveland's election victory in 1892 brought a Democratic administration to power in Washington, and Mahan lost a powerful ally with the departure of Secretary Tracy. Cleveland's choice for secretary of the navy was Hilary A. Herbert, a congressman from Alabama, who, despite his background, favored a battleship navy. Unfortunately, the panic of 1893 and the ensuing depression precluded any significant shipbuilding for the next few years. For Mahan, the change in administrations raised the spectre of sea duty, for he was now at Admiral Ramsay's mercy. Mahan frantically enlisted the aid of Theodore Roosevelt, Henry Cabot Lodge, retired Admiral Luce, and his publisher John M. Brown in an effort to persuade Secretary Herbert that his pen was more valuable to the navy than his sword, but Herbert, new to the office, was reluctant to become enmeshed in naval politics. Ramsay even rejected the offer of several naval officers to go to sea in Mahan's place, and on May 11, 1893, Mahan found himself in command of the USS *Chicago*, lying in the New York Navy Yard.

For a change, it was Ramsay's vindictiveness, rather than Mahan's, that backfired. "It is not the business of a naval officer to write books," Ramsay had proclaimed in response to the entreaties by politicians and naval officers to spare Mahan from sea duty. Assigned to the North Atlantic Station, Mahan managed to convert his two-year European cruise into the equivalent of an author's signing tour, and he took advantage of a stopover in England to do research on a new book, a biography of Lord Nelson. The duty assignment, Mahan later chortled, was "one of the luckiest things that . . . happened in my career, a boomerang for any who wished me ill."

Mahan was in his element when hobnobbing with the royalty and aristocrats of Europe. In England by August 1893, he was invited to dinner by Queen Victoria, who had arranged a meeting with her cousin, Kaiser Wilhelm of Germany. The Kaiser had dismissed his great minister Otto von Bismarck in 1890 for being too inward-looking and had embarked on a naval shipbuilding program. On reading Mahan's *Sea Power* book the Kaiser pronounced: "It is a first class work and classical in all points. It is on board all my ships and constantly quoted by my captains and officers."

At home in the drawing rooms of royalty, Mahan was as nervous and fretful as ever at sea. He worried constantly that he might run the ship aground on an uncharted shoal or collide with another vessel while in harbor. The year 1896 would be his fortieth in the service, and he was determined to retire when he reached that mark. The *Chicago* was scheduled to return to New York in the spring of 1895 to be decommissioned, and even the homeward-bound journey was a nightmare for Mahan. The "rickety" engines of the eight-year-old vessel required constant servicing, and the ship had to pass inspection in New York before it could be decommissioned. Any deficiency in gear or crew risked bringing down the wrath of Ramsey and a final black mark on his seagoing career. He kept the crew busy for a month polishing and trimming before departing home from the Mediterranean. "The approaching inspection is ever on my mind," he wrote Elly in a frightful lather, "and though I confess gratefully that I have so far been safely brought through every trouble, I cannot get rid of the fear that some censure will fall on me."

In fact, all went well. The *Chicago* anchored off Staten Island on March 24, and three days later the Board of Inspection climbed on board. After a meticulous canvass the board pronounced itself satisfied with the condition of the ship and expressed particular pleasure in "the subordination and respect shown by the crew." Secretary Herbert also proved surprisingly compliant. After the decommissioning ceremony on May 1 he gave Mahan two months' leave and then placed him on special duty in New York and Newport until Mahan went onto the retired list on November 17, 1896. He thus had a sabbatical of nearly a year and a half to complete his biography of Lord Nelson. Little, Brown published the book in 1897.

In the same year Little, Brown published Mahan's fourth book, a compendium of the magazine articles he had written since 1890. The thesis of the book was in its title, *The Interest of America in Sea Power, Present and Future*, and its applicability was revealed in the chapter titles: "Hawaii and Our Future Sea Power," "The Isthmus and Sea Power," and "Preparedness for a Naval War." A plea for an American empire bound together by a powerful navy, the book met a more critical reception than his earlier works, which at least purported to rest on history. One reviewer wrote:

> The spirit of the book is so plain that he who runs may read. Military glory and far reaching domination are the great ends of man's aspiration. To give opportunity for these, the United States must have numerous distant, outlying possessions, each sticking out like a sore thumb to be hurt by whatever passes, each wanting its impregnable fortifications and its great garrison to defend it, each demanding its fleet to scour the adjacent seas, and great reserve armies and navies at home besides, to overpower every possible antagonist.

British reviewers were even more critical, for in order to justify an American navy the size of Britain's, Mahan had to portray Britain as a potential foe, perhaps with respect to the annexation of Hawaii,[3] possibly in the construction of an Isthmian canal.

3. Hawaii had experienced a pro-American revolution in 1893, but the Cleveland administration had rejected a treaty of annexation. The islands would be formally annexed during the Spanish-American War in 1898.

A Prophet in His Own Time

With a captain's retirement pay of $3,375 a year and a fairly steady income from books and magazine articles, Mahan looked forward to a retirement of gracious living. He purchased a four-story house on 86th Street on Manhattan's fashionable Upper West Side, and he and Elly built a summer cottage on the beach on Long Island. Although Mahan envisioned an active role in New York's high society, neither Elly nor their daughters (who had been raised under Mahan's stern, puritanical eye) had the personality and social graces for life among the Four Hundred.[4] Neither daughter would ever marry. Lyle Evans Mahan, who had passed his formative years while his father was at sea, was the most sociable member of the family. With a first-class education at Groton and Columbia, he entered into a successful financial and legal career in New York.

The Republican Party platform in 1896 had promised the annexation of Hawaii, and shortly after taking office President McKinley sent a new annexation treaty to the Senate. It languished for almost a year, despite the joint efforts of Roosevelt, Lodge, and Mahan. Concentrating on Hawaii, Mahan failed to see a developing crisis in the Spanish colony of Cuba, where the Cubans had taken up arms for independence, and Spain's incarceration of civilians in prison camps was arousing American public anger. Even after the American battleship *Maine* exploded and sank in Havana harbor on February 15, 1898, Mahan did not foresee war. Nor was he consulted when Roosevelt and Lodge decided to send secret instructions to Commodore Dewey, commanding in the Pacific, to attack the Spanish fleet in the Philippines in the event of war. Mahan had been planning to take his family to Europe that spring, and they sailed in March without any thought of impending war.

Upon McKinley's request, Congress passed a declaration of war on April 19, and Spain reluctantly did the same on April 25. On that day Mahan, touring Rome, received a telegram from the secretary of the navy, John D. Long, ordering him home. Leaving his family in Italy, Mahan hurried home on British passenger ships. He landed in New York on May 7, a scant week after Commodore Dewey, carrying out Roosevelt's secret instructions, destroyed the Spanish Pacific fleet in Manila Bay. Secretary Long put Mahan on the Naval War Board, newly created to give advice on war strategy. In a series of quick naval strikes and two fleet engagements (Manila Bay on May 1 and the Battle of Santiago, Cuba, on July 3) the United States achieved its objectives in a mere 115 days of fighting—the independence of Cuba and the acquisition of an assortment of island possessions: Puerto Rico in the Caribbean and in

4. The Four Hundred were the cream of New York society, the number determined by the capacity of the Astor Ball Room.

the Pacific, Hawaii (Congress approved the annexation treaty in May), the Philippines, Guam, and Midway.

With these territorial acquisitions Mahan's prewar book, *The Interest of America in Sea Power*, suddenly seemed prophetic. The *Chicago Times-Herald* was shocked "to glance over these articles and recognize their startling nearness to events as they have happened." The *Brooklyn Citizen* was delighted that Mahan had instructed even "the backwoods Congressmen" on the point that military strength was "essential to our national prestige and . . . to our national life." A columnist in the New York magazine *The Criterion* wrote that Mahan's "arguments showing the necessity for the United States becoming a great naval power, though written long ago, have been singularly championed by recent events." Mahan's biographer, Robert Seager, has nicely captured the irony: "Mahan at last became a prophet in his own land, and in his own lifetime, as the result of a war that he did not encourage, did not see coming, and for which he had made no personal or professional provision."

Mahan lived the role of national icon for the next fifteen years. He continued to write, publishing chapters of *Sea Power in Its Relations to the War of 1812* serially in *Scribner's* magazine in 1904 and 1905. But he remained backward-looking on matters of national strategy and naval technology. He only dimly perceived the potentiality of the submarine and naval aircraft, and he strongly opposed innovations in naval gunnery, such as armor-piercing shells and self-correcting sights that adjusted to the pitch and roll of the ship. He served on the American delegation to the Hague Conference of 1899—the first of many twentieth-century arms limitation conferences—and persuaded his colleagues to cast the sole national vote against the outlawing of poison gas projectiles. The conference was doomed to failure because neither Britain nor Germany had an interest in naval limitations. Mahan and the American delegation, though a voice of less importance, likewise refused to discuss limitations on shipbuilding.

In the ensuing naval arms race that preceded World War I, Mahan, ever the Anglophile, enthusiastically applauded the British efforts. In a 1912 article in the *North American Review* he surveyed the wars of the past half-century and found moral purpose in them all. The American Civil War was justified by the freeing of the slaves; Prussia's wars against Demark, Austria, and France resulted in the unification of Germany; the elimination of Spanish rule in Cuba and the Philippines in 1898 answered the call of humanity; and Japan's attack on Russia in 1904 was "not without reason" because it guaranteed her "national self-preservation."

When the world war broke out in August 1914, Mahan signed a contract with Joseph Pulitzer Jr., editor of the *New York World*, to publish a series of articles on the naval aspects of the war. The first article accused an "evil" Germany of starting the war, and President Woodrow Wilson, fearing that Mahan's attitude jeopardized American neutrality, persuaded Pulitzer and other publishers to bury the rest of the series. Mahan was furious at being muzzled, but declining health was silencing his pen in any case. He died of a heart attack on December 1, 1914.

In its annual meeting later that month, the American Historical Association, of which Mahan had served as president in 1902, adopted a memorial resolution, concluding: "The profundity of his views and the lucidity of his reasoning attracted the attention of statesmen of all nations; and more than any American scholar of his day, he has affected the course of world politics."

Suggested Reading

Robert Seager II's *Alfred Thayer Mahan: The Man and His Letters* (1977) is a well-written, judicious biography. William E. Livezey provides a topical analysis of Mahan's contributions to the development of naval strategy in *Mahan on Sea Power* (1947, 1981). Two very fine studies of the development of the New Navy are by Kenneth J. Hagan, *This People's Navy: The Making of American Sea Power* (1991), and Mark Russell Shulman, *Navalism and the Emergence of American Sea Power, 1882–1893* (1995). Frederick S. Harrod, *Manning the New Navy* (1978), describes the effort to improve the quality of seamen, and Peter Karsten traces the social origins and attitudes of the officer class in *The Naval Aristocracy: The Golden Age of Annapolis and the Emergence of Modern American Navalism* (1972). A dated but still useful study of the interaction of naval development and American foreign policy is Charles S. Campbell's *The Transformation of American Foreign Relations, 1865–1900* (1976).

6

Richard Harding Davis: The Romantic as Journalist

Americans in the 1890s were a literate people. Close to 90 percent could read and write. Since the days of Benjamin Franklin they had fancied newspapers over books—daily or weekly periodicals that were informative, entertaining, and undemanding. With digests of the day's happenings, commercial and financial information, alluring advertisements, and humorous anecdotes, newspapers were an accessible, practical literature for a people on the move. There were about 14,000 weeklies and 1,900 dailies in America in 1890, and circulation was equal to about 25 percent of the population ten years or older. In New York, which had a population of 2,800,000, the combined circulation of its dailies was almost 2,000,000.

Advances in the technology of printing had made such numbers possible. In the 1830s the rotating cylinder press replaced the ancient hand-screwed engraving press and thus made possible mass-circulation dailies priced at a penny. Horace Greeley's *New York Tribune* and James Gordon Bennett's *New York Herald*, the best of the early "penny press" papers, pioneered such innovations as the multiple-columned headline, the society page, and the sports page, all lightened with "spicy" and "saucy" reporting. In the 1880s, the invention of the Linotype machine replaced the hand typesetter with a keyboard operator who could set blocks of letters on a printing face at the speed of a typewriter. About the same time paper mills switched from a rag-fiber base to pulp wood, significantly reducing the cost of newsprint. These twin developments made the penny paper once again feasible and permitted mass-circulation papers to issue multiple editions in a single day.

The first to spot the potential in the new technology was a Hungarian-born veteran of the Union army, Joseph Pulitzer, who settled in St. Louis after the war. After gaining journalistic experience on a German-language paper, he acquired two English-language papers and combined them into the *Post-Dispatch*, which became an instant financial success. Passing through New York in 1883 on his way to Europe, Pulitzer learned that financier Jay Gould wished to sell a money-losing paper, the *World*. Pulitzer bought it and quickly proclaimed a new style in journalism. The *World*, he said, would be a paper "not only cheap but bright, not only bright but large, not only large but truly Democratic—dedicated to the cause of the people rather than that of purse-potentates—devoted more to the news of the New than the Old World—that will expose all fraud and sham, fight all public evils and abuses—that will serve and battle for the people with earnest sincerity."

The *World* never lived up to these ideals, but Pulitzer built circulation by focusing on the fortunes and misadventures of ordinary people, human interest stories introduced with such seductive headlines as "Screaming for Mercy," "All for a Woman's Love," "A Bride but Not a Wife," "Death Rides the Blast," and "A Preacher's Perfidy." By the next year, when the *World*'s Sunday circulation reached one hundred thousand, he had a hundred-gun salute fired off in City Park and gave every employee a silk hat. By 1890 Pulitzer's eyesight was failing and he had developed a hypersensitivity to noise, but his journalistic style was attracting emulators.

Among these was a dissolute Harvard student, William Randolph Hearst, whose semiliterate father had struck it rich in the gold and silver mines of Nevada and got himself elected to the U.S. Senate from California. The elder Hearst had purchased the *San Francisco Examiner* to enhance his political career but was losing money on it. Young Hearst, expelled from Harvard in his junior year (he had given chamber pots to faculty members with their names engraved on the bottom), persuaded his father to let him take over the *Examiner*. To learn the trade, he spent what would have been his senior year at Harvard as a reporter for Pulitzer's *World*.

Using Pulitzer's methods of dramatizing the most drab of stories, combined with various stunts and promotions, Hearst built the *Examiner* into the "Monarch of the Dailies" in San Francisco. After his father died, leaving a fortune of $7,500,000, Hearst cast his eye upon New York where he purchased a money-losing daily, the *Journal*. Taking over the paper in November 1895, he cautiously built up circulation, using Pulitzer's sensationalist approach to the news but without his florid headlines. When the *Journal's* circulation reached one hundred thousand after a year, he was ready to declare war on Pulitzer. He began by stealing the editor of the *World*'s Sunday magazine, who had a peculiar genius for mass appeal; the magazine's entire staff followed their boss to the *Journal*. A bidding war ensued for the services of top editors and reporters. The climax came when Hearst lured into his employ R.F. Outcault, an artist who had created the *World*'s most popular comic strip, "Hogan's Alley." The *World*'s Sunday comics were printed in color (another innovation), and the hero of "Hogan's Alley" was an urchin dressed in a gown of bright yellow. Pulitzer retaliated by hiring another artist to continue its own version of the strip, and New Yorkers were soon treated to two "Yellow Kids" in their Sunday comics. That inspired an editor of one of the city's more conservative papers to slap the label "yellow journalism" on the type of reporting engaged in by Pulitzer and Hearst, and the name stuck.

The success of Pulitzer and Hearst in New York's circulation wars prompted others to imitate their lurid style, and "yellow" papers appeared in Boston, Philadelphia, St. Louis, and Chicago. Conservative papers that disdained scandal and sensation, like the *New York Times*, managed to survive in the larger cities, but in places like Minneapolis and Detroit, where the public had a choice of only two papers, both were likely to be of a lemony hue.

A further result of the Pulitzer–Hearst competition was the growing recognition of the commercial value of reporters who had an eye for human interest and a knack for distinctive prose. To compete for these talented individuals Pulitzer and Hearst began rewarding them with bylines, even putting their names in the headlines when they scooped the other papers. Well-known reporters became makers of news as well as recorders of it. The best-known of these new-style journalists—a man who seemed as much at home on a distant battlefield as in Delmonico's in Manhattan—was Richard Harding Davis.

A Mother's Son

Rebecca Blaine Harding grew up in Wheeling, West Virginia, and still unmarried at the age of thirty, she turned to writing. Her first story, completed in 1861, was entitled "Life in the Iron Mills." The protagonists are an iron puddler who aspires to be an artist and a crippled girl who adores him. Together they become involved in a foolish theft, and he is sentenced to prison. Rather than go to jail, he slashes his wrists with one of his own tools. The plot is less important than the author's realistic look at the industrial poor—the world of vice-ridden mill workers, living on a diet of whiskey and potatoes. Harding sent the manuscript to the editor of the *Atlantic Monthly* in Boston, the literary vehicle for the cultural Brahmins of New England, and to her surprise it was accepted.

With "Life in the Iron Mills" Rebecca Harding embarked on a literary career, though her later products never came close to the quality of her first. Her first publication also led to marriage. In Philadelphia the story was read by a young attorney who hated the law and aspired to a career in journalism. Clarke Davis sent her a fan letter and later visited the Hardings in Wheeling. They were married in March 1863 and settled in Philadelphia where Clarke had obtained a job as editor of a law journal. Their first child, named Richard Harding Davis after his maternal grandfather, was born on April 18, 1864.

Thrown into a society that she came to dislike but never got to know, Rebecca lost her West Virginia edge of realism and began writing mawkish stories for sentimental monthly magazines. She was soon facing more rejection slips than acceptances. The family prospered, however, as Clarke Davis in 1870 became managing editor of the *Inquirer*, the city's

Theodore Roosevelt and Richard Harding Davis, 1898. (Photograph from Culver Pictures.)

leading newspaper. Rebecca gave birth to two more children, Charles in 1865 and a daughter, Nora, in 1872. But she seemed to dote upon her firstborn, who exuded a special charm even in infancy. The effect was lasting. As Davis's biographer, Arthur Lubow, notes, all the crucial decisions that Richard Harding Davis made in his life—his vocation, his delay in getting married, his choice of a bride—"bear the imprint of his formidable mother."

From his youth Richard seemed to view the world as a stage. "Every little incident is a 'venture,'" Rebecca noted when he was seven, "every twopennysworth of candy becomes a tea party, every pleasure the most trifling is converted into a surprise." He had already by then become "the most entertaining of storytellers," sometimes embroidering his tales with half-truths to his mother's dismay.

Although his parents imbued Richard with a strong sense of right and wrong, the doting mother and pliant father were never able to convey the importance of education. (Although his published works obviously benefited from scrupulous editing, Davis's private correspondence throughout his life was riddled with spelling and grammatical errors.) When Richard brought home a steady stream of failing reports, his distraught but unassertive parents pulled him out of Philadelphia's Episcopal Academy and entrusted him to the care of his uncle, Wilse Harding, a bachelor professor of physics at Lehigh University in South Bethlehem, Pennsylvania. Boosted by his uncle's instruction and a year in a college preparatory school, Davis entered Lehigh University in September 1882 on a trial basis.

Lehigh was not the place for a young man of poetic temperament and minimal background in mathematics. The school had been founded in 1865 by the mogul who had built the Lehigh Valley Railroad through the anthracite country of eastern Pennsylvania. He had envisioned a practical university that focused on engineering. With seeming indifference to his somber colleagues, Davis began to cultivate the romantic persona that would define his life. He would strut the campus in a "straight military walk" in English-inspired dress—gloves, Norfolk jacket, knickers, tam-o'-shanter cap. On a person of slighter stature the costume would have invited ridicule, but Richard had grown into a tall, well-built young man with a strong-featured, handsome face. He managed to carry it off, but not surprisingly, he had few friends.

Lehigh's colorless engineers accepted Davis in part because of his prowess on the athletic field. He quickly adapted to the crude formations and bloody violence of the newly invented game of football. He starred in Lehigh's first intercollegiate game, in which the school lost to the University of Pennsylvania 16–0 in a rain-drenched game on a grassless field that turned into mud eight inches deep. Despite the loss, Davis persuaded his teammates to adjourn after the game to a photographer's shop where they posed in their mud-spattered, rain-soaked uniforms.

For all his posturing, Davis still lacked the patience and perseverance to pursue his studies. Even though he avoided the engineering curriculum and adhered to the liberal arts, he repeatedly failed courses. In English, his future vocation, he was fifty-fourth in a class of sixty-nine. At the end of his junior year the faculty suggested that he withdraw from school. He replied with adolescent bravado: "You do not think me worthy to remain in this school. But in a few years you will find that I have gone further than you will ever go."

The Ladder of Fame

Besides athletics, the only avocation that attracted him at college was working for the school newspaper, and he returned to Philadelphia to find employment as a reporter. After a couple false starts he landed a job with the *Press* in December 1886. Convinced that he had found his life's work, he applied himself for a change. As a cub reporter he was often drafted to produce an obligatory piece on a holiday. He spent one Christmas at a home for retired actors, Easter at the zoo, Thanksgiving in a hospital, and each time he managed to sniff out a human element that gave some sparkle to his story. He continued to remain aloof from his peers, preferring to sit quietly and scan literary journals between assignments. When one cheeky new recruit demanded to know his first name, Davis replied "Mister."

After almost three years with the *Press* he had learned the reporter's trade, and in 1889 he moved to New York, the mecca for an ambitious newspaperman, especially one with social aspirations. With the help of a friend, Arthur Brisbane, he landed a job on the *Evening Sun*.

Under the editorial direction of Horace Greeley-trained Charles A. Dana, the *Sun*, a morning paper, was regarded as the best-written paper in America. In 1887, Dana started up an afternoon paper, the *Evening Sun*, and put in charge of it an editor with more vulgar tastes. Even before Pulitzer arrived in town, the *Evening Sun* was scrounging news from the police blotters and carrying lurid stories of street fights and tenement fires. Brisbane, six months younger than Davis, had become editor only a few months before Davis arrived in town. The son of Alfred Brisbane, a socialist who had helped Horace Greeley found Fourierist communities in the 1840s, Arthur was a fun-loving rebel, sharing Davis's love of rich clothes and punctilious manners.

Six-feet tall, 180 pounds, with square face and clean-shaven jaw, Richard Harding Davis appeared too unblemished to be a New Yorker, and as he approached the ramshackle building that housed the *Evening Sun* on his first day as a reporter he was accosted by a con man. The stranger identified himself as the nephew of Philadelphia department store mogul George Wanamaker. "Wanamaker" wanted to show Davis some samples of woolen cloth, and the scam eventually involved a card game in which Davis was asked to put up $1,000. Davis went along with the swindle until the nature of it was clear. He then tackled "Wanamaker" on the sidewalk and held him in a neck-hold until a policeman appeared. In police court "Wanamaker" was identified as one of the city's most notorious con artists. When the judge asked Davis his profession, he replied "reporter on the *Evening Sun*," and the court room broke up in laughter. The *Sun* ran Davis's account of the incident on its front page under the headline "Our Green Reporter." Rival papers published their own amusing versions of it, and the story helped establish a central feature of the Richard Harding Davis genre—an adventure yarn in which Davis himself is the principal character.

Cut from the same mold, Davis and Brisbane became fast friends, and Brisbane introduced him to the New York high life, which included afternoons at the race track and evenings at Broadway theaters. Davis's brother Charles, who worked for the Pennsylvania Railroad, often came up from Philadelphia to visit, and the brothers would take in a Broadway musical. Davis loved the singing and dancing, but he never tried to date a chorus girl. Despite his youth, his behavior toward women was always scrupulously correct, and in the worldly society of New York he maintained an aura of sexual innocence.

Davis, however, did not let the city's cultural attractions deter him from his newly found profession. Reporters were expected to work a six-day week, but if they managed to put together in advance a feature for Saturday's paper, they could take the day off. Davis used these two-day vacations to write short stories, to be printed in the *Evening Sun* side-by-side with the lighter, gossipy part of the news. The character he created was a simulation of the persona that Davis had created for himself—fashionably dressed, a sociable bachelor of independent means, and a clubman with time to resolve the inane problems of friends and relatives. His name was Cortlandt Van Bibber, and he first appeared on March 1, 1890, to citywide applause. Davis churned out Van Bibber stories at the rate of about one a month, and in 1892 he published the collection in book form, *Van Bibber and Others*. The first edition of four thousand copies was sold out by noon on the next day.

While working on his first Van Bibber story in the spring of 1890, Davis was putting the polish on a second piece that would establish his literary reputation. Based on an experience that Davis had in Philadelphia, the story involved a young reporter, Gallagher, who stumbles upon a crime scene and, though innocent, is arrested by police. He escapes, steals a waiting cab, and makes it to the newspaper office with the police in hot pursuit. He writes up his story just in time to make the paper's next edition. Davis titled the story "Gallegher" and sold it to newly founded *Scribner's Magazine* for $175 (the editor did not correct Davis's misspelling). The magazine published the piece in August 1890, and it immediately made Davis a leading literary figure in New York's "high society."

"Perhaps it never rains but it pours," Davis wrote his mother in the spring of 1890, and while he was referring to New York's unusually wet spring, he might also have been talking about his rising tide of fortune. The artist Charles Dana Gibson, creator of the primly dressed, delicately beautiful, and cooly sophisticated "Gibson girl," was retained by Scribner's to do the illustrations for the "Gallegher" story. When he met the broad-shouldered, square-jawed, clean-cut Davis, Gibson immediately recognized him as the perfect companion for the Gibson girl. Davis happily posed for him, and in May 1890 Gibson began publishing a series of drawings that established the paradigms for both male and female beauty for the remainder of the decade. The characters that Gibson drew were never engaged in business nor lacking for money. Invariably dressed in evening clothes, they were pictured together at dinner, around a piano, or at the opera. In some scenes Davis is the escort; in others he is being seductively eyed by a lady dissatisfied with her boorish companion. Male perfection in fantasy and literary potentate in reality—Davis himself could not have invented a more satisfying persona.

Editor at Large

Harper's Weekly was in trouble. Founded in the 1850s by the nation's leading publishing firm, Harper Brothers, it had been placed under the editorship of George William Curtis, who went politically from Lincolnesque antislavery to civil service reform to mentally numbed old age, losing his Republican audience in the process without gaining any Democrats or liberals. The Harper Brothers clearly needed new editorial blood. The rival publishing house of Charles Scribner had started up a sprightly competitor, *Scribner's Magazine*. In December 1890 the Harpers hired Scribner's star author, Richard Harding Davis, as their new managing editor. The incidental effect was that Davis would have to submit his short stories thereafter to his new employer.

For Davis, the step up the journalistic ladder was a mixed blessing. He had no experience as an editor, although, fortunately, he could depend on underlings to cover up his spelling and grammatical deficiencies. In addition, an editor's job involved drudgery, without the compensating feeling of creativity, and it lacked the social glamour of the littérateur. Even so, for Davis, there were compensations. *Harper's Weekly* was a magazine of political importance and literary substance, and the title of managing editor on one's calling card guaranteed entrance to the homes of the rich and the offices of the mighty. Another perk was expenses for travel, which, in turn, would generate articles for the magazine and perhaps books with royalties.

After a year of plodding editorial work, Davis worked out a deal with the Harper brothers. He would tour the West by train, return to New York briefly, and then sail off to London. He was to be paid $1,000 for each article he wrote, plus expenses. The western trip, which resulted in a book, *The West from a Car-Window*, was unheroic, but Davis managed to find colorful nuances—a gunfight involving a sheriff in Texas, "Sooners" snatching government land in Oklahoma, Indians living on government-supplied rotten beef. The trip to London in 1892 was followed a year later by an extended visit to the Mediterranean where he trolled Morocco, Egypt, and Greece in pursuit of the vivid and the whimsical. This tour resulted in a book, *About Paris*, but in the meantime the ruling Harpers decided that they were not getting their money's worth out of their nomadic editor. On his return in the fall of 1893 he was demoted to the position of associate editor, a part-time job that netted a mere $75 a week. Quietly humiliated, he accepted the position. There seemed few alternatives in the midst of the depression that had begun that spring.

The financial hard times turned into a mental depression, aggravated, one suspects, by the fact that he turned thirty in 1894. The persona that Davis had created for himself was based on eternal youth and strength, and the reality of his human frailty would produce periodic bouts of depression throughout his life. He spent much of the year "in the blues," as he put it. His spirits revived in December when a friend he had met in England, the twenty-year-old heir to the duchy of Beaufort, encountered him in Delmonico's and suggested a Caribbean and Central American tour. Another youthful and wealthy American was added to the group, and the "three gringoes" spent much of 1895 touring Cuba, Central America, and Venezuela. Davis's resulting book, *Three Gringoes in Venezuela and Central America*, was perhaps his best travelogue, a blend of fetching jungle scenery and farcical human comedy.

Shortly after returning from Central America, Davis was approached by William Randolph Hearst. It was November 1895, only a month after Hearst had purchased the *New York Journal*. He asked Davis to cover the Thanksgiving Day football game between Yale and Princeton. Football had come a long way since Davis's collegiate years, and the annual clash between ivied powers attracted much attention because so many of their alumni lived and worked in New York. Davis would have preferred to cover the game for a more prestigious paper, but, rather than give the little-known Hearst a flat "no," he demanded the outrageous sum of $500. To his surprise, Hearst agreed. The sum is thought to have been the highest amount ever paid to a reporter for a single event.

Hearst knew his audience and got his money's worth. He printed Davis's account, with pencil sketches of the action, across the front page of the Sunday edition of the *Journal*, and it sold out. Thereafter Hearst pursued Davis avidly, offering to make him a foreign correspondent and asking him to name his terms. Davis was amenable because he wanted to visit Europe again. A fitting occasion was the coronation of Nicholas II as "Czar of all the Russias," scheduled in Moscow for May 1896. "A hundred years from now there will be no more kings and queens," Davis had written in one of his stories, and he descried a *fin de siècle* poignancy in the crowning of Nicholas and his German-born czarina, Alexandra.

President Cleveland rejected Davis's request to attend the Russian ceremony as an accredited representative of the United States, and he traveled to Europe in the spring of 1896 with nothing more than commissions from the *Journal* and *Harper's Weekly*. When he arrived in Moscow, he discovered that only twelve correspondents would be allowed to attend the coronation (out of ninety in town), and he had to bribe his way into a seat. Davis's account of the five-hour ceremony occupied the first two pages of the *Journal*, and Hearst, now fully alive to the marketing value of his correspondents, ran a sketch of Davis together with a drawing of a lovely half-American girl who served as maid of honor to the czarina. In bold-face type Hearst assured readers that the author was "easily the ablest of the army of correspondents now gathered in Moscow." Davis's next assignment was to cover a revolution in Cuba.

Cuba

In the first two decades of the century Latin American colonists had taken advantage of Spain's preoccupation with the Napoleonic wars and began revolutions for independence. By 1830, Cuba and Puerto Rico were the last vestiges of the once mighty Spanish empire. From 1868 to 1878 Cuban revolutionaries fought a Ten Years' War for independence but failed in their goal. Many of the rebels moved to America and settled in cities of the eastern seaboard where most found employment in tobacco factories. In 1894 a change in American tariff policy suddenly placed Cuban sugar planters in ruinous competition in the American market with Hawaiian sugar and domestic beet growers. A new revolution broke out in February 1895, financed and directed principally by exiles in New York.

Over the next year news correspondents, most of whom never left Key West, reported pitched battles and heavy casualties on both sides, but in reality battles were rare and casualties few. The Spanish general, Maximo Gomez, had only a few thousand men at his command and was short of guns and ammunition. He avoided combat and had no intention of trying to capture rebel strongholds. The arrival of General Valeriano Weyler in February 1896 seemed to herald a change in Spanish strategy. Weyler had a reputation as a ruthless soldier, and within days after his arrival the yellow press had labeled him "Butcher Weyler." Although Weyler would eventually become infamous for incarcerating Cuban civilians in concentration camps, his initial crimes, so far as the American press was concerned, were preventing correspondents from accompanying Spanish troops on their forays and censoring dispatches cabled from Havana.

The Cuban conflict was fodder for the American press, and shortly after Davis returned from Europe Hearst offered him $3,000 plus all expenses for a month of reporting on Cuba. Because the Spanish authorities were suspicious of people with cameras and arrested as a spy anyone caught photographing military installations, American editors often sent sketch-artists to accompany their reporters. Sparing no expense, Hearst persuaded Frederic Remington to accompany Davis. Remington was justly famous for his action-packed drawings of cowboys and Indians. He was also acquainted with Davis, for he had done the illustrations for Davis's book, *The West from a Car-Window*. In addition to Hearst's stipend, Davis lined up a $600 commission from *Harper's Magazine* and a book contract with another publisher. He and Remington went by train and boat to Key West in December 1896, and after seemingly endless delays caused by unseaworthy craft and bad weather, they reached Havana on January 9.

The American consul in Havana introduced the Americans to General Weyler, who, according to Davis, received them "with courtesy and consideration." He granted the Americans permission to travel wherever they liked, including, apparently, visits to rebel-held territory. The pair of reporters departed by train for the eastern end of the island, but after a week Remington decided that he had had enough. The month he had promised Hearst had expired, and there was no fighting to be seen. He cabled Hearst: "Everything is quiet. There is no trouble here. I wish to return. Remington." Hearst's reply is one of the most famous in the history of journalism: "Please remain. You furnish the pictures, and I'll furnish the war. W.R. Hearst."

Remington left Cuba anyway on January 15, and Davis was delighted to see him go. Overweight and given to complaining, Remington was not a good traveling companion. He was crudely macho (at Yale he had dipped his football uniform in a pool of slaughterhouse blood) and a caustic racist, who thought the Cuban people were a bunch of "damned niggers who are better off under the yoke" of Spanish rule. To Davis, travel through Cuba was primitive enough without having to coddle Remington. "I would rather manage an Italian opera company than him," he said. Hearst in the meantime was getting his money's worth from the expedition. The departure of Davis and Remington had rated front page headlines. On January 17 the *Journal* carried a follow-up article claiming that Davis and Remington were with the rebel army. When General Weyler read that piece, he sent spies to follow Davis.

Davis, meantime, was having a pleasant excursion through the Cuban countryside. At the eastern end of the island, where the rebels were strongest, he encountered burning cane fields and smoking villages.

In order to prevent the rebels from obtaining supplies and recruits in the rural villages, Weyler had adopted a policy of *reconcentrado*, that is, herding the villagers into fortified camps while burning their fields and villages. The result, Davis wrote, was that the able-bodied men joined the insurgents, and the *reconcentrado* policy inflicted "terrible suffering" on the women and children, who were "absolutely innocent of any intent against the government." Atrocities against women and children were exactly what Hearst wanted to hear, and Davis's reports were printed with screaming headlines in the *Journal*.

Davis left Cuba in early February 1897, and aboard ship he chanced upon a woman who had been exiled from Cuba for aiding the rebels. She told Davis that she and her companions had been put in a special cabin aboard ship and searched for messages they might be carrying. They even had to take off their shoes and stockings. In Tampa, Davis filed a report of the incident, newsworthy because Spanish authorities had intruded upon an American vessel. Hearst spotted the potential and printed the report under the headline: "Richard Harding Davis Describes . . . Refined Young Women Stripped and Searched by Brutal Spaniards While Under Our Flag. . . ." Accompanying the article was a five-column drawing by Remington of a woman with a bare backside standing among leering Spanish soldiers who were searching her clothing. When he saw the article, Davis was outraged. He had never said that the women were naked or that they had been searched by men. Even if that had been the case, his fastidious disposition toward women would have prevented him from reporting it. He vowed never to work for Hearst again.

The atrocities-against-females angle, which Davis had initiated, was too luscious a story for Hearst to drop. Later that year, while Davis was in the Mediterranean covering a war between Greeks and Turks, *Journal* reporters uncovered the case of Evangelina Cisneros, a "pretty girl of seventeen years," who was languishing in a Cuban jail as a rebel suspect. Hearst leaped on the story, shouting to his managing editor: "Telegraph to our correspondent in Havana to wire every detail of this case. Get up a petition to the queen regent of Spain for this girl's pardon. Enlist the women of America. Have them sign a petition. . . !" With public interest at a fever pitch, a Hearst reporter slipped into the Cuban jail, freed Evangelina, and stowed her aboard an American vessel. (Since, by the reporter's own admission, it took him two days to saw through the bars of the cell, his jailbreak must have been accompanied by a Hearstian douceur to the Cuban guards). Evangelina was smuggled into New York and made a dramatic appearance in the offices of the *Journal*. Historians cite the story as the epitome of yellow journalism.

What Davis thought of this bit of journalistic exploitation we do not know. He was in Greece that summer, attending a war in which, at last, there was some real fighting. While accompanying the Greek army he suffered an acute attack of sciatica (an inflammation of the sciatic nerve, which passes from the spine down the back of each leg), an ailment that would shadow him the rest of his life. He returned to Athens aboard a hospital ship full of severely wounded men. "They groaned all night, and so did I," Davis wrote. "Then when the sun rose they sang, which was worse." He nevertheless was ecstatic over his Greek adventure. The editor of the *London Times*, to whom he sent his dispatches, told him that it was the best writing of the war. From Italy he wrote his parents: "It was the most satisfactory trip all around I ever had. I have been twenty years trying to be in a battle and it will be twenty more before I will want to be in another."

That autumn in New York he undertook to fulfill another lifelong ambition, the writing of a full-length play. He gave up after the first act, however, when a Broadway producer told him, somewhat ambiguously, to go back to work on it. In December he returned to Europe, and he was in Paris on February 15, 1898, when the USS *Maine* exploded in Havana harbor, triggering the chain of events that led to the Spanish–American War.

With Roosevelt and the Rough Riders

Although the yellow press was screaming for war from the moment the *Maine* exploded, President McKinley delayed until April before sending his war message to Congress. In the interim, McKinley appointed a commission of inquiry to visit Havana and determine the cause of the explosion. The commission's report was inconclusive, both as to the explosion (whether an internal fire or an external mine) and as to who was at fault. McKinley also felt the need to win over the American business community, which was just emerging from a depression and feared that war might disrupt the economy.

The delay gave Davis time to make arrangements for covering the expected conflict. He renewed his commission with the *Times* of London, and when that paper contracted to share his dispatches with the *New York Herald* and its fourteen-paper syndicate, he demanded and got a pay raise to $400 a week, plus expenses. In New York he arranged with *Scribner's* to provide three magazine articles at the rate of ten cents a word. In London and New York he purchased an elaborate war outfit, which included boots, a shooting jacket, revolver and holster, and a stylish hat. Predictably, he had himself photographed in the costume, and publication of the shot produced much journalistic merriment. "If he were cut up into small pieces," chuckled one editor, "he would furnish the insurgents with arms and equipments for a whole winter."

After Congress declared war, President McKinley ordered a naval blockade of Havana harbor. Sailing from Key West in a yacht owned by the *New York Herald*, Davis managed to get aboard the battleship *New*

York. However, other correspondents protested this seemingly favorable treatment, and the secretary of the navy ordered all correspondents to be put ashore. Davis departed for Tampa where the army was assembling an invasion force. There he renewed his acquaintance with Theodore Roosevelt, who commanded a regiment of cavalry that styled itself the Rough Riders. Roosevelt, the publicity-hungry politician, and Richard Harding Davis, the storyteller who loved giving leading roles to himself and well-bred friends, were made for one another. Davis paved the road for Roosevelt's journey to the White House; Roosevelt reinforced Davis's reputation as the greatest newsman of his day.

Roosevelt and Davis were already well-acquainted. In his rise through Republican Party ranks, from civil service commissioner to president of the New York police board, Roosevelt had assiduously cultivated journalists. To enliven his duties as police commissioner, Roosevelt had instituted night patrols in the city's slums to bolster the morale of the cops on the street. Davis and other reporters were invariably invited along. When the war began, Roosevelt resigned his position as assistant secretary of the navy and recruited a volunteer cavalry regiment. Because of Roosevelt's reputation, the first volunteers to step forward were football players and wrestling champions from Harvard and Yale. Feeling the need for recruits who could ride a horse, Roosevelt went to San Antonio and personally signed up an assortment of cattlemen and ranch hands. He then led his First Volunteer Cavalry to the embarkation center at Tampa. There Roosevelt modestly declined command of the regiment because he lacked military experience, and command went to Colonel Leonard Wood, a veteran soldier and competent tactician.[1]

By the end of May about 25,000 men had gathered at Tampa. Most of them were volunteers. The regular army had been limited by law to 28,000 soldiers, and nearly all were assigned to frontier outposts. Something like 125,000 men responded to the president's call for volunteers, and it would have been most efficient if the army had used its regulars as a cadre to train and lead the volunteers. Politics prevented any such sensible outcome. State National Guard officers (many of them politicians) wanted to keep their units intact, even though they lacked training or experience, and the army had neither the time nor the money to bring in regulars from the frontier. Commanding the motley force that assembled in Tampa was Brigadier General William R. Shafter, a veteran of the Civil War who had done little of late but grow fat (he weighed nearly three hundred pounds). His second-in-command, "Fighting Joe" Wheeler, was

1. Association with the Rough Riders also brought Leonard Wood within sight of the presidency. He was the favorite in the Republican presidential convention of 1920 until party managers chose instead the dark horse, Warren G. Harding.

an ex-Confederate general who kept confusing the Spaniards with the "Damn Yankees."

From the secretary of war on down no one thought that military exercises or practice shooting was important for the expeditionary army being assembled in Tampa. In fact, the War Department expected its force to sail some time in May, which would not have left time for training, in any case. The departure was delayed, but not by military exercises. There simply were no troop transports. Neither the army nor the navy had any; the government had to rent them from private passenger services, which also provided the seamen. The navy never thought to put its own officers on board, and the merchant seamen, more concerned for the safety of their vessels than the welfare of the troops, caused massive confusion during the invasion.

Lieutenant Colonel Roosevelt need not have bothered to recruit cowboys for his cavalry unit because General Shafter, intent upon squeezing as many men as possible upon his limited number of transports, ordered all horses, except those for the highest officers, to be left in Tampa. Roosevelt somehow managed to squirrel two mounts for himself on board; the rest of the Rough Riders would fight the war on foot.

After several false starts and much confusion, an army of sixteen thousand was finally jammed aboard thirty-two troop ships on June 14, and the flotilla crept out of Tampa Bay. Davis was one of eight journalists allowed aboard General Shafter's ship; most of the other eighty-nine accredited correspondents traveled on a boat reserved for the press. The Spanish fleet, which had caused a war scare on the American coast when the U.S. Navy failed to track its whereabouts in the North Atlantic, holed up in Santiago Bay on the southeast coast of Cuba, and that, rather than Havana, became the new target of the American landing. Because the civilian mariners hired by the navy had no sense of squadron order and kept meandering off by themselves, the voyage to Santiago lasted a week, twice as long as it should have. "No words can tell the discomforts and beastliness and boredom of the troop ship," Davis complained to his parents. "The food is impossible and it is so overcrowded that never for an instant are you alone."

On June 20 the fleet hove to off the Cuban coast, eighteen miles west of Santiago, and Shafter, accompanied by Davis and three other correspondents, went inland to visit the rebel commander, Calixto Garcia, to determine a point where the Americans should land. Because the mountain trail was steep and the temperature scorching, the Cubans found a burro for General Shafter (they later claimed its legs had been permanently bowed). Suffering from sciatica, Davis also rated a mount. Acting on General Garcia's advice, the American army landed at the village of Daiquiri, sixteen miles to the east of the entrance to Santiago Bay.

The troop transports anchored well off the beach, and the soldiers had to be dropped into launches for the trip to shore. The sea was rough, and a number of craft turned over in the surf. Several horses were drowned, including one of Colonel Roosevelt's. Had the Spanish contested the landing, there would have been severe casualties, but the Spanish commander instead withdrew his forces to the hills surrounding the city of Santiago. He also left undefended the fishing hamlet of Siboney, some eight miles closer to the mouth of the bay, and when the Americans learned of this, the transports moved westward and finished unloading there. Arriving at Siboney in company with the Rough Riders on the evening of June 23, Davis described the scene as more like Coney Island on a hot Sunday than an invasion beach. "The men still to be landed from the 'prison hulks,'" he wrote, "were singing in chorus, the men already on shore were dancing naked around camp-fires on the beach, or shouting with delight as they plunged into the first bath they had been offered in seven days."

Santiago lay at the head of a long narrow bay, so even at Siboney the American force was about fifteen miles from its target. An American fleet under Admiral William T. Sampson blockaded the harbor, but he was unwilling to enter it for fear of underwater mines and Spanish coastal artillery. At dawn on June 24 two regiments of army regulars struck out on the road from Siboney to Santiago. The Rough Riders were ordered to take a mountain trail about a half mile to the west of the main road. Davis, still lame from his nerve ailment, was allowed to accompany the march on one of the government's precious mules. Roosevelt and Colonel Wood had the only other mounts. The trail was so narrow and the jungle so thick that the regiment was strung out in single file.

In mid-morning the regiment suddenly came under fire from an unseen enemy using smokeless cartridges. As the men fanned out into the brush to locate the Spaniards, Roosevelt rode up to Davis, and both men studied the hill in front of them searching for the enemy. Suddenly Davis said, "There they are Colonel; I can see their hats near that glade." Roosevelt put this statement into his own history of the war, *The Rough Riders*, and added: "It was Richard Harding Davis who gave us our first opportunity to shoot back with effect. He was behaving precisely like my officers, being on the extreme front of the line, and taking every opportunity to study with his glasses the ground where we thought the Spaniards were."

While part of the regiment drifted to the east to try to link up with the regulars on the main road, the remainder started creeping toward the Spanish position. "The advances were made in quick desperate rushes," Davis wrote, "sometimes the ground gained was no more than a man covers in sliding for a base." Caught up in the excitement, Davis grabbed a carbine from a wounded soldier and began shooting in the direction of the Spanish. The Spanish troops began a slow retreat, and Davis, his sciatica apparently forgotten, joined the advancing American skirmish line. After about an hour of fighting the army regulars joined the fray, and the Spanish fled. When the firing ceased, the Cuban insurgents suddenly made an appearance and began scavenging the packs and bedrolls thrown off by the Rough Riders.

This fight on a nameless jungle path caught the public imagination when described by Davis and other journalists. A few reporters pointed out that Wood and Roosevelt had blundered into an ambush, but Davis emphasized the intrepid courage of the regiment and its leaders in pressing the attack under heavy fire. The partnership of Theodore Roosevelt and Richard Harding Davis had been born.

For the next week the American army closed in on Santiago through torrential summer rains. In Tampa the soldiers had been issued the army's standard woolen uniforms, and these were soon discarded in the heat and humidity of the Cuban jungle. As the soldiers marched they could see in the distance the Spanish digging trenches and setting up fortifications on San Juan Hill, behind which lay the city. General Shafter was prostrate from the heat much of the time; Wheeler and another general were felled by malaria. Colonel Wood replaced a sick general in charge of a brigade, and Roosevelt took command of the Rough Riders.

On the afternoon of June 30 General Shafter divided his army. The cavalry regiments were to assault San Juan Hill, while the remainder of the army wheeled around the hills to attack the city from the northeast. The cavalry regiments marched until midnight and camped on the banks of the San Juan River. Davis, once more suffering from sciatica, was carried to the front in a wagon. From the campsite he could see the lights of Santiago three miles away. Throughout the week-long march he had become increasingly critical of General Shafter. He had particularly noticed the lack of artillery. The entire American army had only sixteen three-inch guns—sixty more had been left behind in Tampa. "It was like going to a fire with a hook and ladder company," he fumed, "and leaving the hose and the steam-engines in the engine-house." If Wood's regiments had been able to pound San Juan Hill with artillery, the infantry assault, Davis was certain, would have suffered far fewer casualties.

San Juan Hill lay about five hundred yards beyond the river. To the right of the hill, and somewhat closer, was a smaller elevation on which were some ranch buildings and a conspicuous iron kettle, causing the men to dub it Kettle Hill. At dawn on July 1 the cavalry regiments waded across the river and entered a field of tall grass. They were immediately pinned down by a rain of gunfire from the hills. The Rough Riders, holding the extreme right of the American line, took cover in a sunken trail near the river bank. Davis became lost in the confusion and ended up amidst the Tenth Cavalry, a black regiment. The Americans were trapped. They could not return the fire because they could not see the Spanish snipers, and they had no orders to advance farther. For an hour they waited in the grass and died—"an hour," wrote Davis, "of such hell of fire and heat, that the heat in itself, had there been no bullets, would have been remembered for its cruelty."

Davis finally located Roosevelt, who was in a rage for lack of orders and threatening to act on his own. At that moment a messenger arrived with orders to move out and attack the two hills. Roosevelt leaped on his horse and rode through his regiment, mobilizing as he went. Moving forward, Roosevelt encountered soldiers of the First and Ninth Cavalry hiding in the grass. He told the ranking officer that he had been ordered to charge the hills and asked for support. When the officer hesitated, Roosevelt swept him aside, saying (according to Davis), "If you don't wish to go forward, let my men pass, please." As the Rough Riders pushed through, the other cavalrymen rose and joined the skirmish line. Davis's report to the *Herald* captured the drama of the moment: "Roosevelt, mounted high on horseback, and charging the rifle-pits at a gallop and quite alone, made you feel that you would like to cheer. . . . No one who saw Roosevelt take that ride expected he would finish it alive. As the only mounted man, he was the most conspicuous object in range of the rifle pits, then only two hundred yards ahead. It looked like foolhardiness, but, as a matter of fact, he set the pace with his horse and inspired the men to follow."

The skirmish line of blue-clad men broke and wavered under a relentless Spanish fire. A few men led the advance; the remainder crept up the hill, slipping and scrambling in the wet grass. "It was much more wonderful than any swinging charge could have been," Davis continued his account. "They walked to greet death at every step, many of them, as they advanced, sinking suddenly or pitching forward and disappearing in the high grass, but the others waded on, stubbornly, forming a thin blue line that kept creeping higher and higher up the hill. It was as inevitable as the rising tide." When the Americans neared the top, the Spanish soldiers stood up, silhouetted against the sky, and then fled.

While Roosevelt and the Rough Riders were assaulting Kettle Hill, the regular cavalry regiments, led by General Hamilton S. Hawkins, attacked the Spanish positions on San Juan Hill. From the crest of Kettle Hill Roosevelt watched this action for a time, and then, wanting to be in on the finish, he dashed across the basin between the two hills. With only a handful of Rough Riders behind him he reached the crest of San Juan Hill just as the Spanish were retreating. Two diehards broke from the trenches and opened fire just as Roosevelt arrived. Roosevelt drew his revolver, missed one and killed the other. The Spanish, who fought gallantly throughout the battle, retreated in good order to a stronghold at the outskirts of the city. From there they opened a deadly artillery and rifle fire on the trenches they had so recently lost to the Americans. Davis followed Roosevelt up San Juan Hill and was the first correspondent to reach the top. He arrived with some artillerymen, whose smoke-belching shots (Americans were still using black powder) immediately drew Spanish fire. "The artillery ran away after occupying the crest three minutes," Davis wrote home. "I occupied it about three seconds."

The Spanish gunfire continued for the next two days, inflicting hundreds of casualties after the Americans had seemingly won the battle. In all, American losses amounted to about 10 percent of Shafter's army of fifteen thousand men engaged in combat. The remainder were far too exhausted, wet from torrential rains, and hungry to mount another assault. Reinforcements were still sitting in Tampa. On the morning of July 3 Shafter sent a flag of truce across the lines with a bluffing demand that the Spanish surrender the city. The Spanish commander refused, and messengers with white flags passed back and forth through the rest of the day. The flags appeared so frequently that the men began comparing them to the various editions of a daily newspaper: "Has that ten o'clock edition gone in yet?" Or "Is this the baseball edition coming out now, or is it an extry?"

While General Shafter dithered and talked, Davis exploded. After touring the trenches he concluded that "It is as impossible to take Santiago with the infantry now overlooking its walls as to open a safe with a pocket pistol." Davis described soldiers who had not slept or eaten properly in several days. And he had no doubt who was to blame. "Truthfully the expedition was prepared in ignorance and conducted in a series of blunders. Its commanding general has not yet even been within two miles of the scene of operation. . . . The presence of some man with absolute authority is necessary at the front." When the *Herald* printed this dispatch on July 7, rival papers accused Davis of treason.

On July 4 the Spanish fleet broke the impasse by sailing out of Santiago Bay and into the arms of Admiral Sampson. In a running sea fight every Spanish warship was either sunk or run aground. But by July 7, when Davis's harsh criticism broke and Shafter received a summary of it, the Spanish in Santiago had still not capitulated. Yellow fever broke out in the army on July 6, and it would ultimately carry away more Americans than had died in battle. The Spanish commander finally suspended hostilities on July 11, and a formal ceremony of capitulation took place at a point midway between the lines on July 17. While the American flag was being raised at the governor's palace later that day, a *New York World* reporter invaded the ceremony and got into a shoving match with General Shafter. Davis did not witness this final indignity. He was at Guantanamo Bay on the eastern end of Cuba waiting to embark for the invasion of Puerto Rico.

The army sent from Tampa to reinforce Shafter was commanded by General Nelson Miles, a veteran of the Indian Wars, who had been recommending a landing on Puerto Rico from the outset of the war. When he arrived in Cuba on July 11, hostilities had ceased, and the War Department promptly diverted him to Puerto Rico, the final Spanish possession in the Caribbean. Davis went along, in part to collect more material for a book on the war and in part to see another commander's handling of an island campaign. Although Davis sent home a string of dispatches favorable to Miles, the general's initial decision was a highly questionable one. The Spanish were concentrated around the city of San Juan on the north (Atlantic) coast of the island. Worried that the Spanish might have been alerted to the invasion by American news reports, Miles decided instead to land on the south (Caribbean) side of the island. That meant a march of seventy miles across mountain roads to reach San Juan. Had the Spanish contested the route, it would have been a bloody affair.

Miles's invasion fleet made several landings in the vicinity of the picturesque village of Guanica at dawn on July 25. While the troops were disembarking, a battery of sailors, meeting no resistance, started inland. The immediate target was the city of Ponce, about two miles from the beach. The American army had established other beachheads, and companies of sailors and soldiers converged on Ponce from several directions. Davis reported that the city surrendered officially and unofficially on four separate occasions. "It was possessed of the surrender habit in a most aggravating form," he wrote. "Indeed, for anyone in uniform it was most unsafe to enter the town at any time unless he came prepared to accept its unconditional surrender."

With Puerto Ricans happily siding with the Americans and no Spanish troops in sight, the march across the island became a frolic. For Davis the high point of the campaign was the capture of the village of Coamo in the mountains that formed the central spine of the island. He and three other correspondents had overslept one morning and hurried to Coamo to witness an expected fight. Finding a shortcut, they galloped into town without realizing that they were ahead of the army. They were greeted by a surrender committee, carrying white flags and gifts of rum, wine, and cigars. The alcalde surrendered the town to Davis, giving him the key to the cartel and a Spanish flag. For twenty minutes, Davis wrote, until the Sixteenth Pennsylvania Volunteers came down the road, Davis was in sole command of the city.

Fortunately for his historical reputation (which had been amply tarnished by the massacre of Sioux Indians at Wounded Knee), General Miles did not have to assault the Spanish defenses at San Juan. Spain offered an armistice on August 12, and the War Department immediately cabled Miles, "Suspend all hostilities." The fate of Puerto Rico would be decided at a postwar peace conference. The humorist Finley Peter Dunne, speaking through his fictionalized Irishman, Mr. Dooley, summarized the campaign: "Porther Ricky . . . Gin'ral Miles' gran picnic an' moonlight excursion."

No one benefited from the war more than Roosevelt and Davis. As a war hero (a public perception created largely by Davis) Roosevelt was placed on the Republican ticket with McKinley in the presidential election of 1900, and when an assassin's bullet felled McKinley in September 1901, Roosevelt acceded to the White House. Davis collected the magazine articles he had written for *Scribner's* into a book, *The Cuban and Puerto Rican Campaigns*. It was greeted with critical acclaim and remains today his best-known work.

Although neither man leaned upon the other after 1900, they maintained a sociable correspondence. For example, during the furor occasioned in 1901 by Roosevelt's luncheon invitation to the black educator, Booker T. Washington, Davis wrote to congratulate Roosevelt, saying, "I would not insult you or myself, by saying you were right to ask to your table a gentleman who has done as much for his people, and through them, for the good of his country, their country, yours and mine, as has Booker T. Washington."

Yielding to Time

Returning from Cuba, Davis landed in New York on August 20, 1898, aboard an army hospital ship. He immediately headed for his family's summer home in Marion, Massachusetts, a seaside resort on Buzzard's Bay. He was thirty-four, moderately wealthy, and had proved his courage in combat. His thoughts now were on marriage.

Among the best friends of the Davises in Marion was the Clark family, whose patriarch, John Marshall Clark, was a Chicago businessman. Davis had known the Clarks' daughter Cecil since she was a teenager. She was now in her early twenties and a portrait painter of some note. Although not strikingly beautiful, she was a fine athlete who loved dogs, rode horses, and excelled at billiards. After spending the summer and fall in Marion, Davis wrote to John Clark, asking for his daughter's hand in marriage. The Clarks were enthusiastic, but Cecil was hesitant—a warning signal that Davis would have done well to heed. He nevertheless pursued the courtship, though periodically hospitalized by bouts of sciatica and malaria. They were married in Marion on May 4, 1899.

Then she dropped her bombshell. "A girl needs someone to take her about," she is supposed to have told Davis. "We will simply be as brother and sister." She insisted from the outset on having her own bedroom, and they eventually lived in separate houses. The fault may not have been entirely Cecil's. As a quasi-sister she was less of a rival to the possessive Rebecca and more easily incorporated into the Davis family. It is interesting that neither of Rebecca's other children married until after their mother died in 1910, and Richard, though utterly estranged from Cecil by that date, did not dare to divorce her until after his mother died. Life must have been difficult. When he took Cecil to Japan in 1903, she insisted upon a stateroom for herself, and because the ship was crowded, Davis had to share a berth with a stranger.

In 1905 Davis bought a large tract of land in Westchester County, New York, and began building a house that matched the persona he had created for himself. They named it the Crossroads Farm, and he may have hoped to trigger some romance amidst the rural seclusion. To pay for the house and the constant accretions of land to maintain his privacy, Davis began turning out plays and novels at a frantic pace. His novels at this time were simple adventure stories with rather wooden characters, and they were more often greeted with derision than praise. But they made money because of his personal fame and Scribners' marketing methods. (They bound his volumes in leather and sold them as sets.)

The marriage failed anyway, and in 1907 they reached what Davis termed a modus vivendi. He spent most of his time thereafter in the city, promoting his books and producing his plays, and Cecil stayed at the farm, with her easel, her horses, and her dogs. Divorce was still rare in America, but it was on the rise, as women gained confidence through their clubs and public appearances on behalf of social reforms. After Davis's mother died, Cecil returned to Chicago to live with her parents. Because Illinois's divorce laws were more lenient than New York's, she filed for divorce there. Her ground was simply desertion. Davis did not contest it, and Cecil did not demand alimony. The decree was signed on June 18, 1912. Three weeks later Davis married a Broadway chorus girl, Bessie McCoy. He was forty-eight, she was twenty-four.

Davis had known Bessie for four years, and he had been rapturously in love from the moment he met her. Never one to be casual when it came to women, Davis from the outset planned to marry her. Only his mother and his marriage stood in the way. Both obstacles were removed by July 1912, and he carried Bessie to the Westchester farm. Whether he gained or lost by the change of mates remains uncertain. Cecil had given him little emotionally, but she had demanded little in return. She had participated in his professional life, accompanying him to battlefields and hosting dinner parties. She was a "modern" woman who thought her painting was as important as her marriage. Bessie, on the other hand, knew nothing of life beyond the Broadway theater district. She was uncomfortable with Davis's wealthy friends, and she detested the Crossroads Farm. She was bored when he was there, frightened by the isolation when he was not. Bessie did enjoy travel, however, and she accompanied him to Europe at the outbreak of World War I.

On January 4, 1915, Bessie gave birth to a daughter, whom they named Hope. Davis adored her, though he would know the child for only a little more than a year.[2]

2. After Davis's death, Bessie, who always retained the name Mrs. Richard Harding Davis, returned to Broadway and starred in one of Florenz Ziegfeld's musical reviews, *Miss 1917*. She died in 1931, having preserved Davis's fortune for her daughter. Hope tried to maintain the family tradition by becoming a writer and failed. She died by her own hand in 1976.

Davis's talents as a journalist held up better than his literary skills in the years after the Spanish–American War. But the foreign correspondent was no longer the public figure that he had been in the 1890s, when he felt able to give advice to generals and swing confidently aboard battleships. It was the Russo–Japanese War that brought home this diminished status. When war broke out in the summer of 1903, Davis was off and running like a firehouse Dalmatian. He signed a contract with Rob Collier, whose muckraking weekly, *Collier's*, had a circulation in the millions, for the fantastic sum of a thousand dollars a week. Collier expected to get his money's worth. "I find that of all the people who write for us we get better returns from your work," he told Davis.

With pockets full of money, Davis outdid himself in assembling a battlefront kit. It included a table, chairs, a bathtub, and a folding bed. Accompanying him and Cecil were three black servant boys, one of whom was assigned the sole duty of polishing boots, shoes, and belts. When Davis arrived at the Japanese War Office in Tokyo, General Fukushima asked to see his outfit and then "borrowed" some of the choice items. Replicas later appeared in the Japanese army.

After a few weeks of pacing the floor of his hotel, Davis realized that the Japanese general staff had no intention of letting foreign correspondents visit the battlefront. Having carefully planned their assault on the somnolent Russians, they feared publicity and tended to view reporters as spies. In May 1904, Davis complained to President Roosevelt that the Japanese had "imposed restrictions that put us a little higher than naughty children and a little lower than spies." When Davis finally did reach the war zone in Manchuria, Japanese officers flatly denied the existence of a battle that was then in progress, and Davis returned home without witnessing the only important battle of the war. He predicted that in the next war the Japanese method of dealing with the press would be widely copied.

In 1911, with the experience of the Russo–Japanese War still firmly in mind, Davis wrote an obituary to his own profession. Journalists would still be sent to wars, he predicted, but their activities will be sharply curtailed. A worldwide cable network forced nations at war to censor or delay each dispatch so "that it will furnish information neither to the enemy nor to anyone else." And, in order to monitor the dispatches, military authorities would have to control the movement of journalists. In addition, Davis went on, the reporter was no longer free to develop the human interest in his story. He was never beyond the editor's reach; he "moved with a cable from the home office attached to his spinal column, jerking him this way and that."

Disgust with his situation, however, did not prevent him from responding to the drums of conflict. When war broke out in Europe three years later, Davis hurried across the Atlantic with commissions from *Scribner's* and a newspaper syndicate. The French in August 1914 were not permitting any reporters near the front, and the British allowed only one accredited American. Fortunately, Davis was not the one chosen, for the British promptly placed the American far to the rear of their operations. From London, Davis pushed on to Brussels where he would have a free hand watching the war from neutral Belgium. As luck would have it, the Germans invaded Belgium just at that moment in a sweeping "end run" around the French armies. On August 20, three days after Davis arrived in Brussels, the Belgian king sent word to the city's gendarmes to lay down their arms and surrender. At 10:00 in the morning an advance guard of the German army swept down the Boulevard Waterloo, followed by column upon column of infantry.

Davis watched for a while and then returned to his hotel to send off a six-hundred-word dispatch to New York. What struck him at first was the lack of human personality in the grey-green torrent of men flowing through the Belgian capital. "The grey of the uniforms worn by both officers and men," he wrote with characteristic emphasis on clothing, "helped this air of mystery. . . . All moved under a cloak of invisibility."

Having sent his initial dispatch, he returned to watch the marching columns with a mixture of fear and fascination. In his hotel room over the next few days he composed an article for *Scribner's*, seeking to capture in his prose the repetitive, devastating effect of the German advance:

> All through the night, like the tumult of a river when it races between the cliffs of a canyon, in my sleep I could hear the steady roar of the passing army. . . . This was a machine, endless, tireless, with the delicate organization of a watch and the brute power of a steam-roller. And for three days and three nights through Brussels it roared and rumbled, a cataract of molten lead. The infantry marched singing, with their iron-shod boots beating out the time. In each regiment there were two thousand men and at the same instant, in perfect unison, two thousand iron brogans struck the granite street. It was like the blows from giant pile-drivers. . . . For three days and three nights the column of gray, with fifty thousand bayonets and fifty thousand lances, with gray transport wagons, gray ammunition-carts, gray ambulances, gray cannon, like a river of steel cut Brussels in two.

With its impressionistic images and poetic meter, Davis's account of the German army's passage through Brussels was an instant classic, and for decades after the war it was standard fare in anthologies compiled for journalism students. A more immediate problem for Davis was smuggling his article out of the city. The Germans prohibited reporters from leaving the city until their armies had passed through, and even then all dispatches would be subject to inspection. Davis employed a loyal young

Englishman, who carried the story to Ostend, where he caught a refugee boat to England.

Davis then had to get himself out of Belgium, a ticklish problem because he had no journalistic accreditation. The Belgian government had fled by the time he reached Brussels. Without papers, the Germans might mistake him for a spy. He got out of Brussels by taxi and then set off on foot for neutral Holland. He lost his way and was captured by a German patrol. As Davis later told the story, the Germans assumed he was an English spy because of the London cut of his clothing. However, when the Germans were momentarily distracted, he furtively checked the label of his hat. It was, luckily, purchased in New York. He then showed the hat to the Germans and persuaded them that no Englishman would purchase, much less wear, a hat from New York. The Germans agreed and gave him a pass to Holland. Whether or not the story is true, to be arrested and then released exclusively on the basis of his outer garb is vintage Davis!

From Holland he went to London and then back to Paris, arriving in time to report on the series of battles, Soissons, the Marne, where the French stopped the German advance short of Paris in September 1914. He was back in New York by the end of the first week of October.

He returned to Europe a year later. The fighting by then had settled into trench warfare. The French, eager to publicize their success in holding the Germans and refusing to let them pass, gave Davis a three-day tour of the trenches. He then sailed to the Mediterranean to report on the fighting on the Balkan front. Throughout this tour he was bothered by abdominal pains. He diagnosed it as food poisoning, but it was, in fact, angina pectoris, an inflammation of the heart. On April 11, 1916, he was stricken by a massive heart attack.

Richard Harding Davis is little known today largely because his literary efforts were scorned even before he died. His romantic tales of adventure, thin in plot and character, were utterly out of place in a new age of literary realism, where the giants were Theodore Dreiser, Stephen Crane, and Jack London. Henry Louis Mencken, the caustic critic of American culture in the 1920s, joked that in the great Baltimore fire of 1904 the only things he lost were "a suit of clothes, the works of Richard Harding Davis, and a gross of condoms."

Another generation would provide a better perspective. The great historian of American literature, Van Wyck Brooks, writing in 1952, suggested that Davis

> was one of those magnetic types, often otherwise second-rate, who establish patterns of living for others of their kind, and the notion of the novelist as war-correspondent which prevailed so long in American writing began in the early nineties undoubtedly with him. It was . . . he who convinced Frank Norris that the

> journalist came in closer touch with the raw material of life than other people. . . . There was something of Davis too in Jack London and Stephen Crane, . . . and his legend was part of the atmosphere in which John Reed grew up, like Vincent Sheean, like Ernest Hemingway. . . . One of the most influential of writers, not as a writer but as a man, Davis was like the reporter who made himself king, for he was the hero of college boys who gathered from him that the journalist's life was the most picturesque and exciting of all careers.

Suggested Reading

An excellent biography, sprightly written and thoughtful in its judgments, is Arthur Lubow's *The Reporter Who Would Be King: A Biography of Richard Harding Davis* (1992). Charles H. Brown, *The Correspondents' War: Journalists in the Spanish-American War* (1967), describes the role of Davis and other journalists in the war. Ivan Musicant's *Empire by Default: The Spanish-American War and the Dawn of the American Century* (1998) is the most recent, and by far the most detailed, study of the war. Roosevelt's part in the war is examined by H. Paul Jeffers in *Colonel Roosevelt: Theodore Roosevelt Goes to War, 1897–1898* (1996). A look at the yellow press is provided by George Juergens, *Joseph Pulitzer and the New York World* (1966), and W. A. Swanberg, *Citizen Hearst* (1961).

7

John Hay: "Echoes of Glory and a Legacy of Duty"

"I wish we had a perfectly consistent foreign policy, and that this policy was that ultimately every European power should be driven out of America, and every foot of American soil, including the nearest islands in both the Pacific and the Atlantic, should be in the hands of independent American states, and so far as possible in the possession of the United States or under its protection."

Those were not the words of a bombastic member of the United States Senate, nor, in fact, of any government official. They were the sentiments of Theodore Roosevelt, a not-too-ordinary citizen in a very ordinary post, that of police commissioner of the city of New York. The Spanish–American War and the virtual elimination of European holdings in the New World were still several years in the future. Yet Roosevelt was giving voice to the feelings of many Americans in the mid-1890s.

Roosevelt's wish had in fact been the essence of American policy toward Europe since the beginnings of the republic. From Jefferson's acquisition of Louisiana to Seward's purchase of Alaska, the United States had been slowly pushing the Old World out of the New, while Latin Americans had been simultaneously freeing themselves from the yoke of Spanish and Portuguese rule. Bound up with this policy of exclusion was an insistence on America's isolation from Old World conflicts. That, too, was as old as the republic. It found expression in the warnings of Washington and Jefferson against foreign entanglements, and it was carved in stone by President James Monroe's embrace of the doctrine of separate spheres in his annual message of December 1823.

Disengagement from the corrupt monarchies of Europe had the additional advantage of preserving America's moral authority. Like their Puritan ancestors who expected to reform the world by shining example, Americans of the nineteenth century thought of their democratic society and republican institutions as a model for the world. When they did treat with Britain, or Russia, or some other power, to preserve the Atlantic fisheries, for instance, or limit the slaughter of fur seals in the north Pacific, it was for some higher moral purpose, the benefit of all.

Just as disengagement characterized American policy toward Europe in the nineteenth century, the principle of free trade was at the root of American policy in the Pacific and Far East. That, too, was grounded on moral principle—justice and fairness. Americans demanded only a level playing field in their business dealings with other nations. The legal concept was that of "most favored nation," and it was embodied in America's first treaty with China in 1844. The principle helped pry open Japan to foreign trade in the 1850s, and after the Civil War it was incorporated in treaties with the Pacific island kingdoms of Hawaii and Samoa. When two countries are bound by a "most favored nation" trade agreement, any concessions (tariff preferences, for instance) granted to a third party by one automatically redound to the benefit of the other. The effect is freedom of trade, or equality of opportunity, for no country could be more favored—in the China market, for instance—than the United States.

The Spanish–American War wove together all of these strands of American policy and principle. It eliminated the last vestiges of the Spanish empire in the New World and brought under American control an assortment of island possessions, from Puerto Rico in the Caribbean to Hawaii and the Philippines in the Pacific. And all this was accomplished under the idealistic banner of extending to other peoples the blessings of American law, justice, and freedom. The war also launched the United States onto the stage of world power with new duties and obligations. In the words of Theodore Roosevelt, whom the war propelled into national office, the guns of war "left us echoes of glory, but they also left us a legacy of duty." Responding to these new obligations while preserving the moral authority of America's traditional policies toward Europe and the Far East was the task of John Hay, who as secretary of state to two presidents, guided American foreign policy from 1898 until his death in 1905.

Middle-Western Aristocrat

John Hay was molded in the same environment as his idol, Abraham Lincoln. His father, Charles Hay, a physician, came from the vicinity of Lexington, Kentucky, moved to Indiana in 1829, and a decade later settled in the Illinois village of Warsaw, on the Mississippi River. Along the way Charles married the daughter of a Baptist minister, who bore him six children. John Hay, born on October 12, 1838, was their third.

Warsaw, across the river from Keokuk, Iowa, was a bustling steamboat stop and a major crossing point for pioneers headed west into Iowa and Missouri. "The years of my boyhood were passed on the banks of the Mississippi, and the great river was the scene of my early dreams," Hay recalled many years later. "The boys of my day led an amphibian life, in and near its waters in the summertime, and in the winter its dazzling ice bridge, of incomparable beauty and purity, was our favorite playground." Dr. Hay's medical business thrived, and he was able to send his son to a private academy in Pittsfield, the seat of a neighboring county. Founded

John Hay holding a copy of Henry Adams's Democracy *(1883). (Photograph from the Massachusetts Historical Society.)*

by emigrants from New England, Pittsfield had a sizable German population, and among the friends Hay made there was John George Nicolay, whose family had come from Bavaria. Six years older than Hay, Nicolay had become the editor of the village newspaper and a cog in county politics. They would be lifelong friends.

At the age of fourteen, John and his elder brother Leonard were placed in the hands of their maternal grandfather, who resided in the state capital, Springfield. The boys were placed in a college preparatory school (later Concordia College), and from there John went on to his grandfather's alma mater, Brown University in Providence, Rhode Island.

John had proved to be an unusually bright scholar, and, although there were Baptist schools closer by, Brown was famed for its quality. The move stretched the family resources—his uncles helped with the tuition—but it was squarely within the midwestern (not to say Lincolnesque) tradition of upward mobility.

He emerged from Brown with the tastes and social attitudes of old-time New England Federalism. Congregational Yale and Unitarian Harvard could not have done a better job on a son of the Illinois prairie. He returned to Illinois upon graduating in 1858, not because he wanted to, but because there was nowhere else to go. "My father, with more ambition and higher ideals than I," he grumbled one dreary day in January 1859, "has dwelt and labored here a lifetime, and even this winter does not despair of creating an interest in things intellectual among the unshorn of the prairies. I am not suited for a reformer. I do not like to meddle with moral ills. I love comfortable people. I prefer, for my friends, men who can read." That attitude was reinforced in later years by his association with the great gentlepeople of Europe. And his friends, all his life, were few. Besides Nicolay, his closest associates were the Harvard historian, Henry Adams, and the Yale-trained geologist, Clarence King.

When Abraham Lincoln was elected president a year later, he took John George Nicolay to Washington as his private secretary. Nicolay, in turn, invited Hay to come along as his assistant. Because the laws at the time did not provide for an assistant secretary, Nicolay found a position for him as a clerk in the Interior Department, detailed for special service at the executive mansion. The salary was $1,600 a year. Hay was delighted to escape Springfield, where he had been studying law with his uncle, but he was no great admirer of Lincoln. The president was a mite too homespun for Hay's college-honed tastes. However, he slowly came to appreciate both Lincoln's qualities as a leader and the importance of the Union cause. By 1864 he was able to write, "As in spite of some rudeness, Republicanism is the sole hope of a sick world, so Lincoln with all his foibles is the greatest character since Christ." By that date both Nicolay and Hay were preserving correspondence and memorabilia with an eye to writing some day a comprehensive biography of Lincoln.

By the end of the war he was heartily sick of Washington and contemplating a return to the "vineyards" of Warsaw when, in March 1865, Secretary of State Seward offered him the post of secretary of the legation at Paris. Hay leaped at the offer, explaining to Nicolay that he feared that service in the nation's capital was leading him into "a red tape career." A tour of duty in Europe, moreover, would complete his education and further refine his appetites. After two years in Paris he elected to stay on in the foreign service. Openings in the world of business were not abundant in the postwar years, and the government was a dependable paymaster. He followed his Paris service with similar secretarial positions in Vienna and Madrid.

By 1870 he had come to two realizations. One was that he had no future in the diplomatic service without political connections in Washington, and after Seward left office he had none. The other was that he had some talent as a writer. While in Spain he began a series of travelogues that would ultimately be published as *Castilian Days*. In 1870 he returned home, stopping in New York to talk to Whitelaw Reid, whom he had known during the war as a Washington correspondent and who was now second in command of the *New York Tribune*. Horace Greeley had built the *Tribune* into the most respected paper in the country, and he was slowly turning over the editorial reins to Reid. Reid immediately offered Hay a job, and the aspiring writer settled in New York. He would remain with the *Tribune* for the next five years.

Hay had dabbled with poetry ever since leaving Brown, and he managed to blend that with his editorial duties. Within a year he had five poems published in the *Atlantic Monthly* and six in *Harper's Weekly*. At the end of 1871 his poems were published in pamphlet form under the title *Pike County Ballads and Other Pieces*, 167 pages of verse priced at twenty-five cents. It was an instant success because Hay made use of his youthful experience with Mississippi River gamblers, ruffians, and boatmen, and wrote in a dialect that anticipated the later works of Mark Twain. The publisher of *Pike County Ballads* also announced, somewhat breathlessly, the imminent appearance of *Castilian Days*, and that too was a popular hit. As a witty travelogue, it came to rival Mark Twain's *Innocents Abroad*, published two years earlier. In a single year Hay had leaped to the forefront of American letters, and he would rest on those literary laurels for the rest of his life. Fame also brought him to the attention of Mark Twain and the Harvard historian Henry Adams, both of whom opened a correspondence with him that would last many years.

Besides being a commercial success, *Castilian Days* revealed a streak of youthful idealism in Hay. Whether at Brown or in Lincoln's household, he had absorbed the American sense of mission, that the New World republic was destined to change the world through example, and, like Jefferson a century earlier, he could not resist comparing the Spanish countryside with that of his homeland. He was distressed at the poverty of the Spanish people and the decadence of their institutions. In every chapter of *Castilian Days* he lashed out at the Catholic Church, the idle aristocrats, and the inept monarchy. He professed admiration for the Spanish people and thought they had a great future if properly led. In phrases that echoed Jefferson he wrote on the flyleaf of the book: "There are those who think the Spaniards are not fit for freedom. I believe that no people are fit for anything else."

With his editor's salary augmented by royalties, Hay moved uptown from the *Tribune* offices and took lodgings at 111 East 25th Street, a neighborhood that introduced him to the more elegant social life of the city. Henry Holt, founder of one of New York's most distinguished publishing houses, fondly recalled a dinner party in which Hay sat at one end of the table and Clarence King, newly returned from his first geological survey of the forty-second parallel, sat at the other end. The repartee went back and forth so rapidly that the other guests could only share in the laughter. "I don't think it's because I am a very old man that I think the talk was better then than now," Holt wrote wistfully in his eighties, "for there was better stuff to talk about."

It was at one such party that Hay met Clara Louise Stone of Cleveland, Ohio, who was visiting her uncle in New York. He saw her often thereafter in the winter of 1871–1872, and he followed up with visits to Cleveland. They were engaged in March 1873 and married a year later in Cleveland. Hay described her to Nicolay as "a very estimable young person, large, handsome, and good." Unmentioned was the fact that her father, Amasa Stone, a railroad builder with connections to both John D. Rockefeller and William H. Vanderbilt (his Lake Shore Line in Ohio became part of the New York Central System), was immensely wealthy. That inheritance enabled John Hay to live the life of genteel indolence to which he had clearly aspired since leaving college. He left the *Tribune*, and for the next twenty years he clipped bonds and managed a stock portfolio, while making frequent trips to England to hobnob with the gentry in their London homes and country castles. His introduction to this social circle was Henry Adams, whose own initiation had occurred while his father, Charles Francis, had served as Lincoln's ambassador to Britain during the Civil War.

Hay's description of Clara as an "estimable" and "good" woman was right on the mark. She was the model Victorian wife and mother, managing the household, disciplining the children (they had two boys, Adelbert and Clarence), hosting dinner parties, arranging for the upkeep of a lakeside cottage in New Hampshire, buying railroad tickets, and shepherding her husband to a church that he never joined—all performed unobtrusively and without eliciting public comment. Hay, in turn, proved to be a typical Victorian husband and father, preoccupied with the marketplace, later with politics, and, at home, a benevolent despot with little time for the particulars of child rearing. They settled in Cleveland, where Clara's father had most of his investments, and purchased a sizable house on Euclid Avenue, becoming neighbors of the Rockefellers and other newly rich Cleveland tycoons.

The idealism and empathy for the downtrodden that Hay had revealed in his *Castilian Days* suffered a severe shock during the great railroad strike of 1877, which eventually had to be suppressed by federal troops. Five hundred workers of his father-in-law's Lake Shore and Michigan Railroad walked off the job, and the strike pretty well halted railroad traffic between Chicago and the East Coast. Hay thought the strike was pure "insanity," caused by lazy workers and professional agitators. "The very devil seems to have entered the lower classes of working men," he wrote, "and there are plenty of scoundrels to encourage them to all lengths." Hay detested labor unions and Democrats ever after, and he often seemed to equate the two.

His newfound venom found expression in his next literary work, a novel entitled *The Bread-winners*, which he wrote over the next five years, completing it during a tour of England in 1882. He set the story of the novel in the year 1877, and the principal character is an irrational labor agitator who shrieks, "We are going to make war on capital. We are going to scare the blood-suckers into terms." The novel, nevertheless, was more than an antiunion tract, for Hay had a larger point to make. The country was sinking, he claimed, because corrupt political machines, dependent for votes on immigrants and labor unions, controlled the city and state governments. The power of political bosses was uncontested because the wealthy, the keepers of the old values of honesty and deference, refused to become involved in petty politics and local organization.

The Bread-winners appeared in 1883 to mixed reviews, and Hay never essayed another venture into fiction. With Nicolay, he spent the remainder of the decade completing the long-promised biography of Abraham Lincoln. Serial publication in *Century* magazine began in November 1886, and the monumental, ten-volume work finally appeared in 1890. Although in many respects a Republican tract, the biography was well-received by those with the stamina to wade through it, and it remains today an indispensable source for the inner workings of the Lincoln presidency.

In 1886, seemingly taking to heart his own advice in *The Bread-winners*, Hay moved to Washington and began taking a more active part in politics. He and Henry Adams had purchased adjoining lots on the corner of H and 16th streets, just across Lafayette Square from the White House. They employed the leading architect of the day, Henry H. Richardson, to design a multistoried duplex, with Hay's doorway opening onto 16th Street and Adams's around the corner. (There was no interior passageway between the two residences.) The result was a massive brick bastion with all the Richardson trademarks—trimmings of light-colored stone, numerous windows, and imposing stone steps leading up to arched entryways and carved wooden doors. The twin addresses—800 Sixteenth Street and 1603 H Street—were soon to become the social center of the city. Adams, who had left a professorship at Harvard in order to devote himself to research and writing in Washington, once remarked wryly that his address was the only position of importance he had attained in life.[1]

In the nation's capital Hay plunged into Republican politics, particularly after Democrat Grover Cleveland captured the presidency in 1884

1. The house has since been replaced by the elegant Hay-Adams Hotel.

The Hay-Adams residences in Washington, D.C. (Photograph from the Collections of the Library of Congress.)

and then repeated the feat for a second term in 1892. By the early 1890s Hay was a major contributor to Republican war chests. By 1893 he had decided that Ohio congressman William McKinley was the man to beat the pathetic Cleveland, who was cursed with "a vast, diffused, circumambulent talent . . . for being an ass." Hay immediately proved useful as McKinley in that year suddenly found himself liable for the debts of a friend, whose notes he had countersigned. Hay responded with a substantial gift, and McKinley wrote: "I have no words with which to adequately thank you. . . . How can I ever repay you & other dear friends."

Within another year Hay was actively involved in Mark Hanna's organizational drive to control the 1896 Republican convention in McKinley's behalf. Hay not only contributed money but he did some "missionary work" among Southern delegates, who, having no constituencies of their own, were quite susceptible to Mark Hanna's blandishments. After McKinley won the election he named Hay to the highest post in the government outside the cabinet, ambassador to the Court of St. James, in London. Hay thus returned to public service at the age of sixty with considerable experience in the world of finance and foreign affairs (he had been assistant secretary of state in 1879–1881) and a solid circle of friends and acquaintances among the decision makers of Europe. He had only eight more years to live, but in that short time he would carve his name indelibly in the annals of history.

The Philippines and the Peace Treaty

Although the Republican platform in 1896 pledged the party to the independence of Cuba, Hay had few thoughts on the subject—and none that he expressed publicly. His friends Clarence King and Henry Adams visited Cuba in 1895, shortly after the revolution began, and returned with a passionate urge for American intervention on behalf of the rebels. Hay ignored their entreaties and seemed to think that the developing crisis in the Caribbean had no bearing on his ministerial duties in Britain. Indeed, he spent much of the summer of 1897 touring Scotland and being entertained in the castles of its tartaned lords. He and Clara were touring Egypt in the company of Henry Adams when the *Maine* exploded in Havana harbor in February 1898. Rather than rushing back to the London post, they spent several more days among the pyramids and then a week in Athens before sailing for England. Hay had asked for a sixty-day leave, and he consumed every minute of it, arriving back in London on March 21. His insouciance did not go unnoticed. In Washington, Theodore Roosevelt, whom McKinley had installed as assistant secretary of the navy at the request of Senator Lodge, fumed that he could not "understand how John Hay was willing to be away from England at this time."

While remaining silent on the subject of Cuba—it was, after all, not his problem—Hay prepared for war in another way, by cultivating an Anglo-American rapprochement. At an Easter dinner, hosted by the Lord Mayor of London on April 21, 1898, he gave an address that anticipated Rudyard Kipling's poem "The White Man's Burden."[2] Britain and the United States, he declared, "are bound by a tie which we did not forge and which we cannot break; we are joint ministers of the same sacred mission of liberty and progress, charged with duties which we cannot evade by the imposition of irresistible hands." A few weeks later he wrote Senator Lodge that "the interests of civilization" were "bound up in the direction the relations of America and England are to take in the next few months."

On May 7, after news of Commodore Dewey's victory at Manila Bay reached London, Joseph Chamberlain, colonial secretary in the ministry of Lord Salisbury, invited the Hays to dinner (Chamberlain's American wife was a good friend of Clara's), and Chamberlain pointedly asked Hay whether the independence of Cuba was the sole condition of peace. Hay had no instructions on the question of whether the United States would make additional demands on Spain and cabled Chamberlain's inquiry to Washington. When the cable arrived the McKinley administration was in some disarray. McKinley had given no prewar thought to the Philippines and in fact knew nothing about them. He later confessed: "When we received the cable from Admiral Dewey [announcing the victory] . . . I looked up their location on the globe. I could not have told where those darned islands were within 2,000 miles!" Nor was the State Department of much help to the president. He had initially given the post of secretary of state to Senator John Sherman of Ohio—in order to vacate an Ohio senate seat, so it was rumored, for his friend Mark Hanna. Sherman (brother of the Civil War general) was at the end of a long political career and showing signs of senility. In the spring of 1898, when McKinley realized he needed someone at the State Department who could do more than open the daily mail, the president replaced Sherman with his assistant, another Ohioan, William R. Day. Day had been a competent assistant, but as secretary he lacked the élan needed to move a hesitant and ill-informed president.

McKinley and Day pondered Hay's cable for a month, and on June 3 wired Hay some tentative conditions for peace: the evacuation of Cuba; the surrender of Puerto Rico in lieu of an indemnity for the cost of the war; the yielding of a naval base in the Philippines, which otherwise could remain under Spanish control; and the conveyance of an island and coaling station in the Ladrone Islands (a reference to Guam, which the navy had already captured). Hay saw nothing wrong with the peace

2. This poem was first published in the United States in *McClure's* magazine in February 1899. Roosevelt sent a copy to Lodge, saying "rather poor poetry, but good sense from the expansionist standpoint." Lodge even liked the poetry.

terms, except with respect to the Philippines. Here his thinking was heavily influenced by English friends, notably Cecil Spring Rice. Rice was Britain's ambassador to Germany, and in Berlin he had developed a healthy mistrust of Germany's ambitions in the Far East.[3] Even before the United States declared war Rice told Hay that the United States ought to annex the Hawaiian Islands lest Germany move in while the United States was preoccupied with Spain. Hay conveyed this advice, and it helped persuade the president to resubmit the Hawaiian annexation treaty to the Senate.

Upon receiving word of Dewey's victory at Manila Bay, Rice blurted to Hay, "Let us try what we can to secure what we can for God's language," adding that "it was the divine instinct ingrained in the race which has brought us to where we are." In July, after an interview with the German ambassador in London, in which the German pointed out that there were so many islands in the Philippine archipelago that the United States could afford to let the Germans have a couple, Hay concluded that McKinley must demand more of the Spanish than an American coaling station in the islands. He conferred with Lord Salisbury himself and received assurances that Britain would have no objections if the United States laid claim to the Philippines. Hay promptly relayed this information to McKinley and Secretary Day.

That was the state of Hay's mind when, on August 15, the day hostilities ceased, President McKinley decided to send Day to Paris as a peace commissioner and offered John Hay the State Department. He accepted, in part because it was the culmination of his life, but with a deep sense of foreboding. "I am longing to see you," he wrote Clara after he arrived in Washington, "and yet I feel so dull and worthless I almost dread to have you come and plunge into this life of dreary drudgery. It is going to be vile—the whole business. The men [foreign diplomats] are bad enough—their wives are worse."

Even so, by the time he reached Washington his mind was pretty well settled on the terms of peace. "I fear you are right about the Philippines," he wrote an old acquaintance, "and I hope the Lord will be good to us poor devils who have to take care of them." Cables from Admiral Dewey in the course of September and October indicated that the Philippines were going to require a great deal of care. Spanish administration had collapsed, Dewey reported, "the natives appear unable to govern," and there was general anarchy outside the city of Manila with reports of "inhuman cruelty." These reports convinced McKinley, and the president ordered the peace commissioners to demand cession of the entire archipelago. The peace treaty, signed in December, assured the independence of Cuba and the cession to the United States of Puerto Rico, Guam, and the Philippines.

3. Rice would be Britain's ambassador to the United States during World War I and is widely credited with helping to bring the United States into the war.

Some months later McKinley told a group of visiting clergymen how he had reached his decision on the Philippines. He had paced the floor for several nights and finally fell upon his knees and prayed to God for guidance. And the light came. The destruction of Spanish rule in the islands had created a vacuum that might be filled by another European power, such as France or Germany. This was unacceptable, as was the notion of independence, for the Filipinos "were unfit for self-government." As a result, said McKinley, "there was nothing left for us to do but to take them all, and to educate the Filipinos, and uplift and civilize, and Christianize them, and by God's grace to do the best we could by them."[4]

John Hay lacked the president's missionary zeal, but his motives in wanting possession of the Philippines were otherwise much the same. He was more concerned even than the president about Germany's ambitions in the region, and he agreed that the Filipinos were incapable of self-government. When, a few months later, the Filipinos rose up in rebellion against American rule, Hay had nothing but scorn for their military abilities and the quality of their leadership. He ranked the rebel leader, Emilio Aguinaldo, in the same gallery with his other rogues—labor agitators, Populists, and William Jennings Bryan—misguided, avaricious, and without much popular support.

Although some modern historians have argued that, in seizing the Philippines, McKinley and Hay were serving as agents of American businessmen who viewed the islands as a stepping-stone to the China market, there is little evidence of business influence in the papers and statements of the president and his secretary. Hay did have a profound faith in American capitalism, and he was convinced that American trade and investment would benefit the islands. But the potential of the China market for American commerce does not seem to have ranked high in his thinking. On the other hand, once annexation of the Philippines became a fact, as it did upon Senate ratification of the peace treaty in February 1899, Hay was forced to give attention to the Far East as he never had before, and he was instantly struck by the threatened partition of China among European colonial powers. The result was the formation of a policy for which he is best known, the Open Door.

The Open Door Policy

The island kingdom of Samoa helped draw Hay's attention to the region. The largest island of the archipelago, Tutila, possessed what many regarded as the finest natural harbor, Pago Pago, in the entire South Pacific.

4. Since the main religion in the Philippines had been Roman Catholic for almost four hundred years under Spanish rule, what the Pope thought of McKinley's missionary zeal has mercifully gone unrecorded.

As early as 1872 the U.S. Navy had leased the harbor for a coaling station, and a treaty negotiated later in that decade tied Samoa commercially to the United States through a most favored nation trade agreement. In the 1880s Germany began its imperial expansion in the South Pacific, staking a claim to the Caroline Islands and parts of Samoa. By a treaty of 1889 the United States, Britain, and Germany set up a tripartite supervision of the Samoan islands, while guaranteeing their independence and the right of the natives to select their own king. There was intermittent warfare for the next ten years, as the colonial powers backed rival aspirants for the island throne.

In the spring of 1899 Germany suggested a division of the islands, and more leery of British imperialism than American, it proposed that the United States be given possession of Tutila and the adjacent islets. Hay agreed, explaining to a friend that he was very happy to "get out of the tripartite business and keep Tutila." He added, "We must keep our foothold there in the interest of our Pacific work." The British were equally happy to let the Americans have Pago Pago, and Hay simply sat on the sidelines while Britain and Germany compensated one another by staking claims to other peoples' lands elsewhere in the Pacific and in Africa. Hay's phrase "our Pacific work" clearly referred to the Aguinaldo revolution in the Philippines and the developing crisis in China.

When he took command of the State Department, Hay's knowledge of China was that of the ordinary educated American. Beginning with a trade in ginseng and sea otter pelts, American interest in China had been purely commercial. In the Opium War of the 1840s Britain had acquired Hong Kong and commercial concessions in South China, but the United States limited its demands on China to a trade agreement in 1844. The treaty gave American traders all they thought they needed—"a fair field and no favor." China thereafter vanished from the American consciousness until the 1890s when the imperial powers of Europe carved up Africa and turned covetous eyes on China. Jealous of the sphere of influence that Britain had established in south China, Germany in 1897 obtained territorial and commercial concessions in north China and Russia occupied Port Arthur, the gateway to Manchuria.

Worried about these incursions, Britain in the fall of 1898 conveyed a series of informal notes to the McKinley administration suggesting a joint Anglo-American attempt to preserve the integrity of China against partition and keep an "open door" in China to traders of all nations. McKinley ignored the overtures, in part because he was preoccupied with Spain and in part because Lord Salisbury was riding two horses—he wanted to preserve Britain's commercial hegemony in the Hong Kong hinterland and the Yangtze valley, while enlisting American support for free trade in the rest of China.

By the summer of 1899, however, Hay was viewing China in a new light. Republican newspapers and magazines had begun running articles on the potential of the China market for American business, and railroad men wanted construction concessions in China that were being blocked by the European "spheres." Realizing the need for an American statement of policy, Hay turned to William W. Rockhill, who had been ambassador to Greece while Hay was in London and who now was his principal advisor on Far Eastern matters. Rockhill advised adopting the British policy of an "open door" without crediting the British. The United States could thus demand equality of commercial opportunity throughout China, and if Britain followed this lead, so be it—Britain would merely strengthen an American initiative. Hay agreed, and with only perfunctory notice to President McKinley (neither Hay nor McKinley anticipated the importance that the Open Door policy would have in the twentieth century), Hay sent notes to Britain, Germany, and Russia in September, with follow-up messages (apparently an afterthought) to France, Italy, and Japan in November.

The notes merely reminded the European powers that China had preserved her right to trade with all nations, even while granting spheres of influence to certain European powers. Hay simply asked that the powers respect China's rights in this regard. Hay did not demand a revision of earlier treaties or joint action; he simply placed the United States on high moral ground and dared anyone to object.

Predictably, no one rejected Hay's overture, but, not surprisingly, no one accepted. Britain expressly reserved the right to monopolize Kowloon (the Chinese province opposite Hong Kong island), but endorsed the idea of commercial equality in any future spheres carved out of China by Europeans. Germany agreed to Hay's proposal only if everyone else did. The Russian response was so murky that it gained nothing by being translated into English. Despite this disappointing reaction, Hay kept the moral high ground. On March 20, 1900, he calmly issued a statement that all the powers had agreed to the principle of commercial equality in China and that he considered the assent "final and definitive." And he made public the American notes, whose existence had previously been only a matter of speculation.

The Open Door policy, as it became popularly known—even though Hay did not coin the phrase or use it in his notes—was well received by the press and public precisely because it appealed to the American sense of honorable behavior. Hay was basking in the sunshine of diplomatic success when in June 1900 China erupted. Chinese traditionalists (known as Boxers[5]), who resented the activities of Christian missionaries as well as the importunate demands of foreigners for special privileges, rose up to drive the "foreign devils" out of the country. The attack centered on the foreign legations in Peking, and by the mid-

5. The name of the anti-foreigner society translated literally as "righteous, harmonious fists," which some wit reduced to "Boxer."

dle of June most of the foreigners had taken refuge inside the Tartar City. The Boxers laid siege to the walled enclave, cutting off outside communications, and Western governments feared that their diplomats had been slaughtered.

The Powers hastily put together a successful relief expedition. Because neither the Europeans nor the Americans (who were tied up in the Philippines) had a significant number of soldiers in the area, the relief army was made up mostly of Russians and Japanese. This was of further concern to Hay because Russia and Japan had been the most aggressive of the Powers seeking slices of China. Hay feared that the powers would seize this opportunity to dismember China altogether, and American interests were certain to suffer in the ensuing melee. Of further concern to Hay was that the Democratic presidential convention was scheduled to meet in July with the likelihood of nominating the anti-imperialist William Jennings Bryan. The Democrats were certain to exploit any American embarrassments in China.

Hay's response was a second Open Door note, or rather, in this case, a circular letter, dated July 3, 1900, to be delivered by American diplomats in the capitals of the Powers. Without using the phrase "open door," the circular endorsed the "principle of equal and impartial trade in all parts of the Chinese Empire," which was a much stronger affirmation than he had ventured in his notes of the previous year. With respect to the immediate emergency, the circular announced that it was the policy of the United States "to seek a solution which may bring about permanent safety and peace to China [and] preserve Chinese territorial and administrative entity." The circular did not require a response and hence it stood unchallenged, growing ever more revered (at least in principle) with the passing years. The preservation of the territorial and administrative integrity of China thus became the cornerstone of American policy in the Far East until the outbreak of World War II.

Unfortunately, it was not so well honored in Hay's lifetime. The presence of American troops (spared from the Philippines) in the army that rescued the foreigners in Peking on August 14 gave the United States an unprecedented opportunity to back Hay's diplomacy with force. Hay himself recognized the limitations of his moral stance and the advantages of a military presence in China. "The talk of the papers about 'our preeminent moral position' giving us the authority to dictate to the world is mere flapdoodle," he told his assistant secretary, Alvey Adee. Unfortunately, Hay's desire to buttress his Open Door policy with a show of force required the cooperation of both the British and President McKinley. And both failed him. The British became involved in a war with the Boers of South Africa in the summer of 1899 and were inclined to let Japan counter the thrusts of Russia and Germany in China. President McKinley, engaged in a reelection campaign, was more susceptible than usual to public opinion, and the American public, suffering the usual postwar letdown, was demanding a return to "normalcy."[6] Although Hay protested as strongly as he dared, McKinley was determined to withdraw the American troops as soon as the Boxer emergency was ended.

With Hay's hands tied by American politics, Britain's bent toward realpolitik became the rule in the Far East. In 1902 Britain and Japan entered into a formal alliance aimed primarily at countering Russian advances into Manchuria. In response to pointed questions from the Japanese ambassador in the spring of 1903, Hay confessed that the United States had no intention of using military force for the preservation of China. A year later Japan attacked the Russian naval base at Port Arthur, and its armies pounded the Russians in Manchuria, while the United States and Britain looked on benevolently. By that time, John Hay, ill and at death's door, had essentially turned over the reins of policy decision making to President Roosevelt.

The Isthmian Canal

The territorial acquisitions in the Caribbean and the Far East achieved by the Spanish–American War reawakened American interest in a canal across the isthmus of Central America. A "path between the seas" was essential to both the operations of the U.S. Navy and the expected expansion of American trade. American interest in such a passage, like its fascination with China, dated from the first half of the century. In 1846, when war with Mexico brought California into the American orbit, the government negotiated a treaty with New Granada (later Columbia) that granted American citizens the right of transit across the isthmus of Panama. The gold rush of '49 inspired thoughts of a canal across Central America, and because Britain had colonial claims in the area, it was thought provident to get Britain's agreement. The Clayton-Bulwer Treaty of 1850 provided for joint Anglo-American control over any future canal, and it further provided that any canal would be unfortified, open to all nations, and completely neutral, even in time of war.

Thus, Britain appeared to be the first hurdle to overcome when President McKinley broached the subject of an American-built canal in the autumn of 1898. Hay immediately asked his chargé d'affaires in London to make inquiries of Lord Salisbury, and word came back that Britain had lost interest in a Central American canal now that it had Suez and that Britain had no objections to an American-built passageway, so long as it remained open to all countries. With characteristic faith in British competence and impartiality, Hay asked Sir Julian Pauncefote, the British

6. The term "normalcy" was coined by Warren G. Harding (the proper word is normality) during the election campaign of 1920.

ambassador to Washington, to draft a revision of the Clayton-Bulwer Treaty. That was a mistake, for Hay's own staff might have been more sensitive to senatorial and public opinion than the genteel Englishman. As a result, to Hay's embitterment toward the Senate, the Hay-Pauncefote Treaty ran into a hornet's nest.

The Pauncefote draft, which Hay accepted virtually without change, modified the Clayton-Bulwer Treaty only to the extent that it allowed the United States alone to construct and manage the ship canal. The waterway otherwise would remain unfortified and open to all. Senators immediately pounced on the defenseless waterway provision. If the canal had no armed guards, what was to prevent local bandits from seizing it? someone asked. When the Senate finally approved the treaty in December 1900, it added amendments allowing the United States to employ its own forces for the defense of the canal and "the maintenance of public order." Although he fumed at the Senate for irresponsibly endangering the treaty, Hay did his best to persuade the British to accept the revised version. He failed, as the British insisted on adherence to the neutral canal envisioned by the Clayton-Bulwer Treaty. Hay and Pauncefote were back where they started.

Hay tendered his resignation, but McKinley, who began a second term in office in March 1901, declined to accept it. Hay then went gamely back to work. The ministry in London was now more receptive to American demands. The British government was suffering a barrage of protests from the continent of Europe over its treatment of the Boers in South Africa. In the Far East Australia was shucking off its colonial bonds and forming a federated dominion, modeled on that of Canada. Lord Salisbury was in need of friends. He knew he had one in John Hay. The Anglo-American understanding, which began with A. T. Mahan's histories and John Hay's ministry to London, was sealed by the second Hay-Pauncefote Treaty. It would prove to be, at least arguably, the most important force of the twentieth century.

By late summer Hay could report considerable progress on a new draft of the treaty. Then, in September, came the shocking news of the president's assassination while on a speaking engagement in Buffalo. Theodore Roosevelt rushed to Buffalo to be sworn in as president and then returned to Washington with the funeral train. When the train pulled into the Union Station on the evening of September 16, Hay was standing on the platform to pay his respects. Roosevelt went up to him and asked him to remain as secretary of state. Hay, deeply touched by Roosevelt's earnest request, said he would. The new treaty was ready by November, and it contained the language demanded by the Senate the previous year. The United States was at liberty to do whatever was necessary to protect the canal "against lawlessness and disorder." The Senate approved the treaty on December 16 by a vote of seventy-two to six.

With the unilateral right to build a canal settled, the next question was where. During the gold rush of 1849 much of the traffic across the isthmus had passed through Panama, which afforded the shortest route between the seas. A forty-seven-mile railroad had been completed across the isthmus in 1855. By 1900 the railroad was owned and managed by Americans. The further advantage of Panama was that it had a partially completed ditch, begun by the French canal engineer, Ferdinand de Lesseps, who had built the Suez Canal in 1869. De Lesseps's company went bankrupt in the early 1890s and had ceased digging. The company was then reorganized for the purpose of selling its canal rights (it had leased land from Columbia), its ditch, and its machinery. Among the new stockholders was Philippe Bunau-Varilla, who would become a lobbyist in the United States for the Panama route in an effort to recoup the company's losses.

The alternative route—and the one seemingly preferred by the press and Congress—lay through Nicaragua. This involved a longer transit from sea to sea, but the crossing benefited from a huge lake whose western shore was a scant nine miles from the Pacific. The lake drained eastward into the Atlantic through a sometimes navigable river. Commodore Vanderbilt had run steamboats up the river and across the lake in the 1850s. The biggest advantage of Nicaragua was that it was four hundred miles closer to the United States than Panama. President Roosevelt set up a commission to evaluate the routes, and the commission reported that Nicaragua route was practical from an engineering point of view.

In early 1902 the French company priced its assets in Panama at $40 million, which was much lower than previously hinted figures, and Bunau-Varilla embarked upon a speaking tour of the United States. Among his stops were visits to key congressional leaders, including Senator Mark Hanna, whose railroad holdings included the Panama Railroad. In mid-summer Congress passed an act directing the president to negotiate with Columbia a perpetual lease on land for a canal across Panama. If Columbia balked, the statute authorized the president to turn to Nicaragua.

John Hay had no preferences as to the route of the canal, and if Roosevelt had not impetuously intervened and helped bring about a revolution in Panama, it is likely that Hay would have played Columbia and Nicaragua against one another until he got the best deal possible. That, however, was not in the cards. Pursuant to the statute, he began talks with the Columbian chargé d'affaires in Washington, Dr. Tomas Herran, and in early 1903 they signed a treaty by which the United States leased a zone of land across Panama with a down payment of $10 million and annual payments of $250,000. The Senate approved the treaty without amendments. The Columbian senate, however, refused its assent. Its motives were essentially patriotic. Some thought that the financial terms were much too low; others saw an infringement upon Columbian sovereignty in a grant of land on which the United States could do what it wished in perpetuity.

Roosevelt, Hay, and many other Americans saw a more venal motive in the Columbian reaction. The French lease in Panama was due to expire in 1904. Its property, including the unfinished ditch, would revert to Columbia, and then Columbia, presumably, could collect the $40 million the United States was prepared to pay for the French company's rights. Although there is no evidence that officials in Bogotá actually subscribed to this line of reasoning, Roosevelt and Hay, neither of whom had much regard for the integrity of Latin Americans, assumed it was true. Roosevelt denounced the Columbians as "contemptible little creatures" and "foolish and homicidal corruptionists." Hay actually outdid the president, predicting that the "greedy little anthropoids" were courting a revolution.

In June 1903, William Nelson Cromwell, a New York lawyer retained by the French canal company, had a "long conference" with the president at the White House. Cromwell then talked to a reporter of the *New York World*, and the next day the *World* carried a story that "President Roosevelt is determined to have the Panama canal route. He has no intention of beginning negotiations for the Nicaragua route." The story concluded: "Information has also reached this city [Washington] that the State of Panama, which embraces all the proposed Canal Zone, stands ready to secede from Columbia and enter into a canal treaty with the United States." The White House reacted with silence.

In early September Hay told the president that he considered a revolution in Panama "altogether likely," but he advised caution lest the United States appear to have too big a hand in it. He also reminded Roosevelt that the Nicaragua route was still an alternative. Later that month Bunau-Varilla returned to New York and took lodgings at the Waldorf-Astoria, room 1162. On September 24 Dr. Manuel Amador knocked on his hotel room door. Amador was the leader of a handful of Panamanians who were seeking independence from Columbia. Bunau-Varilla later claimed that the two men happened to be in New York "by pure chance," but the meeting had almost certainly been arranged by Cromwell. In that and in subsequent meetings the two men plotted the revolution. (Despite much coming and going Bunau-Varilla always managed to secure room 1162, which he called in his memoirs "the cradle of the Panama republic.")

On October 10 Assistant Secretary of State Francis B. Loomis escorted Bunau-Varilla into the White House for a conference with the president, after which the Frenchman rushed back to New York to give additional assurances to Dr. Amador. On October 16 he was back in Washington where he procured an audience with Secretary Hay. Hay assured him (according to Bunau-Varilla) that American warships had been ordered to make an appearance off the coast of Panama. Hay then began talking about a novel he had recently read by Richard Harding Davis. Entitled *Captain Macklin*, the story was about an idealistic West Point graduate, who had gone off to South America to aid in popular revolutions. Hay gave Bunau-Varilla a copy, and the Frenchman interpreted the gesture as a "subtle symbol, the password exchanged between Mr. Hay and myself."

Bunau-Varilla hurried back to New York and had a final meeting with Dr. Amador. He handed the doctor a revolutionary kit, which amounted to a flag and a code for use in cables between Panama and New York. They agreed on November 3 as the date for the revolution. It also happened to be Election Day in the United States. On October 30 Bunau-Varilla had a "chance" encounter with Assistant Secretary Loomis on Lafayette Square, and later that day a cable went out to Kingston, Jamaica, where the gunboat *Nashville* lay birthed. The ship's captain, Commander Hubbard, was ordered to proceed to Colon, the seaport on the Caribbean side of the isthmus.

The *Nashville* steamed into Colon harbor on the afternoon of November 2. Unfortunately, the Columbians had word of the impending revolution, and later that night a Columbian warship sailed into the harbor with a complement of five hundred soldiers. The Columbians landed the next morning, and their vessel fled when the *Nashville* aimed its guns at the beach. The Columbian general in command demanded to be taken across the isthmus to Panama City, the regional capital. During the night the American manager of the Panama Railroad had sent all but one of his trains to the Pacific side. However, he had an engine and a single coach left, and he obligingly offered to transport the Columbian general and his staff across the isthmus. The general agreed, and when he arrived in Panama City on the afternoon of November 3, Amador and his cohorts ran up the Panama flag, declared independence, and clapped the surprised Columbians in jail. That was the Panama "revolution"—much fanfare and little bloodshed. The "revolutionaries" never amounted to more than a couple dozen, and the only casualty was a Chinese man sleeping in his bed at home who was struck by a stray shot from a Columbian warship in the harbor.

Back in Colon the next morning Commander Hubbard offered the leaderless soldiers $8,000 to take passage back to Columbia on a British mail steamship that was passing through. The cash came from the office safe of the Panama Railroad. Unfortunately, it emptied the safe, and when the British purser demanded $1,000 for tickets, Hubbard had to sign a chit obligating the U.S. government for the amount.

Elected president of the new republic by his handful of cohorts, Amador sent a coded message to Bunau-Varilla conveying news of the success of the revolution and adding—to Bunau-Varilla's horror—that he and a delegation were on the way to Washington to negotiate a canal treaty. In his earlier talks with Amador in room 1162 Bunau-Varilla had extracted the promise that, as a price for his efforts to involve the American government, Amador would name him the Panama republic's ambassador to the United States. Amador had only reluctantly agreed since Bunau-Varilla could not claim citizenship in either Columbia or Panama. On receiving Amador's message, Bunau-Varilla realized that the Panamanians had no concern for the interests of the French company, and he could see a double cross in the steamship smoke on the horizon.

At 11:30 on the morning of November 6 a cable from the American consul in Panama declaring the success of the "Isthmian movement" was delivered to the White House. Slightly more than an hour later Secretary Hay extended diplomatic recognition to the Republic of Panama. A week later Bunau-Varilla was in Washington and was ushered into the Blue Room of the White House where the president read a formal declaration recognizing Panama's independence. Two days later John Hay sent Bunau-Varilla, who was staying at the Willard Hotel, a copy of the Hay-Herran Treaty with some penciled changes making it applicable to Panama. Bunau-Varilla made additional changes favorable to the United States to ensure ratification by the Senate. The most important of these was a provision granting the United States all the rights within the canal zone that it would "possess and exercise if it were the sovereign of the territory." And where the earlier treaty granted the United States only a hundred-year lease, Bunau-Varilla's new language granted the canal zone "in perpetuity." The Frenchman sent the document back to Hay on the morning of November 17—the day that the steamer from Colon was scheduled to arrive in New York.

That same morning Hay received a friendly note from Richard Harding Davis saying that he had been planning a novel about a foreign adventurer who had stolen Panama from Columbia. "The day I started to write the story," said Davis, "Panama became a republic, and somebody owes me the money I lost on the story."

Hay was delighted with the new draft of the treaty. In a confidential note to Senator John Spooner, Hay explained that the new document was far more advantageous to the United States than the earlier pact with Columbia, "and we must confess, with what face we can muster, not so advantageous to Panama. . . . You and I know too well how many points there are in this treaty to which a Panamanian patriot could object."

Distrusting Bunau-Varilla, Dr. Amador had cabled him from Panama giving instructions to do nothing until the Panama delegation arrived in Washington. On the morning of November 18, with Amador and his delegation boarding a train in New York, Bunau-Varilla urged Hay to move swiftly. Hay invited Secretary of War Elihu Root and Attorney General Philander Knox to lunch, and the three of them reviewed the treaty. After lunch Hay sent Bunau-Varilla a note requesting that he call at his house at 6:00 that evening. Bunau-Varilla was at the portal of 800 Sixteenth Street at 6:00 sharp, and they signed the treaty in Hay's library.

Later that evening Bunau-Varilla was standing on the platform as Dr. Amador and his two companions stepped off the train. The Frenchman greeted them with the words: "The Republic of Panama is henceforth under the protection of the United States. I have just signed the Canal Treaty."

The Panamanians were outraged and dashed off the next morning to protest to Hay. While Hay tried to soothe them with a promise to make any changes in the treaty they desired, Bunau-Varilla cabled the text of the treaty to Panama's new minister of foreign affairs, along with a note indicating that the Panama delegation was behaving very badly and was an embarrassment to the new republic. Apparently mollified by Hay's promises, Dr. Amador and his companions accompanied Bunau-Varilla back to New York where, in room 1162 of the Waldorf-Astoria, they placed the treaty in an envelope, wrapped the envelope in a Panamanian flag, placed the package in a small safe, and sent it by steamship to Colon. The provisional government of Panama ratified the treaty on December 2, a month almost to the day after the revolution. Bunau-Varilla made arrangements with the House of J. P. Morgan to handle the transfer of the $40 million the United States owed the French canal company and then sailed to France. He never set foot on Panama.

Although both Hay and Roosevelt publicly insisted that the revolution had been the work solely of the Panamanians and that the American naval commander in Colon had acted with complete impartiality, the press was skeptical. The faculties of Yale and several other institutions adopted resolutions criticizing America's conduct. Roosevelt was sufficiently concerned about public opinion that he planned to devote his entire annual message to the subject of Panama. In preparing the message, he first tested his explanations on the cabinet. After a lengthy statement of his position he glanced around the table and settled upon Elihu Root. "Well," he demanded, "have I answered the charges? Have I defended myself?"

"You certainly have, Mr. President," replied the nimble-witted secretary of war. "You have shown that you were accused of seduction and you have conclusively proved that you were guilty of rape."

Figurehead

Hay's biographer, Tyler Dennett, is of the opinion that Hay ought to have resigned from the State Department and gone into retirement in 1903. In 1900 he had been diagnosed as having an enlarged prostate gland, and he suffered periodic bouts of cold and flu thereafter. His health deteriorated markedly after 1903 and by 1905 he was unable to perform even routine tasks in the State Department. In addition, the president, beginning with the Panama affair, increasingly asserted his own control over foreign policy. After 1903 the foreign policy landmarks of the Roosevelt presidency—the treaty ending the Russo-Japanese War, the assertion of an American right to take over the finances of Latin American countries that get into trouble with European creditors (the "Roosevelt Corollary" to the Monroe Doctrine), and the agreement to allow Japan to establish an economic sphere of influence in Manchuria—all bore the marks of Roosevelt's personal diplomacy. In 1909, after he left the presidency, Roosevelt complained that Hay had been a mere "figurehead" as secretary of state. That was certainly not true of Hay's earlier service under McKinley and Roosevelt, but it may have been a fairly apt description of him after 1903.

Hay gave several important speeches on Roosevelt's behalf during the election campaign of 1904 and then collapsed into bed with an acute bronchial infection. In March 1905, Clara Hay, with the help of Henry Adams, booked passage to Europe in the hope that an ocean cruise would revive her husband. He did improve temporarily, but in London he was unable to maintain the social schedule expected of an American secretary of state. He did manage to have lunch at Buckingham Palace with King Edward, but that was his limit. The Hays were back in New York on June 15, and Hay was dead two weeks later. Despite Roosevelt's disparaging comments on his effectiveness as secretary, he had presided over the emergence of the United States as a world power. That was monument enough for any man.

Suggested Reading

The principal biography, Tyler Dennett's *John Hay, From Poetry to Politics* (1933, 1963), is dated but judicious in its conclusions. Kenton J. Clymer's *John Hay: The Gentleman as Diplomat* (1975) is a more recent study, but it is organized topically ("Hay and Race," for instance) and will be tough going for most readers. Ivan Musicant's *Empire by Default: The Spanish American War and the Dawn of the American Century* (1998) is a richly detailed study of the war and the peace negotiations. Thomas J. McCormick's *China Market: America's Quest for Informal Empire, 1893–1901* (1967) is a modern critique of Hay's Open Door policy. David McCullough's *The Path Between the Seas: The Creation of the Panama Canal, 1870–1914* (1977) is a splendidly written account of the Panama revolution and the subsequent construction of the canal.

PART III

Progressives

Thus while the liberal philosophy is concerned with the reform of the laws in order to adapt them to the changing needs and standards of the dynamic economy, while the agenda of reform are long and varied, no one must look to liberalism for a harmonious scheme of social reconstruction. The Good Society has no architectural design. There are no blueprints. There is no mold in which human life is to be shaped. Indeed, to expect the blueprint of such a mold is a mode of thinking against which the liberal temper is a constant protest.

Walter Lippmann, *The Good Society* (1937)

8

Louis D. Brandeis: The "People's Lawyer"

It began as a tale of three families—Dembitz, Wehle, and Brandeis. They were Jewish, educated, relatively well-to-do, and lovers of the arts. They resided in Prague, capital of Bohemia, which was then part of the Austrian empire. All three families suffered minor, but intensely irritating, disabilities, in part because they were Jewish and in part because they were subject to the arbitrary caveats of functionaries in a decadent monarchy. Sigmund Dembitz was a surgeon who was not allowed to practice in Austria because he had been trained in Germany. He and his wife, Fanny Wehle, wandered from village to village in Germany and Poland, educating their daughter, Fredericka, as best they could. After Fredericka finished high school, she went to live with the Wehles in Prague. Across the street from the Wehles lived the Brandeis family, who owned a cotton-printing mill. The Brandeises were not doing well in the 1840s, in part because Jews were subject to special taxes and restrictions. In 1848 Fredericka Dembitz and the Brandeises' son Adolph were engaged to be married.

After a Bohemian revolution against Austria failed in that year, the three families decided to emigrate to America, the promised land of freedom and opportunity. Adolph Brandeis went on ahead to select a location. He decided that the most promising future lay in the bustling river cities of the Midwest. He took a job in a grocery store in Cincinnati and summoned the others. The three families—with children and governesses totaling a party of twenty-six—sailed for New York in April 1849. Their baggage included cases of books, boxes of music, and two pianos. Shortly after they landed Adolph and Fredericka were married, and the couple ultimately settled in Louisville, Kentucky, setting up a grocery and feed store in partnership with the Wehles. The Brandeises had two daughters, Fanny and Amy, a son Alfred, and on November 13, 1856, a second son, Louis Dembitz Brandeis.

Louis Brandeis thus grew up in a home full of books and music, where learning was revered, and in a city that was so busy making money that it had no time for intolerance. It was not a religious household; Adolph and Fredericka blended with the secular Christianity of their neighbors, exchanging greetings and gifts at Christmastime. They ignored formal religion and instead imbued their children with the Judaic ethic—high moral standards, love of humanity, and a desire for self-improvement. Louis was sent to private academies in Louisville where he received training in classical languages, French and German, mathematics, and science. His most important tutor, however, was his uncle, Lewis Dembitz, who had become a prominent lawyer in Louisville. Dembitz was an ardent abolitionist and follower of Lincoln, an amateur scientist who contributed articles to encyclopedias, and, some years later, the author of a textbook on Kentucky jurisprudence. Determined to follow his uncle into the law and brimming with the fruits of family environment and private academies, Louis Brandeis gained admission to the Harvard Law School in 1875 without ever attending college.

Boston Brahmin

In 1875 the philosopher Ralph Waldo Emerson and the poets James Russell Lowell, John Greenleaf Whittier, Henry W. Longfellow, and Oliver Wendell Holmes Sr. were all alive and active, carrying on the literary "flowering of New England" that had begun thirty years before. Still active also were idealists such as Thomas Wentworth Higginson, who had left his Unitarian pulpit to command the first African-American regiment that had enrolled in the Union Army, and Julia Ward Howe, author of "Battle Hymn of the Republic." And relative newcomers, philosopher William James and historian Henry Adams, were beginning to make their mark. Boston businessmen, many of them heirs to old wealth, shared the reformers' sense of responsibility for the welfare of one's fellow citizens. This mercantile and intellectual elite had been given the respectful label "Brahmins," after the highest, and most intellectual, caste in India. Because of the elite's leadership and sense of social responsibility, Massachusetts pioneered in the mid-nineteenth century many of the social reforms that other states struggled with during the Progressive movement—regulation of the working hours of women, restrictions on child labor, prison and asylum reform, and state inspection of factory working conditions.

In law school Brandeis became a close friend of Samuel Warren, whose forebears had been prominent in the American Revolution and who gained him admittance to the best of Boston homes. Brandeis had no difficulty blending with the Brahmins. The ethics of his home training in secular Judaism were little different from the philosophy of Emerson and Boston's Unitarian ministers: self-reliance coupled with a sense of responsibility for one's fellow citizens. Brandeis attended a lecture by the aged Emerson and another by the youthful Harvard historian Henry Adams. At one reception, he wrote home excitedly, he "saw" Longfellow and Holmes and "just missed" Whittier.

Law school was as stimulating as Boston society. Instead of the casual approach of "reading law," which usually meant the commentaries of Blackstone and Coke, Harvard had set up a rigorous curriculum of courses—contracts, torts, procedure, taxation, wills, and the like—that had to be taken in sequence. Instruction was by the case method, where students derived general principles from specific court decisions. In three years Brandeis compiled the highest scholastic record that any Harvard law student has ever achieved. When he was due to graduate in 1877 (after the normal term of two years), the faculty was embarrassed to discover that he was not yet twenty-one years of age. Because school rules provided that no one under the age of twenty-one could graduate, President Charles Eliot ruled that Brandeis must wait a year. The trustees intervened and suspended the rule, allowing Brandeis to graduate cum laude at the head of his class.

Louis had gone off to Boston with $100 in his pocket loaned him by his brother. His father's grocery business had suffered during the depression that began in 1873, and he was unable to sustain his son in law school. Louis worked his way through school by tutoring faculty children and proctoring exams. He continued these occupations for a year after graduating, while taking additional courses in the law school. By the spring of 1878 he had saved enough money to repay his brother and purchase a $600 railroad bond. All his life he shunned the stock market as a form of gambling. He invested his savings instead in relatively secure (if low yield) railroad and utility bonds. Returning to the Midwest—but, significantly, not to the cradle of his extended family in Louisville—he obtained a job in a law office in St. Louis. He detested the city that was evolving from uncouth river town to crass railroad hub, and within a year he was back in Boston, a place that he was to call home for the rest of his life.

He was admitted to the Massachusetts bar "without examination and contrary to all principles and precedent," he wrote jubilantly to his brother, and formed a partnership with his friend Samuel Warren. The partnership thrived initially on Warren's social connections among Boston merchants, but Brandeis gradually developed clients of his own among the city's German-Jewish merchants. The Brahmins were quite tolerant of Jews who were Harvard-connected and intellectually gifted, but the Jewish shopkeepers were inclined to throw their legal business to one of their own. Brandeis, who was comfortable in both worlds, responded by joining, and contributing financially to, German-American clubs. The law firm flourished. By 1890 Brandeis was earning $50,000 a year, at a time when 75 percent of the country's lawyers earned less than $5,000. His net assets exceeded $1 million by 1907, and he was worth $3 million by the time of his death in 1941.

Brandeis's financial success was the more remarkable because of his self-imposed ethical standards. The legal profession was undergoing a profound change in the 1880s and 1890s. Under the ancient adversary system, lawyers had accepted any client on a theory that everyone had a right to representation. They had then presented the client's case and hoped to persuade a judge or jury that it had merit. As more and more lawyers were retained full-time by large corporations, they mutated from the role of adversary to that of counsel, advising the client how to manage the law, at times evade it, without regard to the moral issues involved. This Brandeis refused to do. He had many commercial clients, but he would not take a case unless he was sure of the moral soundness of his position. When potential clients were clearly in the wrong, Brandeis would tell them so and point out that it was in their own interests to behave honestly.

The People's Lawyer

In 1891 Brandeis married his second cousin, Alice Goldmark. It was a happy and lasting marriage; they had two daughters, Elizabeth and Susan. Alice shared his humanitarian instincts, and he relied on her a good deal for advice. She was a very private person who could host dinner parties and receptions but shunned the public stage. She broke her rule of privacy only once when in 1913 she gave an interview to the *Boston American* favoring women's suffrage. Alice was also physically frail and suffered intermittently from mysterious aliments that the family described only as "the vapors." Brandeis relieved her of many household duties. He paid the bills, contracted for home repairs, and arranged an annual summer cottage.

Brandeis's sense of moral obligation, his desire to be counsel to the cause, rather than the client, led him to undertake public service work. Few lawyers of the time gave any thought to serving the public directly, and Brandeis suspected that this was one reason the profession had such a poor public image. "Instead of holding a position of independence between the wealthy and the people," he wrote in 1905, "able lawyers have, to a large extent, allowed themselves to become adjuncts of great corporations and have neglected their obligation to use their powers for the protection of the people. We hear much of the 'corporation lawyer' and far too little of the 'people's lawyer.' The great opportunity of the American Bar is and will be to stand again as it did in the past, ready to protect also the interests of the people."

When he undertook to serve as counsel in a public cause, he refused to accept a fee. Almost alone among his profession at the time, he believed in the Latin law phrase *pro bono publico*. With what his friend Oliver Wendell Holmes Jr. described as Brandeis's "exquisite moral susceptibility," Brandeis recognized that his law firm would suffer from his pro bono public work. He accordingly insisted upon reimbursing the firm—and hence his partners—for billable hours that he devoted to public service.

He began his public career in the 1880s with Sunday school lectures on subjects such as taxation and women's suffrage (he opposed it at the time) in Boston's Unitarian churches. He also did battle against local monopolies that involved collusion between city officials and favored businessmen. In 1893 he became involved in a contest that would last more than a decade with street railway companies. A company that owned a series of trolley lines wanted to run a track across the Boston Common. Such franchises were then in the hands of the legislature, rather than the city, and Brandeis went before a legislative committee to protest a private inroad on public park land. He won that fight, and the city relieved the traffic congestion by building a subway under Tremont and Boylston Streets.

Then in 1897 another street railway company quietly obtained from the legislature a long-term franchise to run street cars on many of the city's streets at a price of five cents a passenger. Brandeis went to war against the terms of the franchise, which violated all precedent, and the price of transportation, which exceeded that of most other cities. Brandeis helped to form a Public Franchise League to mobilize the public on the issue, and he won a victory in 1902 when the legislature modified the street railway franchise.

He came away from the street railway traction fight with the same lesson that La Follette had learned in Wisconsin—that there was an insidious alliance between businessmen needing favors and party bosses in need of money to oil their machines. Brandeis, nevertheless, remained skeptical of La Follette's mechanisms for popular participation in government—the primary, the referendum, and recall of officials. Brandeis feared that such devices could be subverted by the party professionals, and he preferred instead to educate the people on an issue and then mobilize them. In the wake of the traction fight he drafted a bill making it illegal for legislators to seek favors from quasi public corporations. He then formed a Good Government Association to promote the measure and got it enacted into law in 1906.

By that date he was engaged in a fight on a national scale—this time with the life insurance industry. Since its inception early in the century, life insurance had been a method of savings for the middle class. It afforded a shopkeeper a way of making provision for his family when he died. After the Civil War insurers appealed to the less well-to-do with "industrial policies," which could be sold to factory workers who were paid a weekly wage. Premiums were collected weekly in person by an insurance agent. Premiums were fixed by age—a one-year-old child was insurable for ten cents a week—and they rose in multiples of five cents. Unfortunately, if a worker lost his job—a common occurrence in the depression of the 1890s—his policy lapsed, and the insurer paid nothing. If he made payments for as long as twenty years, the worker might surrender an industrial policy and receive $165. Three companies—Metropolitan of New York, Prudential of New Jersey, and John Hancock of Boston—wrote 94 percent of industrial life insurance in 1904, and out of the nearly three million policies that ended in that year, as a result of death, surrender, or lapse, they made a payment in only one-eighth of the cases. And the payments that were made averaged $140.

In 1905 a catfight broke out among officers of the New York-based Equitable Assurance Company. Tales reached Boston of an Equitable vice president who charged the company for the services of his gardener and entertainments at his chateau in France. The Bostonians organized the New England Policy-Holders' Protective Committee and hired Brandeis. As was his custom, he immersed himself in the books of the insurance companies and unearthed the scandalous statistics cited above. Brandeis calculated that if a male worker paid a fifty-cent weekly premium for life insurance from the age of twenty-one to the average life-expectancy age of sixty-one, his family would collect $820. If the same payments had been made into a savings bank, the inheritance, at an average annual interest rate of 3.5 percent, would amount to $2,265 after forty years. The further advantage was that the savings could be withdrawn at any time and would not be forfeited by a lapse in weekly payments.

Brandeis accordingly proposed a law that would allow savings banks to open insurance departments. This, he hoped, would induce insurance companies to rewrite their own policies on a savings bank model. To educate the public and mobilize opinion he outlined his plan in a lengthy article in *Collier's* magazine, and then alerted Massachusetts newspapers of the forthcoming publication and induced them to reprint it simultaneously. In the meantime, the policyholders who had retained him originally formed the Massachusetts Savings Bank League, which reprinted the *Collier's* article and blanketed the state with copies. When the insurance companies objected that the Brandeis plan was utterly impractical and represented nothing but the ravings of a socialist who knew nothing about the insurance business, Brandeis appeared before a legislative committee and calmly laid out the figures he had collected from the companies' own books. To ensure that even small savings banks would be able to live up to their insurance policy obligations over an extended period of time, the legislature inserted a provision in the law establishing a General Insurance Guaranty Fund to supervise the entire industry.

The bill passed and was signed into law in June 1907. As Brandeis anticipated, the corporate giants reformed their policies on the savings bank model, and the methods of an entire industry were revolutionized. Brandeis long regarded this as his most important achievement. "Far more has been accomplished by the savings bank insurance movement," he wrote to Lincoln Steffens, "than even its most ardent supporters dared hope for." More important than eliminating the scandalous practices of life insurers, he felt, was the assurance he gave to workers that, with modest foresight, they and their families need not be penniless in their old age.

The Brandeis Brief

Brandeis barely had time to return to private practice when, in the fall of 1907, he was approached by Florence Kelley, secretary-general of the National Consumers League, the most powerful of the women-led Progressive reform organizations. Accompanying Kelley was Josephine Goldmark, Brandeis's sister-in-law and an officer of the league. The two women wanted to retain Brandeis in a case then pending before the United States Supreme Court, *Muller v. Oregon*, which involved a state law regulating the hours of working women. Brandeis agreed on two conditions. He must be the chief counsel for the state of Oregon and therefore in charge of the defense, and not merely a friend of the court filing a brief on behalf of the league. Secondly, he must work without a fee. Kelley agreed, as did the state of Oregon. Brandeis thus embarked upon the drafting of a lawyer's brief that would earn him a national reputation and become a landmark in American legal history.

In 1903 the Oregon legislature had passed a law limiting to ten hours the workday for women employed in factories and mechanical service establishments. Curt Muller's Grand Laundry in Portland broke the law by requiring a female employee to work more than ten hours. The court found Muller guilty of a misdemeanor and fined him $10. In an attempt to overturn the law Muller took his case all the way to the United States Supreme Court.

The validity of the Oregon statute under the U.S. Constitution turned on the applicability of the developing doctrine of "substantive due process." In *Lochner v. New York* (1905) the Court overturned a New York statute regulating hours of labor on grounds that it impaired the freedom of contract between worker and employer that was protected by the due process clause of the Fourteenth Amendment. The decision in that case evoked Justice Holmes's famous warning that the court was writing laissez-faire economics into the Constitution.

Brandeis, though he agreed with Holmes's dissent, spotted a loophole in the majority opinion in *Lochner* that Holmes missed. Justice Rufus W. Peckham, writing for the court majority, held that the Constitution guaranteed the right of workers to labor as many hours a day as they chose, and the state, which did have the right to protect its citizens' health, morals, and welfare, could interfere with the constitutional right to work only if it could prove that the regulation was necessary to protect the public health and welfare. New York, Peckham wrote, had failed to meet this burden.

Aha! thought Brandeis. If Oregon could meet this burden, by demonstrating that excessive hours were detrimental to the health and morals of women, the Court would have to accept its statute as constitutionally valid. And it so happened that such data was available. Under the influence of Benthamite reformers (who thought that government should promote "the greatest good for the greatest number"), the British government had been collecting statistics on the health of factory operatives since the 1830s. The Massachusetts legislature had been collecting similar data since the 1870s, and it had used the statistics to justify its laws limiting the hours of labor.

The National Consumers League helped Brandeis gather this mountain of data, and in 1908 he submitted a brief in the case of *Muller v. Oregon*. Only two pages of the brief were devoted to legal precedents, most of them taken from *Lochner*. Instead of contesting *Lochner*'s assertion that freedom of labor contract was a constitutional right, he cited it as authority for the proposition that a state could limit that right upon a showing that it was exercising its "police powers" with respect to the health, safety, and morals of its citizens. The remainder of the brief was ninety-five pages of labor statistics arranged under such headings as "The World's Experience upon Which the Legislation Limiting the Hours of Labor for Women in Based" and "Bad Effect of Long Hours on Health." The strategy worked. The Court upheld the validity of the Oregon law and specifically complimented Brandeis on his approach.

It was a landmark decision because, for the first time, an American court had accepted social statistics as legal evidence. Brandeis had shifted the focus of legal argument from treatises on the relevance of legal precedents to the presentation of factual information designed to educate judges about the needs of modern society. As historian Melvin Urofsky has written, "The real brilliance of the Brandeis brief lay in its attempt to harmonize the law with the need for social progress. The great strength of the law is its proximity and relevance to life, and in *Muller* Brandeis prodded the law into the first step on the road back to that relevance."

Modern women might object to being singled out for special legislation on grounds that their health and morals are more frail than those of men. It should be remembered that Brandeis was a Progressive, not a feminist.[1] And the frailty of women was a common assumption of the day, among both sexes. One result of the *Muller* decision was the passage of laws regulating the hours of women in most of the Northern and Western states. In 1917 the Supreme Court, confronted with a brief of more than a thousand pages of statistics, upheld an Oregon law limiting the hours of working men.

1. A better measure of Brandeis's attitudes is the encouragement he gave his daughters to pursue professional careers. Susan became a lawyer and Elizabeth obtained a Ph.D. in economics under the venerable John R. Commons at the University of Wisconsin. Elizabeth married another Commons Ph.D., Paul Raushenbush, and together they helped Professor Commons draft the nation's first unemployment compensation law (1931), adopted with the aid of Governor Philip La Follette.

Such change did not come easily, to be sure. Confronted with a massive brief from the state of Washington on behalf of employment legislation, Chief Justice Edward D. White (a Louisiana sugar planter appointed by Grover Cleveland) grumbled that he could "compile a brief twice as thick to prove that the legal profession ought to be abolished." The long-range effect of the Brandeis brief, nevertheless, was the acceptance by the Supreme Court in the school desegregation cases of the 1950s of statistical data showing the deleterious effect of segregation on African-American children.

The Brandeis brief also contributed to a developing concept in the legal community that the Constitution was more than a rigid set of strictures, drafted in 1787, and applicable to all eternity. It was, instead, an organic being, capable of adjusting to the needs of modern times. In a series of published essays Dean Roscoe Pound of the Harvard Law School and Justice Holmes had been telling the legal world that laws were the product less of logic than of experience and that courts ought to exercise self-restraint in the face of legislative innovation. In his brief Brandeis had forced the Supreme Court to accept, however tentatively, the legal relevance of social data. In *Muller v. Oregon* the Supreme Court by no means abandoned its Jesuitical approach to the sanctity of the Constitution, but it left an opening for the intrusion of factual reality. In 1903 Justice Holmes outlined the organic view of the Constitution that he and Brandeis would seek to instill over the next three decades:

> When we are dealing with words that are also a constituent act like the Constitution of the United States, we must realize that they have called into life a being, the development of which could not have been foreseen completely by the most gifted of . . . [the founding fathers]. It was enough for them to realize or to hope that they had created an organism; it has taken a century and has cost their successors much sweat and blood to prove that they created a nation. The case before must be considered in the light of our whole experience and not merely in that of what was said a hundred years ago. (*Missouri v. Holland*)

Woodrow Wilson and the New Freedom

In May 1911 the United States Supreme Court enforced the Sherman Antitrust Act and ordered the Standard Oil Company broken up on grounds that it had engaged in "unreasonable" restraints of trade. The Court, as was often its wont, was engaging in judicial legislation because the qualification "reasonable" was nowhere to be found in the Sherman Act. In addition, the "rule of reason," as it came to be called, had the potential for emasculating the statute. It implied that the mere existence of a "trust" (most so-called trusts were actually holding companies at this time), that is, mere bigness, was not illegal. The corporation had to abuse its size in an unreasonable way in order to suffer the punishment threatened by the act. The political fallout of the "rule of reason" was to give judicial blessing to Theodore Roosevelt's stance on the trust issue. Though not yet a declared presidential candidate in 1911, Roosevelt had enunciated a philosophy that he called the "New Nationalism." Instead of "busting" the trusts, he would tolerate big business because of the economic advantages it afforded and instead use governmental power to regulate its behavior.

Woodrow Wilson, governor of New Jersey and by mid-1911 the likely Democratic nominee for president, had worried about the trusts for some years but never found a solution to the problem. When he first heard of Roosevelt's approach, he thought it made sense. A congressional investigation into the results of the trend toward business consolidation and the ideas of Louis Brandeis changed all that. Wilson in 1912 was searching for intellectual guidance; Brandeis lit the way.

"Big business" became a source of public concern as a result of the consolidation movement that began in the early 1890s and reached a crescendo after the Republicans gained control of both the presidency and Congress in 1897. Business organizers no longer favored the trust, which had proved unwieldy and suffered a tattered reputation after passage of the Sherman Act. The new device, instead, was the holding company. A New Jersey statute of 1889 permitted the creation of corporations whose sole purpose was the holding of stock in other corporations. James B. Duke was one of the first to take advantage of the new law by consolidating a number of small cigar and cigarette manufacturing companies into the American Tobacco Company. American Tobacco did not manufacture anything; it merely owned the companies that did. In 1893 investment banker J. P. Morgan followed the same model in creating the General Electric Company (GE).

The role of J. P. Morgan in creating GE is revealing, for he was a banker who knew nothing about electric power and lighting. The establishment of a holding company required a huge reservoir of capital. Buying up other corporations was expensive, even if one purchased only a controlling interest, rather than 100 percent of the stock. Only an investment banker like Morgan could tap into that kind of capital. Morgan's reward was a substantial chunk of stock in the holding company and a seat on its board of directors. Morgan's greatest triumph was combining the Carnegie Steel Company with several of its competitors to create the United States Steel Company (1901), the nation's first billion-dollar corporation.

Besides using a new device, the holding company, the wave of business mergers that crested between 1897 and 1904 had a new purpose. Consolidation in the 1880s—the Standard Oil trust, for example—was aimed at vertical integration, that is, placing under a single management all the stages of production, from oil well or coal mine to retail outlet. The purpose of consolidation at the turn of the century was horizontal integration, that is, the elimination of competitors. The specter of monopoly is what concerned middle-class Progressives, including businessmen who feared that they were being squeezed out of competition.

The Progressive movement coincided with a period of general prosperity, which meant rising prices. Consumers tended to blame the price increases on business monopolies—a suspicion on which Democrats capitalized in the election of 1910. After Democrats gained control of the House of Representatives, the House Banking and Currency Committee (chaired by Representative Arsene Pujo) in 1912 investigated the results of the consolidation movement and reported that J. P. Morgan and two bankers allied with him held 341 seats on the boards of directors of 112 corporations—banks, railroads, public utilities, and insurance companies. The combined assets of these corporations amounted to more than $22 billion, a figure that equaled the value of all of the real estate and physical property in the twenty-two states west of the Mississippi.

Brandeis mistrusted size of any sort, whether in business or government. He regarded monopolies as inefficient because, lacking competition, they had no motive for streamlining their operations. Ten years after the formation of U.S. Steel, for example, the United States had fallen behind Germany in updated methods of steel production. Brandeis also regarded huge corporations as inhumane because no single executive felt responsible for faulty or dangerous products or hazards to workers. And, most importantly, he regarded them as dangerous because they wielded more power than even the government. The capitalization of the United States Steel Company in 1901, for instance, was enough to run the federal government for two years.

Brandeis had no faith in Roosevelt's approach to the trust issue because he was certain that the trusts would dominate the regulatory agencies. A regulatory agency was effective only if staffed by Progressives, and there was no certainty of that. In the 1890s, for instance, Presidents Harrison and McKinley had routinely named railroad executives to the Interstate Commerce Commission. In 1911 Brandeis helped La Follette draft an antitrust bill in response to the Standard Oil decision. The bill, which La Follette introduced to the Senate, attempted to define the "rule of reason." Any business combination that controlled more than 40 percent of an industry was presumed to be unreasonably restraining trade, and, by the terms of the bill, the burden was on the "trust" to prove that it was acting reasonably.

Among the individuals called upon to testify before the Senate committee considering the La Follette bill was George W. Perkins, a partner in J. P. Morgan and Company. Perkins, who would later be a prominent figure in Roosevelt's presidential campaign, claimed that bigness was not a problem because large corporations were inherently superior economically—they could afford to hire the most talented executives, for instance, and finance the research that produced new and better products. But Perkins also felt that businessmen needed government oversight to ensure that they competed fairly. All any competent executive wanted was a level playing field. It was an ingenious argument, and it showed the extent to which business management had become professionalized since the tumultuous days of Rockefeller and the South Improvement Company. (The first business school, Harvard's, was founded in 1920.)

Brandeis, however, would have none of it. He followed Perkins on the witness stand and argued that trusts were neither efficient nor humane. He also pointed out that stockholders were, in effect, absentee landlords, who took no responsibility for the antisocial behavior of the creature they owned. Neither House nor Senate acted on the La Follette bill, but Brandeis was sufficiently impressed to announce his support for La Follette in the approaching presidential campaign. Reading of La Follette's Philadelphia debacle while campaigning for him in Chicago, he wrote his wife: "My thoughts have been much with you and Bob and the children, and I long to be East where I may hear something authentic. Only make Bob take the rest he needs. . . . When he comes back we will take up the good fight again together."

When he finally became aware of the extent of the damage done at Philadelphia, Brandeis concluded that Woodrow Wilson's candidacy was the best chance for the survival of Progressivism. After the Democratic convention nominated Wilson, Brandeis declared the selection "one of the most encouraging events in American History." On August 1, 1912, Brandeis, who had never met Wilson, wrote the governor to compliment him on his campaign pledge to reduce customs duties. Wilson promptly issued an invitation to get together, and the two met at Sea Girt, New Jersey, where the state maintained a summer residence for its governors. The two men talked for three hours, and rarely has there been such a meeting of minds. Wilson, the son, grandson, and nephew of Presbyterian ministers, was a moral Calvinist who believed in both the free enterprise system and the clear-cut delineation between good and evil. With theological barriers erased by modern secularism, the two men had only their ethical heritage on which to rely—and they saw eye to eye.

Wilson, the ex-college professor, was an open chalice—Brandeis poured in the wine. Brandeis by this time had modified his position. He still favored "busting" the trusts, but he now thought that, in addition, there should be some government oversight of the pieces. Wilson resisted the idea of regulation, fearing that to succeed in an oversight role, the government would have to be as large and tyrannical as the corporations. Nevertheless, his speeches were soon echoing two other Brandeisian ideas: unrestricted competition resulted in monopoly, and monopoly was inefficient and inhumane.

In September, Wilson's campaign manager, William Gibbs McAdoo, suggested that Brandeis publish his theories in the form of articles; this would educate the public without committing Wilson on the details. Brandeis agreed, and through the election campaign and after he published, first in *Collier's* and then in *Harper's Weekly*, a succession of articles publicizing the findings of the House Pujo Committee and outlining his own remedies. In 1914 the series was consolidated into a book entitled *Other People's Money*. Wilson read the articles carefully and was soon proclaiming that Roosevelt was a paternalist who thought he knew what was best for the people, when it was the people themselves who understood best what was right and just. Midway through the campaign he conferred the label "New Freedom" on his program. Brandeis had given him the focus, the tactical opening, and the live ammunition. After he won the election Wilson told him, "You were yourself a great part of the victory."

Journalists and editorial writers generally assumed that Brandeis would be offered a place in the president's cabinet. Wilson felt obliged to award the top jobs to influential Democrats. Bryan became secretary of state and McAdoo secretary of the treasury. Progressives thought that Brandeis might be offered the post of attorney general to prove that the president was serious about curbing monopolies, and Wilson might have yielded had Brandeis pressed for the job. But he did not. He had long shunned public office, realizing that it would compromise his moral authority and reduce his influence. The *Detroit Times*, a voice of midwestern Progressivism, thought it understood. Hearing that Massachusetts Progressives wanted to run Brandeis for the U.S. Senate in 1912, the *Times* opined that he was "bigger than a senatorship" and unlikely to win election because he was too honorable. "Anyone who has ever heard him hurling thunder at a public hearing," the paper went on, "must realize how little the senatorial toga would add to the stature of a real statesman, patriot, and lover of his kind."

Brandeis's biographer, Philippa Strum, agrees that the man was more influential and more content as an elder statesman without administrative duties: "He was able to jump into whatever fray appealed to him. He could continue to read whatever caught his fancy at the moment, moving from economic reports and Greek history to biographies and tracts on social reform. He could spend the leisure time that he enjoyed so much with his family, rigorously limiting his work hours and safeguarding his August vacations."

As a result of the Pujo Committee hearings, both Brandeis and Wilson were convinced that the "money trust" was the most pernicious of all because it enabled bankers to control the national economy. Reform of the banking system was top priority in the "New Freedom." A more flexible currency than the rigid gold-fettered National Bank notes was a parallel need. In early 1913 Representative Carter Glass of Virginia drafted a bill creating twelve reserve banks, which would function as a stabilizing backup to the nation's banking system. The reserve banks would be in private hands, and the currency they issued would be in the control of the Federal Reserve Board, which was itself elected by bankers.

Although, as secretary of state, his principal duties related to foreign policy, Bryan regarded himself as an authority in matters of banking and currency. He objected to the Glass bill on grounds that the proposed reserve banks were privately owned and without government supervision. He wanted a presidentially appointed board to supervise the reserve system and the issuance of currency, thus making the money supply a governmental function, as it was elsewhere in the Western world. Wilson, who claimed to know nothing of banking (except that bankers in general had too much power), turned to Brandeis. Brandeis had to agree with Bryan. Banking was too important to the economy to be left to the mercy of private interests. He persuaded both the president and Carter Glass that there must be a Federal Reserve Board, appointed by the president, with power to set the interest rates that reserve banks charged (known today as the "rediscount rate") and hence, indirectly, to govern the amount of money in circulation. In addition, the bill, as redrafted by Glass, provided that the currency issued by the Federal Reserve banks would be backed only in part by gold and in part by commercial paper (i.e., IOUs, bonds, drafts, and other obligations issued by American businesses). The money would thus have some "elasticity," in the sense that the quantity in circulation would vary with the amount of business being transacted. The bill passed, and though the powers of the Federal Reserve Board had to be increased substantially during the 1930s depression, it remains Woodrow Wilson's finest monument.

Although most of Wilson's cabinet wanted to delay action on the trust issue until the business community had digested the impact of the changes in the banking system, Brandeis wanted to press ahead with antitrust legislation. He had by this time, however, modified his position. In one of his magazine articles he had proposed the establishment of an "Interstate Trade Commission" to investigate unfair business practices and determine whether any business arrangement was in restraint of trade. This, he felt, would be a constructive step, "which will show that the business man is as much the subject of governmental solicitude as are the farmers and the working man." Such a watchdog agency would reinforce the antitrust laws by preventing the sort of unfair competition that led to the growth of monopolies.

While Wilson pondered this new approach in the spring of 1914, the House Judiciary Committee, chaired by Henry D. Clayton of Alabama, drafted a new antitrust measure designed to strengthen the Sherman Act. The bill prohibited specific practices, such as the purchase of stock by one corporation in another when the effect is to reduce competition.[2] The bill also, at the insistence of Brandeis, prohibited interlocking directorates in competing corporations. The only controversial feature of the bill was an exemption of labor unions from the antitrust laws, something for which Samuel Gompers and the AF of L had long fought. By the time Congress passed the Clayton Act in June, Wilson had endorsed Brandeis's idea of a Federal Trade Commission. Congress obligingly passed that bill as well, and Wilson signed the two antitrust measures into law in September and October 1914.

The passage of the antitrust measures rounded out the New Freedom, and Wilson thereafter seemed to lose interest in reform. One reason is that he became increasingly preoccupied with foreign affairs and the need to preserve American neutral rights in the war that had broken out in Europe. He was also afraid of making more enemies in the business community that might jeopardize his chances of reelection in 1916. He was, after all, a minority president who had received less that 50 percent of the popular vote in 1912. Congress, rather than the president, provided the impetus for the last vestiges of Progressivism: the La Follette Seamen's Act (1915) and the Adamson Act (1916) requiring an eight-hour day for railroad workers. To Brandeis's disgust Wilson loaded the Federal Reserve Board with bankers and appointed conservative businessmen to the Federal Trade Commission.[3] Brandeis left Washington for his seaside vacation in August 1914 thoroughly disheartened by Wilson's change in attitude, and by the end of the month he had a new humanitarian mission—Zionism.

The Zionist Movement

For centuries European Jews had dreamed of reestablishing their homeland in Palestine—the ancient Zion that had existed in covenanted alliance with God. There had always been some Jews in Palestine, though they were a minority in a land dominated by Arabs and governed by Ottoman Turks. In the 1880s a band of Russian Jews, fleeing the pogroms that had deprived them of their land and possessions, settled in Palestine and purchased land from their Arab neighbors. Other refugees came

2. In the 1970s, for example, federal courts forced DuPont to divest itself of stock it held in General Motors (GM) because DuPont was using its leverage to persuade GM to use DuPont paints on its cars.

3. In the 1920s Presidents Harding and Coolidge continued the practice of naming businessmen to the Federal Trade Commission. At one point the chair of the commission declared governmental "hands off" and said that business could regulate itself. The FTC did not become a viable watchdog agency until the presidency of Franklin Roosevelt.

from Poland and Germany. An international Zionist congress convened in Basle, Switzerland, in 1897 and met annually thereafter. Although the Turkish sultan refused to give the Zionists a charter for a state of their own, he had no objection to individual settlements. By 1914 the Jewish population in Palestine numbered some ninety thousand, about half being recent settlers from Europe. The war halted the flow of refugees, and a British blockade (Ottoman Turkey sided with Germany in the war) deprived the settlers of their only source of income, the export of citrus fruits and wines.

British Zionists began touring the United States in search of funds for the relief of the settlers and to finance new settlements. On August 30, 1914, American Zionists asked Brandeis to attend an emergency conference. Neither he nor his family had ever shown much interest in Judaism and none at all in Zionism. "My early training was not Jewish in a religious sense, nor was it Christian," he had written in 1910. "While naturally interested in their race, my people were not so narrow as to allow their religious belief to overshadow their interest in the broader aspects of humanity." Although Brandeis was generous with his money, his donations to Jewish charities had been minute.

In 1910 he served as counsel during a garment workers strike in New York, which acquainted him with the Jewish working class, and he began to express sympathy for the establishment of a Jewish state in Palestine. The Zionists invited him to their August 1914 meeting because he was a known humanitarian and a confidant of President Wilson. Brandeis accepted because he was disillusioned with Wilson and saw an independent Palestine, populated with self-reliant pioneers, as an ideal testing ground for social experimentation.

The conference created a Provisional Executive Committee for General Zionist Affairs, and Brandeis agreed to serve as chair. Brandeis set up an emergency fund, and within a few weeks he reached his goal of $100,000. Most of the money was sent to the Zionist organization's office in Palestine for the purchase of land. By mid-1915 he was helping to subsidize the emigration of Jews from Eastern Europe, who were caught between the German and Russian armies and suffering from anti-Semitism on both sides. However, he never conceived of Palestine as a homeland for American Jews. It was not large enough to accommodate them, in the first place, and they were reasonably free, assimilated, and prosperous in the United States. He urged American Jews to learn about the Zionist movement and study Jewish history and culture, but they should otherwise stay home.

Brandeis did not hesitate to use his connections within the American government to further his cause. Particularly valuable was his friendship with Henry Morganthau, the American ambassador to the Ottoman government in Constantinople. Morganthau helped channel American money into Palestine, and he served as a conduit for messages to Zionists in Eastern Europe. Bryan permitted the Provisional Committee to use the State Department's cipher facilities, though departmental bureaucrats fretted about violations of American neutrality in dealing with the Turks.

Although Brandeis resigned his offices with the Zionist movement when he became a Supreme Court justice in 1916, he remained intensely interested in the creation of a Jewish state. His most important contribution may have been to encourage British interest in the project. He met the British foreign secretary, Arthur Balfour, at a Washington reception shortly after the United States entered the war in April 1917, and he conferred with Balfour twice in the next couple weeks. The British had a self-interest in the establishment of a Jewish state. A British army was marching on Jerusalem from Egypt, and the British wanted to control the Levantine Coast in order to protect the Suez Canal. The settlement of a Jewish population in Palestine, tied to Britain by sentiment and financial investment, was certainly in Britain's short-term interest.

Brandeis and Balfour discussed a formal statement of British policy, and Brandeis obtained President Wilson's approval. Balfour issued his declaration on November 2, 1917, saying that the British government viewed with favor the establishment in Palestine of a national home for the Jewish people. France and Italy associated themselves with the policy a few months later. The peace treaty that ended the war broke up the Ottoman Empire, and in 1920 Britain obtained a mandate from the League of Nations to govern Palestine. Two years later the U.S. Congress adopted resolutions approving the formation of a Jewish state. Brandeis and his wife visited Palestine in 1919, but he refused the Zionist demand that he quit his job on the court and move to Palestine permanently. Criticized by the European Zionists for this stand, he severed all connections with the movement in 1921.

"Holmes and Brandeis in Dissent"

Wilson never sensed Brandeis's disillusionment, and relations between the two men remained cordial after 1914. Wilson performed favors for the Zionist movement whenever asked, and in 1915 he used his influence to gain Brandeis admission to an exclusive club in Washington, which had resisted his membership on grounds that he was a political radical. When a vacancy appeared on the United States Supreme Court in 1916, Wilson did not hesitate to nominate Brandeis. It was a courageous stroke, for Brandeis was certain to be opposed by Republican conservatives and businessmen.

The Supreme Court's resistance to progressive social legislation had called public attention to the Court's political conservatism. As a result, presidents began considering the ideology of potential nominees in ways they seldom had before. It was the beginning of the Court's demeaning role as political football, a burden that it has carried into the twenty-first century. President Taft, with the Standard Oil case pending, deliberately loaded the court with legal conservatives. (He had the opportunity to name six justices during his four-year term.) In 1912 Roosevelt's Progressive Party pledged itself to constitutional changes that would empower legislatures to overturn court decisions. After the election Democrats introduced a bill in Congress increasing the number of Supreme Court justices, so that Wilson might have an early opportunity to reconstruct the Court. Level heads prevailed, and it failed to pass.

Before making his nomination public, Wilson first had to get Brandeis's consent. That turned out to be remarkably easy. Although Brandeis had consistently rejected offers of public office, the Supreme Court was another matter; it was the culmination of a legal career. At the age of sixty, he rationalized that a Court seat would be appropriate for his "retirement" years. Wilson then consulted Bob La Follette to determine if Republican Progressives would support the nomination, and La Follette gave a resounding "yes." Wilson submitted Brandeis's name to the Senate on January 28, 1916. A friend wrote to ex-president Taft (who desperately wanted the Court seat himself): "When Brandeis's nomination came in yesterday, the Senate simply gasped. . . . There wasn't any more excitement at the Capitol when Congress passed the Spanish War Resolution."

The tumult went on for four months, with charges and countercharges filling the newspapers, the records of the Senate Judiciary Committee, and finally the Senate journal itself. The main accusation was Brandeis's alleged radicalism, but because he was the first Jew considered for the Supreme Court, anti-Semitism was never far from the surface. The Senate finally confirmed him on June 1 by forty-seven to twenty-two, a party-line vote except for La Follette and a handful of Republican Progressives. Wilson never regretted his choice. After the United States entered the war, advisers urged the president to use Brandeis for special missions. Brandeis would obligingly offer to resign from the Court, whereupon Wilson would reply: "Not on your life. On that Bench you are more important to the Country than you could possibly be elsewhere. It was too difficult to get you there to take a chance on losing you through a temporary arrangement."

Supreme Court sessions occupied only a few months out of each year. Louis and Alice Brandeis held on to their Boston home and rented an apartment in a fashionable complex on Connecticut Avenue. Justice Holmes lived only a block away, and the two friends regularly walked to work together. The two men were both Progressives, and they agreed that courts should be tolerant of legislative attempts to respond to the social problems presented by the swift advent of industrialization and urbanization. But they differed in their approach to the law. Brandeis thought the law ought to rest on the facts, with courts seeking justice as the situation warranted. Holmes found the key to jurisprudence in philosophy. He viewed the Constitution in a pragmatic and organic way, but he preferred to apply principles of justice to specific situations. Nevertheless, on a Court loaded with hide-bound conservatives, given to a mechanistic view of the Constitution and such judicial constructs as "substantive due process," Holmes and Brandeis often found themselves in the minority. The phrase "Holmes and Brandeis dissenting" became a commonplace of law review articles, though their dissents were usually in carefully chosen and highly publicized cases.[4]

The first important decision in which Brandeis participated involved, ironically, one of the last vestiges of Wilsonian Progressivism, a federal child labor act. State regulation of child labor in the late nineteenth century had been on humanitarian grounds, an effort to limit the hours of work and mitigate dangerous working conditions. After 1890 the objective changed, as a middle-class, city-bred, increasingly professionalized society concluded that children belonged in school up to the age of sixteen, rather than in the factory. Thereafter, child labor laws and compulsory school attendance laws went hand in hand. In 1912 Roosevelt's Progressive Party pledged itself to the enactment of a federal law prohibiting child labor. In 1916 Congress passed a law prohibiting the interstate shipment of the products of mines that employed children under the age of sixteen and the products of factories that employed children under the age of fourteen. Other provisions regulated the hours of children in mills and mines, again under the guise of prohibiting the interstate shipment of child-made products.[5]

The validity of the statute was at issue in the case of *Hammer v. Dagenhart* (1918). In a five-to-four vote the Court held the statute unconstitutional on grounds that Congress had no power to regulate working conditions in mines and mills. Even though the statute purported to regulate products shipped in interstate commerce, the real intent—and here the Court claimed the authority to examine Congress's hidden motives—was to regulate labor, specifically that of children, and that it had no power to do so. Holmes dissented, joined by Brandeis and two others, pointing

4. In twenty-three years on the court Brandeis participated in 528 decisions and dissented from the majority, or differed in nuance by "concurring," 74 times.

5. Because the Constitution does not expressly give Congress power to fix working conditions of labor, it has to rest such legislation on its power to regulate interstate commerce. Unfortunately, the Supreme Court, in an antitrust case in 1894, had declared that factories are sedentary and do not move across state lines; therefore neither the factory worker nor the owner was involved in interstate commerce. Congress in 1916 attempted to circumvent this by focusing its restrictions on products made by child labor that were subsequently shipped across state lines.

out that there was no such limitation on the commerce power in the Constitution, and he chided the Court majority for allowing its political predilections to override the will of elected legislators. In the Senate La Follette called for a constitutional amendment allowing Congress to override Supreme Court decisions and depriving lower federal courts of the power of judicial review altogether. Samuel Gompers, president of the AF of L, and consumer advocate Florence Kelley publicly supported the measure. The judicial roadblock nevertheless held fast. Congress did not succeed in enacting child labor legislation until 1938.

American entry into World War I brought a new issue before the Supreme Court—freedom of speech. Eager to unite the country behind the war effort, the Wilson administration employed hundreds of "Four Minute Men," who traveled around the country giving brief, patriotic speeches on street corners. Congress, never behindhand on matters of patriotism, joined the frenzy. In 1917 it passed an Espionage Act that, in addition to making spying and sabotage criminal acts, provided criminal penalties for public criticism that could be considered detrimental to the morale or operations of the military. A year later it enacted a Sedition Act that prohibited the "uttering, printing, writing, or publishing any disloyal, profane, scurrilous, or abusive language" against the government or the armed forces. Under these laws the government banned from the mails all magazines and newspapers that opposed the war, and the courts gave jail sentences to Socialist congressman Victor Berger of Milwaukee and perennial Socialist presidential candidate Eugene Debs.

The constitutionality of the Espionage Act came before the Supreme Court in the case of *Schenck v. United States* (1919). Albert Schenck had been arrested for circulating antidraft leaflets outside an army base. His lawyer appealed his criminal conviction on grounds that the statute violated the First Amendment guarantee of free speech. It is a measure of the limited role that government played in American society in its first hundred years that this was the Court's first opportunity to analyze the First Amendment.

Oliver Wendell Holmes wrote the opinion for a unanimous court in upholding the law. The right of free speech, he pointed out, has never been absolute. "Free speech," for instance, "would not protect a man in falsely shouting fire in a theater, and causing a panic." Holmes held that the government similarly had a right to limit freedom of expression when the nation was in a "clear and present danger," as in time of war. Realizing the breadth of this doctrine, Holmes sought to delineate clearly what was permissible and what was illicit in time of war. Applying a "rule of proximate causation," he said that whether speech could be limited depended on the immediate circumstances; the danger in the offending utterance must be obvious and immediate.

Although Brandeis joined in concurring with this opinion, he almost immediately regretted it. "I have never been quite happy about my concurrence," he told his friend, Felix Frankfurter. "I had not then thought the issues of freedom of speech out—I thought at the subject, not through it." The problem with the "clear and present danger" test—which would lead the Court to abandon it altogether in the 1960s context of the Cold War—was measuring the immediacy and extent of the nation's danger when the peril arose from the lone voice of a civilian far removed from military operations.

Both Holmes and Brandeis had a chance to rethink the problem the following year in a series of cases in which they dissented. In the most important of these, *Pierce v. United States* (1920), Brandeis, with Holmes this time concurring, revealed the extent to which he now rejected the *Schenck* notion that the mere existence of war might make certain speech illegal. As in *Schenck*, persons had been arrested for distributing a Socialist pamphlet that allegedly interfered with the war effort and caused insubordination in the military. The problem was that the pamphlet had been distributed to civilians, and, though it contained some "lurid pictures," Brandeis could not see that it contained anything that would induce a person of ordinary intelligence to commit such serious crimes as insubordination and mutiny. Certainly, there was no "clear and present danger" that this would result. The court majority, perhaps anticipating his dissent, did not even seek to apply the "clear and present danger" test and instead invoked a "bad tendency" doctrine. It ruled that the pamphlet might well "have a tendency to cause insubordination, disloyalty, and refusal of duty in the military and naval forces of the United States." It therefore found the Sedition Act constitutional in this instance. In a ringing dissent, Brandeis argued for the preservation of "the fundamental right of free men to strive for better conditions through new legislation and new institutions" without regard to whether the nation was at war or at peace.

Prohibition of the manufacture and sale of alcoholic beverages, authorized by the Eighteenth Amendment to the Constitution in 1919, raised new questions of civil rights in the 1920s. Because the act failed to outlaw the consumption of liquors, demand remained steady and bootleggers filled in the supply side of the equation. Federal agents faced enormous difficulty in enforcing the law. The issue in the case of *Olmstead v. United States* (1928) was the legitimacy of government wiretapping in light of the Fourth Amendment's prohibition of "unreasonable searches and seizures." For five months federal G-men had tapped the home and office telephones of men suspected of bootlegging liquor. The men were convicted and appealed their case on the basis that evidence gathered by wiretapping was tainted by a violation of the Fourth Amendment.

Chief Justice William Howard Taft, whom President Harding had placed on the bench, writing for the court majority, upheld the convictions. Because government officials had not actually entered the men's homes or offices and nothing physical had been seized, there had been no "unreasonable search." No one had forced the men to talk over the telephone; the Fourth Amendment had not been violated. Brandeis, in dissent, found wiretapping a clear invasion of privacy; it amounted to an illegal search even though the telephone had not been invented when the Fourth Amendment was drafted. With remarkable clairvoyance, Brandeis wrote: "The progress of science in furnishing the Government with means of espionage is not likely to stop with wire tapping. Ways may some day be developed by which the Government, without removing papers from secret drawers, can reproduce them in court, and by which it will be enabled to expose to a jury the most intimate occurrences in the home." One of Brandeis's working folders for the *Olmstead* case contained a newspaper clipping reporting on some scientist's invention of a contraption called television.

While limitations on the rights of citizens involved the immediate specter of governmental tyranny, Brandeis had long been concerned, as well, for the potential for tyranny in the mere size of government. He accordingly viewed Franklin Roosevelt's New Deal with mixed emotions. The centerpiece of the First New Deal (the legislation of 1933–1934 aimed largely at recovery from the Depression) was the National Recovery Administration. The statute creating the NRA—one of the most poorly conceived statutes in American history—envisioned a government agency that would manage the economy, somewhat on the order of the war mobilization agencies created by Woodrow Wilson. It suspended the antitrust laws and allowed businesses to collaborate on price-fixing on a theory that higher prices would stimulate manufacturing and end the depression. Without specific powers, the NRA was put in charge of this vague recipe for prosperity.

Brandeis had welcomed some features of the New Deal, such as banking and securities legislation, and Roosevelt had courted him as a friend. Roosevelt, who enjoyed giving nicknames to people, referred to him in private as "Old Isaiah." Roosevelt was accordingly stunned when Brandeis joined a unanimous court in declaring the NRA unconstitutional in 1935. Turning amorphous areas of power over to a federal agency was contrary to his long-held fear of centralization. For Brandeis the turning point in the case was the testimony of an oilman being prosecuted for ignoring an NRA regulation who claimed he did not know of the law's existence. The man testified that the only copy of the regulation "was in the hip pocket of a government agent who came down from Washington to Texas." Under questioning from Brandeis, a government lawyer admitted that there was no general publication of NRA edicts.

Brandeis resigned from the court in 1939, saying that, at age eighty-three, "the time has come when a young man should assume the burden." Roosevelt honored him by replacing him with Felix Frankfurter, a long-time friend and Progressive protégé. In 1913 Brandeis had persuaded the Harvard Law School to hire Frankfurter and had helped raise the money to fund the professorship. Brandeis also left a rich legacy of law clerks who revered him. One remembered, "I never understood Jesus Christ until I met Brandeis." They carried on the philosophy that human development is unlimited if individuals are given the freedom to hear and think and speak. Among his many clerks who became decision makers in the mid-twentieth century was Dean Acheson, secretary of state to President Truman at the outset of the Cold War. At Brandeis's funeral, Acheson said in eulogy, "To him truth was less than truth unless it were explained so that people could understand and believe."

Suggested Reading

Philippa Strum has written two recent biographies of the justice, *Louis D. Brandeis, Justice for the People* (1984) and *Brandeis: Beyond Progressivism* (1993). The books are well-researched and judicious in interpretation but rather wooden in writing style. A bit more sprightly is Melvin I. Urofsky's *A Mind of One Piece: Brandeis and American Reform* (1971), though it is an examination of his ideas, rather than a life story. A more recent intellectual study is Stephen W. Baskerville's *Of Laws and Limitations: An Intellectual Portrait of Louis D. Brandeis* (1994). The most recent study of his compatriot on the Court is G. Edward White's *Justice Oliver Wendell Holmes: Law and the Inner Self* (1993). A provocative interpretation of the two Progressive presidents is by John M. Cooper Jr., *The Warrior and the Priest: Woodrow Wilson and Theodore Roosevelt* (1983). William G. Ross examines the conflict between Progressives and the courts in *A Muted Fury: Populists, Progressives, and Labor Unions Confront the Courts, 1890–1937* (1994).

9

Carrie Chapman Catt: Progressivism and Women's Suffrage

The reformers of the mid-nineteenth century argued among themselves as often as they fought their opponents. The disputes invariably pitted moderates against "ultras." The antislavery movement divided between abolitionists, who demanded the immediate uncompensated freeing of slaves, and Free-Soilers, who would tolerate slavery where it existed and simply try to prevent its expansion. The peace crusade divided between pacifists who would oppose any war and those who felt that a nation had a right to defend itself when attacked. The temperance movement split between enthusiasts who demanded total abstinence and moderates who would tolerate beer and wine. The only movement that did not divide within itself prior to the Civil War was the drive for legal rights for women, including the right to vote, that began with the Seneca Falls Convention of 1848.

The push for women's rights did not suffer schism prior to the war in part because it was so tiny. The number of prominent leaders of the movement could be counted on one hand, and most of the rank-and-file activists were Quakers who shied from conflict. The women had, moreover, no formal organization that might serve as a forum for disputes over tactics, and they were fairly successful in obtaining property and legal rights for women in the Northern states. After the war, on the other hand, the grant of suffrage to freedmen of the South created a dilemma for the feminists that did split their movement. The Fourteenth Amendment, which went into effect in 1868, threatened a reduction in the congressional representation of states that failed to give black males the right to vote. (This was the first reference to gender in the Constitution.) It occurred to Susan B. Anthony and Elizabeth Cady Stanton, leaders of the women's rights movement, that it would be easy enough for the drafters of the amendment to scratch the word "male" and thereby extend the vote to any citizen. This would have the effect of extending the vote to white women as well as the freedmen. Anthony so testified before a committee of Congress, but she got nowhere.

Male reformers who supported women's suffrage asked the women to stand aside for the moment and not complicate the drive to give African-American men the vote. Lucy Stone and her husband Henry Blackwell, who had divided their speaking engagements before the war about equally between women's rights and antislavery, agreed with this view. And that split the women's movement. In 1869, after Congress approved the Fifteenth Amendment, which expressly prohibited the states from denying the vote to black males, Anthony and Stanton formed a Suffrage Association to lobby for a sixteenth amendment that would grant the vote to women. The following year Stone and Blackwell formed their own, more conservative organization, which favored working with the states individually to secure the vote for women. Their model was the Territory of Wyoming, which granted the vote to women in 1869. For the next twenty years the two suffrage organizations battled one another. The Stanton–Anthony association was by far the more radical of the two, addressing, in addition to the vote, such taboo issues as prostitution, birth control, labor unions for women, and the male-oriented Bible.

In 1890, realizing that they were squandering their energies fighting one another, the two organizations merged to form the National American Woman Suffrage Association (NAWSA). The first task of the new association was to create a grassroots organization. Its model was the Women's Christian Temperance Union (WCTU), the largest female-led pressure group in the nation. Its president, Frances Willard, had built a federal structure with tactical decision making left to local organizations. Willard herself controlled the direction of the movement, which went well beyond the issue of laws prohibiting the sale of liquor. By 1889 the WCTU had thirty-nine departments, reflecting concerns for women's health, labor unions, morals, and world peace, in addition to temperance. NAWSA needed an organizational genius of Willard's caliber, and it found one in Carrie Chapman Catt.

Apprenticeship of a Leader

She was born Carrie Lane on January 9, 1859, in Ripon, Wisconsin, a village whose sole distinction, to that point in time, was a claim to be the birthplace of the Republican Party. Her parents, Lucius and Maria Lane, were of New England stock, and they were among the Yankee pioneers who had drifted westward in the first half of the century. They had settled in Wisconsin's fertile Fox River valley, where Lucius took up farming. In 1866 the Lanes resumed their westward trek, moving to Charles City, Iowa, where Catt spent the years of her youth that she remembered best.

Unfortunately, few of those memories survive, for Catt, who valued her privacy all her life, destroyed nearly all of her personal papers. She attended the one-room schoolhouse near the family farm and then went to high school in town. After graduating from high school, she was determined to go to college. Her father, seeing no value in a collegiate education for a person whose only future was motherhood, offered to pay

Carrie Chapman Catt. (Photograph from the Collections of the Library of Congress

only $25 a year for her expenses. Iowa State Agricultural College at Ames, a beneficiary of the Morrill Land Grant College Act of 1862, did not require much more than that. Tuition was free, board was $2.50 a week, and a room could be had for $2 to $3 a term. Carrie made up the difference between her needs and her father's niggardly benevolence by teaching school, and she graduated in 1880.

Although Carrie Catt's relationship with her parents remained cordial all their lives, the parental influence on her, as biographer Booth Fowler has observed, was essentially negative. Her father fought her every effort to enter the world on an equal footing with men, and her mother accepted without complaint her subordinate role in the family. During the election of 1872, when Carrie was thirteen, she was shocked to discover that her mother could not vote. Shock turned to anger when both parents told her that this was only right, and neither could give a sensible reason for women's inferior status. In later life Catt often said that no revelation in her youth angered her more. It also helped establish a lifelong objective.

In the fall of 1881 she received an offer of a teaching job in the newly built Mason City high school. She accepted the position and soon found a joy in teaching and a talent for administration. By the end of her second year she held the combined jobs of high school principal and superintendent of the city's schools. While working on the town's Decoration Day committee she met Leo Chapman, the owner-editor of a weekly newspaper, the *Republican*. Chapman was an ardent believer in both temperance and women's suffrage, and the two were soon very much in love. Carrie Lane resigned her positions as teacher and school superintendent because married women were not allowed to teach in Iowa, and the two were married in February 1885.

Carrie became a coeditor of the *Republican* and initiated a feature entitled "Woman's World," in which she explored feminist issues from suffrage to the right of working women to strike for better pay and conditions. Before long the Chapmans ran afoul of the conservative editor of another of the city's papers, and he sued them for libel. Unable to afford the legal costs of a trial, the Chapmans sold their paper and prepared to move to San Francisco. In May 1886 Chapman took a train to California to arrange for a job and housing, but before Carrie could join him he died of typhoid fever.

Carrie Chapman lingered in San Francisco for a year, supporting herself with freelance writing for various journals. She moved back to Charles City, Iowa, in August 1887 with intent to begin a new career as a public lecturer. She was soon drawn into the temperance movement, where she honed her organizational skills on Frances Willard's system. Because regulation of liquor could be achieved only by political means, Carrie quickly moved from temperance to women's suffrage. Her talent for public speaking and gift for organization made her a fast-rising star. In 1889 she was elected secretary of the Iowa Woman Suffrage Association and head of field operations. The following year she attended the national convention that united the suffrage organizations and was invited to give an address. The aging Lucy Stone, who had heard her give a talk in Iowa, predicted: "Mrs. Chapman will be heard from yet in this movement."

After the NAWSA convention Carrie traveled west again, this time to Seattle to marry George Catt. She had known Catt in high school, and their friendship had been renewed in San Francisco. The thirty-year-old Catt was now a successful engineer who was in charge of building most of the railroad bridges and trestles in the state of Washington. Carrie had again chosen a soul mate, and their marriage was one of equals. "We made a team to work for the cause," she wrote some years later. "My husband used to say that he was as much a reformer as I, but that he couldn't work at reforming and earn a living at the same time; but what he could do was to earn living enough for two and free me from all economic burden, and thus I could reform for two. That was our bargain and we happily understood each other." This was soon demonstrated, for within a few weeks after their wedding she ventured off to South Dakota to supervise NAWSA's first state suffrage referendum.

Although Susan Anthony still preferred the strategy of securing an amendment to the Constitution, that goal was more distant than ever. It had been more than a decade since a suffrage amendment was introduced into one of the houses of Congress, and securing the necessary two-thirds vote seemed all but impossible. Anthony thus acquiesced in the strategy of appealing to the states; it was state legislatures, after all, that determined who could vote. Unfortunately, the prospects for that strategy were almost equally dim. The Utah Territory had joined Wyoming in giving women the vote, but Congress had taken away that right in 1886 in an attempt to curb the political power of the polygamous Mormons. (They feared that a man with nine wives would have, in effect, ten votes.) No other state had acted.

South Dakota had scheduled a referendum on women's suffrage for the fall election of 1890. To Catt and other suffrage leaders it seemed a propitious opportunity. The rhetoric of Populism was thundering across the plains; the Farmers Alliance was strong in the Dakotas and favored giving the vote to women. NAWSA's strategy was to blanket the state with speakers. Catt was among a dozen women who traveled the state's rutted roads by wagon, through farmland parched by a late-summer drought, speaking night after night in dust-blown villages. While the Alliance men found the suffragists food and lodging, neither of the main political parties offered any help. Susan Anthony had raised $8,000 for the effort; liquor interests countered with a war chest of $500,000. Not surprisingly, the suffrage item went down to defeat in the referendum, although, ironically, the same referendum extended the vote to male Indians. Catt's experience in California had turned her against the Chinese and other aliens, who showed no interest in women's rights; a tour through a dismally poor Sioux reservation in South Dakota extended her prejudices to Indians. After the South Dakota vote was tallied, she grumbled, "Only idiots, insane persons, traitors, Chinese, and women are now disfranchised."

In 1892 George Catt won a contract to dredge Boston Harbor, and his invention of a more efficient dredging device led to other contracts on the East Coast. The Catts moved to New York and purchased a house in Bensonhurst, then a fashionable section of Brooklyn.

In the NAWSA convention of that year President Anthony created a special committee to recruit and educate suffragists who would operate through a network of organizer-lecturers. Appointed chair of the committee, Catt became responsible for hiring speakers, planning their trips, and fostering the formation of local clubs.

The next target was Colorado where a determined band of women, working on a budget of $25, had persuaded a friendly politician to quietly introduce a suffrage referendum bill into the state legislature. The women had taken turns monitoring its silent passage through legislative committees, and the governor signed it into law. The women had come to Anthony for help with the referendum. After her South Dakota experience, Catt was reluctant to visit another sparsely populated frontier. But then she learned that Colorado used the Australian ballot (preprinted and secret), which ensured a relatively honest election. A poll of the state's newspapers indicated that three-fourths were willing to publish the suffragists' materials. Catt arrived in Denver in September 1893, and over the next two months she traveled through the high plains and mountains, speaking two or three times a day and organizing fifty local clubs. On November 7 the voters approved the suffrage law. It was the first time that women had won the vote through their own campaigning.

Catt put a similar effort into a referendum in Kansas the following year, and when it failed to pass, she decided it was time to modernize the staid suffrage movement. Anthony, too, realized the need for youthful energy in the organization and had spotted Catt's leadership potential. Given a choice spot on the 1895 convention program, Catt blasted the suffrage movement for its timidity, lax leadership, and overall lack of success. She put before the convention a three-pronged table of organization: a special committee to raise money for state campaigns; a new standing committee to coordinate national, state, and local suffrage work; and a cadre of specially trained organizers to lead state campaigns. The convention endorsed the idea, and Anthony put Catt in charge of the new Organization Committee. Within four years Catt could report a branch in every state, hundreds of local clubs, and dozens of paid organizers. Suffrage referenda in Idaho and Utah were successful, raising to four the number of states allowing women to vote. In the NAWSA convention of 1900 Anthony announced her retirement and lobbied delegates to make Catt her successor. After the votes were tallied, Anthony introduced the new president and hailed her as "my ideal leader."

Progress and Disillusionment

In 1900, the year that Carrie Catt was elevated to the presidency of the suffrage association, urban Americans generally were seeking to order their lives through community clubs, professional societies, and social improvement associations. The nation had built factories and cities and tied them together with a network of railroads, but in the advance of modernity something had been lost—the quiet rhythm of rural life and the comforting ethos of the village community. Feeling that a decent world, where traditional values mattered, was being lost, Americans sought new forms of association that would preserve their values and promote their interests. The Farmers Alliances provided rural people with both social interaction and political cohesion. Women, confined to the home by cultural norms and deprived of political action, formed voluntary organizations that provided outlets for their energies and vehicles for social improvement. The General Federation of Women's Clubs, formed in 1890, numbered more than a million members by 1914.

Professional organizations experienced a similar surge. The American Medical Association, formed by a handful of physicians in the 1840s, reorganized itself into a federation of locals in 1901, and within a decade its membership numbered more than seventy thousand. Lawyers formed the American Bar Association in 1878, and during the 1880s scholarly disciplines asserted their individuality with the formation of the American Historical Association, the American Economic Association, and the American Political Science Association. As Louis Brandeis discovered in Boston, organizations of civic-minded individuals were the key to Progressive reform. As president of NAWSA in 1900, Carrie Chapman Catt was on the crest of this wave.

Unfortunately, the organization she headed was in near atrophy in 1900. The historic convention of that year was held in a church basement, and its delegates ranged from the middle-aged to the very elderly. All middle class, all moderately wealthy, all white. Although the convention elected Catt president with near unanimity, it retained in office Anthony's vice president and close friend, Anna Howard Shaw. It also rejected Catt's choice for the all-important Organization Committee, Mary G. Hay. Hay was a gifted organizer and Catt's best friend, but her quick intelligence too often resulted in an abrasive impatience. As a result, Catt functioned under the stern, though usually supportive, eye of Susan Anthony.

Catt nevertheless diligently went to work reviving the organization. She increased membership and convention attendance and harvested enough donations to place NAWSA on a sound financial footing. She helped to found an International Women's Suffrage Association in 1902 and served as its first president. But she made no progress with the state legislatures, even though she was almost constantly on the road giving talks and forming local clusters. Despite the rising tide of reform in the cities and states, often prompted by women's consumer leagues, no state would grant suffrage to women until 1910. In 1904 Catt abruptly resigned, citing exhaustion and ill health. Adding to her personal problems was the declining health of her husband, who died after a series of heart attacks in 1905, and her mother, who died in 1907.

Catt spent much of the next five years abroad, leading the international suffrage movement with some success. Finland, in 1906, was the first country in the world to grant women the vote, followed soon after by Norway, Iceland, and Australia. In 1911–1912 she capped her international efforts with a trip around the world—from Europe to South Africa, India, and China. She arrived in China in August 1912, a little more than a year after a revolution led by the reformer Sun Yat Sen overthrew the emperor and established a republic. Chinese women, among the world's worst oppressed, had formed societies to win legal and property rights and to seek education and job opportunities. Catt met several able and articulate women in Peking and participated in their meetings. The brief feminist revival in China was quickly crushed, but the experience was a revelation to the xenophobic Catt. She realized, she later wrote, that America did not have "a monopoly on all that stands for progress," and that women around the world, regardless of race and religion, had the same aspirations as American women.

The death of Susan Anthony in 1906 memorialized the passing of the old guard, and NAWSA, infused with youth and energy, grew in numbers and technique while Catt was busy bridging the Atlantic. From 11,000 members at the time of Catt's resignation NAWSA grew to 117,000 by 1910. In 1908 some NAWSA speakers borrowed from the radical British suffragists the tactic of speaking from soapboxes on street corners. Although they had to compete with missionaries, Socialists, and political ward heelers, the women thought it "the ideal auditorium for those who are trying to push an unpopular cause, who have in their pack no drawing cards, and lack money to 'go hire a hall.'" While in New York Catt was invited to address an open-air street meeting, but she declined. She was unable to overcome the cultural bias against women in undignified public stations. The soapbox oratory nevertheless continued. "It is no longer considered bad form to hold street meetings," intoned the *New York Times* toward the end of 1908. "On the contrary it is considered bad form not to."

In that same year NAWSA initiated another tactic that was to become one of the standbys of the suffrage movement—a giant petition campaign. This tactic Carrie Catt firmly approved, though she had no illusions that petitions would sway either Congress or a state legislature. The "chief benefits of petitions," she wrote, are "the education which their circulation carries into homes, clubs, churches, and all varieties of community gatherings." In 1910 a petition campaign that aimed for the signatures of a million women was promoted "chiefly for its agitational value."

In 1910, Western suffragists overcame the problem of vast distances by using the automobile in their campaigns. The Northern California College Equal Suffrage League owned a seven-passenger Packard, which it named the "Blue Liner" because of its colorful decorations. The young women crisscrossed the state, staging songs and speeches from the back seat of the open-air vehicle. The range of movement afforded by the automobile was widely credited with suffrage victories in Washington in 1910 and California in 1911—victories that ended the legislative "doldrums" that had existed since 1896.

In the East the automobile made street parades safer for women. New York City militants had been experimenting with parades since 1908, but they sometimes met harassment from male bystanders. In 1910 they set up a parade of ninety automobiles to proceed down Fifth Avenue in protest of the legislature's failure to approve a suffrage referendum. Emboldened by the vehicular shield, several thousand women marched behind the automobiles. NAWSA president Anna Howard Shaw had some concern about public demonstrations, but she overcame her misgivings and rode in one of the cars.

Carrie Catt was initially opposed to parades of any sort, whether they involved automobiles or not. "We do not have to win sympathy by parading ourselves like the street cleaning department," she said. She was converted, however, while visiting London in 1910 when she witnessed a parade that demonstrated a solidarity that cut across class lines. University women in academic gowns marched arm in arm with factory operatives in their overalls. The effect was to disprove one of the insults that NAWSA had battled from the outset—that suffrage was a sport for wealthy whites. She returned to New York, so she claimed, "burning with desire" to replicate the tactic in America.

The British suffragist movement was far more militant in tactics than its American counterpart. British visitors, in fact, pioneered both the soapbox oratory and the street parade in America. Disappointed at the slow progress of the state referendum strategy and bewildered by the growing intransigence among the male population, younger suffragists concluded that the complaisance of the male-dominated establishment needed to be shaken by more aggressive tactics. Feminist militancy, unfortunately, risked a male rejoinder, and together they posed violence. That likelihood split the women's suffrage organization once again and ultimately brought Carrie Chapman Catt back to the forefront of the movement.

Alice Paul's Challenge

Alice Paul, like Susan B. Anthony, was of Quaker lineage, and she grew up in a culture that assumed women, with the same heavenly destiny as men, were the equal of men. She was a graduate of Swarthmore, a college that her grandfather had helped to found. In 1905 she received a master's degree in sociology from the University of Pennsylvania, and she was working on her Ph.D. (a degree she received in 1912) when she came to the attention of the Women's Suffrage Association. In doing research for her doctoral degree Paul traveled to London where she came into contact with the British suffrage movement. Despite her Quaker pacifism, she enthusiastically participated in the militants' marches and open-air meetings, suffering a short stay in prison for her efforts.

Returning to the United States, Paul asked to address the American Suffrage Association at its annual meeting in May 1910. Challenging NAWSA's cautious methods, Paul described the exhilaration that British women felt in seizing their rights after years of patient petitioning. "The cringe was gone from their souls," she said. "Woman the supplicant had become the rebel."

NAWSA ignored her for the moment because it was developing a new and more forceful ideology of its own. In the 1890s women had demanded the vote on the basis of natural rights. They contended that because the Declaration of Independence had affirmed that all men (i.e., persons) are created equal, women were entitled to equality of suffrage. Opponents had relied on the age-old assumption of inequality, citing the Bible as authority for the notion that women are inherently frail, morally as well as physically. By 1910 the economic and professional advancement of women had rendered the equality debate moot. As early as 1900 more than five million women were working outside the home; they constituted about one-fifth of the nation's work force. At that date 40 percent of Stanford students and 52 percent of students at the University of Chicago were women. And women attending the University of Chicago made up 56 percent of Phi Beta Kappa initiates. By 1910 many of these women had entered the legal and medical professions and demonstrated that they could compete equally with men.

With equality of skill no longer at issue, suffragists began emphasizing the value of the ballot—it would enlarge women's interests and intellect by giving them part of the responsibility of running the government. The right to vote would also make women better mothers because they would have firsthand experience in the meaning of citizenship and thus be better able to raise their children to be public-spirited constituents of the republic. In an open bid for Progressive support, suffragists also pointed out that women's organizations, such as Florence Kelley's National Consumer's League, had been in the forefront of improvements in urban facilities, from sewers to schools, and in the enactment of pure food and drug legislation.

This new set of proofs at first seemed to work. In 1912 three more Western states—Oregon, Kansas, and Arizona—extended the vote to women. The following year Illinois yielded—the first state east of the Mississippi to do so. Illinois allowed women to vote only in presidential elections, but suffragists took comfort in the thought that women's participation in the presidential electoral vote might give them some leverage toward federal action.

In 1913 NAWSA asked Alice Paul and her friend Lucy Burns, a Brooklyn-born veteran of the London wars and British prisons, to form the Congressional Committee to revitalize the drive for an amendment to the federal Constitution. NAWSA president and Anthony-disciple Anna Howard Shaw agreed to the new venture, but she informed the young women that they had to raise their own funds. Paul and Burns promptly turned to friends in New York City and got immediate help from Crystal Eastman, a graduate of New York University Law School and state investigator of industrial accidents, and Mary Beard, professional historian and wife of Columbia University professor Charles A. Beard.

Paul and Burns's first project was to organize a gigantic suffrage parade in Washington, D.C., the day before Woodrow Wilson's inauguration on March 4, 1913. The idea was to demonstrate that women's suffrage was an issue of national importance that could no longer be ignored by Congress. Thousands of women answered the call, including members of the Federation of Women's Clubs (that, at last, endorsed suffrage in that year), Red Cross volunteers, representatives from the WCTU (whose membership still outnumbered NAWSA), and Kelley's Consumer's League. Paul organized them into seven divisions, with twenty-six floats and ten bands. Carrie Catt led the first division, which was called the Worldwide Movement for Woman Suffrage. Bringing up the rear was a twenty-five-member contingent from the National Association for Colored Women, a breakthrough of sorts because NAWSA had evaded the issue of suffrage for African-American women in its effort to win support among Southern legislators.

Even though the women had a permit to march from the Capitol to the White House, the police were openly hostile. Male spectators, taking a cue from the attitude of the police, began harassing the marchers, shoving the women, stealing their banners, and shouting obscenities. Secretary of War Henry Stimson[1], whose sister-in-law was a member of the parade committee, called in a troop of cavalry to clear a path for the marchers.

In a protest meeting immediately following the parade, Catt and others urged Congress to investigate, claiming that many of the spectators along the line were drunk enough to be locked up and that the police had clearly failed in their duty. After a four-day Senate hearing, the Washington chief of police was fired. Although that satisfied no one, NAWSA got an enormous amount of sympathetic publicity. The *New York Times*, although opposed to women suffrage, denounced the "abominable ill-treatment" meted out to women who were only exercising a right (i.e., to

1. Henry L. Stimson, who lived until 1950, served as Herbert Hoover's secretary of state, and though a Republican, he served as Franklin Roosevelt's secretary of war through World War II, having a major say in the development of the atomic bomb.

parade) "the legality and legitimacy of which [is] beyond question." A further result of the Washington episode was that middle-class women around the country were stirred into action. Too shy to parade, too homebound to become NAWSA activists, they contributed what they could—money, lots of it. By 1916 NAWSA's annual budget stood at $100,000, and it was able to maintain professional lobbyists to work for the constitutional amendment.

To Alice Paul the lesson of the near-riot in Washington was that the perception of suffragists as martyrs boosted the cause. She was determined more than ever to "keep the people watching the suffragists." In April 1913 she expanded the Congressional Committee into the Congressional Union, which, while technically a subdivision of NAWSA, operated quite independently. Anna Howard Shaw's hapless decision to force Paul to raise her own financing deprived NAWSA of any practical oversight of Paul's activities.

In the off-year congressional election of 1914 the Congressional Union targeted Democrats in the Western states where women had the vote, demanding that candidates publicly endorse women's suffrage or be voted out of office. The Democratic Party organization resisted, telling the Eastern organizers to go home. But Western women listened. Of the forty-three Democrats up for election in those states, only twenty won. Republicans, of course, were delighted, but for the first time, women's suffrage had become a central issue in a national election. In January 1915 Congressional Union delegations began demanding interviews with President Wilson, and when he claimed to be too busy to see them, they camped in his waiting room for days at a time. In March the Congressional Union severed itself from NAWSA altogether and became an independent association.

Anna Howard Shaw, whose own feckless leadership of NAWSA had set the stage for the schism, was the leading critic of Alice Paul and her militant tactics. Shaw denounced the women who went over to Paul as "blank fools" and claimed that the Congressional Union was damaging the movement by its divisiveness and militance. Carry Catt was less critical. She deplored the split in the organization, but she could see potential in Paul's emphasis on a constitutional amendment. Through the years of Paul's rise to prominence, 1913–1915, Catt was preoccupied in winning New York to the cause of women's suffrage, hoping that a victory there would trigger a chain reaction among Eastern states. The stunning failure of that campaign converted Catt to the strategy of a federal amendment.

New York Debacle

Catt had begun organizing suffrage groups in both New York City and New York state as early as 1909. Her approach was a refinement of the collaborative techniques she had devised in the 1890s, but progress was slow due to her travels abroad. In 1913 she set up an Empire State Campaign Committee, which she herself chaired, to coordinate the efforts of the local groups. Not satisfied with a simple coordinating committee, she undertook to model her organization "exactly after the dominant political parties in order to measure swords with them." She built it precinct-by-precinct throughout the state so that every house in every neighborhood could be canvassed by her volunteers. To broaden her base of support, she sent multilingual recruiters into the immigrant ghettoes of New York City to arrange meetings and hand out literature. She established "suffrage schools" to train recruiters in the arts of organizing locals, addressing legislators, and maintaining good relations with the press.

New York, along with Pennsylvania, New Jersey, and Massachusetts, had scheduled a suffrage referendum for 1915. Although the referendum was a central feature of the Progressives drive to "cure the ills of democracy with more democracy," cynical legislators had discovered that it was also a convenient way of dodging responsibility for a controversial matter because it placed the onus—for passage or nonpassage—on the voters. Legislators could thus claim credit in areas where the law was popular and disclaim responsibility where it was not. Unfortunately, promoters of the referendum like Bob La Follette had never considered the role of money in an appeal to the people. Clever advertisements in mass circulation journals could reach more voters with superficial proofs than could an army of house-to-house volunteers.

The liquor industry, witnessing the ties between the WCTU and NAWSA and the number of states that had voted themselves "dry" after giving women the vote, decided to shore up the opposition in New York. The industry poured millions into the campaign, dwarfing the $95,000 that Catt had raised dime by dime. Catt countered by arranging spectacular events. Ten days before the November 2 election she organized a gigantic parade in New York City. An Irish visitor described the scene: "About 30,000 marched up Fifth Avenue in the teeth of a bitter wind, which swept down their banners remorselessly. It took them over three hours to pass any point. . . . Some 5,000 men were also in the march. It was a great demonstration."

Although the parade drew more than a million spectators, Catt, in retrospect, wondered whether such marches were truly productive, especially after discovering that, after the march, the Union League Club, a Republican organization dating from the Civil War, garnered more donations from its members than her entire war chest. The referendum was defeated by a margin of sixty to forty, and the votes in the other Eastern states suffered the same fate.

The night before the election Anna Shaw reminded Catt that opponents were predicting that defeat would set the suffrage movement back by ten years. Shaw then asked, "How long will it delay your fight, Carrie?" The response was, "Only until we can get a little sleep." Two days after the election Catt organized a new campaign under the slogan "Victory in 1917." And she was developing a new strategy. Although the referenda in the four Eastern states had lost, a million and a quarter votes had been cast in favor of women's suffrage. It was time, Catt decided, to pressure Congress for an amendment to the Constitution. In December 1915 she accepted the presidency of the National Woman's Suffrage Association.

The "Winning Plan"

Catt truly did not want the presidency of NAWSA. But Anna Howard Shaw, who had served since 1904, announced her retirement, and no one but Catt had the stature to be a satisfactory replacement. "I am an unwilling victim," she told the convention. Drawing herself up, she persuaded the convention to adopt her new strategy of pushing for a constitutional amendment. The language was framed with classic simplicity: "The right of citizens of the United States to vote shall not be denied or abridged by the United States or by any state on account of sex." Like the Fifteenth Amendment, which purported to give male African-Americans the vote, it was phrased in the negative as a restriction on the states because the states, since the beginning of the republic, set the standards (wealth, race, age, sex) for those qualified to vote.

Catt's first task was to heal the rift in the suffrage movement. Alice Paul and Lucy Burns agreed on the amendment stratagem, but citing their success in embarrassing the Western Democrats in 1914, they insisted on the tactic of holding the party in power responsible for passing the amendment. They wanted commitments from Democratic candidates on the threat of blocking their election. Catt agreed with the strategy of commitment, but she disagreed with the whimsical notion that victory can be achieved by bringing about the defeat of a potential friend. She met with Alice Paul in an effort to build a cooperative strategy for putting pressure on Congress, but they were unable to reconcile their differences in tactics.

With a presidential election looming in the fall, both flanks of the suffrage movement descended on the party conventions that met in June 1916. Catt's goal was the insertion of a suffrage plank in the platforms of both parties. The Republicans, having healed their rift and absorbed the remnants of Theodore Roosevelt's Bull Moose Party, were more amenable to women's suffrage than they had been. Roosevelt's Progressive Party had boldly approved a suffrage amendment in 1912. A thunderstorm was raging outside the convention hall on the day that the platform committee took up the issue of the suffrage plank. An opponent of suffrage was assuring the committee that women did not want the vote when the doors burst open and hundreds of dripping and bedraggled women, bedecked in yellow ribbons (the color symbol of the movement), poured into the hall. The committee approved a suffrage plank but diluted it by leaving the decision up to the states.

At the Democratic convention in St. Louis a week later, six thousand suffragists, dressed alike in white with yellow sashes and yellow parasols, lined both sides of the street between the convention hall and the hotel. Embarrassed but unintimidated, the Democratic delegates matched the Republicans by approving a plank in favor of women suffrage by state action. Carrie Catt reacted with a mixture of anger and apprehension. She feared that "Congress would hide behind those state rights planks and shut us out from Congress forever." Adding to her concern was division within the ranks of NAWSA, as some women still preferred the state-by-state method. This was especially true of women from the Democratic states of the South and West, who felt that the antics of Alice Paul's Congressional Union had rendered congressional action on a constitutional amendment hopeless.

While the Democratic Convention was still in session, the executive board of NAWSA met and called for an emergency convention to meet in Atlantic City in September. Catt's purpose was twofold—to unite the suffrage association on a single strategy and to set forth a "Winning Plan" for carrying it out. Catt opened the convention with a lengthy address in which she rehearsed the sad history of the organization's attempt to extract the right to vote from state legislatures. She insisted that the right to vote could come only by constitutional amendment, and that could be brought about only by utmost cooperation and unceasing effort.

In a later address she laid out the dual strategy—aim for a federal amendment but build support for it by hard work at the state level. She assigned each state organization a particular task. In those states where women had the vote, the legislatures should pass resolutions pressuring Congress to act. In states like New York where a referendum was scheduled, NAWSA would work for success at that level. In reluctant states, women should press for whatever they could get, at a minimum the vote in presidential elections. In the South, where NAWSA was weakest, its locals should seek the vote in party primaries. This was what Catt called her "Winning Plan."

Woodrow Wilson made an appearance on the last evening of the convention. It was the first time a president had ever addressed a suffrage convention, though his impact was limited because he was frustratingly enigmatic. Complimentary and optimistic, Wilson gave the delegates the standard politician's advice that their goals could be achieved only through unity and hard work. His concluding words were a masterpiece of obfuscation:

> It is all very well to run ahead and beckon, but after all, you have got to wait for them to follow. I have not come to ask you to be

> patient, because you have been, but I have come to congratulate you that there was a force behind you that will, beyond any peradventure, be triumphant and for which you can afford a little while to wait.

Asked by Catt to respond, Anna Shaw challenged the president, saying, “We have waited long enough for the vote, we want it now, and (facing the president) we want it to come in your administration.” Wilson smiled enigmatically and bowed, while the convention cheered. He would not openly endorse women’s suffrage for almost another year.

By the early weeks of 1917 Catt faced a new problem: the steady drift of the United States into the vortex of the European war. Catt, as with many suffragists, was a pacifist at heart; she hated war. All wars. At the same time, the drum of patriotic rhetoric that accompanied the preparedness campaign of 1916 and the outburst of public belligerence that followed Germany’s resumption of submarine warfare in February 1917 convinced her that public opposition to the war would doom the suffrage movement. After the Wilson administration severed diplomatic relations with Germany on February 3, 1917, Catt summoned a special convention of NAWSA to meet in Washington on February 23. By a vote of sixty-three to thirteen the delegates approved a letter to President Wilson pledging their support for the war and offering their services to the government if needed.

The women were not sure what they could do for the government, and the Wilson administration was even less sure what it could do with them. After the United States declared war in April 1917, Catt wrote the president offering NAWSA’s services. Wilson passed it on to Secretary of War Newton D. Baker, who came up with the classic bureaucratic solution—he created a Women’s Committee of the Council of National Defense. The committee was given a number of busywork assignments, all of which Catt regarded as a waste of time. “The thing I remember about the Great War more distinctly than anything else,” she later wrote to Wilson’s Secretary of the Navy Josephus Daniels, “was the day when some of us, representing the new Woman’s Council of National Defense, went to see you by appointment in order to learn what was expected of us. We asked what we were to do, and your answer was something like this: ‘Take the women off our backs. Here is about a bushel basket full of letters from women asking what they can do. Take it away and tell those women to keep quiet till we get the war going.’ As I look back on the work of the Woman’s Committee, entertaining the women was the main object we performed!” Daniels never denied it.

The gesture of cooperation nevertheless gained Catt’s branch of the suffrage movement some favorable publicity. This stood in stark contrast to the opprobrium heaped upon Alice Paul and her branch, now reincarnated as the National Women’s Party. Although Paul did not publicly oppose the war, she saw no reason to let up the pressure on the president. In January 1917 the Women's Party began picketing the gates of the White House carrying banners demanding the president's support for suffrage. Wilson at first greeted them with bemusement, nodding and tipping his hat as he passed through the gates. However, by early summer the Washington police began arresting the pickets on charges of "obstructing traffic." Given a choice of fines or a three-day jail sentence, the women chose jail and made national headlines.

Catt thought the tactics of Alice Paul's group were "unwise and unprofitable to the cause," and it is a matter of dispute to this day whether the picketing tactics helped or delayed the suffrage amendment. Catt was particularly apprehensive about the attention given Paul's tiny band of extremists. Paul's militants, which never numbered more than fifty thousand, were threatening to undo the work of NAWSA's two million. On the other hand, Paul's radicalism helped make NAWSA respectable. As important, perhaps, as the activities of either suffrage group was the unheralded contribution of the women who went to work on farms and factories during the war, relieving men for military duty. The ability of women to do "equal work" removed for many any last doubt that they were entitled to political equality.

Despite the distractions of the war effort, Catt's attention that year was centered on New York, where the referendum scheduled for the fall election was thought to be critical. If New York yielded, Catt reasoned, Congress would have to act on the suffrage amendment. She had begun the organizational effort shortly after the defeat of 1915. The state organization, which Catt also headed, analyzed the 1915 vote and decided that the fate of any future referendum depended on New York City. The city's immigrant population was resistant to the liquor lobby, and its huge underclass of female factory operatives was an untapped resource. Distasteful as it was to many middle-class suffragists, they began working the street corners of working-class neighborhoods and distributing literature at labor union meetings. Catt told a legislative committee that her volunteers in the New York tenement districts had been forced to learn scraps of twenty-four languages.

No significant number of working-class women ever became suffrage organizers or volunteers; they simply lacked the time. But they did recognize the importance of having the vote. They needed the vote for the same reason they needed their labor unions, to protect themselves against the dominance of wealth and power. And, for a change, Carrie Catt had the financial resources to educate and mobilize the poor. In 1914 Mrs. Frank Leslie, heiress to a fortune derived from a popular nineteenth century magazine, died and left her entire fortune of $2 million to Carrie Catt, to be used in the cause of women's suffrage. Family heirs had fought the bequest, and lawyers' fees had gobbled up all but $900,000 by the time Catt's right to the legacy was established in 1917.

She used the money to set up the Leslie Bureau of Suffrage Education, which became a crucially important press and publicity agent for NAWSA. The Leslie Bureau's immediate objective was educating the working-class women of New York City.

By 1917 the liquor lobby in New York was less powerful than it had been. State after state was voting itself dry, and a constitutional amendment authorizing the prohibition of the manufacture and sale of alcoholic beverages (the eighteenth) was working its way through Congress. Although the "dries" in New York were potential allies, Catt, who personally had no objections to liquor, carefully kept the two movements separate. She did not want to antagonize the liquor interests, lest they pour more money into the anti-suffrage campaign, and she certainly did not want to offend any male voter who might favor both women's suffrage and drinking.

In late October, as the referendum vote neared, Catt staged the largest parade yet in New York City. Twenty thousand women marched up Fifth Avenue from Washington Square to Sixty-second Street. Factory operatives walked side by side with nurses, lawyers, teachers, actors, and journalists. It was a striking demonstration of gender solidarity, but as so often happened in New York politics, it was the city machine that clinched the victory. A few days before the November 6 election the bosses of Tammany Hall, several of whose wives were suffrage neighborhood captains, put out the word that the election was to be fair. For a change, there would be no cemeteries voting, no pre-marked ballots. A little before midnight on November 6 the *New York Times* flashed a signal that suffrage had won. Catt was jubilant. "The victory is not New York's alone," she shouted over the laughter and cheers at suffrage headquarters. "It is the nation's. The 65th Congress will now pass the federal amendment!"

The Nineteenth Amendment

Earlier in 1917, Ohio, Indiana, Rhode Island, Nebraska, Michigan, and Arkansas had granted the vote to women in whole or in part, and Congress could see the script on the wall. In September the House of Representatives created a Woman Suffrage Committee to consider the constitutional amendment. Suffrage bills had previously been buried in the Neanderthaloid Judicial Committee. The new committee reported favorably, and a vote was scheduled for January 10, 1918. That "wonderful day," as Catt referred to it, was marked by long and tedious speeches while the suspense built. Because a two-thirds approval was needed for a constitutional amendment, the vote was certain to be close. At the last minute one congressman with a broken shoulder straggled in, having delayed getting it set lest the anesthetic put him down, three more left sickbeds, and one was carried in on a stretcher to cast his vote. All were needed, for the amendment carried with only one vote to spare, 274 to 136.

The next day Catt wrote to her state chairs, asking them to bring pressure on their U.S. Senators. The Senate, however, could not be hurried. It scheduled a vote for May 10 and then called it off at the last minute. Catt was thoroughly exasperated. She had made thirty trips to Washington in the last six months. In June she called on President Wilson for support, and the president obliged with a public letter endorsing the suffrage amendment. Catt then persuaded him to amend his statement by urging the Senate to vote in the present session. The Senate took offense at the presidential interference and postponed its vote until the autumn. Catt was in the gallery on October 1 when the Senate, after weeks of debate and a personal appearance by the president, brought the amendment to a vote. The balloting was sixty-two to thirty-four, two votes short of the two-thirds majority. Catt returned to New York in disgust and resolved never to attend another Senate session.

In the off-year election of 1918 the Republicans returned to power in both houses of Congress (inaugurating a period of Republican dominance that would last until 1932), and the prospects for the suffrage amendment were dimmer than ever. There was still a chance for the lame-duck session of the old Congress, but the Senate in February 1919 fell short of approving the amendment by one vote. President Wilson called the new Congress into session as soon as it was sworn in on March 4, ostensibly to deal with military affairs, but suffrage was high on the agenda. By this time seven million women had secured the vote through state action, and congressmen, regardless of party, could no longer resist the tide. The House repassed the Nineteenth Amendment in May, and the Senate followed suit in June.

Catt, staying at home, received the news by phone, and she immediately wired her state chairs to mobilize for ratification. There was some instant success because several state legislatures happened to be in session that spring. Illinois and Wisconsin, each eager to be the first, ratified within a few days after learning of the Senate vote. Illinois won the race by forty-five minutes, but Wisconsin reached Washington first by putting a special messenger on the train. Michigan ratified that same day, and three more states followed within a week. By the end of September seventeen of the necessary thirty-six states had ratified. Then things bogged down. Several states refused to call their legislatures into special session; three Southern states rejected the amendment.

In October Catt organized a "Wake Up America" tour of NAWSA executives. An old-fashioned railroad electioneering tour, the women organized meetings in state capitals and met with governors and legislatures. During the winter and spring of 1920 state after state fell in line until, at last, ratification rested on one Southern state, Tennessee. Its legislature had scheduled a vote for August 1920, and Catt spent the summer on a speaking tour of the state. The state senate gave its approval on August 10, and the house voted a week later. With a simple majority needed, the House appeared to tie, at forty-eight to forty-eight. But at the last moment a twenty-four-year-old first-term legislator from a rock-ribbed county in the heart of the mountains reversed his vote on the pleas of his mother, and the Nineteenth Amendment was part of the Constitution.

Even before ratification was complete Catt had foreseen the need to educate women politically so they could vote intelligently. Although she no longer felt that giving the vote to women would necessarily advance social reform—such arguments had done more harm than good in the past—she did believe that the political liberation of women would lead to more honest, responsive government if women were politically informed. Anticipating ratification of the amendment, the executive board of NAWSA called for a victory convention to meet in Chicago in February 1920. That meeting formally dissolved NAWSA and created in its place the League of Women Voters. In proposing the plan for the league to the seven hundred women in attendance, Catt emphasized that the purpose of the league was not to seek power for itself but to promote useful legislation. The league's own constitution simply stated that its object was "to foster education in citizenship and to support improved legislation."

Catt by 1920 was already shifting her interests to the cause of world peace and she had no intention of running the new organization itself. Although Catt would have preferred to have new faces in charge of the league, she soon realized that practical experience was the primary qualification. Consequently she persuaded the delegates to elect as president Maud Wood Park, who had been in charge of congressional lobbying for NAWSA. Catt agreed to be honorary chair of the league, a post she held until her death.

Although Carrie Chapman Catt is revered today as the founder of the League of Women Voters, any active role in the league ended with its founding. She had a new cause at hand, world peace, and a new agency, the League of Nations. Woodrow Wilson had persuaded the European powers to insert the charter for a League of Nations into the Versailles Treaty that ended the war. When the issue reached the Senate, American attitudes toward a world organization dominated the debate over the treaty. Amidst a growing public distaste for America's role as world power, the Senate refused to ratify the treaty. Although the Democratic presidential ticket of James M. Cox and Franklin Roosevelt stumped the country in the fall of 1920 on behalf of the league, the election of Republican Warren G. Harding precluded any chance of American entry into the League of Nations.

Two weeks after the election, still fuming over the defeat, Catt attended a dinner of the League of Women Voters. Asked to address the dinner guests, she recklessly denounced the partisanship and cowardice of the Republicans who had killed the League of Nations. Her listeners were shocked, for the League of Women Voters, though it favored such reforms as the elimination of child labor, was determinedly nonpartisan. "She blew the cover off the soup pot and spilled the whole contents," groaned a friend. While one Republican woman resigned from the league's executive committee and others threatened to, Catt rather shamefacedly boarded a ship for Europe to attend a peace get-together in London. She followed the league's fortunes with interest thereafter, occasionally addressed it and contributed money, but for the rest of her life her attention and skills were devoted to the cause of world peace.

The Price of Peace

For the next few years Catt resumed the peripatetic life she had led before becoming president of NAWSA. She mixed peace meetings with conferences of the International Woman's Suffrage Association in Geneva in 1920, Luxembourg the following year, and Rome in 1923. In January 1925 she helped organize a conference in Washington, D.C., on the Cause and Cure of War. The 450 delegates to the conference represented nine worldwide sponsoring organizations with five million members. Catt opened the meeting with the statement: "The Conference opens with the conviction, firmly fixed, that war is a relic of barbarism whose abolition should have been achieved years ago." In the course of the convention Eleanor Roosevelt, a delegate from the General Federation of Women's Clubs, spoke twice on behalf of the establishment of a world court that could settle international disputes and treat war as a form of murder. The conference closed by forming a National Committee on the Cause and Cure of War that continued to function until the United States entered World War II.

The cultural atmosphere of the mid-1920s was not a friendly one for peace crusaders. The ultra-patriotism created by government propaganda during the war had resurrected Americans' latent biases against foreigners and alien ideologies. The Bolshevik coup in Russia in November 1917 sent a shock wave through American society. Abetted by opportunistic politicians, a Red Scare seized the public in 1919–1920, and hundreds of aliens were deported, allegedly for the crime of being Socialist/Communists (the distinction between the two was still rather fuzzy). By the mid-1920s the American Legion (made up of war veterans) and the Daughters of the American Revolution (DAR) were on the hunt for subversives who would undermine the American way and persons who advocated social welfare reforms or world peace filled the bill. Giants of the Progressive movement like Jane Addams and Florence Kelley were branded as dangerous radicals.

Intent on the world peace movement and anxious to avoid exposing herself to the witch-hunters, Catt refused to support the lingering issues of social reform, such as equal employment opportunities for women, abolition of child labor, and women's efforts at birth control. In 1928 Catt, who had lived in various places in New York, built her final residence in New Rochelle and spent increasing amounts of time in her yard and garden.

The depression, which began with the stock market crash the following year, silenced for the moment the superpatriots of the DAR, but, ironically, it did not improve the climate for world peace. At a peace conference in Geneva in 1932 several delegates reported that unemployed workers thought they could benefit from "a good rousing war." Catt resigned as chair of the Committee on the Cause and Cure of War at that conference. Her final address was a homily on survival: "A reformer always knows that he is going to win, but he never does know whether it is in his day or that of somebody else. He is completely satisfied that victory will one day crown his labors."

The peace movement began to disintegrate in the late 1930s, with the rising specter of Nazism in Germany and Japan's attack on China. When the United States entered the war after the attack on Pearl Harbor, Catt supported the president as she had in 1917. In her eighties, she could do little but follow closely the wartime efforts to prevent future conflicts—the signing of the General Agreement on Tariffs and Trade, creation of the World Bank, and formation of the United Nations. As befitted a lifetime of serving humanity, she died peacefully on March 9, 1947.

Suggested Reading

Jacqueline Van Voris's *Carrie Chapman Catt: A Public Life* (1987) is a conventional biography, sensible in its judgments but rather plodding in style. More sprightly is Robert Booth Fowler's *Carrie Catt, Feminist Politician* (1986), but it is organized topically (for example, chapters on organization, leadership, and private life), which may be confusing to some readers. The recent studies of the suffrage movement supply added details or nuances of interpretation to Aileen S. Kraditor's classic, *The Ideas of the Woman Suffrage Movement, 1890–1920* (1965, 1971). Recent studies include Jane Jerome Camhi's *Women Against Women: American Anti-Suffragism, 1880–1920* (1994), Suzanne M. Marilley's *Woman Suffrage and the Origins of Liberal Feminism in the United States, 1820–1920* (1996), Sara Hunter Graham's *Woman Suffrage and the New Democracy* (1996), and Linda J. Lumsden's *Rampant Women: Suffragists and the Right of Assembly* (1997). Alice Paul's militant movement is the subject of Linda G. Ford's *Iron-Jawed Angels: The Suffrage Militancy of the National Woman's Party, 1912–1920* (1991). A superb perspective on the Progressives' reliance on organization is Robert H. Wiebe's *The Search for Order, 1877–1920* (1967).

10

John Muir: Nature's Evangelist

In its report of 1890 the United States Bureau of the Census informed the nation that the frontier had vanished—there was no significant area of the United States that contained fewer than two people per square mile (the bureau's definition of "frontier"). The era of westward expansion, which dominated American thought and culture for nearly three hundred years, had ended. Three years later historian Frederick Jackson Turner read a paper entitled "The Significance of the Frontier in American History" before the American Historical Association meeting at the Columbian Exposition in Chicago, a world's fair that was honoring the glory of a "White City" and the marvels of urban landscape planning. Ignoring the paeans to urbanization that echoed around him, Turner proffered a theory that the wilderness environment and the frontier encounter had shaped the American character, that qualities that made Americans exceptional—self-reliance, individualism, equality, political democracy—were forged in the pioneer experience.

In that same year, 1893, the Boston publishing house of Houghton and Mifflin began republishing the works of Henry David Thoreau, gaining Thoreau more public recognition than he had received in his own lifetime. Like Turner, but from a different perspective, Thoreau called attention to the value of wilderness. He had even argued for its preservation through "national reservations" for the protection of wildlife and human "inspiration." By the 1890s, when Thoreau's works were republished, the nation had begun to experiment with wilderness preserves, but the objectives were hardly what Thoreau envisioned. In creating the nation's first national park, Yellowstone, in 1872, Congress was concerned less with its aesthetic and spiritual qualities than with preventing developers from exploiting its mineral baths and geysers. Similarly, when New York created the Adirondack Forest Reserve in 1885, the purpose was not to preserve wilderness or wildlife but to ensure a steady water supply for the Erie Canal.

The works of Turner and Thoreau together with the novels of Jack London and Ernest Thompson Seton were part of a literary groundswell at the turn of the century that dwelt on nature and "the call of the wild." Joining this groundswell and helping to divert it into an appreciation of wilderness for its own sake was John Muir. In an 1897 essay he wrote: "The forests of America . . . must have been a great delight to God, for they were the best he ever planted. The whole continent was a garden, and from the beginning it seemed to be favored above all the other wild parks and gardens of the globe." The notion of America as an earthly Eden, a paradise regained, was as old as the concept of a "New World," but Muir was using it to counteract the spoliation of the continent that had been going on with increasing destructiveness since the Civil War. Muir added a mystical note to the idea of preservation, a note that resonated with Americans' deep-seated religiosity. "Climb the mountains and get their good tidings," he advised his fellow Americans. "Nature's peace will flow into you as the sunshine into the trees. The winds will blow their freshness into you, and the storms their energy, while cares will drop away like autumn leaves." Both an apostle of nature and a prophet of doom upon its destruction, John Muir is the father of the modern drive for ecological preservation.

From Farm Boy to Naturalist

John Muir was born in the village of Dunbar, Scotland, on April 21, 1838, the third of eight children (and oldest boy) delivered to Daniel and Anne (Gilrye) Muir. Daniel Muir was a fairly prosperous grain merchant and an adherent of a splinter sect of the Presbyterian Church that believed in an austere Calvinist God who graced a fortunate few with salvation and condemned most of humanity to eternal damnation. Daniel Muir's concept of child rearing was to treat his son as a miniature adult and to administer a severe whipping whenever the child's social or ethical behavior fell short. The masters of the school to which John was sent operated on much the same theory. Muir later recalled how well the instructors confirmed the "all-sufficing Scotch discovery that there was a close connection between the skin and the memory, and that irritating the skin excited the memory to any required degree."

When John Muir was eleven, his father joined an American-born Campbellite sect (later Disciples of Christ), which sought to revive the simple ways of the primitive church that was thought to have existed after Christ's ministry. Daniel then took the older children to America, where Campbellites were more numerous, leaving Anne and the younger children to come later when he was settled. Learning that Wisconsin was prime wheat country, the emigrants traversed the Erie Canal and Great Lakes to Milwaukee. Daniel purchased a farm in the Fox River valley, built a house, and sent for the remainder of his family. John Muir's memories of his youth in Wisconsin were as bleak as those of Scotland. The children cleared the land, plowed the fields, weeded, and harvested the crops, as their father kept watch from the window of his house while reading his Bible. "We were all made slaves through the vice of over-industry," Muir recalled bitterly.

John Muir in 1873. (Photograph from the State Historical Society of Wisconsin.)

Although the workday began at 4:00 in the morning, Daniel allowed his oldest son to do what he wished if he arose earlier. Muir discovered that he could get by with only three or four hours of sleep, and he borrowed books from neighbors to read from 1:00 till 4:00 in morning. He also poured through the family Bible, memorizing huge portions of it, for he had discovered that biblical citations were his best weapons in arguments with his father. Somewhere in those early-morning hours he also found time to whittle. Fascinated by mathematics, he worked out problems of algebra and geometry with chips of wood. Mathematics led him to the principle of the pendulum, and he went from there to carving the gears and mechanisms of clocks. At the suggestion of a neighbor, he took his "inventions" (two clocks and a thermometer) to Madison where locally made mechanisms were being put on exhibit at the state fair grounds. The year was 1860, and the fair grounds were soon to be converted into an army training camp. A reporter for the *Wisconsin State Journal* visited the exhibit and wrote: "We will venture to predict that few articles will attract as much attention as these products of Mr. Muir's ingenuity."

Acquaintance with Madison—and no doubt the taste of freedom from farm labor—inspired Muir to wish for a university education. In January 1861, as the age of twenty-three, Muir journeyed to Madison and took a series of odd jobs, hoping to earn enough money to enter the university. When a student told him he could board himself at the university for as little as a dollar a week, he applied for admission. That proved to be easy, for the university, well aware of the deficiencies in the state's public education system, maintained a preparatory division taught by the university faculty. Within a few months he was one of the 180 youths that constituted the university's student body. He was never classified as a regular student, and he realized that, for lack of money, he would not be able to remain in school long enough to graduate. Instead, he picked out those courses that seemed most useful to him, principally science and mathematics, with a smattering of Greek and Latin.

In his two and a half years at the university Muir took enough literature courses to become acquainted with the writings of Emerson and Thoreau, whose works he would pore over in later years. But he concentrated on chemistry, physics, and botany, and his professor in these fields, Ezra S. Carr, would be a lifelong friend and mentor, as would Carr's wife Jeanne, who rivaled Muir's own mother in his affections. Older than most other students and already sporting the beard that would become his trademark, Muir was soon known as a campus character. And his room reinforced the image. Its walls were lined with shelves that contained geological and botanical specimens, and scattered around the floor was a collection of carved wooden gadgets. The most interesting of these was a bed equipped with clock gears, which tipped and expelled its occupant at an appointed hour. Muir also had a clock-geared study table, which plopped a book in front of him, left it there for an hour's study, and then replaced it with another.[1]

1. Muir's geared study table is on permanent exhibit in the State Historical Society of Wisconsin, Madison.

John Muir's study desk and clock that he used while a student at the University of Wisconsin. (Photograph from the State Historical Society of Wisconsin.)

Muir left the university after the spring semester of 1863, apparently feeling he had absorbed whatever the school had to offer. He spent the summer and fall on a botanical excursion down the Wisconsin River and before leaving, he registered for the draft. The bloody battles in Virginia had dried up the source of volunteer soldiers, and Congress in July 1863 passed a military conscription law. By the spring of 1864 the supply of eligible men in Muir's Fox Valley district was virtually exhausted, and rather than risk his life in a war that was not of his making, Muir decided to "skedaddle" to Canada. He found a job in a Canadian sawmill and spent his leisure hours gathering plant specimens in the Ontario woods.

When the war ended, he returned to the United States and got a job in a shop that made carriage parts in Indianapolis. He was soon offering advice on the improvement of the shop's saws and lathes and receiving regular promotions. He was on the road to wealth when an industrial accident changed his life. A tool he was using spun off a machine and struck him in the eye. With one eye damaged and the other failing in a sympathetic reaction, he feared for the total loss of sight. Although his eyes healed, he resolved to take up the career that interested him most, the study of nature. "I could have become a millionaire," he later wrote, "but I chose to become a tramp."

From Florida to California

His initial ambition was to follow the journey of the great physical geographer, Alexander Humboldt, who had trekked through Central and South America at the beginning of the century. Lacking money for transportation to South America, Muir decided to set off on foot for Florida. Before departing, he paid a visit to his family in the summer of 1867. He was, more than ever, a mote in the eye of his father with his useless education, idle hands, and "creedless" cast of mind. It only made things worse when Muir reminded his father of his walks in the woods and claimed, "Father, I've been spending my time a lot nearer the Almighty than you have!" When John was preparing to depart, Daniel demanded that he pay for the board and lodging of his visit. Muir handed his father a gold coin and said quietly, "Father, you invited me to come for a visit. I thought I was welcome. You may be very sure it will be a long time before I come again." Over the years Muir corresponded frequently with his mother and sisters, but he did not see his father again until Daniel lay on his deathbed.

John Muir began his walk to the Gulf of Mexico on September 2, 1867. From Indianapolis he headed south to Louisville and then plotted from there a "rough hewed course" south and east. He planned "simply to push on a general southward direction by the wildest, leafiest, and least trodden way I could find." He traveled light, as he would all his life. He carried his belongings in a rubberized bag—his plant press, toilet articles, a change of underwear, his journal (entitled "John Muir, Earth-Planet, Universe") and four books: a botany handbook, the Bible, the poems of Robert Burns, and John Milton's *Paradise Lost*.

His route took him over the steep hills of Kentucky and across the mountains that divided the Cumberland River from the Tennessee. He skirted the Smokies at the western tip of North Carolina and entered Georgia, which, he noted, had been turned into a botanical wasteland by the fighting. He arrived in Savannah on October 8 and wired his brother Dan, with whom he had left his money, to send him $100. He expected that sum, which took several weeks to arrive, to see him to South America. To avoid the swamps and coastal wetlands of southeastern Georgia, he took a coastal steamer to Florida. Finding that state too "watery and vine-tied" for a pathless walk, he struck off walking on a railroad bed westward to the Gulf Coast. The sight of alligators along the way inspired a new step in his developing thought. "Many good people will believe that alligators were created by the Devil," he wrote in his journal, "thus accounting for their all-consuming appetite and ugliness." But, if nature is God's creation, it is likely that "these creatures are happy and fill the place assigned to them by the Creator of us all. Fierce and cruel they appear to us, but beautiful in the eyes of God." Continuing the thought after a bear crossed his path he wrote, "If a war of races should occur between the wild beasts and Lord Man I would be tempted to sympathize with the bears."

His destination on the gulf was Cedar Key, an island about seventy-five miles southwest of Gainesville that is now a national wildlife refuge. He arrived suffering from malaria and lay in bed for weeks. He refused to give up his dream of reaching South America, however, and when a sailing vessel bound for Cuba put into the harbor, he engaged passage. In Havana, renewed bouts of the fever changed his mind and he caught an orange freighter to New York. Unable to discover a vessel of any sort bound for South America, he decided to go to California instead. He booked passage on a packet headed for Panama.

Meandering through San Francisco, Muir accosted a man on Market Street and asked the best way out of town. "Where do you wish to go?" the stranger asked. "Anywhere that's wild," Muir replied. The man directed him to the Oakland ferry. There is a double entendre in Muir's report of this conversation in his journal. Oakland, at one time a nest of pirates, was indeed an unruly place, but anyone aiming for the wilderness of the Sierra Nevada first had to cross the bay to Oakland and Berkeley.

Yosemite

Muir's objective from the outset was probably Yosemite where the Merced River drops in a spectacular waterfall off the crest of the Sierras and winds through flower-strewn meadows in a dramatic rock-walled canyon. Originally federal public land, Congress in 1864 had granted the valley to California as a state park. Artists and photographers had brought it to public attention; geologist Clarence King had suggested that the valley might have been shaped by glaciers. Muir and a companion he had met on shipboard spent eight or ten days in the valley gathering plant specimens, but his initial reaction was more one of awe than delight. After returning to the central California valley, he wrote Jeanne Carr that "the magnitudes of the mountains are so great that unless seen and submitted to a good long time they are not seen or felt at all." He was nevertheless determined to return to the mountains, and for the next year he took a succession of jobs on sheep and cattle ranches while saving his money for an extended stay.

While in college Muir had become acquainted with the works of the Swiss-born Harvard naturalist Louis Agassiz, who, as early as the 1830s, had theorized (after spotting smooth, rounded stones in the Rhone Valley of France) that a gigantic ice sheet had at one time covered northern Europe and part of North America. In his spare time, while working on a ranch, Muir read *The Yosemite Book* (1868) in which Josiah D. Whitney, the state geologist of California, heaped scorn on the theory of glaciation and claimed that Yosemite had been formed when "the bottom of the Valley sank down to an unknown depth, owing to its support being withdrawn from underneath" by a movement of the mountains. Muir was hardly a trained geologist, but as an enthusiastic amateur, he was prepared to leap into the middle of this scholarly mud puddle when he returned to the mountains in the fall of 1869.

Several small hotels had been built in the Yosemite, and Muir obtained a job at one of them, receiving $90 a month and board. He was to operate a water-powered sawmill and use the lumber to build tourist cabins. Muir began by building a one-room cabin for himself at the foot of Yosemite Falls. With his customary ingenuity, he installed "indoor plumbing" by diverting a small stream from the base of the falls through the cabin "with just current enough to allow it to sing and warble in low, sweet tones" to aid in his sleeping. So efficiently did he work the sawmill that his employer allowed him to take off for days at a time to tramp the valley and the surrounding mountains. His principal errand was to search for evidence of glaciation, telltale scratches in the granite walls of the valley that had been carved by moving, grit-filled ice. He found them in abundance, as well as the gravelly mounds of the glaciers' moraines. On these treks he carried only a bag for his plant and rock specimens and a small sack of flour to make unleavened bread over the campfire. His diet was confined to bread and water; he did not bother with blankets even on wintry nights.

Spring brought the season's first tourists, and the job of guide was added to Muir's duties. Muir was scornful of the tourists because they insisted on riding and saw little of the tiny floral wonders along the trail. "They climb sprawling to their saddles," he wrote to Jeanne Carr, "like overgrown frogs pulling themselves up a stream bank through the bent rushes, and ride up the valley with about as much emotion as the horses they ride on." The University of California had enticed Professor Carr away from Wisconsin, and Jeanne Carr began sending a stream of notables to Muir's cottage. Among these was Ralph Waldo Emerson, whose party arrived in the valley in May 1871. Emerson was lodged in a hotel some distance from Muir's, but he rode over to Muir's cottage on the first day of his visit. The two men were utterly entranced with one another, and Emerson returned each of the four days he was in the valley. Muir's only disappointment was that Emerson declined to go camping, pleading old age.

Years afterward Muir would identify his meeting with Emerson as one of the finest moments of his life. They corresponded regularly after Emerson returned to the East. Muir sent the philosopher-poet a packet of flowers and received in return a two-volume collection of Emerson's essays. Although he read and reread Emerson's works, Muir never accepted the philosophy of transcendentalism. Emerson's acquaintance with nature was from the window of his study in Concord; Muir immersed himself in nature and became at one with it. Nature confirmed for Emerson the existence of a transcendent oversoul; to Muir nature and God were synonymous. Even so, Emerson influenced Muir more than any other writer, with the possible exception of Thoreau, and gave a direction to Muir's thoughts. It is perhaps significant that Muir began writing his first essay for publication shortly after Emerson departed.

Entitled "Yosemite Glaciers: The Ice Streams of the Great Valley," Muir sent the article to the *New York Tribune*, which published it on December 5, 1871. It was a curious outlet, but Muir probably thought he would be shunned by the professional journals because of his lack of academic credentials and the novelty of his theory. On the other hand, Horace Greeley had expressed an interest in glaciation, and his newspaper was the most widely read in the country. "The Great Valley itself, together with all its domes and walls," Muir boldly asserted, "was brought forth and fashioned by a grand combination of glaciers, acting in certain directions against granite of peculiar physical structure." He continued with an even bolder claim: "All of the rocks and mountains and lakes and meadows of the whole upper Merced basin received their specific forms and carvings almost entirely from this same agency of ice."

The essay, which was published anonymously, would probably have been forgotten, had not the president of Massachusetts Institute of Technology visited the valley that autumn and spent several days discussing glaciers with Muir. In the spring of 1872 the Boston Society of Natural History heard a series of presentations on Yosemite glaciers that were based on Muir's essay and letters. Simultaneously, Jeanne Carr sent Muir's letters describing glacial action to a San Francisco-based periodical, the *Overland Monthly*. California's testy state geologist, Josiah D. Whitney, would have preferred to ignore the upstart amateur but found he could not. He denounced Muir with his usual blend of sarcasm and scorn, thus initiating a controversy that continued for years. Assessing this controversy, Dennis R. Dean, a modern student of the history of geology, concludes that Muir "was partly right, whereas some of those who bullied him with their more impressive professional credentials were wholly wrong."

Publication and a certain amount of national recognition pointed Muir to a new career—an apostle of nature. He began carrying scraps of paper on his daily treks to record, in abbreviated fashion, his reaction to his surroundings. Sitting before a campfire in the evenings, or in his gurgling cabin, he would elaborate upon the rough notes in his journal. He would later—sometimes years later—fashion the journal pages into essays and chapters of books. His initial reaction to the mountains, for instance, entitled *My First Summer in the Sierra*, was not published until 1911.

In addition to botanical observations and notes on glaciation, he recorded his emotional reactions to his surroundings. At some point in the early 1870s he experienced an epiphany of sorts. He later remembered that his body seemed as "transparent as glass to the beauty about us, as if truly an inseparable part of it, thrilling with the air and trees, streams and rocks, in the waves of the sun—a part of all nature, neither old nor young, sick nor well, but immortal." He compared the feeling to the Christian experience of salvation—Paul on the road to Damascus, Martin Luther in a monastery at Wittenberg, even his Calvinistic father. "How glorious a conversion," Muir continued rapturously, "so complete and wholesome it is, scarce memory enough of old bondage days left as a standpoint to view it from! In this newness of life we seem to have been so always."

Nature's Evangelist

Toward the end of 1873 he emerged from the mountains and set up a temporary residence in Oakland. He spent the next ten months converting the notes in his journal into essays, which were published in the *Overland*. The series of essays was entitled "Studies in the Sierra," and it was serious geology although Muir avoided the Latin vocabulary and arcane terminology that cluttered the work of the professionals. Although Muir erred in adhering to the Agassiz theory that there was a single ice sheet some twenty thousand years ago (the glaciers that shaped Yosemite were local and did their work three thousand to four thousand years ago), his work is now accepted in the scientific community as a seminal contribution to the theory of glaciation. It did not immediately establish his reputation as a scientist, however, because his vehicle, the *Overland Monthly*, was unknown outside of California. Muir intended to publish the series of articles as a book, but he never got around to it. The

Sierra Club finally published *Studies in the Sierra* in book form more than thirty years after his death.

In September 1874 he sent the final installment to the *Overland* office and bolted for Yosemite, crying "I'm wild once more." He now began to extend his travels throughout the Sierra Range. In November he climbed Mount Shasta in northern California, where Clarence King had found living glaciers a few years earlier. While he stood on the mountain's massive glacier, an early snowstorm swept down upon him. He crept off the ice, slipped into a crevice in the rocks, and covered himself with pine boughs. He lay there for four days, while friends down in the valley gave him up for lost.

In the summer of 1875 Muir trekked south from Yosemite to see the giant sequoias in what is today King's Canyon National Park. Conventional wisdom was that the thousand-year-old trees were relics of the past, in Muir's phrase the "mastodons of the vegetable kingdom," doomed to extinction. To his surprise he found the forest of giants to be thriving, with numerous small trees waiting their turn in the sunlight. At the same time, he discovered that the forest was in mortal danger at the hands of humans. Loggers were cutting down the unprotected forest, and sheep herders were setting fires to create new pasture. Where once he had operated a sawmill without misgivings, he now described a mill on the Kaweah River as a sinister intruder, "booming and moaning like a bad ghost, [it] has destroyed many a fine tree from this wood." Sheep, he concluded, were even more destructive than the loggers because they stripped the forest floor of every living thing, from wild flowers to seedling trees. "Hoofed locusts," he called them.

The experience added to his sense of religious mission. He had previously felt his purpose in life was to celebrate nature by describing it, to entice people to look more closely at its loveliness. He had often compared himself to John the Baptist, preaching the good tidings of wildness. After 1875 his writings were more akin to the pessimistic Jeremiah, warning humankind of the barren future it faced if it continued its destructive ways. He kept the voice of the prophet muted, however, and sought to convey his message with poignant stories and gentle humor. In "The Douglas Squirrel of California," for instance, he did a character sketch of an animal that he considered a "master forester." He began sending his essays to such eastern magazines as *Harper's* and *Scribner's*, and by the end of the decade he had gained a national reputation for nature writing.

His writings also gained him invitations to the homes of prominent Californians, and he began to realize how lonely was his life in the woods. Among the invitations was one from the Strentzels, who owned a 2,600-acre ranch of orchards and vineyards. Muir and the Strentzel's daughter, Louisiana ("Louie"), discovered a mutual love for trees and flowers, though in other ways they were opposites. She was quiet and diffident, where he was voluble and outgoing. She was prim and careful in dress; he often appeared at the house with ragged trousers and unkempt beard. By the spring of 1879 they were engaged to marry, though it cannot be said that Muir was smitten with love. In communicating news of his wedding to a friend, he neglected to mention the name of his future wife. He also insisted that, before he settled down to married life, he had one more trip to make—to see the active glaciers of Alaska. That he did in the summer and fall of 1879. The wedding finally took place in April 1880.

As a wedding present, Dr. Strentzel (a Polish immigrant with a medical degree) gave the couple a ranch house on his property and twenty acres of orchards surrounding it. Muir rented more land, planted vineyards, and compulsively set himself to the work of farming. He prospered, as he did in every career he undertook, and even managed to find time for an occasional trek into the mountains or a visit to Alaska. (He visited the nation's recent acquisition a total of seven times.) In the next few years Louie gave birth to two daughters whom they named Wanda and Helen.

Muir nevertheless could not elude the siren call of the wild, and Louie sensed this. While he was in Washington climbing Mount Rainier, she wrote him of a decision she had made. "A ranch that needs and takes the sacrifice of a noble life, or work," she wrote, "ought to be flung away beyond all reach and power for harm. . . . The Alaska book and the Yosemite book, dear John, must be written, and you need to be your own self, well and strong, to make them worthy of you. There is nothing that has a right to be considered beside this except the welfare of our children." Muir had made a good deal of money in his orange groves and vineyards, and he had prudently deposited it in several San Francisco banks. With this insurance, he was happy to return to the life of nature writer and mountain climber. They sold part of the ranch, leased part of it, and when Dr. Strentzel died two years later they moved into his Victorian farmhouse so that Louie could look after her mother. In 1891 Muir's sister Margaret and her husband gave up a dusty homestead in Nebraska and moved west to manage the part of the ranch that John and Louie retained.

Yosemite National Park

In May 1889, Robert Underwood Johnson, editor of *Century* magazine, a journal with a readership of 200,000, came to San Francisco hoping to squeeze a story out of aged prospectors of 1849. He contacted Muir, and Muir promptly issued an invitation to come to the ranch. Another invitation resulted in a camping expedition to Yosemite. Johnson was suitably impressed with the grandeur of the falls and the sheer walls of the canyon, but he noticed the absence of the carpet of wildflowers that

Muir had so lovingly described in his earlier writings. "No," said Muir, "we don't see those any more. Their extinction is due to the hoofed locusts." Muir went on to describe the devastation in the mountains caused by grazing sheep, by the fires set by sheep herders, and by wasteful logging practices.

Johnson, always ready for a crusade that would promote useful projects while selling magazines, said: "Obviously, the thing to do is make a Yosemite National Park around the valley on the plan of the Yellowstone." Muir knew the power that Johnson wielded in shaping public opinion, and over their campfire they struck a deal. Muir would produce a pair of articles for *Century*, together with pictures. Johnson would publish them and then seek out friends in Washington. Coinciding with the Census Bureau's announcement that the frontier had ended, the timing of a proposal for another national park could not have been more propitious.

In March 1890 a California congressman introduced a bill to create the Yosemite park, but Muir felt the prescribed area much too limited. It included only part of the Merced watershed (the main valley was still a California state park), and it did not include the Tuolumne River canyon to the north, which Muir felt was as beautiful as the Yosemite. He finished his articles, the second of which was a plea for an enlargement of the proposed park, and went off to explore the Muir Glacier in Alaska, which he had discovered on a previous trip. His essays, which appeared in the August and September issues of *Century*, caused a sensation, generating newspaper editorials and hundreds of letters to congressmen. Spotting a potential tourist attraction, officers of the Southern Pacific Railroad quietly threw their considerable influence behind the park bill. A substitute bill with boundaries that corresponded closely to the limits proposed by Muir (and amounting to 1,512 square miles) passed both houses and was signed into law by President Harrison on October 1, 1890.

That autumn Congress fulfilled another of Muir's dreams by creating the Sequoia National Park to protect the giant trees. Although this park amounted to 604 square miles, Muir regarded it as much too small because it did not include the sequoia groves in King's Canyon and the Tule River. Muir rushed to completion an article describing King's Canyon as "a rival of the Yosemite," but a bill establishing that park died in congressional committee (creation of that park would be delayed until 1940). Muir's article, however, gave Secretary of the Interior John W. Noble another idea. He assigned an assistant to draft a sixty-word amendment to an obscure bill to revise the general land laws. Subsequently known as the Forest Reserve Act, the amendment gave the president authority to reserve by proclamation any forest land within the public domain. Both Noble and his congressional allies realized that Western timber interests would bitterly oppose any such preservation plan. Consequently, the amendment was surreptitiously attached to the public lands bill as a rider in a conference committee of the two houses. Referred back to the House and Senate, the package slipped through without a close reading at the end of the congressional session, and President Harrison signed it into law. Prompted by Noble, President Harrison, before leaving office in March 1893, set aside more than sixteen million acres of western forests, including a belt of four million acres in the Sierras that covered the entire sequoia woods from Yosemite Park south to Bakersfield.

It was almost immediately evident that a protective association was needed to watch over the parks and forest reserves. The statute failed to specify the purpose of the reserves, and the government had no police force to keep out sheepherders and loggers. The National Park Service was not created until 1916, after Muir's death. When Johnson, nudged by Secretary Noble, suggested a private watchdog club, Muir declined to take the lead. "I would gladly do anything in my power to preserve Nature's sayings and doings here or elsewhere," Muir told the editor, "but have no genius for managing societies." Muir did, however, circulate the word among friends on the faculty of the University of California, and by the spring of 1892 the fledgling organization was in place and had a name, the Sierra Club. The club listed 182 charter members, and at its first meeting Muir was elected president, a post he would hold for the rest of his life.

Over the next year Muir accompanied Johnson to New York, visited Emerson's home in Concord and Thoreau's Walden Pond, and made a quick trip to Scotland to reacquaint himself with Edinburgh and Dunbar. On his return he went to work on a book that he had promised Johnson and his publishing house, Century Company, a compilation of his early essays, much revised and edited. *The Mountains of California* appeared in 1894. It was his first book, and many still regard it as his finest.

His description of an ascent of Mount Ritter that he made in 1872 is characteristic. Camping for the night at 11,000 feet, he was treated to "one of the most impressive of all the terrestrial manifestations of God," a starlit glow that basked the mountains in "a rapt religious consciousness." Proceeding the next day up a sheer rock face just shy of the summit, he experienced a failure of mind and courage that convinced him he was doomed to fall. At that moment a preternatural spirit seized him, restored his confidence, and he scampered up the cliff to the 13,000-foot summit of the mountain. With a view of the entire Sierra Nevada range all the way to Mount Whitney, he sensed an Emerson-like concord, a harmony composed of "Nature's poems carved on tables of stone—simplest and most emphatic of her glacial compositions." Camping in the woods on another occasion, he lay on a bed of pine boughs and saw the stars sparkling like blossoms on the upper branches of the trees.

Charles S. Sargent, director of the Harvard Arboretum, wrote Muir: "I have never read descriptions of trees that so picture them to the mind as yours do. Your book is one of the great productions of its kind." Coinciding with the republication in Boston of Thoreau's works, *The Mountains of California*, helped to mobilize public sentiment in favor of conservation. As an indication of how young the movement was, the term conservation itself had come into use, as applied to nature, in only the past ten years.

Preservation vs. Conservation

In 1896, Charles S. Sargent, Robert Underwood Johnson, and a young forester named Gifford Pinchot persuaded the National Academy of Sciences (a nonprofit scientific adviser to the secretary of the interior) to name a National Forestry Commission that would, in Pinchot's words "put government forestry on the map" and devise ways to protect the forests from herders and loggers. In the summer of 1896, Muir, Pinchot, and several commission members traveled through the West, from the Black Hills to the Bitteroot Range of Idaho, and south to the Grand Canyon. Everywhere they went they found publicly owned forests ravaged by grazing, fires, mining operations, and illegal logging. Attracted to one another from the outset, Muir and Pinchot spent long evenings walking and conversing over the campfire. Of one such midnight amble, Pinchot wrote in his memoirs, "It was such an evening as I have never had before or since."

In January 1897 the National Forestry Commission sent to President Cleveland a recommendation that he create thirteen new forest reserves and two more national parks, Mount Rainier and Grand Canyon. The parks would have required congressional action, but Cleveland had no qualms about setting aside the forest reserves by proclamation. On Washington's birthday, two weeks before he was to leave office, Cleveland withdrew from the public domain (and hence from public land office sales) the thirteen reserves recommended by the commission, totaling twenty-two million acres. Neither politicians nor the public had been prepared for such a dramatic quarantine, and the West exploded in alarm. Gifford Pinchot would call it "the most considerable storm in the whole history of forestry in America." Lumbermen, railroad men, and ranchers feared that the lands were going to be locked up tight, which of course is what John Muir would have preferred. Cleveland's failure to explain the purpose of the reserves, which intensified the hullabaloo in the West, gave Gifford Pinchot, secretary of the Forestry Commission, an opportunity to step in with his brand of conservation. The final report of the commission, issued in May 1897, assured westerners that the reserves would not be "withdrawn from all occupation or use," that instead they would be "made to contribute to the welfare and prosperity of the country."

Gifford Pinchot had a background of family wealth that enabled him to attend Phillips Exeter Academy and Yale University. Because neither Yale nor any other American college had a school of forestry, he went to Europe to attend the French Forest School in Nancy. He returned to America thirteen months later imbued with the European philosophy that forests were a crop that could provide a sustained yield with proper management. He also believed that proper management could be obtained only through government regulation of private cutting. In Switzerland, for instance, he had seen how the government controlled logging so as to prevent erosion of mountainsides.

Pinchot's work with the Forestry Commission brought him to the attention of President McKinley's secretary of the interior, who appointed Pinchot his "special forest agent." Pinchot immediately encountered the bureaucratic irony that, while the Department of Agriculture had a Division of Forestry (created in the 1880s) and employed the only professional foresters, the presidential forest reserves were under the jurisdiction of the Department of the Interior. He resolved the dilemma by engineering his appointment as head of Agriculture's Division of Forestry the following year. An able administrator and shrewd lobbyist with Congress, Pinchot expanded his two-room office and tiny staff into the Bureau of Forestry by 1901.

As Pinchot rose to power, John Muir began to recognize the danger he posed. In 1897 Congress, responding to the western uproar over Cleveland's actions, passed a Forest Management Act that suspended Cleveland's proclamation for a year, allowing the government to survey the projected reserves. The statute yielded to Western demands to allow logging in the reserves, but it prohibited the forest land from ever being sold. And it gave the secretary of the interior power to devise measures to protect the forests.

Enraged by this compromise, Muir went to war with the only weapon he had, his pen. In the course of 1898 he published three articles, one in *Harper's Weekly* and two in the *Atlantic Monthly*. "Any fool can destroy trees," he fumed in the first essay. "They cannot run away, and if they could, they would still be destroyed—chased and hunted down as long as fun or a dollar could be got out of their bark hides, branching horns, or magnificent bole backbones." It had taken three thousand years to grow some of the giants of the West, he reminded his readers. God had protected them from natural disasters through all these millennia, "but he cannot save them from fools—only Uncle Sam can do that." In another essay he insisted that "not only should all the reserves established be maintained, but every remaining acre of unentered forest-bearing land . . . should be reserved, protected, and administered by the Federal Government for the public good forever." In 1901 these essays would become the core of Muir's second book, *Our National Parks*.

In the meantime the developing feud with Gifford Pinchot came to a head. In early 1898 Muir came across a newspaper article quoting Pinchot to the effect that sheep grazing in the government's forest reserves did no harm. Both men were touring the West at the time, and they happened to stop at the same hotel. Muir accosted Pinchot with the newspaper article and asked if he had been correctly quoted. When Pinchot admitted that he had, Muir replied: "Then, I don't want anything more to do with you." The ideological division within the conservation movement would long outlive both men and is still very much evident today. The contest in the short run, however, depended on who gained the attention of President Theodore Roosevelt.

By the time he took office upon McKinley's assassination on September 14, 1901, Roosevelt had read *Our National Parks*, and Muir's philosophy blended with the president's growing grasp of Populist/Progressive rhetoric—that unbridled entrepreneurship was raping the American landscape and bringing profits only to the wealthy few. A month after Roosevelt took office the chief of the U.S. Biological Survey wrote Muir: "The President is heartily with us in preserving the forests and keeping out the sheep. He wants to know the facts and is particularly anxious to learn them from men like yourself." Roosevelt followed up by making conservation a principal theme of his first annual message in December 1901. "The western half of the United States," he declared, "would sustain a population greater than that of our whole country today if the waters that now run to waste were saved and used for irrigation. The forest and water problems are perhaps the most vital internal questions of the United States at the present time."

Roosevelt's tendency to lump forest and "water problems" together reveals his rather muddled view on conservation. The "conservation" of water with dams so that it would be publicly "useful" (e.g., for irrigation) was well within Gifford Pinchot's definition of conservation. In 1902, with Pinchot at his ear, Roosevelt strongly endorsed a Reclamation Act, which provided for the government construction of dams to provide irrigation that would be paid for by the water users. A newly created Reclamation Service became an engineering agency for damming the rivers of the West.

Roosevelt saw no inconsistency between these actions and Muir's gospel of preservation. In early 1903 Robert Underwood Johnson wrote Muir that the president was planning a visit to California and wanted Muir as a guide through Yosemite. Muir replied enthusiastically, "Should the President invite me, I'll go and preach recession like . . . a *Century* editor." By recession he meant the return of the state park in the middle of Yosemite to federal control, which had become his latest concern. Soon thereafter Roosevelt wrote Muir: "I do not want anyone but you, and I want to drop politics absolutely for four days, and just be out in the open with you." Roosevelt in his youth had spent several years working

John Muir and Theodore Roosevelt at Yosemite Park, 1903. (Photograph from the Bancroft Library, University of California, Berkeley.)

on a ranch in the Dakotas, and he prided himself on his skills as an outdoorsman.

Roosevelt landed in San Francisco on May 14, and Muir met him the next day. The presidential party rode by train and stage coach to the edge of the sequoia reserve, where Roosevelt and Muir planned to camp for the night. Learning from aides that his luggage had been sent to a hotel in a nearby town, where park officials and local politicians were planning a testamentary dinner, Roosevelt snapped "Git it!" Muir later remembered, "Never did I hear two words spoken so much like bullets."

Muir built a campfire under the giant trees and put together beds of ferns and pine boughs. "It was clear weather," Roosevelt later described the venture for *Outlook,* "and we lay in the open, the enormous cinnamon-colored trunks rising about us like the columns of a vaster and more beautiful cathedral than was ever conceived by any human architect." That metaphor was almost certainly inspired by Muir, who often referred to Yosemite as "a cathedral." The two talked far into the night, and Roosevelt emerged firmly convinced of the need to place all of Yosemite in a single national park.

The next day they rode by horseback to Glacier Point on the south rim of the valley. Stopping that night in a pine grove, they cooked steaks over the campfire—steaks that had been stored at the site by presidential aides, who presumably were also lugging around the presidential baggage. Sniffing the steaks and the brewing coffee, Roosevelt burst forth with his favorite expression, "Now this is bully!" That night their blankets were covered with four inches of snow, and the president awoke crying: "This is bullier yet! I wouldn't miss this for anything." For the third evening the politicians had planned a hotel banquet with fireworks. Roosevelt again shooed his aides away, and the twosome camped on Bridalveil Meadow near the foot of the falls. This was on land managed by the state, and it had been so abused by grazing, plowing, and orchards that Roosevelt emerged more committed than ever to recession to the federal government. On parting after the fourth day, Roosevelt took Muir's hand and said, "Goodbye, John. Come and see me in Washington. I've had the time of my life."

Rear-Guard Battles on the Retreat

After camping with the president Muir went on a long-planned world cruise, climaxing with a tour of giant trees in the temperate rain forests of Australia and New Zealand. Gifford Pinchot, during this time, ingratiated himself with the president. He was a member of the president's "tennis cabinet," as newspapers labeled it, and the two frequently played tennis, rode horseback, and took long walks along the Potomac. In order to pursue his agenda of forest management, Pinchot first had to bring the reserves under his jurisdiction. He won the support of western ranchers and politicians by promising that, under his control, the forests would be opened to public use; he also opposed the creation of new national parks that would prevent commercial use of the land. In 1905 Congress approved a law that transferred the national forests—which, with Roosevelt's additions, now totaled 86 million acres—to a newly christened Forest Service headed by Pinchot.

Pinchot's concept of "wise use" was actually a compromise of competing interests. He opened the forest reserves to ranchers but attempted to prevent overgrazing through a system of permits and fees. Influential ranchers approved of the system because it assured long-term protection of the open range. Pinchot also permitted timber cutting in the national forests but only for local needs. The great lumber companies, like Weyerhauser and Georgia Pacific, would have to do their harvesting on their own lands. Valuable though much of his work was in the context of the time, Pinchot's slogan "wilderness is waste" was certain to irritate John Muir more than ever.

Realizing that his was at best a rear-guard holding action, Muir, upon his return from his world tour, concentrated his energies on the creation of new national parks. Unlike the forest reserves, parks were preserved because of their pristine wonder and beauty, though of course they would be used (and abused) by tourists and campers. Muir's earlier advocacy had helped in the creation of Mount Rainier National Park in 1899 and Crater Lake Park in Oregon three years later. In 1904 Muir and the Sierra Club focused their energies on a bill in the California legislature to return Yosemite Valley below the park back to the federal government.

As with the original creation of the Yosemite National Park, the lobbying influence of the Southern Pacific Railroad was crucial in this new endeavor. Muir was well acquainted with the president of the railroad, Edward H. Harriman, having been a guest of Harriman's on a private scientific cruise along Alaska's coastline in 1899. The businessman reacted favorably to Muir's plea for help, and the lower house of the state legislature passed the bill in February 1905 by a goodly margin. It squeaked through the senate, however, by a single vote, validating Muir's theory that the "love of Nature among Californians is desperately modest, consuming enthusiasm almost wholly unknown."

Muir's wife Louie died in the summer of 1906 and the loss profoundly affected Muir. After a rather cool beginning, their relationship had become one of utter devotion, and Muir, at sixty-eight, felt the loss keenly. Earlier that summer his older daughter Wanda had married a civil engineer whom she had met at the university in Berkeley, and the newlyweds moved into the old adobe structure that had been built by the original owner of the ranch. Muir, his daughter Helen, and an aging Chinese servant rattled around in the great Victorian mansion of the Strentzels.

By 1906 Roosevelt and the Congress were struggling over railroad regulation, and conservation was no longer one of the president's priorities. While this battle went on, Representative John F. Lacey, a Progressive from Iowa, managed to secure passage of an Antiquities Act, which empowered the president to set aside public lands of special scenic, scientific, or historical interest. Because such sites were comparatively small in size, the act did not arouse the attention of ranchers and lumbermen. But Muir could see its potential. He immediately called the president's attention to the petrified forests of Arizona, whose 200 million-year-old logs were being sawn up by the Santa Fe Railroad for tourist souvenirs. In 1908 Roosevelt designated the Petrified Forest a national monument (it would become a national park in 1962), and that same year he designated a portion of the Grand Canyon as a national monument, a step toward its becoming a national park in 1919.

By 1908 the western distaste for federal interference of any kind was beginning to jeopardize even Gifford Pinchot's version of conservation. His management program by then extended to the efficient mining of minerals, government control of waterpower development, and the regulation of grazing and lumbering. Believing that the nation needed a unified policy to make its natural resources available to the people as efficiently as possible, he persuaded the president in 1908 to summon a conference of state governors to develop a national policy. Congress refused to appropriate funds for the conference, and Pinchot paid most of the expenses out of his own pocket.

The conference was launched with a good deal of fanfare and speech making, but the only result was Roosevelt's appointment of a National Conservation Commission. Pinchot was made chair of the commission's executive committee. John Muir was not invited to the conference, nor was he named to the commission. He would not have been satisfied with the result, in any case, for the commission's report was devoted to management activities, such as forest fire control, reforestation of cutover lands, and leasing of federal lands with coal deposits. Even these programs ran into solid opposition from Congress, which refused to appropriate funds. The commission soon died, and with it went any commitment to conservation that Roosevelt might have had.

As the terms "preservation" and "conservation" both fell into disfavor, even among Progressives, Muir sought to keep his philosophy before the public with his pen. The next four years were the most productive of his life in terms of pages published, and he continued his political holding action by trying to fend off a new threat to his beloved Yosemite. Muir's final battle—a losing one at that—involved a lovely little valley in the northwest corner of the park, a valley carpeted with ferns and wildflowers that the Indians had named Hetch Hetchy.

Hetch Hetchy

The Tuolumne River, whose canyon made up the northern half of Yosemite National Park, descended into another canyon, Hetch Hetchy, before dropping into the Central Valley and emptying into the San

Joaquin River below the city of Modesto. The city fathers of San Francisco, eager to free themselves from a privately owned city water monopoly, began casting about for potential dam sites on the streams that emerged from the mountains. Personnel of the U.S. Geological Survey informed them that the federally owned Hetch Hetchy valley, with its high walls and narrow exit, was an ideal site for a dam that would provide both water and electric power. Because the dam and the flowage behind it would be on park land, Roosevelt's secretary of the interior rejected the city's application to dam the river.

Muir and the Sierra Club learned of the city's designs on the valley in 1905 when Gifford Pinchot endorsed the city's plan for a dam. Aware that President Roosevelt equated dams and reservoirs with "conservation," Muir and the Sierra Club began a campaign of letters, magazine articles, and public speeches to draw attention to the threat to the national park. The controversy, which went on for the next eight years, became the centerpiece of the entire issue of preservation of the nation's natural resources.

In its baldest form the issue at stake was the welfare and growth of a city that represented "civilization" versus the preservation of a "wilderness" that few people saw and even fewer had any use for. Muir and the Sierra Club countered the stunted growth argument by pointing out that there were several locations on both the Tuolumne and the Merced rivers in the Sierra foothills that could serve as a water supply reservoir. It then became apparent that the city's real interest in Hetch Hetchy was the potential for electric power, which the city could profitably sell. Unwilling to confess openly this materialistic aim, the dam's proponents argued that Hetch Hetchy was only one of many lovely valleys in the Sierras and that its insect-ridden meadows could be turned into a lovely lake. In response to this form of economics, John Muir could only fall back on his natural religion. "Hetch Hetchy Valley," he wrote, "far from being a plain common rock-bound meadow, as many who have not seen it seem to suppose, is a grand landscape garden, one of Nature's rarest and most precious mountain temples." To turn it into a reservoir would be a scandalous desecration. In addition, a natural cathedral such as Hetch Hetchy was of practical utility. People, Muir wrote, need "beauty as well as bread, places to pray in and play in, where Nature may heal and cheer and give strength to body and soul alike."

Such arguments, together with the Sierra Club's barrage of communications to Congress, prevailed for the moment. In January 1909 the House Committee on Public Lands pigeonholed a bill to allow San Francisco to trade some marginal lands for the floor of Hetch Hetchy. The committee admitted that its action was the result of a loud protest "by scientists, naturalists, mountain climbers, travelers, and others."

William Howard Taft, who was inaugurated two months later, had fair credentials as a Progressive and he was initially friendly to the concept of conservation—though it would turn out that his notion of what constituted "conservation" was as foggy as Roosevelt's.[2] In September 1909 the president visited California and asked Muir to give him a tour of Yosemite. Having been entertained by San Francisco politicians with their version of the Hetch Hetchy issue, Taft was well apprised of the controversy when he and Muir rode into the valley. The president was awed by the view from Glacier Point and was determined to preserve the integrity of the park. But he could not resist teasing the earnest Scotsman. Gazing around as they rode along the Merced River, Taft observed that the locale would make an excellent farm. "Why!" Muir exploded, "this is Nature's cathedral, a place to worship in!" Delighted with getting the rise out of Muir that he had expected, the president pointed to the rock gateway where the Merced poured out of the valley and suggested that it would be an excellent site for a dam. Realizing at last that he was being razzed, Muir exploded again, but this time with mock horror. When he and the president rode out of the park, Muir knew that he had an important ally.

The San Francisco Board of Supervisors also recognized that their plans for Hetch Hetchy had little support in Washington, and they put everything on hold. Publicly they announced that the site needed more study; privately they hoped for a change in administrations in 1912. The respite gave Muir time to complete four popular books: *Stickeen* (1909), a series of short stories based on his experiences in Alaska; *My First Summer in the Sierra* (1911), recounting his wonderment in the experience of 1868; *Yosemite* (1912), in which his philosophy of preservation reached full maturity; and *The Story of My Boyhood and Youth* (1913), describing his early acquaintance with nature on the moors of Scotland and woodlands of Wisconsin.

In 1911 Muir realized his youthful dream of following the footsteps of Alexander Humboldt, journeying to South America to see the tropical rain forest of the Amazon and the mountains of Chile. Although his doctor had told him he was too old to travel, especially alone, Muir seemed to thrive on it. From Montevideo he caught a steamer to Cape Town, visited Victoria Falls, and steamed up the east coast of Africa to the Red Sea. He returned home by way of the Mediterranean in early 1912.

The election of Woodrow Wilson later that year doomed Hetch Hetchy. The president had no firm ideas on the subject of conservation, and the Democratic Party's strength was in the South and West where

2. Taft lost favor among conservationists and Progressives generally when his secretary of the interior, Richard A. Ballinger, became embroiled in a controversy with Gifford Pinchot over the leasing of public forest lands to timber companies. John Muir stood aside altogether from this imbroglio.

the term alone was a form of blasphemy. Roosevelt carried California in 1912, and the state would be crucial to Wilson in 1916. Wilson may have thought that giving Hetch Hetchy to San Francisco was a small price to pay.[3] The new president signaled his attitude when he nominated as secretary of the interior Franklin K. Lane, who had served as city attorney for San Francisco and was an enthusiastic supporter of the Hetch Hetchy dam. A bill to grant San Francisco a permit to dam the Tuolumne at Hetch Hetchy came to a vote in the U.S. House of Representatives in the fall of 1913. The bombardment of protests from Muir and the Sierra Club embarrassed the legislators, but it did not stop action on the bill. It passed the House 183 to 43, with 205 members absenting themselves. The Senate approved it forty-three to twenty-five with twenty-nine senators absent or abstaining. President Wilson signed it into law. It was John Muir's starkest and saddest defeat.

Depicted in the San Francisco press as a churlish old codger, Muir ceased public appearances and devoted his last days to his family and to Sierra Club outings. He was working on a final book, *Travels in Alaska* (which would be posthumously published), when he died of a stroke, complicated by pneumonia, on Christmas Eve, 1914. His death ended the first chapter of the American conservation movement. The last chapter of the movement he authored, wilderness preservation, which nowadays goes by the name of "deep ecology," has yet to be written.

Suggested Reading

John Muir is far more popular today than he was in his own time. In the decade of the 1980s at least sixty-seven books and articles were published on his life and work, and the number of biographies has continued to mount. *John Muir, Apostle of Nature* by Thurman Wilkins (1995) can be recommended as fairly recent, relatively brief, and nicely written. *John Muir: Life and Work* (1993), edited by Sally M. Miller, is a collection of excellent essays by scholars in a variety of fields, from geology to journalism. A nice introduction to Muir's own works is *John Muir: His Life and Letters and Other Writings* (1996), edited by Terry Gifford. Douglas H. Strong, *Dreamers & Defenders: American Conservationists* (1988), has well-written sketches of Muir, Gifford Pinchot, and other naturalists from Henry Thoreau to Rachel Carson. An excellent overview of the preservationist movement is Max Oelschlaeger's *The Idea of Wilderness, From Prehistory to the Age of Ecology* (1991).

3. Arthur S. Link's *Woodrow Wilson and the Progressive Era, 1910–1917* (1954), the standard authority on the domestic side of the Wilson presidency, does not even mention Hetch Hetchy. California's electoral vote provided Wilson his margin of victory in 1916.

11

William E. Burghardt DuBois: The African-American's Dilemma

The Burghardts were a respected and much-extended family in Great Barrington, a village that sits astride the Housatonic River in the Berkshire Hills of western Massachusetts. They shunned the mills that tended to employ recent immigrants from Ireland and eastern Europe. Past generations of Burghardts had been farmers; at the end of the Civil War most were employed as domestic servants, barbers, house painters, or coachmen. They were thus on the lower edge of the middle class and shared the puritanical ethics of their fellow New Englanders. They were also black.

The Burghardts owed their status and their surname to a distant ancestor, Tom, the African-born slave of a Dutch planter in the Hudson River Valley who had earned his freedom through service in the Revolutionary army. Mary Silvina Burghardt, great-granddaughter of Tom, was about thirty-five years old when the Civil War ended. She lived an isolated existence, scorned by her family because she had given birth to an illegitimate child, fathered by a Burghardt cousin whom she could not marry because of consanguinity. Where and how she met Alfred DuBois is not known. Alfred, who wandered into Great Barrington some time in 1867, was the son of a wealthy physician of New York, who in turn was descended from a French Huguenot planter of Haiti and a slave mistress. Alfred DuBois, who had deserted from the Union army toward the end of the war, remained in Great Barrington long enough to wed Mary Silvina and father a child. He then disappeared, never to return. Rumor had it that the Burghardts chased him out of town. Mary saddled her son with a string of commemorative family names. William Edward Burghardt DuBois was born on February 23, 1868. He was blessed, he would write later in his autobiography, "with a flood of Negro blood, a strain of French, a bit of Dutch, but, thank God! no 'Anglo-Saxon.'"

From Great Barrington to Berlin

There were perhaps thirty families of African descent in the Great Barrington vicinity, most of them with the surname Burghardt. Although much lighter-skinned than other members of his family, Willie (as the family called him) would grow up with a perception of racial differences but without the feeling of being beaten down, as he would have been if he had been born in Georgia or Mississippi. He could be a competitor in school without the sense of being a combatant, and as he wrote in one of his several autobiographies, he pursued "knowledge like a sinking star." By the time he reached high school he realized that academic achievement was the ticket out of his family environment of service occupations. Fortunately, his high school principal recognized his scholarly abilities and urged him upon graduation in 1884 to go on to college.

DuBois, one of only two students in the college preparatory course at Great Barrington High, aimed for Harvard, but that proved too lofty a goal. One problem was a lack of money, especially after his mother, who had been employed as a housekeeper, died in the spring of 1885. Another was that his high school training, even with personal attention from the school principal, was not up to Harvard's admission standards, and the lily-white faculty of the college was unwilling to bend the rules for a "Negro," even a brilliant one. Spurred by Willie's high school mentor, the Congregational ministers of Great Barrington proposed an alternative, a preparatory experience at Fisk University, a Congregational school for Negroes in Nashville, Tennessee. The village's four churches each pledged $25 a year to finance DuBois's further education. He would supplement that income with summer teaching in rural Tennessee.

Fisk Free Colored School had been founded by the Freedmen's Bureau in 1866, and it had since been taken over by Congregationalist missionaries, who elevated its status to Fisk University. By 1885 it was regarded as the best teacher-training school for Negroes in the country. Because his secondary education was superior to that of his fellow students, DuBois was admitted as a sophomore. He earned a degree three years later with enough background in Greek and Latin, as well as physics, chemistry, and literature, to resume the pursuit of his dream—admission to Harvard. His entry into Harvard in 1888 was, however, only a new beginning. His educational odyssey would last another eight years.

In his autobiographical writings DuBois described his Harvard years as a cakewalk of academic success, in which "scholarships and prizes fell into my lap" whenever he needed money. He recalled reading Kant's *Critique of Pure Reason* in the study of Professor George Santayana, and he remembered William James as a personal friend who invited him occasionally to dinner. The reality of the Harvard world was a bit more harsh, for the school was a citadel of Anglo-American Protestants who looked upon Catholics, Jews, and Negroes with condescension bordering on contempt. Although he impressed his professors well enough to win admission to the august Philosophical Club and took his meals at the nonexclusive Foxcraft Club, DuBois avoided social contact with his white classmates. He adopted a "voluntary race segregation" and fought off condescension with the cloak of "brusquerie." He graduated cum

W. E. B. DuBois and family, 1897. (Photograph from the W. E. B. DuBois Library, University of Massachusetts, Amherst.)

laude on June 25, 1890, and was selected as one of six student commencement orators.

Although DuBois majored in philosophy as an undergraduate, his grades in that field were lower than those he received in history, particularly in the classroom of Professor Albert Bushnell Hart. He accordingly petitioned the Harvard Academic Council for scholarship assistance to pursue a Ph.D. in social science. The topic of his proposed dissertation was "The Suppression of the African Slave Trade in America," and upon Professor Hart's recommendation, the council awarded DuBois a handsome fellowship of $450. After obtaining his master's degree in 1892 DuBois decided that he would benefit from some graduate study in Europe. The thought was perhaps inspired by the establishment of a Fund for the Education of Negroes, which offered to subsidize the European education of "any young colored man in the South whom we find to have a talent for art or literature." Although DuBois hardly qualified as a Southerner, he applied for a grant and received the princely sum of $750. His ambition soaring, DuBois decided to pursue his doctoral degree at the University of Berlin, whose international prestige overshadowed Harvard to the extent that Harvard overshadowed Fisk. To return to the United States with a German Ph.D. would guarantee his professional success and serve as a racial milestone.

The professors who attracted him in Berlin were neither historians nor philosophers, but economists. The Berlin school of political economy scorned the grandiose systems of both Karl Marx and Herbert Spencer. Following the lead of Johann Gottlieb Ficte, the first rector of the university, the Berlin scholars conceived of a guardian state, managed by highly educated Prussian bureaucrats, protecting the citizenry from the abuses of the marketplace, preserving capitalism while keeping in check its tendency toward monopolies and cartels. In America, twenty years later, this thinking would be picked up by Herbert Croly and Theodore Roosevelt and given the name "New Nationalism."

DuBois launched on a comparative study of agriculture in Germany and the American South, apparently (the thesis has not survived) comparing the planter/sharecropper system in the South with the landlord/peasant system in Germany. His fellowship was renewed in 1893, and he purportedly completed the thesis in December of that year. He had by then completed three of the four semesters of residence that the university required for its Ph.D., and he expected to defend the thesis in the fall semester of 1894. Unfortunately the Negro Fund declined to renew his fellowship in the spring of 1894, and the Berlin faculty insisted on a rigid adherence to its four-semester rule. DuBois left Berlin empty-handed, and, after a tour of England, returned home in the steerage of a vessel loaded with immigrants.

Pioneer in Social Science

Back in Great Barrington, DuBois sent letters of inquiry to every Negro college in the country, including Howard, Hampton, Fisk, and Tuskegee. From the president of Tuskegee, Booker T. Washington, as yet little known to white America, DuBois received an offer to teach mathematics. He accepted instead a chair of classical language at Wilberforce University in western Ohio.

The community of Tawawa Springs, twenty miles south of Dayton by wagon road, had originally consisted principally of a luxurious hotel frequented by Southern planters as a summer retreat. In 1852 Methodist missionaries acquired the hotel, renamed it after Britain's leading abolitionist, William Wilberforce, and incorporated it as a college. During the Civil War the African Methodist Episcopal Church bought the school, and in 1887 the Ohio legislature created a "Normal and Industrial Department" at Wilberforce University, thus making it one of the few schools in the country that received both governmental and religious support. The legislature's price for this modest gesture was racial segregation throughout the state's system of higher education.

Although asked to teach English, German, and history, in addition to Latin and Greek, DuBois found time to complete his Ph.D. dissertation on a topic that he had started under Professor Hart at Harvard, "The Suppression of the African Slave Trade to the United States of America, 1638–1870." Hart placed his signature of approval on the work on June 1, 1895, and recommended it for selection as the leadoff monograph for the newly established *Harvard Historical Studies*. It appeared in print the following year. The book was a landmark in the developing "science" of history that had been pioneered by Henry Adams—ingenious interpretations founded on dry facts quarried from statutes, censuses, naval reports, court decisions, and newspaper accounts. Although the import of slaves from Africa was prohibited by law in the United States after 1808 and internationally condemned, DuBois built a solid case demonstrating American participation in the ghastly commerce in human beings from the seventeenth century to the late nineteenth. His one error was to attribute the dramatic increase in the black population to the slave trade, without taking into account the natural increase. The birth rate among black slaves exceeded the death rate in the Chesapeake by about 1720, and through the early nineteenth century the Chesapeake planters were selling their surplus labor to the cotton planters of the Southwest. Although DuBois did not recognize it, the internal slave trade was far more important than the import of newcomers from Africa.

Life at Wilberforce was a trial. The college was frequently swept by the fires of religious revival, and the president required daily public prayer sessions. DuBois, whose contact with religion had been limited to the liberal Congregationalism of rural New England, firmly refused to lead the student body in prayer and escaped censure only because of his endless capacity for work and his growing reputation as a scholar. No more than a year after he arrived at Wilberforce DuBois began bombarding Professor Hart with pleas for help in finding a new job. In the meantime he found his classroom brightened by the presence of Nina Gomer, daughter of a Negro hotel chef and his deceased German wife, of Cedar Rapids, Iowa. "A slip of a girl," DuBois wrote of her in his autobiographical *Darkwater*, "beautifully dark-eyed and thorough and good as a German housewife." They were married in Cedar Rapids in May 1896. Three weeks later he received a telegram offering him a one-year appointment at the University of Pennsylvania. The offer bore the fingerprints of Albert Bushnell Hart.

Although it released him from the confines of Wilberforce, the appointment at Penn was less than it seemed. He was given neither an office nor teaching responsibilities; he was not even listed in the school catalogue. The school had received money to conduct an investigation of the living conditions of Negroes in the city's tenement district, the heart of which was the nation's first African Methodist Episcopal Church. As an expendable black man with some credentials in social science, DuBois was brought in to do the job.

Years later DuBois would treat the university's racial snobbery with sardonic humor, but at the time he saw nothing but opportunity in the research appointment. The inspiration and some of the money came from the Philadelphia Settlement, which occupied four residence halls and a kitchen/coffee house on Lombard Street in the city's Seventh Ward. The idea of urban settlement houses had originated in England as a sort of religious mission to the urban ghetto. When the concept spread to the United States—Jane Addams's Hull House in Chicago was the most famous—the religious motivation was dropped in favor of secular humanitarianism, and women became the principal organizers. The idea was to have college-educated women (and some men) live and work among the urban poor, earning a living by teaching or nursing, and gathering data on living conditions. Their experience and knowledge, it was expected, would lead to the formation of a leadership cadre essential to social reform, and in the meantime they would "bring brightness and help to a limited neighborhood."

The project that brought DuBois to Philadelphia was a study of the city's Seventh Ward, which had the highest proportion of Negroes (about 30 percent) of any ward in the city. The ward also had some of the city's highest unemployment and crime rates. The proposal of the Settlement House reformers, joined by the Sociology Department of the university, was to investigate the relationship between race, poverty, crime, and political corruption. DuBois was scornful of the hidden bias in the reformers' agenda—they thought, he later wrote, that the city "was going to the dogs because of the crime and venality of its Negro citizens"—but he found in the project a grand opportunity to harness social science to the cause of racial advancement. Philadelphia was a perfect laboratory in which to apply the goal he had set himself when embarking upon his graduate work—to study the science of society "with a view of the ultimate application of its principles to the social and economic advancement of the Negro people."

Ignoring the bias inherent in the university's charge to him, DuBois set out simply to "find out what was the matter with this area and why" by gathering data from city records, censuses, and interviews with residents. It was a daunting task because there were no methodological precedents in America. American sociology in the 1890s was dominated by the theoretical speculations of Herbert Spencer and William Graham Sumner, both of whom tended to place Africans at the primitive end of the evolutionary scale without adducing any empirical evidence for their conclusions. DuBois accordingly turned to England for models for his research and hit upon a work in progress that would ultimately go to seventeen volumes, Charles Booth's *Life and Labour of the People of London* (1889–1902), which investigated the nature and causes of poverty in London. The choice of Booth for a model was an inspired one because Booth had no occasion to consider the factor of race. DuBois could therefore use Booth's research methods to explore his thesis that "the problems of Negroes are the problems of human beings."

With help from the university's Sociology Department, DuBois devised a questionnaire to hand out to the residents of the Seventh Ward. He recorded the responses on preprinted schedules and then personally "visited and talked with 5,000 persons." In addition, he later explained, "I went through the Philadelphia libraries for data, gained access in many instances to private libraries of colored folk and got individual information. I mapped the district, classifying it by conditions; I compiled two centuries of the Negro in Philadelphia and in the Seventh Ward."

DuBois was able to divide the African-American population into four classes or "grades." At the top was the "aristocracy"—277 families numbering approximately three thousand persons out of the city's Negro population of forty thousand. These were nuclear families with a male head who had a respectable job and earned sufficient income to live well. Next came the "respectable working class," persons with steady work, usually in service occupations. Grade three was the working poor, "honest although not always energetic or thrifty." And at the bottom were the chronically unemployed and the criminals, what DuBois called the "submerged tenth." Interestingly, he discovered that the prevalence of poverty in the black population was not due to unemployment. He found that 78 percent of black men in the Seventh Ward were gainfully employed, which was a higher percentage than existed among the white population. The problem instead was white racial bias, which confined Negroes to the most menial and poorly paid jobs. He concluded that the seemingly complex "Negro Problem"—dysfunctional families, cultural backwardness, poverty, disease, and crime—could be traced to slavery and the racial prejudices that lingered after it was abolished.

The cure, however, was not solely the responsibility of white progressives. An elitist by temperament and training, DuBois argued that the Negro's progress in the past had been driven by the elite of educated persons with responsible occupations, and it was the ethical standards and aspirations of this miniscule element that would determine the future of the race. This argument, which would lead within a few years to his concept of leadership by the "talented tenth," assured a respectful hearing for the book among the scholarly community. Had he done nothing more than blame the "Negro Problem" on slavery and white attitudes, the book would have been ridiculed by the arbiters of thought and taste.

When it made its appearance in 1899, *The Philadelphia Negro, A Social Study*, received favorable treatment by reviewers. The American Historical Review was pleased that the author was "perfectly frank, laying all necessary stress on the weakness of his people." A scholar writing in the *Yale Review* called it "a credit to American scholarship, and a distinct and valuable addition to the world's stock of knowledge concerning an important and obscure theme." In a little more than a half-century historians, sociologists, and anthropologists would all applaud it as a seminal work in their developing disciplines. On the other hand, the *American Journal of Sociology* ignored the monograph altogether, and that in itself was a measure of the obstacles that lay ahead for DuBois, the elite on which he depended, and black folk generally.

The Souls of Black Folk

DuBois's research into the problems of Philadelphia Negroes drove him into a new line of thinking long before he completed the book. The mere presentation of statistical data, he concluded, would not convey a true feeling of what it was like to be a Negro. In the spring of 1897 he took up his pen to write a magazine article to which he gave the title "Strivings of the Negro People." Abandoning the scholarly prose of his *Suppression of the Slave Trade* and *The Philadelphia Negro* (in progress), he adopted the highly personal, yet lyrical, style of his journal and student notebooks. When the article appeared in the *Atlantic Monthly*'s August 1897 issue, it marked a new departure in Negro literature.

Blending art with social science, DuBois provided both an analysis of the "Negro Problem" and an enduring metaphor—the Veil. The Negro, he wrote, unlike other races, from Egyptian to Indian, Teuton, or Mongolian, was "a sort of seventh son, born with a veil, and gifted with second sight in this American world—a world which yields him no true self-consciousness, but only lets him see himself through the revelation of the other world." His explanation provided focal images for African-American literature for the next century (e.g., Ralph Ellison's *Invisible Man*, 1952):

> It is a peculiar sensation, this double-consciousness, this sense of always looking at one's self through the eyes of others, of measuring one's soul by the tape of a world that looks on in amused contempt and pity. One ever feels his twoness—an American, a Negro; two souls, two thoughts; two unreconciled strivings; two warring ideals in one dark body, whose dogged strength alone keeps it from being torn asunder.

DuBois's word-pictures were meant to evoke a thoughtful, as well as emotional, response in his audience and demonstrate that the "Negro Problem" was a very human one. "How does it feel to be a 'Problem?'" he wrote. Nothing the black man tried, nothing he aspired to, seemed to work. The great wealth of the country and its growing stockpile of scientific knowledge served only to tantalize, for "to be a poor man is hard, but to be a poor race in a land of dollars is the very bottom of hardships." The article was DuBois's debut before a national audience, and it marked the next step in his intellectual odyssey—from social scientist to racial advocate to political radical.

A few weeks before the *Atlantic Monthly* essay appeared in print the DuBoises were visited by the president of Atlanta University, Horace Bumstead, a kindly Congregationalist from New England who was building a first-rate black college amidst the intellectual ruins of Populist Georgia. A Boston philanthropist had given the university a stipend to study the living conditions of Negroes in the South, and Professor Hart had strongly recommended DuBois for the research grant. It was another timely opportunity, for the University of Pennsylvania position was due to expire on January 1, 1898. Bumstead's offer of employment arrived at the moment the *Atlantic Monthly* article appeared, and DuBois gratefully accepted. Nina was seven months pregnant, and to escape Philadelphia's pestilential ghetto, she returned to Great Barrington to have her child. Burghardt DuBois was born on October 2, 1897. His father, busy winding up his Philadelphia research before moving to Atlanta, was unable to be in attendance.

Like Fisk University, Atlanta University had been established by Congregationalist carpetbaggers immediately after the Civil War. Its Yankee faculty had first sought to make it into a model of a Northern liberal arts college, though it eventually compromised with its students' needs for industrial training. The school attracted white as well as black students (both of whom were treated as pariahs by Atlanta's unreconstructed whites), and its graduates staffed the school systems of the South for many years, including (DuBois would later note smugly) the faculty of Booker T. Washington's Tuskegee. Assigned to teach economics, history, and sociology, while directing and editing the *Atlanta University Studies*, soon to become one of the nation's most respected social science publications, DuBois remained at the school for twelve years.

DuBois used the philanthropist's grant money to sponsor an annual conference of scholars, whose papers were consolidated into an annual publication. The influential *Outlook* Magazine praised the 1898 study as "a valuable sociological publication," and three years later the *London Spectator* took note of the valuable social science work being done "under the inspiration of Atlanta University." DuBois found himself in much demand as a learned society speaker, and scholars of national renown began showing up at his annual conferences. Yet, despite the growth of his national reputation, DuBois felt increasingly dissatisfied. His strenuous efforts to disseminate scientific truth had produced no tangible result. He seemed to have no impact on the rabid racism of the South or the stolid indifference of the Northern public.

A ghastly incident in April 1899 stirred him to the core and accelerated his introspection. A black farmer who lived a few miles outside of Atlanta had shot a white man to death in a dispute over a debt. A white mob made up of men, women, and children hanged the man, took him down alive, and burned him to death, and then fought over the barbecued bones for souvenirs. DuBois was carrying a restrained letter of protest to the offices of the *Atlanta Constitution* when he saw the blackened knuckles of the victim on display in a store window. Numbed with horror, he returned home prepared "to turn aside from my work." He could not, he later wrote, "be a calm, cool, and detached scientist while Negroes were lynched, murdered, and starved."

A month later a more personal tragedy struck the DuBois household. In mid-May, six-month-old Burghardt came down with diphtheria. The inexperienced parents were slow to recognize the seriousness of the disease, and the night before the child died, when DuBois rushed out to find a physician, he discovered that none of the white doctors was willing to visit a black household. The handful of Negro doctors lived on the far side of town, too remote to be of assistance. Nina's emotional health was permanently affected. She detested Atlanta and the South ever after, and she blamed her husband for placing her and her child in such a disease-ridden, uncaring environment.

DuBois felt it was time to move again, but despite his international reputation, his options were few. Booker T. Washington's institute at Tuskegee, Alabama, was the one possibility, though, as a Southern institution, it had no attraction for Nina. Washington was the best-known Negro in America, and his Tuskegee Institute was awash in endowments from Northern philanthropists and businessmen. Washington's fame stemmed from an address he gave at the Cotton States International Exposition in Atlanta on September 18, 1895. Proposing a racial entente in the New South, Washington advised blacks to concentrate on developing skills in agriculture and industry and abandon further demands for "social equality." In return he asked white people to rein in their redneck demagogues and provide jobs for those who have, "without strikes and labor wars, tilled your fields, cleared your forests, builded [*sic*] your railroads and cities." Raising his right hand, the college president captured his audience with a spellbinding image: "In all things that are purely social we can be as separate as the fingers, yet one as the hand in all things essential to mutual progress."

The promise of a permanent black underclass, content with its lot in life and able to perform the grub work of an industrial society, was a message that white America wanted to hear, and overnight, Booker T. Washington became a national icon. Since the curriculum at his Tuskegee Institute was already focused on the agricultural and mechanical arts, persons with money to give, philanthropists and cynics alike, sent endowments to Tuskegee. Before long, the Negro educator had permanent fund-raising organizations in Washington and New York, and he was subsidizing newspapers that trucked his gospel to the counting rooms and ghettoes of the Northern cities.

DuBois did not at first perceive the implications of Washington's philosophy, and when, late in 1899, Washington offered him a position at Tuskegee, he gave it serious consideration. He eventually turned the offer down, however. Tuskegee was no better forum for his scholarship than Atlanta, and he would be under the thumb of the powerful and egotistical Washington. Relations between the two men nevertheless remained cordial until Washington's ghostwritten autobiography, *Up from Slavery*, appeared in 1902.[1]

While novelist William Dean Howells poured unstinting praise on the autobiography in the *North American Review* and industrialist George Eastman sent another $5,000 to Tuskegee, DuBois's review in the literary digest *Dial* pointed out that Washington's ideas were neither sophisticated nor original. The federal government had been subsidizing industrial education for both blacks and whites since the Civil War, and racial accommodation had long been preached in both the North and South. DuBois's focal concern was that Washington's ideas discouraged any sort of intellectual effort on the part of Negroes. The Tuskegee educator had "learned so thoroughly the speech and thought of triumphant commercialism . . . that he pictures as the height of absurdity a black boy studying a French grammar in the midst of weeds and dirt." DuBois's purpose was not only to desanctify Washington but to point out that there was a loyal opposition to him within the ranks of Negroes, a "large and important group" who believed "in the higher education of Fisk and Atlanta Universities; they believe in self-assertion and ambition; and they believe in the right of suffrage for blacks on the same terms with whites." This disclosure—a surprise to whites and a stab in the back from the viewpoint of the Washingtonians—was the opening volley in a decade and a half of warfare between the "Tuskegee Machine" and the "Talented Tenth."

A year later DuBois descried an opportunity to offer an alternative to Washington's philosophy, and at the same time, encourage the development of an African-American culture. The McClurg publishing company asked him for an assortment of essays that could be assembled into a printed volume. He sent McClurg a collection of fourteen essays and stories, and the book was published in 1903 under the title, *The Souls of Black Folk*. Nine of the fourteen had previously appeared in national publications like the *Atlantic Monthly*. The opening essay was decanted from his article "Strivings of the Negro People" and bore the new title "Of Our Spiritual Strivings." After discussing the problem of black identity and

1. Washington's publisher, Doubleday, Page and Company, capitalized Negro throughout the book, a virtually unprecedented move for a major publisher, but a source of satisfaction to DuBois who would make a lifelong crusade of the uppercase *N*. It was important because it gave the race the same status as others, such as Indian, Chinese, Caucasian, and Eskimo.

"two-ness", he opened the second essay with a line that would remain a staple of African-American literature: "The problem of the Twentieth Century is the problem of the color line—the relation of the darker to the lighter races of men in Asia and Africa, in America and the islands of the sea." The remainder of the essay and those that followed explained that "the problem of the color line" was the problem of racial differences and how they had been affected by slavery in the Americas and imperialism in Africa and the Far East. At the root of the problem, DuBois argued, was economic exploitation, which deprived entire peoples of both the fruits of their labor and their cultural identity.

The last half of the book, consisting primarily of new essays and short stories, brought to national attention a Negro-American culture rooted in its African past. Some of the essays, such as "On the Passing of the First-Born" (the death of his son) were intensely emotional; others, such as "Of the Sorrow Songs," were literature of surpassing beauty. Accompanying each selection was a pairing of lines from famous European poets with a few bars of a Negro spiritual. In the opening essay, where he discussed the problem of black identity, he chose lines from the spiritual "Nobody Knows the Trouble I've Seen." In this way he advanced the unprecedented idea that there was a certain parity in cultural creativity across the races.

Taken in its entirety, the book answered the problem of "two-ness" that DuBois had first posed in his 1897 *Atlantic Monthly* essay. There had, in the past, been two solutions to the problem of being a social outcast. Some, like Frederick Douglass, had simply wished the problem away, assuming that full assimilation and racial amalgamation were only a matter of time. Other black writers had found the answer in cultural separation and even expatriation to Africa. DuBois transcended this dialectic between Integrated Society and Negro Zion by proposing a permanent, though benign, tension, in which hyphenated African-Americans could proudly affirm their cultural duality.

Because Booker T. Washington's philosophy endorsed economic exploitation without cultural pride, it was the worst of all solutions, and DuBois devoted the third essay of *Souls* to a scathing indictment of the Tuskegee system. Washington's creed, he argued, was one of submission, or, at best, acceptance of timid, circumscribed advancement. Washington would have his people renounce the fundamental avenues to social standing: political power, civil rights, and higher education. No people in history, DuBois insisted, had ever progressed after making such concessions. "In the history of nearly all other races and peoples the doctrine preached has been that manly self-respect is worth more than lands and houses . . . that a people who surrender voluntarily such respect, or cease striving for it, are not worth civilizing."

In the fifth essay in the book, "On The Wings of Atlanta," DuBois revealed the names of some of the black leaders who opposed Washington, the "large and important group" he had alluded to in his review of Washington's autobiography. Among these were John Hope, Brown University-trained classics professor at Atlanta Baptist College (later Morehouse University), Bishop Benjamin Tucker Tanner of the African Methodist Episcopal Church, Ida Wells-Barnett, a spitfire crusader for civil rights, and Harvard-trained newspaperman, William Monroe Trotter.

This essay and the following one, "Of the Training of Black Men," evolved the following year (1904) into DuBois's best-known essay, "The Talented Tenth." He began the piece with the rhetorical question: "Was there ever a nation on God's fair earth civilized from the bottom upward? Never; it is, ever was, and ever will be from the top downward that culture filters." He continued: "The Negro race, like all races, is going to be saved by its exceptional men." These "quality folk," college educated and employed as doctors, lawyers, journalists, ministers, and educators, would provide leadership for their race and simultaneously a model for emulation. With pardonable optimism, DuBois estimated their numbers at 10 percent of the black population, though a thousandth would have been more accurate (several hundred in a population of nine million). Nevertheless, this was the cadre that would launch both the Niagara Movement and the National Association for the Advancement of Colored People (NAACP).

The NAACP

In June 1905 DuBois drafted a "call" that he sent to about sixty persons, leaders of the Negro community who were not under the influence of Booker T. Washington. He suggested a meeting in Buffalo, New York, to establish an organization of those "who believe in Negro freedom and growth." Racial prejudice on the part of Buffalo hotel owners forced DuBois to find accommodations across the Niagara River at Fort Erie, and on July 10 twenty-nine men (women were invited to join the movement the following year) convened at the comfortable old Erie Beach Hotel. (Because of the change in venue, a spy sent north by Washington never caught up with the convention.) Of the rest of those invited, nearly all expressed support but plead genuine conflicts of schedule.

Denoting itself the Niagara Movement for Civil Rights, the convention established an executive committee with DuBois as general secretary and it adopted a DuBois-drafted "Declaration of Principles," which, in addition to demanding civil and political liberties, denounced the discriminatory practices of both employers and labor unions. The employment of blacks on a temporary basis only, and the outright proscription of them, the report warned, "have accentuated and will accentuate the war of labor and capital, and they are disgraceful to both sides." The Niagara Declaration thus boldly drew up a new program for the leaders of black

America while challenging the leadership and ideology of Booker T. Washington. Washington might have served himself best if he had acknowledged the legitimacy of the Niagara Movement's aims and welcomed well-mannered debate. Instead, he publicly dismissed the "Declaration of Principles" as idle talk and sent thinly veiled threats to the still-neutral members of the "Talented Tenth."

During the next few years betrayals by white politicians and racial atrocities across America swelled the membership of the Niagara Movement. Theodore Roosevelt, despite his much publicized luncheon with Booker T. Washington at the inception of his presidency, appointed fewer African-Americans to federal office than had any of his Republican predecessors, and after winning reelection in 1904 he distanced himself from blacks altogether. In his Lincoln Day address in February 1905 he appealed for white racial purity, and on swings through the South that spring he lectured Tuskegee graduates on the dangers of falling into crime and derided Africans as a "backward race."

In August 1906 several black soldiers were accused of shooting up a bar in Brownsville, Texas (without evidence—spent military cartridges were never found). Without a hearing, President Roosevelt issued a secret order and departed for a photo-op tour of the Panama Canal. When the order was made public after the fall elections (in which Negro votes were crucial to Republicans in New York and the border states), it was found that Roosevelt had discharged an entire battalion of one of the army's black regiments (which had fought against the Sioux, the Spanish in Cuba, and the Filipino rebels), without honor and with forfeiture of pension. Among those discharged were men with twenty-five years of service and six winners of the Congressional Medal of Honor. Booker T. Washington warned Roosevelt of a "great blunder" and begged him to reconsider. Roosevelt replied to his one-time dinner companion: "You cannot have any information to give me privately, to which I could pay heed, my dear Mr. Washington." The black-owned *Cleveland Gazette* drew an ominous conclusion: "Politics will yet KILL the great Tuskegee school. Mark our prediction!"

In September 1906, a month after the Brownsville incident, Atlanta erupted in the worst Southern race riot of the twentieth century.[2] The cause was the tactic of Negro-bashing adopted by the once-Progressive Hoke Smith in a bid for Tom Watson's support in a gubernatorial election campaign. Newspapers took up the cry and began a drumfire of reported assaults by black men on white women. DuBois, who had a speaking engagement in rural Alabama when the riot broke out, rushed to Atlanta by train and sat on the steps of his university residence protecting Nina and their newborn daughter, Yolanda, with a shotgun. The

2. The worst race riots of the century were in Northern cities, after blacks migrated northward seeking jobs in factories.

best estimate of the deaths in a week of rioting is two dozen blacks and four or five whites.

By the spring of 1907 it was evident that Washington's influence was waning and DuBois was on the ascendency. The Afro-American Council, previously an echo chamber for Tuskegee doctrines, voted to censure President Roosevelt for his attitude toward Negroes. At the beginning of the year DuBois, using the presses and editorial help of black journalists in Washington, founded *The Horizon: A Journal of the Color Line*. His essays in this outlet took on more bite, as he ranged from peonage in Alabama to the "diabolic" practices of the Belgians in the African Congo. The magazine was a dress rehearsal for his future career as a leftward-drifting polemical journalist. Describing himself as a "socialist-of-the-path," he pointed out that the Negro's natural allies were "not the rich but the poor, not the great but the masses, not the employers, but the employees." The third annual meeting of the Niagara Movement in Boston's Faneuil Hall attracted an attendance of eight hundred (the movement's largest audience ever).

As DuBois's quest for racial advancement became more political and his voice more shrill, he became increasingly disillusioned with his scholarly career. In 1909 he published a biography of John Brown and at the end of the year he read a paper on the Reconstruction to the annual meeting of the American Historical Association. Both works ran counter to the prevailing thought that dismissed Brown as a lunatic and blamed the excesses of Reconstruction on ignorant blacks and venal carpetbaggers. Unable to sway even learned whites, DuBois concluded that his effort to break the shackles of racial prejudice through scholarship was a lost cause. His scholarly endeavors were also in financial trouble. By the end of 1909 the endowment for the annual conferences that had produced the widely respected *Atlanta University Studies* was exhausted, and the university's trustees were reluctant to devote the school's scarce resources to the social science publication.

On July 5, 1910, DuBois wrote the university's trustees: "Gentlemen, having accepted the position of Director of Publicity and Research in the National Association for the Advancement of Colored People, I hereby place in your hands my resignation." The resignation was a risk born of desperation, for the organization existed only in name and the director of publicity and research was a position without prescribed duties, office, or pay. Realizing that he was jumping ship without a life vest, DuBois obtained the trustees' permission to allow his wife and daughter to retain their apartment in a university residence hall for the coming academic year, while he boarded a train for New York.

The impetus for the founding of the NAACP was an August 1908 race riot in Springfield, Illinois, home of the Great Emancipator. The riot grew out of the migration of blacks from the South to work in the coal mines and railroads of central Illinois. It was the first race riot in a

Northern city since the Civil War, and by the time it was quelled by the National Guard there were six fatal shootings, two lynchings, and scores injured. White Progressives realized that the "Negro Problem" was now a national problem, an "American Dilemma," as Swedish sociologist Gunnar Myrdahl phrased it forty years later.

The initial call for corrective action came from twenty-nine-year-old William English Walling, who had left the University of Chicago to become an Illinois factory inspector and then a resident of New York University's Settlement House. In 1905 he had hurried to St. Petersburg in the heady days of an abortive revolution against the Czar and returned home with a Russian wife. Shocked by the Springfield tragedy, Walling enlisted the support of New York Settlement reformer Mary Ovington and muckraker journalist Charles Russell in the formation of an organization of "fairminded whites and intelligent blacks." Walling subsequently brought into the movement leading Progressives, including the muckraker Ray Stannard Baker, New York Settlement founder Lilian Wald, and newspaper owner Oswald Garrison Villard, grandson of the abolitionist William Lloyd Garrison. In a series of meetings through the year 1909 leaders of the Niagara movement, including DuBois, were absorbed into the developing organization. By the end of the year the movement had jelled into a forty-member National Committee for the Advancement of the Negro. Booker T. Washington was suspicious of the movement but confined himself to backstairs efforts to prevent it from raising money.

A New York City conference in May 1910 attracted reformers of all hues: settlement workers, university professors, Niagara blacks, and suffragettes. To that point the organizers still had not decided whether it was to be a white association dedicated to Afro-American uplift or whether it was to be an interracial phalanx of reformers. Walling insisted that the organization could accomplish little without "a colored leader of national prominence," and he persuaded the conference to offer a job and a salary (without specifics) to Dr. DuBois. The conference then substituted "Advancement of Colored People" for "Negro" in its official title, a change that apparently reflected DuBois's concern that the institution promote the interests of dark-skinned people everywhere.

Although a constitution for the NAACP was not adopted until the following year, the configuration of the organization was set by the May 1910 conference. Walling became the executive chair, journalist-businessman John E. Milholland was made treasurer, and Oswald Villard was named assistant treasurer. On May 25 the all-white executive committee created the position of director of publicity and research with a salary of $2,500. The organization's funds had not yet reached that level when Walling offered the job to DuBois on June 8, and DuBois accepted. "Stepping therefore in 1910 out of my ivory tower of statistics and investigation," he later wrote with lofty conceit, "I sought with bare hands to lift the earth and put it in the path in which I ought to go."

Crusading Editor

Since the NAACP had as yet no office or headquarters, Villard offered DuBois an editor's desk in his *Evening Post* building at 20 Vesey Street, Manhattan. DuBois interpreted his position with the NAACP to include an organization-sponsored magazine, and he arrived in New York with plans for a militant civil rights monthly, to be called *The Crisis: A Record of the Darker Races*. The first issue, which appeared in November 1910, contained the comforting assurance that it was edited "with the cooperation of Oswald Garrison Villard." Villard's name and financial support were crucial, but if he expected to control the new journal, he was sadly mistaken. No one controlled W. E. B. DuBois.

The NAACP obtained a one-year, $50-a-month line of credit to sustain the magazine, and businesses that catered to blacks in New York—hotels, restaurants, drug stores, and real estate agencies—took out full or half-page ads. DuBois priced the sixteen-page journal at ten cents a copy, and the first issue of 1,000 sold out completely. DuBois doubled the number of pages in the December 1910 issue and increased the printing to 2,500. Villard and other journalists thought that 5,000 subscribers were needed to guarantee financial success; DuBois reached that figure by March 1911. By April 1912 monthly circulation was 22,500. By then the African-American colleges (except for Tuskegee and Hampton) were among the growing list of advertisers.

Revealing a natural gift for journalism, DuBois instituted focal sections that appeared in each issue. "Along the Color Line" followed political events of interest to blacks, and "Earning a Living" drew biographical sketches of successful inventors, physicians, architects, and writers that provided the Talented Tenth model that DuBois championed. DuBois's editorials ranged across the spectrum of reform. An early advocate of women's suffrage, he howled with outrage when a mob of men attacked female marchers in Washington on the eve of Woodrow Wilson's inauguration in March 1913. He was also a trenchant critic of Samuel Gompers and the AF of L. "*The Crisis* believes in organized labor," he trumpeted in one issue, but he objected to the growing tendency of labor unions to exclude blacks and the failure of the AF of L to organize unskilled workers. Like Socialist presidential candidate, Eugene V. Debs, DuBois believed that Gompers was building an aristocracy of labor in collusion with capitalists.

For several years DuBois had been telling Negroes to abandon the Republican Party, and he backed Wilson in the election of 1912. Perhaps for that reason he was slow to criticize Wilson's tolerance of racial segregation in federal office buildings. Leadership of that protest fell to the combative Monroe Trotter, who led a delegation to wait on the president in August 1913. DuBois merely reported Trotter's visit without comment. When there was no change in presidential policy, an angry Trotter returned to the

White House in November 1914. Wilson was emotionally distraught over the recent death of his wife, and a nasty argument ensued, during which the president repeatedly sought to break off the interview. After the president finally lost his temper and ordered Trotter out of the building, the outspoken journalist held a press conference on the White House steps, reenacting the debate with verbatim quotes.

It was a remarkable performance in a time when it was considered a great privilege for a black to be granted an audience with the president. DuBois, his conscience now fully awakened, devoted the next issue of *The Crisis* to the complete text of Trotter's exchange with the president and followed with an editorial praising Trotter for voicing "the feelings of nine-tenths of the thinking Negroes of this country." Wilson, DuBois now concluded, was "by birth and education unfitted for largeness of view or depth of feeling" on the race question.

DuBois's break with President Wilson was symbolic of tensions between DuBois and the mostly white board of the NAACP, to which he was formally answerable. DuBois insisted on making all the crucial policy decisions for the format and content of *The Crisis*, and the financial success of the journal reinforced his independence. DuBois came to believe, not unreasonably, that his role in the association, as successful journalist and symbolic black, was essential to its success. Less reasonably, he also regarded any interference in his mission as either racially motivated or pigheaded. It was almost inevitable that he would clash with Villard, an imperious executive with kindred ego. When DuBois began working on a history of the race, which he entitled *The Negro* (published in 1915), Villard grumbled that he was seeking personal profit on company time. DuBois ignored the criticism, but when Villard demanded that *The Crisis*, in the interest of balanced reporting, regularly publish a list of crimes committed by Negroes, DuBois flatly refused. The board sided with DuBois, and Villard somewhat peevishly demanded that his name be removed as a contributing editor.

Tension between DuBois and the board of the NAACP continued throughout his editorship. Not only was the board nearly all white, but about half of its annual budget came from a handful of white philanthropists who felt that DuBois's editorials were too inflammatory. As late as 1920, Florence Kelley, a life-long battler for consumer interests and women's rights, angrily threatened to resign from the board unless the NAACP disavowed a DuBois editorial claiming that social equality was "just as much a human right as political or economic equality."

During these years the NAACP fought two great battles. It won one and lost the other. The victory was a legal one. The NAACP's legal department had gone to court arguing the unconstitutionality of the "grandfather clauses" by which the Southern states, beginning in the 1890s, had sought to deprive blacks of the vote. In 1915, in the case of *Guinn v. United States*, the Supreme Court struck down an Oklahoma grandfather clause on grounds that it was contrary to the Fifteenth Amendment of the Constitution. It was the first time the Court enforced the amendment in its forty-five-year history.

The NAACP's lost battle was sad but inevitable. It involved D.W. Griffith's movie *The Birth of a Nation*, which was based on a Southern racist novel, *The Clansman*. Griffith's production was a landmark in the evolution of motion pictures, but its hidden message was racial bias. A purported history of the Civil War and Reconstruction, it portrayed the postwar South as misgoverned by ape-like black legislators, and it made heroes of night riders such as the Ku Klux Klan. Indeed, the movie inspired the birth of the modern Ku Klux Klan in 1916. In 1915, the year in which it was released, more than one hundred blacks were lynched in the South, a figure that had not been reached in the past decade. The NAACP went to court to have the movie banned, but it invariably ran up against the First Amendment's guarantee of freedom of speech and press. "We are aware now and then that it is dangerous to limit expression," DuBois editorialized during the heat of the battle, "and yet without some limitations civilization could not endure." It was a "miserable dilemma," he conceded.

The irony is that the movie and the NAACP fed upon one another. DuBois himself admitted that the legal fight helped publicize the movie and filled the theaters with curious patrons. The battle also mobilized thousands of blacks, especially in the Northern cities, who had never heard of the NAACP. Monthly circulation of *The Crisis* reached forty-five thousand by mid-1916 and nearly eighty thousand two years later. A new section of the magazine, "The Lynching Industry," tabulated with names, dates, and places the 2,732 African-Americans lynched between 1885 and 1914. "All this goes to show," DuBois mocked Wilson's idealism, "how peculiarly fitted the United States is for moral leadership of the world."

The death of Booker T. Washington in 1916 removed one enemy from the battlefield, but DuBois remained without friends and with a sterile home life. Though she despised Atlanta, Nina remained there for nearly a year after DuBois moved to New York. She wrote him frequently, trying to engage him in the mundane details of her existence, but he seldom answered her letters. She compensated by doting on Yolanda. When mother and daughter finally arrived in New York in the summer of 1911, DuBois was disgusted to find his daughter unmotivated, undisciplined, and grossly overweight. In her command of English, once a source of pride to her father, Yolanda seemed to have slipped backward in the Georgia school environment. Her marks in school did not improve in New York, and in the summer of 1914 DuBois decided to send his thirteen-year-old daughter to an English boarding school, which he hoped would instill some discipline and prepare her for college. Nina decided to join her, despite the outbreak of war in Europe, and found lodgings in a London suburb. Except for a brief visit at Christmastime, DuBois did not see wife or daughter again for two years. When they returned, he ensconced them in a house he had rented on the New Jersey seashore and departed for a vacation of his own in Maine.

Descent into Irrelevance

DuBois welcomed American entry into the war in Europe because he was convinced that the war would destroy Europe's domineering civilization and bring to an end the empires in Africa and Asia. He was prepared to swallow whole the idealistic rhetoric by which the president steered the nation into war. In January 1918 Wilson listed "Fourteen Points" that he hoped would form the basis of a peace settlement, a "peace without victory." Point Five could have been written by DuBois himself: "An absolutely impartial adjustment of all colonial claims, based on the principle that the interests of the population must have equal weight with the equitable claims of the government." Hoping that the peace conference assembling at Versailles would bring an end to the European empires, DuBois joined the entourage of journalists that accompanied Wilson to France in December 1918.

European colonies in Africa had also sent observers to the conference, and DuBois hoped to organize a Pan-African congress in Paris that could speak for the continent with a united voice. Wilson had brought a thousand-strong delegation of journalists, historians, geographers, and economists to the conference, and for three weeks DuBois scurried from one of Wilson's advisers to another "with the American Secret Service at my heels." But he could win no support for an African Congress. British and French governments both expressed their strong opposition. Although a Pan-African congress was eventually held, neither DuBois nor the Africans made any impression on the peace conference. The Versailles Treaty left the European empires intact, and it allowed the victorious allies—Britain, France, Italy, and Japan—to carve up for themselves the German and Turkish empires under a League of Nations mandate.

DuBois returned to a nation more biased and violent than ever. The "Red Summer" of 1919 was a time of violent labor strife and race riots, accompanied by a "red scare" occasioned by the Bolshevik Revolution in Russia and Lenin's 1919 pronouncement of worldwide Communist revolution. By the end of the year 76 black men and women had been lynched in the South, and 250 more had been killed in urban riots. In the autumn J. Edgar Hoover, youthful head of the Justice Department's General Intelligence Division, sent to Attorney General A. Mitchell Palmer a report on "Radicalism and Sedition Among Negroes as Reflected in Their Publications." Hoover's primary examples of subversive publications were A. Phillip Randolph's *Messenger* and DuBois's *Crisis*. DuBois, who regarded Bolshevism as irrelevant to America, treated Hoover's accusations as utter silliness, but he could not anticipate the damage that rumor and innuendo would do in the reactionary postwar era. Circulation of *The Crisis*, which reached a height of 100,000 in 1919, plummeted to half that figure by 1921.

Through the 1920s DuBois was a man swimming against the tide. Congress annually rejected a bill that would have made lynching a federal crime, and racial segregation spread into the North, which had not seen "Jim Crow" laws since the Civil War. In 1921 Harvard banned students of color from its undergraduate dormitories, a body blow to the Talented Tenth, which emulated DuBois in aspiring to send its sons to Harvard. Tuskegee, erstwhile symbol of Negro "progress," won the establishment of a veteran's hospital, but the government staffed it with whites only. *The Crisis* denounced this train of setbacks.

By the mid-1920s DuBois seemed more comfortable traveling abroad. He spent much time in Europe and Africa helping to organize annual Pan-African congresses. In 1926 he visited the Soviet Union, just two years after Lenin's death and Stalin's seizure of power, and he came away impressed with the Leninist doctrine of worldwide class warfare. He concluded that the future lay with the world's repressed masses—the colored folk of Africa and Asia in alliance with laborers of Europe and America. "I am a Bolshevik!" he announced in *The Crisis*, and circulation plummeted to twenty-five thousand.

In the middle of the decade Yolanda, slimmed down and Fisk-educated, experienced a brief marriage to the Harlem poet Countee Cullen (a homosexual), and after divorcing him, she and her mother went to live in Paris. DuBois, who had already had some flings with women of accomplishment, embarked upon an exuberant love life that belied his sixty-odd years. Yolanda returned to the United States in 1930 and took a job teaching at a high school in Baltimore. She married the following year a college football player, Arnette Franklin Williams, whose tuition payments DuBois assumed to ensure that his new son-in-law finish school.

The depression of the 1930s ravaged the NAACP. Its endowment had been blasted away by the stock market crash, and membership shrank to fewer than twenty thousand. The seeming collapse of the capitalist system reinforced DuBois's Marxist philosophy, and he abandoned altogether his faith in the Talented Tenth for a reliance on the awakening of a "black proletariat." He had little use for the bourgeois aims of the NAACP, and the organization, in turn, concluded that he was a liability. He resigned as editor in July 1934. For the next ten years he subsisted on temporary appointments with Atlanta University and research grants from a German foundation critical of Hitler. He produced an important monograph on Reconstruction, which was ignored by the historical profession at the time. Nevertheless, by focusing on black freedom and civil rights, it foreshadowed the scholarly work that was under way at the time of DuBois's death.

In 1940 he published a second autobiographical account (he had published a semi-fictional one, *Darkwater*, in 1920) entitled *Dusk of Dawn*. In this polemic he identified his own life with the progress of the Negro in America, even though the amount of progress to that point was hardly cause for exultation. The "Dawn" was the end of capitalism and its replacement by rational planning and government ownership, a seeming abandonment of Bolshevism and attempt to blend the New Deal with British Socialism.

In 1944 the NAACP, having grown into a national powerhouse with 325,000 members (due, in large measure, to President Roosevelt's wartime support for civil rights), offered the seventy-five-year-old DuBois a temporary position, which he accepted. In that year the NAACP's Legal Defense Fund, headed by thirty-six-year-old Thurgood Marshall, won a Supreme Court case outlawing the Southern "white primary." (Southern states had declared the Democratic Party a "whites only" private club in their latest effort to restrict Negro voting.) This was the first in a series of successful legal challenges to the nation's Jim Crow laws, culminating in the historic school desegregation decision of 1954. DuBois, who had never had much patience for piecemeal reform, paid little attention to the activities of the legal department, and significantly, Thurgood Marshall ignored him. Marshall was of a new generation with a different temperament and a new agenda.

In 1959, an icon of Communists worldwide, DuBois toured the Soviet Union and China, feted wherever he went, and finally established a residence in the Republic of Ghana, a former British colony that was the first in Africa to win its independence. The president of Ghana, Kwame Nkrumah, had adopted an Africanized version of Marxism, and the ninety-two-year-old DuBois apparently saw it as a dream come true. He died on August 28, 1963, the very day on which his old ally, Asa Philip Randolph, organized a march on Washington to bring about "a massive moral revolution of jobs and freedom." Roy Wilkins, executive secretary of the NAACP, conveyed the news of DuBois's death to the throng of 250,000 moments before Rev. Martin Luther King rose to give his timeless "I Have a Dream" address. Wilkins, Randolph, and other black leaders mourned the passing of "the old one," and the crowd observed a moment of silence.

Suggested Reading

The only modern biography of DuBois is a two-volume work by David Levering Lewis, *W. E. B. DuBois: Biography of a Race, 1868–1919* (1993) and

W. E. B. DuBois: The Fight for Equality and the American Century, 1919–1963 (2000). Each volume runs to more than six hundred pages, and the reader can easily become lost in a maze of detail that contains neither time-reference nor chronological order. It is nevertheless thoroughly researched and prudent in its judgments. Less taxing is *Critical Essays on W. E. B. DuBois* (1985), edited by William L. Andrews, which contains a good biographical sketch and several fine analytical essays. Keith E. Byerman's *Seizing the Word: History, Art, and Self in the Work of W. E. B. DuBois* (1994) is a useful analysis of DuBois's writings. Editors Michael B. Katz and Thomas J. Sugrue have put together a fascinating collection of essays on DuBois's most important research study in *W. E. B. DuBois, Race, and the City: The Philadelphia Negro and Its Legacy* (1998).

12

Margaret Sanger: Crusade for Birth Control

Corning was a rather dreary mill town on the banks of the Chemung River in southern New York. The Erie Railroad, whose main line passed through the city, maintained substantial repair shops there, and the city boasted a famous glass works. The factories attracted a labor force of immigrants, chiefly Irish. Michael Hennessey Higgins and his wife Anne settled in the city shortly after the Civil War. Michael, who had been apprenticed to a stone mason in Ireland, emigrated to Canada at the age of fifteen and moved to New York to enlist in the Union army. He settled in Corning hoping to find work as a stone carver in cemeteries. Although both Michael and Anne were of Irish-Catholic lineage, Michael was a hard-drinking freethinker who ventured near a church only when hired to repair its masonry. He would name one of his sons after single-taxer Henry George, and his radical theories, proclaimed loudly from taverns to street corners, cost him many commissions and ensured social ostracism for his children.

Despite his radical politics, Michael Higgins was a creature of his Irish-Catholic cultural background and regarded the siring of children as both a duty and signal of manhood. His wife, a victim of the same culture, had neither the knowledge nor the inclination to practice birth control. As a result she became pregnant almost annually, a total of eighteen times. Of the eighteen pregnancies, she suffered seven miscarriages and delivered eleven children, four girls and seven boys. Margaret ("Maggie" to the family), their third child, was born on September 14, 1879. Anne Higgins had contracted tuberculosis when young, and each pregnancy worsened her condition. By the time she had her last child, Ethel (a lifelong friend and ally of sister Margaret), Anne was so weak she could hardly talk and had to be carried up and down stairs. She died in 1899 at the age of forty-eight.

Maggie's older sisters fled the household when they reached their teenage years and went in search of jobs and husbands. Upon Maggie's shoulders fell the care of the household, including the care of her dying mother and younger siblings. Her brothers themselves suffered a variety of maladies; only three survived into adulthood. While her father spent most of his time preaching in the taverns or roaming the woods with his dogs, Maggie endlessly cleaned, cooked, and washed clothes. She grew up detesting housework and child care, and because she regarded her mother as a victim of her father's lust, she disdained both marriage and men—except when one or the other served her own needs. She also detested Corning and its social environment and recognized that her only ticket out of town was education. The care of her mother gave her some experience at nursing, one of the few occupations open to women. The moment her mother died she borrowed money from her sister Mary and took a train to White Plains, just north of New York City. The hospital there provided living quarters and probationary training for aspiring nurses.

Maggie Higgins Becomes Margaret Sanger

Although blessed with her father's flaming red hair, Maggie, as an adolescent, regarded herself as ungainly and homely. By the time she moved to New York at the age of twenty, however, she had blossomed into a slender, beautiful, auburn-haired woman with a seemingly irresistible allure. By that date she had already had at least two affairs with teenage boys—she called them "trial marriages" in her autobiography. At a hospital dance in early 1902 a friend introduced her to William Sanger, a young architect and aspiring artist who had come up from Manhattan with plans for a new home for one of the White Plains doctors. Sanger was instantly smitten with the auburn-haired beauty, and he began camping daily on the hospital steps to pick her up when she was off duty. He was soon proposing marriage, and when she resisted the idea, he impulsively decided to carry her off. On August 18, 1902, he hired a horse and carriage, picked her up between shifts at the hospital, and drove her to the house of a minister. Despite her insistence that she would marry only in her own good time, Sanger had the minister perform the service. Margaret was back at the hospital in time for her next shift. With mixed emotions she wrote her sister Mary:

> That beast of a man William took me out for a drive last Monday and drove me to a minister's residence and married me. I wept with anger and would not look at him for it was so unexpected. I had an old blue dress on, and I looked horrid. Now the only thing is to make the best of it. . . . He is the loveliest of men but I am mad at him. . . . Good night, dear Mary. I am very sorry to have had this thing occur but yet I am very, very happy.

They kept the marriage secret at first so Margaret could continue her nurse's training. She transferred to a Manhattan hospital, and they took an apartment on the edge of Harlem where rents were cheap. A potential conflict between the need to keep house and the desire to become a nurse was resolved when she became pregnant. The baby was much wanted by both. Margaret didn't expect to become a breeder like her mother, but she thought two or three children appropriate. Unfortunately, the pregnancy caused a latent tuberculosis to flare up, and William placed her in a sanitarium in the Adirondacks. Bored with the restful atmosphere, she escaped, returned home, and gave birth to a son, Stuart. The TB flared up during the delivery, forcing her to return to the sanitarium with the baby.

When she left the sanitarium after nearly three years' residence, they looked for a suburban residence with better air than smoke-drenched Manhattan. Bill bought a half-acre lot in Hastings-on-the-Hudson, an upper-middle-class community in Westchester County. He designed a dream house, and they settled into a life of suburban bliss. Two more children followed at healthful intervals, Grant and Peggy. Margaret's days were filled with card parties and changing diapers, women's club meetings and washing clothes, walks along the river and cooking meals. And she was bored to distraction. She endured six years of it and then insisted on returning to the city, even though her daughter was only a year old.

In 1911 they took an apartment "way uptown" in Manhattan and commuted nightly to participate in the bohemian culture of Greenwich Village. As a painter, William Sanger had extensive acquaintances among the rebels and activists of Manhattan's underground, and through them Margaret met such intoxicating personalities as Eugene Debs, head of the Socialist Party; Robert Reed, the journalist who would later give the world a firsthand account of the Bolshevik Revolution (*Ten Days That Shook the World*); and the incomparable Marxist and feminist Emma Goldman, who for some years had been preaching "voluntary motherhood" while slipping information on contraception to the women of the city's slums. Margaret listened intently to the philosophy of Socialism without ever joining Debs's political party, and she was particularly impressed with Emma Goldman's theory of political change through confrontation—toppling the existing order through violent rhetoric and activist demonstrations (Goldman lived with an anarchist who had served fourteen years in prison for stabbing and shooting Carnegie's lieutenant Henry Clay Frick during the Homestead strike of 1892).

Bill Sanger appreciated artistic bohemians, but he was appalled by the radical doctrines of Emma Goldman and the anarchists she brought to his house. Intellectually and emotionally, the Sangers drifted apart. In the summer of 1912 and again in 1913 Bill rented a cottage on Cape Cod to enable Margaret and the children to escape the heat of Manhattan. In the summer of 1913 she put Emma Goldman's free-love theories to practice by taking a lover, an experience that she later described to a friend as "an affair . . . that really set me free." Bill visited the cottage in Provincetown, heard rumors of the affair, and the two quarreled violently.

During the fall of 1913 they attempted to patch up their frayed marriage by taking a trip to Paris with the children. Because Bill's paintings did not sell very well, they financed the trip with the proceeds from the sale of their home in Hastings. Bill naturally wished to visit the city that was the artist's mecca, but his main purpose in going was to satisfy Margaret's long-expressed yearning for world travel. In her autobiography many years later Margaret claimed she went to Paris to learn about European methods of birth control. In fact, she had not, in 1913, even read the rather extensive American medical literature on contraception. She had listened to Emma Goldman's theories on voluntary motherhood, but, to this point, Margaret Sanger was more enchanted by romantic notions of class warfare. After less than a month in the city she abruptly packed up her children and sailed for New York. Although she did not formally divorce Bill Sanger until 1920, from this point on she would live her life on Emma Goldman's maxim: "It is only individuals that count, not families."

Dawn of the Birth Control Movement

Margaret did encounter some feminist radicals in Paris, and she returned to America with a feminist tinge to her anger at society. "'Virtue,' 'Marriage,''Respectability,'" she wrote in her journal in early 1914, "they are all alike. How glorious too and how impudent the present society—which dares to shut up young girls or women in their 'homes' because that girl defies conventions and fills the longings of her nature. For this she is an outcast. The whole sickly business of society today is a sham; one feels like leaving it entirely or going about shocking it terribly." It was evident that she had chosen the second alternative when in March 1914 she founded the *Woman Rebel*, an incendiary journal aimed at lower class women. At its masthead was the slogan "No Gods, No Masters!" borrowed from the recently founded Industrial Workers of the World, and the IWW members, known as "Wobblies," helped distribute the magazine through its locals. The first issue consisted of eight pages, with a brief essay on each page. Only on the final page was there an article relative to contraception. In that piece Sanger urged the wives of factory workers to limit the number of children in order to frighten the "capitalist class," though she was not yet prepared to discuss specific methods of contraception.

Despite this glimmer of her future, she remained focused for the moment on the misdeeds of the masters of capitalism. After the Ludlow massacre in the Colorado coal strike in April 1914 she assailed John D. Rockefeller, characterizing him as a "blackhearted plutocrat whose soft, flabby hands carry no standard but that of greed." Not until the June issue of 1914 did the *Woman Rebel* use the phrase "birth control," a term that had been coined by one of her poet-playwright friends (Sanger would claim authorship the rest of her life). With that phrase and that issue of her magazine Margaret Sanger at last had found her cause. Although her article on the subject spoke of family limitation in general terms and never described any contraceptive practices, the Post Office Department found that the journal could not be distributed through the U.S. mail because of the Comstock law.

Forty years earlier an obscure Congressman named Anthony Comstock had managed to write Victorian prudery into the United States Criminal Code when he slipped through an inattentive Congress a bill prohibiting the mailing, transporting, or importing of "obscene, lewd, or lascivious" material. While the statute did not define those terms, it specifically banned all devices and information pertaining to "preventing conception." Invoking this law, the New York postmaster declared Sanger's April issue to be unmailable, but he would not tell her which essay he found offensive. Still in her confrontational mode, Sanger decided to force the postmaster to single out an article for suppression, though what that would accomplish is not clear.

Her August issue contained two particularly inflammatory essays. In one Sanger defended two anarchists who had been experimenting with homemade bombs in a house on Lexington Avenue and accidentally blew up both the house and themselves. Another article by an anarchist friend defended the principle of assassination. She had clearly gone too far; neither the Comstock Law nor the U.S. mail was any longer the issue. The government indicted her for publishing indecent articles and inciting to murder. Acting as her own attorney, she won a series of delays in her trial, and when time ran out she fled to Canada and caught a boat to England. She left Stuart enrolled in a boarding school on Long Island. The younger children were deposited with friends in Greenwich Village.

Before leaving, she used the time afforded by the court to write a pamphlet entitled "Family Limitation." The federal indictment had clearly sobered her. She abandoned her flirtation with anarchism, and she would focus thereafter on birth control. Even on that subject, however, she remained on the radical fringe. She told American women—what no one had ever dared say, or even think—that "a mutual and satisfied sexual act is of great benefit to the average woman, the magnetism of it is health giving, and acts as a beautifier and tonic." She would repeat and embellish that theme in lectures and writings for the rest of her life. Among contraceptives, her pamphlet recommended douches, condoms, and diaphragms. The condom, originally a sheath made of sheep's gut, had been introduced to the court of Charles II in the seventeenth century by a Dr. Condom, and knowledge of it had been spread in the following century by the professional lover Casanova. In his autobiography he called them "English overcoats, little preventive bags invented to save the fair sex from anxiety. . . ." The diaphragm, a rubber disk designed to fit over the neck of the uterus, had been invented in Holland in the mid-nineteenth century. Margaret had obtained one for herself on her visit to Paris. American women had long been aware of douches—and of their dubious effectiveness—but no American manufacturer was bold enough to produce condoms or diaphragms. And the Comstock law prohibited their importation from abroad.

With a court appearance looming and a decision to be made whether to stand trial or flee, Sanger searched desperately for a printer. One reflected the fears of many when he told her, "That's a Sing Sing job!" She finally found an IWW member who agreed to stay in his shop after hours and run off 100,000 copies of her pamphlet. After she landed safely in England, Sanger wired him to release the pamphlet. It was distributed around the country by IWW and Socialist Party locals.

Her passage to England was paid by loyal Bill, who had sent her money when he learned of her arrest and trial. Once she reached England, he sent her paintings to sell to support herself. Shortly thereafter Bill was arrested for distributing her pamphlet on "Family Limitation." She could only express annoyance at his interference in her crusade.

Havelock Ellis

Determined that her enforced exile be turned to good account, she spent hours reading the medical literature on contraception in the British Museum in London. Acquaintances there arranged an invitation to tea with Havelock Ellis. In the process of writing the seven-volume *Studies in the Psychology of Sex*, Ellis was the world's leading authority on sexual psychology and abnormality. But he was not simply an arid scientist. He associated in London with the same sort of romantic bohemians that Sanger knew in Greenwich Village. His approach to sex, according to his biographer, held out "the wonderful possibility of a mystical communion."

When Margaret Sanger knocked on Ellis's door in December 1914, she faced a tall man, twenty years her senior, with wavy white hair and a handsome face framed by a spacious beard. The two became instant friends. Ellis later confessed that "he had never been so quickly or completely drawn to a woman in the whole of his life." Margaret in her autobiography claimed "a reverence, an affection, and a love which strengthened with the years."

Ellis shaped her thought in two important ways. First, he insisted that she concentrate on a single issue, birth control, and forget her fulminations against capitalists, marriage, and priests. Secondly, he advised caution and prudence. He had read the *Woman Rebel* and found it both scattershot and inflammatory. It is no use, he advised, "being too reckless and smashing your head against a blank wall, for not one rebel, or even many rebels, can crush law by force." To change the law, he said, "needs skill even more than it needs strength." Under Ellis's tutelage, she began to develop an ideological structure for her crusade that it had previously lacked. Together they sought to harness the science of contraception to the romance of lovemaking.

In January 1915, on Ellis's advice, Sanger journeyed to Holland to visit the government-sponsored birth control clinic in The Hague. The head of the clinic showed her a new and superior type of diaphragm, invented by a German doctor in the 1880s. He also convinced her that, to work properly, the diaphragm must be fitted to a woman by a doctor. Sanger had previously believed—and so wrote in her pamphlet "Family Limitation"—that a single size worked for all and that women could "teach each other" how to use it. Margaret Sanger's acceptance of the idea that dependable contraception was a medical matter gave a whole new direction to the birth control movement.

In September 1915 Sanger returned home, across the submarine-infested Atlantic, a more mature woman. The old combativeness learned from her father would occasionally surface, but she was now prepared to preach love, rather than hatred, and to pitch her message in tones that would attract the moderates, the middle class, the women of education and means who were in a position to actually help her.

Organizational Battles

Before she could put her new philosophy to organizational use, however, she suffered some dark days, the product, in part, of her earlier extremism. In November, a month after she landed in New York, her daughter Peg died of pneumonia. Margaret, who had worshipped her daughter even while largely ignoring her, was distraught. She blamed herself and her absence abroad for the tragedy, even though in those days pneumonia was virtually incurable. For the rest of her life she solemnly observed the anniversary of her daughter's death.

The other problem was the federal indictments that still hung over her head. Her first instinct was to do battle as of old, in order to vindicate her exile and her daughter's death. However, friends pointed out that it was the wrong war on the wrong issue. She had been indicted for advocating public disorder and murder, not for advocating birth control. She would certainly lose at trial, and a jail sentence would inhibit the entire birth control movement. Fortunately, the issue was resolved when, in early 1916, the government decided not to prosecute. The federal attorney apparently decided it was not worth the effort and might give the suffragettes who were picketing the White House a new issue. "We were determined that Mrs. Sanger shouldn't be a martyr if we could help it," he told the press.

This crisis weathered, Sanger turned her attention to the need for organization. Two years earlier she had announced the formation of a birth control league in the *Woman Rebel*, but it existed only in name at the time she fled to England. In her absence Mary Ware Dennett, an interior decorator by trade and a veteran of the suffrage movement, read a copy of "Family Limitation" and formed the National Birth Control League. Most of the members at first were Dennett's wealthy clients in New York City, and the league from its inception directed its appeal to politically moderate women of wealth and social standing. It expressly excluded from membership radicals like Emma Goldman. Taking the position that birth control was a "purely scientific topic," the league worked for the repeal of state and federal laws that treated birth control as obscene.

The sort of women that Dennett enlisted had been practicing forms of birth control for years. Indeed, the decline in the birth rate among the middle class by 1900 had led President Theodore Roosevelt to warn that the fecund immigrants from southern and eastern Europe were threatening to overwhelm the "Anglo-Saxon" portion of the American population. Many of Dennett's wealthy adherents, as a result, joined the league in order to propagate birth control information among the new arrivals and the poor. The eugenics movement, which sought to improve the race by scientific breeding, was another source of money and members for Dennett's league. Margaret Sanger was at first angered by this threat to her preeminence in the movement, but then she remembered Havelock Ellis's advice. She declined an offer to serve on the executive committee of the league, but she would cooperate with it in a sort of joint venture.

In the spring of 1916 she embarked on a lecture tour that took her west to Chicago, Portland, San Francisco, and Los Angeles. She had not appeared in public before, and audiences that were accustomed to the forensic harangues of stocky Emma Goldman and the Wobblies were in for a surprise. Sanger was petite, stunningly attractive, conservatively dressed, and soft-spoken. Her standard oration included a lurid description of a woman who had died of a self-attempted abortion during Sanger's nursing experience. She then pleaded for an abandonment of Victorian prudery and an open discussion of sex and the dissemination of contraceptive information. Blending statistics with anecdotes and exuding personal charm, she captivated her audiences and developed a strongly committed personal following.

As contributions flowed in, Sanger (who never in her life bothered to distinguish between personal income and contributions to her cause) purchased a cottage in the seaside village of Truro on Cape Cod. There, in the summer of 1916, she brought her father, who had been thrown out of an old soldier's home for voicing his radical opinions too loudly and too often. Michael Higgins would reside in the cottage until his death ten years later. Her sons, Stuart and Grant, on vacation from their boarding schools, also spent the summer at the cottage.

In October, Margaret and her sister Ethel Byrne, who was also a trained nurse, opened a birth control clinic in the Brownsville section of Brooklyn. Joining them in the venture was Russian-born Fania Mindell, who would serve the clinic as translator and secretary. Establishment of the clinic revealed a subtle difference in philosophy between Sanger and the National Birth Control League. Sanger was not content with simply seeking repeal of repressive laws; she wanted to challenge them and win change through the courts. In December her New York friends founded the New York Birth Control League to raise funds for her legal battles. The new organization also hoped to change the laws so as to permit physicians to instruct their patients on birth control and to publicly advocate birth control as a means of protecting the health of mothers and babies. This, too, was a subtle but significant shift in strategy from Dennett's National Birth Control League.

The founding of the Brownsville clinic brought the anticipated response. Within days after it opened police raided the clinic and confiscated the condoms and diaphragms that Sanger and Byrne were prescribing. The district attorney then brought suit against Sanger and Byrne under the New York penal code, which made it a misdemeanor to sell, advertise, or distribute "any recipe, drug or medicine for the prevention of conception."

Ethel Byrne's case came before the court first. Her attorney attempted to introduce the expert testimony of a physician who would provide statistics on the high rate of mortality among mothers and children in large families and the tendency to transmit mental and physical defects when fertility cannot be controlled. The Brooklyn court, however, was not willing to follow the Supreme Court's lead in accepting the sociological evidence provided by the "Brandeis brief," and it disallowed the testimony. In January 1917 the court sentenced Mrs. Byrne to thirty days in jail. The trial had the effect Sanger intended, however. Wealthy New York women jammed the court room, and contributions flowed into the Brownsville clinic from around the country. While her sister continued to hold public attention by rejecting food and water and suffering a force-feeding by her jailors, Margaret quietly went to trial and endured a thirty-day sentence of her own.

While the two women were engaged in a legal tussle with the state of New York, Frederick A. Blossom, erstwhile Socialist and Wobbly, who had helped to found the New York Birth Control League, launched a new magazine, the *Birth Control Review*. Sanger joined the *Review* when she was released from jail, and it occupied most of her time for the next few years. Less strident than the *Woman Rebel*, the *Review* printed factual articles on such subjects as child labor, eugenics, and the legal status of birth control. It avoided explicit discussion of contraception, which allowed it access to the mails, and eventually attracted a national circulation. Sanger also began putting her thoughts on birth control into book form. *Woman and the New Race* appeared in 1920 and *The Pivot of Civilization* was published two years later.

All the while she kept her sons in private boarding schools. She claimed that these institutions afforded a better education, but, in truth, she had neither the time nor the inclination to raise them at home. She even reneged on promises to visit them on spring and fall vacations. On Thanksgiving 1918, she told the boys to go to her apartment in Greenwich Village where her maid, Daisy, would cook them a nice dinner. She had time and energy for a succession of bedmates through these years, but no time for her sons.[1]

In the spring of 1921 she met J. Noah H. Slee, a stocky, sixty-three-year-old Dutchman from South Africa, who was a self-made millionaire. Slee was president of the Three-In-One Oil Company and had made his household lubricant a national brand by advertising on roadside barns. (He was the first to conceive the idea of giving a farmer a free barn-painting in exchange for a sign that covered the side facing the highway.) Married to a frigid woman (who is reported to have telephoned her mother the morning after each attempt at sex to report "He did it again!"), Slee developed a self-destructive infatuation for Margaret reminiscent of William Sanger's. He attended her birth control lectures, took her to parties, and sent her flowers every day. He begged her to marry him as soon as he could obtain a divorce. Margaret, as usual, was of mixed emotions. "What do I want with a man like that?" she asked her secretary. "I don't want to marry anyone, particularly a stodgy churchgoer who isn't interested in art or anything. Yet . . . how often am I going to meet a man with nine million dollars?"

The money talked, and they were married in 1922. First, however, she made him sign a document that ranks as the most bizarre in the annals of marriage. By the terms of this prenuptial agreement Margaret was to have her own quarters and servants in his New York City mansion and could come and go as she pleased. He was to telephone whenever he wanted her to come to his side of the house for dinner, and when both were busy, communications would be exchanged through their secretaries. She would also retain the name Sanger because it was so well-

1. Sanger's biographer, Madeline Gray, by exploring Sanger's letters and diaries and interviewing surviving friends and relatives, has identified the individuals that Gray describes delicately as Sanger's "lovers." Gray has identified most by name, some by their initials, and a few by occupation ("anarchist," "journalist"). Curiosity induced me to tally the number, and I came up with a total of eighteen. They span a lifetime, the first some time in her mid-teens, the last when she was sixty-seven. Each affair lasted weeks or months, in some cases for years. The amount of time and energy the woman expended on romance is quite astonishing. It should nevertheless be noted that there is no evidence that she ever used sexual favors to promote herself or her cause. She was simply practicing the liberated life that she preached.

known. They were married in London, and she promptly sent him off to visit museums and cathedrals while she spent her days with her English soulmates, Havelock Ellis and novelist-historian H. G. Wells.

Slee made the best of this curious marital arrangement and became the principal financial support for the American Birth Control League, which Margaret founded in 1921 and served as president. By 1926 the league had a membership of more than thirty-seven thousand, and it was sponsoring regional and national conferences on birth control and demographic problems. By that date also it employed a physician full-time to travel the country and address medical societies. The support of physicians was crucial to the movement because the only dependable contraceptive devices (and that did not require a sexual partner's consent) were those fitted to women by a doctor. And, next to the Catholic Church, physicians were her worst enemies. Most doctors were men raised in a Victorian ethos, and they had little empathy for the special problems of their female patients. They were also highly protective of their newfound professionalism (medicine had been cursed with quackery for centuries), and they were resistant to a practice unrelated to the treatment of illness. It would be another decade before the medical profession would come to Margaret Sanger's aid.

Sanger did, however, find a young female doctor who was willing to operate a birth control clinic in New York. Dr. Dorothy Bocker, who was employed by the Public Health Service of Georgia, came to New York in 1923, and Sanger provided her with an office in the Birth Control League's headquarters on Fifth Avenue. The title on Bocker's door read "Clinical Research" because birth control clinics, as such, were still illegal. With only word-of-mouth advertising the clinic was soon attracting women by the hundreds—Jewish, Italian, and Irish women from the city's tenement houses.

To maintain her supply of diaphragms, Sanger made a bargain with an Italian rumrunner who was smuggling gin from Holland. He owned a speedboat that ran cases of liquor into the harbor from freighters anchored outside the twelve-mile national limit. For a dollar apiece he smuggled diaphragms in liquor bottles. Slee put up the money in exchange for an occasional case of Holland gin. When the Italian quit the smuggling business and opened a candy store, Slee himself undertook to smuggle diaphragms in cartons of oil cans from his Three-In-One factory in Canada. When Slee got cold feet after one of his trucks was stopped and searched at the border, Margaret turned to Herbert Simonds, a chemical engineer whom she had met on one of her lecture tours and had known for years. He opened a shop in uptown Manhattan and perfected a rubber diaphragm that would, in his words, "withstand all kinds of climate." Volunteers carried the devices downtown to Margaret's clinic in suitcases. Years later, when diaphragms became legal, Simonds opened branch factories in Chicago and Los Angeles and grew rich.

Sanger and Simonds remained friends and occasional lovers for the next thirty years.

From Encumbrance to Idol

The American Birth Control League's efforts through the mid-1920s to change state laws outlawing the sale (in Connecticut even the use) of contraceptives were utterly unsuccessful. The league opened an office in Washington to lobby for repeal of the Comstock Law and closed it a month later when not a single congressman stepped forward to sponsor a bill. Even Sanger's drift toward conservatism and attempt to appeal to white, middle-class Protestants failed to work. She continued to argue that birth control information be extended to the lower classes, not to prevent them from being exploited, but to protect the rest of society from fecund immigrants and the "unfit." By "unfit" she meant persons mentally retarded or physically deformed. None of her approaches seemed to work. In 1927 the National Women's Party, the most radical of the feminist organizations, rejected a birth control plank in its platform for fearing of splitting the organization, and three years later the League of Women Voters refused to entertain a resolution calling for a study of birth control.

In 1926 and 1927 Sanger spent eighteen months in Europe organizing a world conference on birth control and traveling with her husband. While she was gone the acting president steered through the board of directors a reorganization plan that reduced the powers of the president. Enraged by this assault on her authority, Sanger abruptly resigned as president. Later in 1928, when the directors proposed that the league's official organ, the *Birth Control Review*, be placed under professional management, Sanger quit as editor. Slee thereafter ceased to fund the organization, and the league slipped into obscurity.

Sanger was left with her Manhattan clinic, and with her husband's money, she established a "National Committee" in Washington to lobby for repeal of the Comstock Law. From 1930 to 1934 her committee annually drafted a repeal bill and found sponsors for it, but it never came to a vote. By 1934 her efforts had been rendered irrelevant by new interpretations of the law in the courts. In 1930 Sanger's old rival Mary Ware Dennett had been taken to court for publishing a pamphlet explaining sexual anatomy and functions to children. A federal circuit court of appeals refused to apply the Comstock Law, stating that the statute was not "designed to interfere with serious instruction regarding sex matters unless the terms in which the information is conveyed are clearly indecent." In 1934 the same court allowed the distribution of James Joyce's novel *Ulysses*, remarking: "It is settled, at least so far as this court is concerned, that works of physiology, medicine, science, and sex instruction are not within the statute, though to some extent and among some persons they may tend to promote lustful thoughts." Two years later the court held that the Comstock Law did not prevent the import and distribution of diaphragms and other contraceptives, "which might intelligently be employed by conscientious and competent physicians for the purpose of saving life or promoting the well-being of their patients."

The change in judicial interpretation reflected a change in public opinion in the 1930s. In 1931 the national organization of the Churches of Christ in America endorsed the idea of birth control. It was the first religious organization to do so. The Roman Catholic clergy continued to denounce contraception as "Satanic" and to recommend abstinence as a means of limiting births, but by 1936 a poll conducted by *Fortune* Magazine revealed that 63 percent of Americans, including 42 percent of the Roman Catholics, believed in "the teaching and practice of birth control."

This shift in public opinion reflected the return of liberal thought that accompanied Franklin Roosevelt's New Deal and had little to do with Margaret Sanger. Indeed, by the mid-1930s she was probably more of a liability than an asset to the birth control movement. Unable to forget her early radicalism, politicians and physicians alike refused to address "Sanger groups." In 1935 she gave up on efforts to repeal the Comstock Law and turned the propaganda efforts of her National Committee on the American Medical Association. The AMA balked until she dissolved her National Committee in 1937; it then publicly endorsed birth control.

The following year the remnants of Sanger's past—the American Birth Control League and the Clinical Research Bureau—joined to form a new organization, the Birth Control Federation of America. Ignoring Sanger altogether, the new organization chose as its president a man—who was also a physician. A few years later, over Sanger's angry protests (she wanted her pet phrase "birth control" retained), the organization changed its name to the Planned Parenthood Federation of America. Professionally managed and well-financed, that organization remains a social force in America today.

Shunted to the sidelines, she began collecting materials for her autobiography. Ghostwriters had produced a preliminary sketch of her crusade, entitled *My Fight for Birth Control*, in 1931, and she retained the same writers to do an *Autobiography* in 1938. Reviewers severely criticized the work, saying it had "the flavor of a hagiography, or life of a Saint." The book presents Margaret as the sole author of birth control and its lonely advocate over the years. She gives no one else any credit. She alludes to her second husband but never supplies the reader with his name. English reviewers were equally critical of the book, and her London mentors, Havelock Ellis and H. G. Wells, were acutely embarrassed.

In 1933 Margaret and J. Noah had purchased a house in Tucson, hoping that the warm climate and dry air would benefit his arthritis and her latent tuberculosis. In the late 1930s they moved permanently to Tucson, while retaining their mansion on the outskirts of New York City. Her sons, who, despite some careless parenting, had grown into normal adults, were successful physicians. Grant, a gynecologist practicing in upstate New York, was married and the father of several children. Stuart did his medical internship in Tucson, and after serving in the army during the war returned to the city and became his mother's physician in her last years.

After settling in Tucson in 1938 Margaret set out to make herself the social hostess of the town. She threw elegant dinner parties and invited celebrities to visit the city. When Eleanor Roosevelt passed through town, Margaret arranged a formal tea. Slee was of no help in this enterprise. He never read anything and had little to say to guests. He died of a stroke in 1942, leaving his millions at her disposal. Her social life became more active than ever, as she divided her time between the house in Tucson and the house in New York. She lived long enough to become an idol of the feminist movement that arose in the 1960s. She died of leukemia in 1966.

A physician friend of her last years thought that Margaret Sanger and Sir Alexander Fleming, the discoverer of penicillin, were the two most important personalities of the twentieth century. "There have been no basic changes in sexual patterns from 1900 B.C. to 1900 A.D.," he wrote. "Then Margaret Sanger caused a sexual revolution by freeing people from the fear of unwanted children, and Fleming gave the world the first real cure for syphilis. . . . Certainly Mrs. Sanger's discovery caused some increase in promiscuity. But then freedom always brings problems. She herself can hardly be blamed. Besides, how many people start a crusade and finish it in their own lifetime?"

Suggested Reading

Madeline Gray's *Margaret Sanger: A Biography of the Champion of Birth Control* (1979) is an excellent piece of work. It was thoroughly researched; Gray is objective in her treatment and judicious in her conclusions. David M. Kennedy's *Birth Control in America: The Career of Margaret Sanger* (1970) is a prize-winning book. More a study of the movement than a biography of Sanger, it is organized topically, which requires much leaping around in chronology and some repetition. The birth control movement is placed in context by Dorothy Schneider and Carl J. Schneider, *American Women in the Progressive Era, 1900–1920* (1994).

Index